The **Rough Guide** to

Vancouver

written and researched by

Tim Jepson

www.roughguides.com

Contents

Eating out in Vancouver colour section following p.156

The great outdoors colour section following p.208

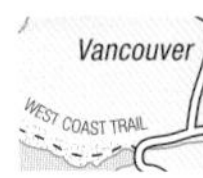

Colour maps following p.280

◀◀ Vancouver ◀ Stanley Park and downtown

Introduction to

Vancouver

One of the world's most beautiful cities, Vancouver is centred on a glitzy downtown, fringed by water and set against a spectacular backdrop of mountain peaks. Its setting and surroundings make it an outdoor-lover's paradise, and locals barely have to move to take advantage of the countless recreational opportunities afforded all year round – whether it's sailing or swimming in crystal-clear English Bay, biking or rollerblading in vast Stanley Park, skiing or boarding on the mountains, or wandering through the forests and canyons on the city's northern shore.

Vancouver's nearly two million residents exploit this spectacular natural setting to the hilt, and when they tire of the immediate region they can travel a short distance to the unimaginably vast wilderness of the British Columbia interior. No wonder, given its superb natural heritage and outdoor facilities, that in 2003 the International Olympic Committee accepted the city's bid to stage the 2010 Winter Olympics.

Vancouver also has plenty that contributes to a cultured atmosphere: top-notch museums, superb restaurants – arguably the best in North America after New York and San Francisco – countless cafés, great parks and gardens, and any number of hip bars and clubs. Summer and winter it's all hedonism and healthy living, typically West Coast obsessions that spill over into its sophisticated arts and culture. Vancouver claims a world-class symphony orchestra, as well as opera, theatre and dance companies at the cutting edge of contemporary arts. Festivals proliferate throughout its mild, if occasionally rain-soaked, summer, and numerous music venues provide a hotbed for up-and-coming rock bands and a burgeoning jazz scene.

Some idea of the city's outlook can be gleaned from a slew of lifestyle surveys which show that, per capita, its inhabitants read more, drink more wine, smoke less, spend more on outdoor gear and support more bars and restaurants than do residents of any other Canadian city.

Not all is devoted to pleasure here, however. Business growth continues apace in Canada's third largest city, much of its prosperity stemming from a **port** that handles more dry tonnage than the West Coast ports of Seattle, Tacoma, Portland, San Francisco and San Diego put together. The port in turn owes its prominence to Vancouver's much-trumpeted position as a **gateway to the Far East** and its increasingly pivotal role in the new global market of the Pacific Rim.

Links across the Pacific, however, are nothing new. After all, the city is closer to China and Japan than it is to Britain, its old colonial master and source of many of its twentieth-century immigrants. And much of the city's earliest immigration focused on Vancouver's extraordinary **Chinatown**, just one of a number of ethnic enclaves – Italian, Greek, Indian and Japanese in particular – which lend the city a refreshingly down-to-earth quality that belies its sleek, modern reputation. So, too, do the city's semi-derelict eastern districts, whose down-and-out population is shockingly at odds with those pursuing pleasant lifestyles in the lush residential neighbourhoods. Low rents and Vancouver's cosmopolitan young have nurtured an unexpected **counter-culture**, distinguished by secondhand shops, avant-garde galleries, and hip bars and clubs.

The city's vibrant feel is catching, its growth and energy almost palpable as you walk the streets. From 2001 to 2006, the date of the last census, the city's population increased by

Natural Vancouver

"Spectacular by Nature" runs the tag line across much of Vancouver's official visitor material, emphasizing (as if emphasis were needed) the city's key attraction: the stunning mixture of cityscape and natural environment. Even if you only walk or cycle around the city, you'll experience some of the thrill of the great outdoors, from glimpses of snow-capped mountains at the end of Downtown streets to the centuries-old forest and ocean views of Stanley Park.

Meanwhile, the string of parks of North Vancouver offers super hiking for all levels, as well as tremendous skiing, snowboarding and other winter activities, all just twenty minutes' drive from the city centre.

Just because the parks are close, don't be fooled into thinking they're tame; most contain areas of real wilderness for which you should be properly equipped. Don't think either that Vancouver's great outdoors stops with the mountains. The ocean provides sailing, kayaking, canoeing and diving, among other activities, some of which, such as kayaking, you can pursue from the city itself.

▲ The Fairmont Hotel

6.5 percent and it remains **Canada's fastest-growing city**: over the next few years the rate of growth is expected to double. In response, the Downtown area is spreading, and the older, run-down districts on its southern and eastern fringes – the areas of Yaletown and False Creek in particular – are feeling gentrification's effect. On the whole, real estate in Vancouver is now more expensive than it is in Toronto. In addition to new residents, film and TV production companies have discovered the city's riches, making it North America's largest production centre after Los Angeles and New York. Yet, in the peculiar way that seems second nature to Canadians, the changes are being handled in a manner that enhances rather than compromises all the city has to offer.

Although there's plenty to occupy you here, you should also aim to visit **Victoria**, easily reached by ferry or seaplane. An eminently charming old town – albeit one that slightly overplays its ersatz Englishness – it has enough sights and interest to merit an overnight stay. En route to the city by air or sea you'll pass the **Gulf Islands**, an archipelago scattered across the Strait of Georgia between the mainland and Vancouver Island. All the islands make peaceful and bucolic retreats, with plenty of laid-back accommodation, good restaurants, sleepy villages and pleasant (and easy) hiking, cycling and other outdoor opportunities. Like Victoria, they also offer tremendous opportunities for whale-watching, increasingly one of the region's most popular visitor activities.

If you hanker for more demanding outdoor pursuits, Vancouver is perfectly placed for excursions into the Coast Mountains to the north, notably the peaks near the year-round ski resort of **Whistler**, and for trips along the mainland **Sunshine Coast** facing Vancouver Island, an area known, above all, for some of the world's best diving.

What to see

Cradled between the Pacific and snowcapped peaks, Vancouver's dazzling Downtown district fills a narrow peninsula bounded by Burrard Inlet to the north, English Bay to the west and False Creek to the south, with Greater Vancouver sprawling south to the Fraser River. Edged around Downtown's idyllic waterfront are fine beaches, a dynamic port and a magnificent swath of green – Stanley Park – not to mention the mirror-fronted ranks of skyscrapers that look across Burrard Inlet and its busy harbour to the residential districts of North and West Vancouver (the North Shore). Beyond these comfortable suburbs, the Coast Mountains rise in steep, forested slopes to form a dramatic counterpoint to the Downtown skyline and the most stunning of the city's many outdoor playgrounds.

You'll inevitably spend a good deal of time in **Downtown Vancouver**, which is where you'll find the city's most visited sights: **Canada Place**, an impressive waterfront complex; the **Harbour Centre** and its panoramic views; and the Neoclassical grandeur of the **Vancouver Art Gallery**, home to the works of celebrated Canadian painter Emily Carr. The Downtown core spills southward into **Yaletown**, a revitalized former warehouse district that's full of cafés, restaurants, galleries and interesting shops.

East of Downtown is its Victorian-era neighbour, **Gastown**, now a renovated and less-than-convincing pastiche of its past. Moving eastward, Gastown blends into edgy **Chinatown**, which could easily absorb a morning – it contains more

◀ Sea kayaking near the city

▲ Hitting the slopes

than its share of interesting shops and restaurants along its busy streets, plus the area's main attraction, the **Dr Sun Yat-Sen Garden**. At the northern tip of the Downtown peninsula, you'll find abundant recreational pleasures in **Stanley Park**, a huge area of semi-wild parkland and beaches.

Beyond the Downtown peninsula in the southern portion of the city are other worthwhile destinations, notably **Granville Island**, by far the city's most tempting spot for wandering and people-watching, situated in the waters of False Creek. Neighbouring **Kitsilano** to the west is home to the **Vancouver Museum** and the other museums of the **Vanier Park** complex, all easily accessible from Granville Island. West of Kitsilano and at the westernmost point of Vancouver lies the sprawling **University of British Columbia** and its formidable **Museum of Anthropology**, flanked by the protected area of **Pacific Spirit Regional Park**.

At a push, you could cram the city's essentials into around three days. If you're here for a longer stay, though, you'll want to venture further from Downtown. Trips across Burrard Inlet to **North Vancouver** are worth making for the views from the SeaBus ferry alone (see p.25) – they also provide a different panoramic perspective on the peninsula and take you into the mountains and forests that provide Vancouver with its tremendous setting. The most popular trips here are to the Capilano Suspension Bridge, something of a triumph of public relations over substance, and to the more worthwhile cable-car trip up **Grouse Mountain** for some staggering views of the city.

The area of Vancouver east of Chinatown is a vast collection of suburbs, lacking in specific attractions and therefore not covered in the guide.

When to go

Vancouver has a reputation for **rain**. About 117cm, 46 inches, falls in the city per year (59cm/23inches in Victoria), a fair amount to be sure; however, only about ten percent of the year's total falls in the summer months of June, July and August. And unlike the rest of the country, Vancouver's generally benign climate means it can be considered a year-round destination.

Viewpoints

A city with a majestic setting demands viewpoints from which it can be admired, and in Vancouver you are spoiled for choice. If you fly here, then you'll enjoy one of the world's great aerial approaches, whether you come in over the ocean or over the mountains. Either way, you'll see the water-fringed skyscrapers of Downtown, the peaks of the Coast Mountains and the great expanse of the Fraser Delta. At some point, budget allowing, you should repeat this experience by taking a floatplane from the city's harbour (see p.28), either as a tour or as means of travelling to Victoria or the Gulf Islands.

Less expensive but only marginally less dramatic aerial views can be enjoyed from the Harbour Centre (see p.43) or Grouse Mountain (see p.98) and from some of the approach roads to protected areas on the city's North Shore, such as Mount Seymour and Cypress provincial parks.

At water level the views can be equally captivating, notably on the SeaBus ferry (see p.25) between Downtown and Lonsdale Quay in North Vancouver. This crossing offers a wonderful close-up look at the city's port, as well as a stunning panorama of the Downtown skyline.

Other views can be more unexpected. Kitsilano Beach, for example, provides a different perspective on Downtown, as do trips over the Lions Gate and Granville Street bridges.

The best time to visit is in **summer** – July and August – when you're likely to enjoy plenty of hot sunny days. "Indian summers" are also common, often prolonging the good weather into September and/or October. Still, the city can also have a sunny June and wet July. The busiest months in terms of visitor numbers are July and August, but the city rarely feels overcrowded. Accommodation prices are highest between June and early September, though many hotels divide the year into four seasons, with appreciably lower rates in even the grandest hotels from December to February.

Winters are mild and damp, but there is little snow in the city. Snow is present on the Coast Mountains, however, allowing you to ski or snowboard just minutes from Downtown. Whistler, one of North America's finest winter-sports resorts, is around two hours' drive away. The winter season here extends to around April, but summer glacier skiing means you can take to the slopes here year-round.

Spring and **autumn** – roughly May to June and late September and October – are temperate, which is to say you can have great days and grim days. Note that the ocean and mountains mean Vancouver has several micro-climates. The nearer you are to the mountains, the wetter you'll be: Grouse Mountain has an annual precipitation of 350cm (140 inches), Downtown receives 140cm (55 inches) of rain, and Richmond (near the Fraser River) just 100cm (40 inches).

Average monthly temperatures and rainfall

	Jan	Feb	Mar	Apr	May	Jun	Jul	Aug	Sep	Oct	Nov	Dec
Average daily temperature												
Max/min (ºC)	5/2	7/4	10/6	14/9	18/12	21/15	23/17	23/17	18/14	14/10	9/6	6/4
Max/min (ºF)	41/36	44/40	50/43	58/48	64/54	69/59	74/63	73/63	65/58	57/50	48/43	43/39
Average rainfall												
no of rainy days	20	15	16	13	10	6	6	8	9	16	18	36
Total in (cm)	21.8	14.7	12.7	8.4	7.1	3.1	3.1	4.3	9.1	14.7	8.3	22.4
Total in (inch)	8.6	5.8	5	3.3	2.8	1.2	1.2	1.7	3.6	5.8	3.3	8.8

things not to miss

It's not possible to see everything that Vancouver has to offer in one trip – and we don't suggest you try. What follows, in no particular order, is a selective taste of the city's highlights: outstanding museums, stunning vistas and vibrant nightlife. They're arranged in five colour-coded categories, which you can browse through to find the very best things to see and experience. All highlights have a page reference to take you straight into the guide, where you can find out more.

01 **Museum of Vancouver** Page **80** • Fronted by an eye-catching fountain, this eclectic civic museum presents a lively account of Vancouver's history, from its earliest aboriginal inhabitants to the burgeoning city of today.

02 Whale-watching Page **221** • The waters between Vancouver and Vancouver Island teem with whales, easily visible either on tours or kayaking.

03 Ice hockey Page **200** • Excitement, finesse and high-speed action are guaranteed at a Vancouver Canucks hockey game.

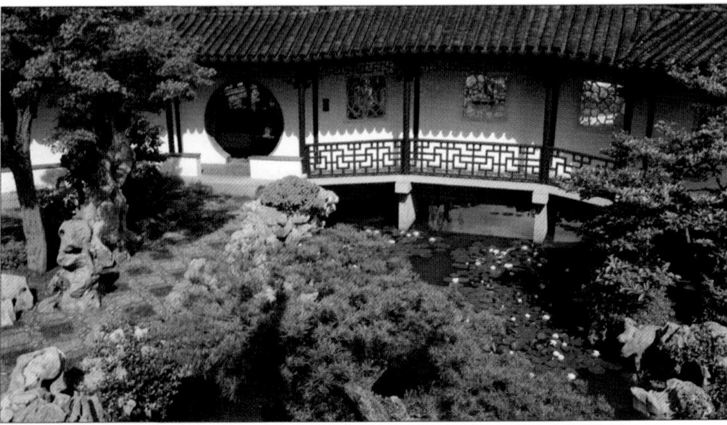

04 Dr Sun Yat-Sen Garden Page **60** • Chinatown's cultural showpiece is the only full-scale classical Chinese garden in the Western Hemisphere.

05 The Royal British Columbia Museum Page **218** • Victoria's showcase museum mixes fascinating historical displays with stunning natural-history dioramas.

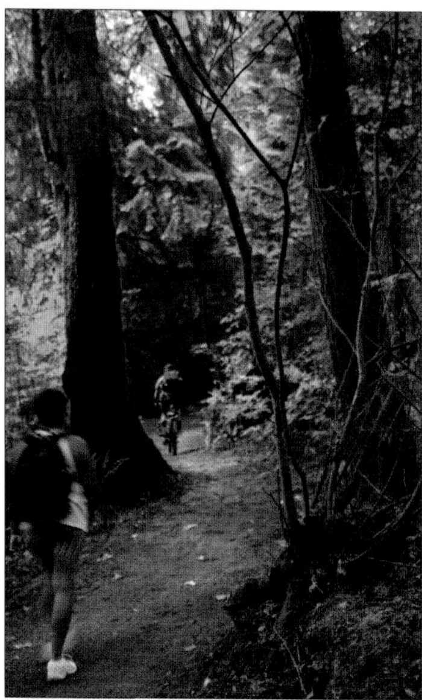

06 Stanley Park Page **62** • North America's largest urban park is a green oasis of woodland, ancient forest, marshes, beaches and peaceful trails.

07 Yaletown Page **49** • This former warehouse district is now a dynamic mixture of funky stores, bars and excellent restaurants.

08 Grouse Mountain Skyride Page **99** • The largest cable cars in North America offer a breathtaking way to reach the top of Grouse Mountain, the city's finest viewpoint.

09 Butchart Gardens Page **223** • More than a million plants and 700 different species are spread across British Columbia's most celebrated gardens.

10 Seaplane ride Page **28** • Leaving from the Downtown waterfront, the seaplane affords glorious panoramas of the city and its surroundings.

11 Vancouver Art Gallery Page **46** • See the imaginative, aboriginal-influenced works of Victoria-born Emily Carr, the highlight of Vancouver's principal gallery.

12 Canada Place Page **42** • Stroll by day or night around the walkways of this striking convention centre, hotel and cruise-ship terminal for wonderful views of Vancouver's port.

13 **Whistler Mountain** Page **245** • Whistler is best known for its skiing and other winter activities, but there is plenty to do here in the summer, too.

14 **Kitsilano Beach** Page **79** • While away a summer afternoon at this popular South Vancouver beach.

15 **Pacific Rim cuisine** Page **130** • Sample the inspired fusion of Far Eastern, Italian and West Coast cooking, a mainstay of *Bishop's* and many other Vancouver restaurants.

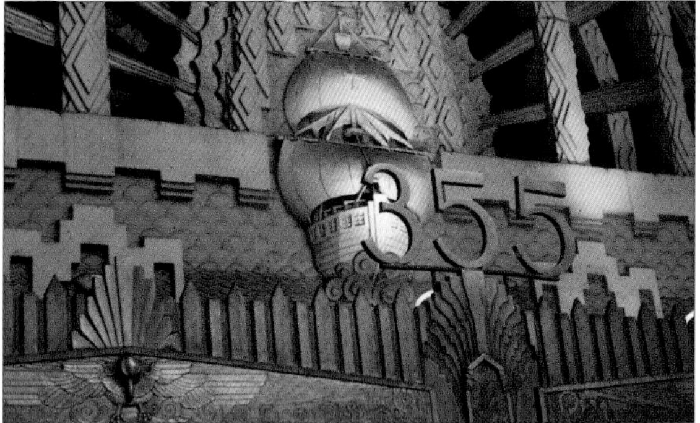

16 Marine Building Page **44** • The city's maritime heritage is celebrated in the motifs adorning Vancouver's only surviving Art Deco skyscraper.

17 Granville Island Page **71** • Fabulous food shops and teeming market stalls are the main attractions of this hugely popular enclave, easily accessible from Downtown.

18 Beacon Hill Park Page **222** • The views from Victoria's lovely city park extend across the Juan de Fuca Strait to the mountains of Washington State.

19 Museum of Anthropology Page **87** • Bill Reid's *The Raven and the First Men* is one of countless outstanding pieces of aboriginal art in Vancouver's most compelling museum.

Basics

Basics

Getting there

As one of Canada's gateway cities, Vancouver is well served by direct air links from all over the world. Flying is the most time-effective option, unless you're already relatively close to the city, in which case there are plenty of road and rail links, including a train service daily from Seattle. From outside North America, flying is of course your only option – unless you're aboard a cruise ship. The main airport is modern and efficient Vancouver International, 13km (8 miles) south of the city centre (see "Arrival" for more).

Flights from the US and Canada

From most of the US and Canada, the easiest and often cheapest way to get to Vancouver is to fly; there are direct flights from larger Canadian cities and from most major US hubs. From the East Coast of the US, you should be able to get the 5hr flight to Vancouver for around US$300 in low season; booking early can sometimes get you a similar summer rate, but count on paying closer to US$600 in high season.

Direct flights from the West Coast of the US will be cheaper, around US$255 in the low season and US$275 in the high season. Competition is fiercer for flights to Vancouver from other Canadian cities than it is for flights originating in the US. A low-season round-trip from Toronto will cost around $440 with a regular carrier or $240 with a no-frills airline such as Westjet (which also flies year-round from Montréal, Winnipeg, Calgary and Las Vegas), while in high season, expect to pay $660 with Air Canada. Low-season fares from Montréal are around $555 with the likes of Air Canada or $275 with the budget airlines; in high season fares from Montréal may be $760 or more with Air Canada, or as little as $305 with a no-frills carrier like Westjet.

The no-frills carriers also offer excellent value from provincial Canada – a low-season round trip from Edmonton or Calgary can cost as little as $115 to $130 (as compared with the regular airlines' $250–300).

Flights from the UK and Ireland

Air Canada, British Airways, Lufthansa, Scandinavian Airlines, Canadian Affair and bmi British Midland all fly direct daily from the UK mainland to Vancouver. Most direct flights leave from Heathrow or Gatwick, with other airports offering add-ons and transfers; Manchester and Glasgow offer the most. It is sometimes cheaper to take a flight from the UK to Seattle and then catch a bus, train or an internal flight than it is to fly directly to Vancouver.

Other non-direct routes include flying via the US to Vancouver, or via Amsterdam with KLM. You can also explore the charter route, though companies offering charters tend to come and go from year to year. A standard return fare from Heathrow direct to Vancouver with Air Canada, the principal carrier, can cost as little as £300 from London in low season and between £485 and £740 or more in high season.

From Ireland you can generally fly direct to Vancouver from Belfast during the summer, and from Dublin via Amsterdam or Frankfurt year-round; the main alternatives are charter flights or routings via the UK mainland or a US hub airport, such as San Francisco or New York. Keep in mind that non-stop flights can often – but certainly not always – cost more than one-stop flights. From Ireland, low-season fares will be around £485 but high-season fares can creep up to £1240 if booked late – if you book early enough, you might get a much more reasonable £500 or £600 fare.

Flights from Australia and New Zealand

Air Canada offers the only direct flight from Australia and New Zealand to Vancouver, from Sydney; travellers in other parts of the continent can either fly via Sydney or break their journey elsewhere. Options are flying with the likes of Air China or Singapore Airlines and connecting in an Asian city such as Hong Kong, Tokyo or Beijing, or going via the US, transferring at Los Angeles with Qantas, United or Air New Zealand; the same applies to charter flights.

Fares vary considerably, depending on the time of year and on the restrictions attached to your ticket. There are, for example, discounts for midweek travel and advance booking. A low-season round-trip fare from Sydney to Vancouver with Air Canada costs around Aus$2000, or Aus$2600 in high season; from Melbourne it's more likely to be Aus$2100 in low season, Aus$2990 in high; if you're travelling from New Zealand in low season, expect to pay around NZ$2000 from Auckland to Vancouver; NZ $2500 in high season.

By car

Getting to Vancouver by car is easy enough if you're in the Pacific Northwest – coming from anywhere else, driving to Vancouver will take a

Six steps to a better kind of travel

At Rough Guides we are passionately committed to travel. We feel strongly that only through travelling do we truly come to understand the world we live in and the people we share it with – plus tourism has brought a great deal of **benefit** to developing economies around the world over the last few decades. But the extraordinary growth in tourism has also damaged some places irreparably, and of course **climate change** is exacerbated by most forms of transport, especially flying. This means that now more than ever it's important to **travel thoughtfully** and **responsibly**, with respect for the cultures you're visiting – not only to derive the most benefit from your trip but also to preserve the best bits of the planet for everyone to enjoy. At Rough Guides we feel there are six main areas in which you can make a difference:

- Consider what you're contributing to the **local economy**, and how much the services you use do the same, whether it's through employing local workers and guides or sourcing locally grown produce and local services.
- Consider the **environment** on holiday as well as at home. Water is scarce in many developing destinations, and the biodiversity of local flora and fauna can be adversely affected by tourism. Try to patronize businesses that take account of this.
- Travel with a purpose, not just to tick off experiences. Consider **spending longer** in a place, and getting to know it and its people.
- Give thought to how often you **fly**. Try to avoid short hops by air and more harmful night flights.
- Consider **alternatives to flying**, travelling instead by bus, train, boat and even by bike or on foot where possible.
- Make your trips "**climate neutral**" via a reputable carbon offset scheme. All Rough Guide flights are offset, and every year we donate money to a variety of charities devoted to combating the effects of climate change.

long time. See p.32 for information on what's needed to cross the US/Canadian border.

From Seattle to Vancouver is approximately 225km. From San Francisco, it's approximately 1520km, or roughly fifteen and a half hours' drive. From Montréal, it's about 4900km, and driving, not counting stops, will take you about two days. From Toronto, it's around 4375km.

You can of course drive your own vehicle, or you can rent a car. If you rent a car in the US, inform the agency that you intend to take the car into Canada.

Trains

Canada's national VIA Rail services operate in and out of Pacific Central Station (Ⓣ604-3772 or 1-888/842-7245, Ⓦwww.viarail.ca), located in a dismal part of the city to the southeast of Downtown off Main Street at 1150 Station St. VIA Rail trains arrive here via Kamloops from Jasper, where there are connections from Prince George and Prince Rupert, and from Edmonton and points east.

There are also daily Amtrak (Ⓣ253/931-8917 or 1-800/872-7245, Ⓦwww.amtrakcascades.com) services from Seattle, with tickets from US$26 and a journey time of just under 4hr, plus a direct two-day route from San Diego with stops at all major West Coast US cities. Amtrak also links with VIA Rail at Winnipeg, Manitoba, if you want to make a much longer rail trip to Vancouver across western Canada.

Rail fares from the US are cheaper than airfares, provided you book ahead; Canadian rail fares tend to be as expensive as normal airfares, if not more so. Deals for students and seniors can offer between 50 and 100 percent off a second fare.

Rail contacts

Amtrak US Ⓣ1-800/872-7245, Ⓦwww.amtrak.com.
BritRail Travel US Ⓣ1-866/BRITRAIL, Canada Ⓣ1-514/733-5247, Ⓦwww.britrail.com.
CIT World Travel Australia Ⓣ1300 361 500, Ⓦwww.cittravel.com.au.
ScanTours US and Canada Ⓣ1-800/223-7226, Ⓦwww.scantours.com.
STA Travel US Ⓣ1-800/781-4040, UK Ⓣ0871/2300 040, Australia Ⓣ134 782, New Zealand Ⓣ0800/474 400, South Africa Ⓣ0861/781 781, Ⓦwww.statravel.com.
Trailfinders UK Ⓣ0845/058 5858, Ireland Ⓣ01/677 7888, Australia Ⓣ1300/780 212, Ⓦwww.trailfinders.com.
VIA Rail Canada Ⓣ1-888/842-7245, Ⓦwww.viarail.ca.

Buses

You can reach Vancouver by long-distance bus from most major cities in Canada. The city's main bus terminal lies alongside the VIA Rail Pacific Central Station and is used by Pacific Coach Lines (Ⓣ604/662-8074, 662-7575 or 1-800/661-1725, Ⓦwww.pacificcoach.com) for services from Victoria and other parts of Vancouver Island, Maverick Coach Lines (Ⓣ604/940-2332, Ⓦwww.maverickcoachlines.bc.ca) from Whistler, Sunshine Coast and Nanaimo, and all Greyhound services (see p.206 for contact information).

Airlines, agents and operators

Online booking

Ⓦ**www.expedia.co.uk** (in UK)
Ⓦ**www.expedia.com** (in US)
Ⓦ**www.expedia.ca** (in Canada)
Ⓦ**www.lastminute.com** (in UK)
Ⓦ**www.opodo.co.uk** (in UK)
Ⓦ**www.orbitz.com** (in US)
Ⓦ**www.travelocity.co.uk** (in UK)
Ⓦ**www.travelocity.com** (in US)
Ⓦ**www.travelocity.ca** (in Canada)
Ⓦ**www.zuji.com.au** (in Australia)
Ⓦ**www.zuji.co.nz** (in New Zealand)

Airlines

Aer Lingus Ⓦwww.aerlingus.com.
Air Canada Ⓦwww.aircanada.com.
Air New Zealand Ⓦwww.airnz.co.nz.
American Airlines Ⓦwww.aa.com.
British Airways Ⓦwww.ba.com.
Bmi Ⓦwww.flybmi.com.
Canadian Affair Ⓦwww.canadianaffair.com.
Continental Airlines Ⓦwww.continental.com.
Delta Ⓦwww.delta.com.
KLM (Royal Dutch Airlines) Ⓦwww.klm.com.
Lufthansa Ⓦwww.lufthansa.com.
South African Airways Ⓦwww.flysaa.com.
United Airlines Ⓦwww.united.com.
US Airways Ⓦwww.usair.com.
Virgin Atlantic Ⓦwww.virgin-atlantic.com.
WestJet Ⓦwww.westjet.com.

Agents and operators

Adventure Center ⓣ1-800/228-8747 or 510/654-1879, ⓦwww.adventurecenter.com. Hiking and "soft adventure" specialists worldwide, with trips to the Canadian Rockies and the Pacific Coast, as well as Vancouver, from about US$1575.

Adventures Abroad ⓣ1-800/665-3998, ⓦwww.adventures-abroad.com. Adventure specialists with a variety of western Canadian trips.

Contiki ⓣ1-888/CONTIKI, ⓦwww.contiki.com. 18- to 35-year-olds-only tour operator with tours taking in Whistler, Vancouver, Jasper and the Rockies.

Cosmos ⓣ1-800/276-1241, ⓦwww.cosmosvacations.com. Planned vacation packages with an independent focus, often leaving afternoons free after active mornings. Offers various Canadian Rockies packages, some with Vancouver components.

ebookers UK ⓣ0800/082 3000, Republic of Ireland ⓣ01/488 3507, ⓦwww.ebookers.com. Low fares on an extensive selection of scheduled flights and package deals.

Maupintour ⓣ1-800/255-4266, ⓦwww.maupintour.com. Luxury independent and escorted land-only tours, including a 10-day escorted tour of western Canada

North South Travel UK ⓣ01245/608 291, ⓦwww.northsouthtravel.co.uk. Friendly, competitive travel agency, offering discounted fares worldwide. Profits are used to support projects in the developing world, especially the promotion of sustainable tourism.

STA Travel US ⓣ1-800/781-4040, UK ⓣ0871/2300 040, Australia ⓣ134 782, Canada ⓣ1-888-427-5639, New Zealand ⓣ0800/474 400, South Africa ⓣ0861/781 781, ⓦwww.statravel.com. Worldwide specialists in independent travel; also student IDs, travel insurance, car rental, rail passes, and more. Good discounts for students and under-26s.

Trailfinders UK ⓣ0845/058 5858, Ireland ⓣ01/677 7888, Australia ⓣ1300/780 212, ⓦwww.trailfinders.com. One of the best-informed and most efficient agents for independent travellers.

Viator ⓦwww.viator.com. Bookings for local tours and sightseeing trips in destinations around the world, including Vancouver and around.

Travel CUTS Canada ⓣ1-866/246-9762, US ⓣ1-800/592-2887, ⓦwww.travelcuts.com. Canadian youth and student travel firm.

USIT Ireland ⓣ01/602 1906, Northern Ireland ⓣ028/9032 7111, ⓦwww.usit.ie. Ireland's main student and youth travel specialists.

Arrival

Vancouver International Airport is linked to most major world and Canadian cities in the world and receives more than 15 million visitors a year, making it the second-busiest airport in Canada after Toronto. Vancouver's bus and train station, Pacific Central Station, is located southeast of Downtown and links the city to many Canadian and a few American cities. Those arriving by car are likely to find the city – and its bridges in particular – rather congested, especially at rush hours.

By air

Vancouver International Airport (ⓣ604/207-7077, ⓦwww.yvr.ca) is situated on Sea Island, 13km south of the city centre. Its often-used coded abbreviation is YVR. International flights arrive at the majestic main terminal; domestic flights at the smaller and linked old Main Terminal.

If you're an international passenger, you'll find a tourist information desk (daily 7am–midnight; ⓣ604/688-5515) as you exit customs and immigration and before entering the terminal's public spaces. Close by are desks for direct bus services from the airport to Victoria (Pacific Coach Lines) and Whistler.

Domestic passengers also have a tourist information desk (daily 7am–midnight) just before the terminal exit.

The best way to get into Vancouver is on SkyTrain (see p.25), the light rail system, on the Canada Line, opened in 2009. Trains run from about 4.50am and 1.05am and take 26 minutes to make the journey to Waterfront station close to Canada Place and the heart of Downtown. Fares are $5 ($2.50 after 6.30pm weekedays and all day Saturday and Sunday and public holidays).

You an also take the private Airporter bus (6.45am–1.10am; $14 single, $12 return; ⓣ604/946-8866 or 1-800/668-3141, ⓦwww.yvrairporter.com), which leaves every 15 minutes from a bay to the left immediately outside the main door of the international arrivals; from domestic arrivals you can walk here if you need Airporter information or wait at the domestic arrivals pick-up outside the terminal. You can buy tickets from the driver or at the bus stop by international arrivals. Resourceful staff and a pamphlet with a useful map help you figure out which drop-offs on the shuttle's three routes are most useful. Returning to the airport, buses run round the same pick-up points, including the bus depot. Taxis into town cost about $25–30.

Pacific Coach Lines (ⓣ604/662-7575 or 1-800/661-1725, ⓦwww.pacificcoach.com) runs direct buses from the airport to Victoria (7 daily; $48) and Whistler (7 daily, $51.45). Other bus services from the airport are run by Perimeter (ⓣ604/717-6600 or 1-888/717-6600, ⓦwww.perimeterbus.com) for services to Whistler; Quick Shuttle (ⓣ604/940-4428 or 1-800/665-2122, ⓦwww.quickcoach.com) to Bellingham Airport, Downtown Seattle and Sea-Tac Airport; and Malaspina Coach Lines (ⓣ604/885-2217 or 1-877/227-8287, ⓦwww.malaspinacoach.com) to the Sunshine Coast, Powell River, Whistler, Pemberton and Nanaimo on Vancouver Island.

By bus

Vancouver's main bus terminal is used by Pacific Coach Lines (ⓣ1-800/661-1725, ⓦwww.pacificcoach.com; for Victoria, Vancouver Island), Malaspina Coach Lines (ⓣ604/885-2217 or 1-877/227-8287, ⓦwww.malaspinacoach.com; for the Sunshine Coast) and all Greyhound services (ⓣ604/482-8747 or 1-800/661-8747, ⓦwww.greyhound.ca; for BC, Alberta, Yukon and long-haul destinations including Seattle and the US). It is in a slightly dismal area alongside the VIA Rail Pacific Central train station at 1150 Station St; ticket offices for all companies are inside on the right as you enter.

It's too far to walk to Downtown from the bus terminal, so bear left from the station through a small park to the Science World–Main Street SkyTrain station, from where it's a couple of stops to Downtown (take the train marked "Waterfront"); tickets ($2.50) are available from platform machines. Alternatively, you could take a taxi Downtown from the station for about $7–9.

By train

Skeletal VIA Rail services operate out of Pacific Central Station (ⓣ1-888/842-7245, ⓦwww.viarail.ca); they run to and from Jasper (3 weekly), where there are connections (also 3 weekly) for Prince George and Prince Rupert, and on to Edmonton and the east. There is one service run by VIA–Amtrak (ⓣ 1-800/872-7245, ⓦwww.amtrak.com) between Vancouver and Seattle.

By car

The approach to Vancouver by road is straightforward from the US and points to the east and north in Canada. From the western US, follow Interstate 5 (I-5) from Seattle and Washington State to the border towns of Blaine (in the US) and White Rock (BC), about 210km from Seattle. You clear Canadian Customs at the Peace Arch crossing in Blaine (open 24hr). If you return this way, you pass through US Customs.

Interstate 5 becomes the Canadian Hwy 99 and leads west from White Rock and then north to Vancouver, where it becomes first Oak Street and then – six blocks after a left turn at Oak and 70th Avenue – Granville Street, a major artery that leads directly to the heart of Downtown. Note, however, that much of Granville is pedestrianized in the centre, and you'll have to be prepared to follow various one-way routes if your destination is in the Downtown core. Hwy 99 is also the route to follow if you're driving from the ferry terminal at Tsawwassen (for ferries from Vancouver Island and the Gulf Islands): Hwy 17 runs from the terminal to connect with Hwy 99 just before the George Massey Tunnel.

If you're heading to the city from points in the east of Canada or from the central US, you should follow the main Trans-Canada Highway (Hwy 1), which crosses the Fraser River on the Port Mann Bridge and then cuts through the suburbs of southeast Vancouver before an exit at Cassiar Street to Hastings Street (Hwy 7A), which leads west about 7km to Downtown. Hwy 1 then continues over the Burrard Inlet on the Second Narrows Bridge before turning west to pass through North and West Vancouver.

If you're arriving from the north (Squamish, Whistler or the ferry terminal at Horseshoe Bay), then you'll follow the Trans-Canada south. If you're headed for Downtown on this route, take the Taylor Way Bridge to Vancouver-Hwy 99 exit (Exit 13) in West Vancouver and cross the Burrard Inlet on the Lions Gate Bridge to Downtown's West End district – note that you can expect delays on this route at busy times of the day.

City transport

Vancouver's public transport system is an efficient, integrated network of bus, light-rail (SkyTrain), catamaran (SeaBus) and ferry services, which are operated by TransLink (daily 6.30am–11.30pm; ⓣ604/953-3333 or customer relations 604/953-3040, ⓦwww.translink.bc.ca), formerly – and occasionally still – known as BC Transit.

Tickets are valid across the system for bus, SkyTrain and SeaBus. Generally they cost $2.50 for journeys in the large, central Zone 1, and $3.75 or $5 for longer two- and three-zone journeys – though you're unlikely to go out of Zone 1 unless you're travelling to the airport from Downtown, which involves crossing from Zone 1 to 2. These regular fares apply in peak hours: Monday to Friday from start of service until 6.30pm.

In off-peak hours – after 6.30pm and all day Saturday, Sunday and public holidays – a flat $2.50 fare applies across all three zones. Tickets are valid for transfers throughout the system for ninety minutes from the time of issue; on buses you should ask for a transfer ticket if the driver doesn't automatically give you one. Otherwise, you can buy tickets individually (or in books of ten for $19 for Zone 1) at station offices or machines, 7-Eleven, Safeway and London Drugs stores, or any other shop or newsstand displaying a blue TransLink sticker (so-called "FareDealer" outlets). You must carry tickets with you as proof of payment.

Probably the simplest and cheapest deal if you're going to be making three or more journeys in a day is to buy a DayPass ($9), valid all day across all three zones (weekly passes are not available). If you buy these over the counter at stores or elsewhere (not in machines) they're "Scratch & Ride" – you scratch out the day and month before travel.

See "Listings" on pp.206–208 for details of car and bicycle rental and taxis.

Buses

You can buy tickets on the bus, but make sure you have the right change (they don't carry any) to shovel into the box by the driver; ask specially if you want a transfer ticket. If you have a pass or transfer, simply show the driver. Normal buses stop running around midnight, when a rather patchy

"Night Owl" service comes into effect on major routes until about 4am. Note that blue West Van buses (Ⓣ604/985-7777) also operate in the city (usually to North and West Vancouver destinations, including the BC Ferries terminal at Horseshoe Bay) – TransLink tickets are valid on these buses as well.

SeaBuses

The SeaBuses ply between Downtown and Lonsdale Quay in North Vancouver, and they're a ride definitely worth taking for its own sake: the views of the mountains across Burrard Inlet, the port and the Downtown skyline are superb. The Downtown terminal is Waterfront Station in the old Canadian Pacific station buildings at the foot of Granville Street. There is no ticket office, only a ticket machine, but you can get a ticket (same price as bus tickets) from the small newsagent immediately on your left as you face the long gallery that takes you to the boats. Two 400-seat catamarans make the thirteen-minute crossing every fifteen to thirty minutes (6.30am–12.30am). Arrival in North Vancouver is at Lonsdale Quay, where immediately to the left is a bus terminal for connections to Grouse Mountain and other North Vancouver destinations. Bicycles can be carried on board.

City ferries

The city has a variety of small ferries run over similar routes by two rival companies: Aquabus (Ⓣ604/689-5858, Ⓦwww.theaquabus.com) and False Creek Ferries (Ⓣ604/684-7781, Ⓦwww.granvilleislandferries.bc.ca). These provide a useful, very frequent and fun service daily 6.30am–10.30pm (until 8.30pm in winter). Aquabus runs boats in a continuous circular shuttle from the foot of Hornby Street to the Fish Docks on the seawalk, to Vanier Park and the museums, to Granville Island (both $2), and to the Yaletown dock by the road loop at the east foot of Davie Street ($3). False Creek Ferries also runs to Granville Island ($2), and also to Vanier Park ($3 from Granville Island, $2 from the Aquatic Centre) just below the Maritime Museum – a good way of getting to the park and its museums (see p.81).

Both companies also offer what amount to mini-cruises up False Creek, with connections from Granville Island to Science World and the Plaza of Nations. You can pick up the Aquabus boat at the Arts Club Theatre on Granville Island, the foot of Hornby Street Downtown or – with False Creek Ferries – below the Aquatic Centre at the foot of Thurlow and northern end of Burrard Bridge, on Granville Island or below the spit and small harbour near the Maritime Museum in Vanier Park.

SkyTrain

Vancouver's light-rail line – SkyTrain – is a model of its type: driverless, completely computerized and magnetically propelled, half underground and half on raised track. It links the Downtown Waterfront Station (housed in the CPR building with the SeaBus terminal) and the southeastern suburb of New Westminster. Only the first three or four stations – Waterfront, Burrard, Granville and Stadium – are of any practical use to the casual visitor. A new 16-station extension, the 26-kilometre Canada Line, serving Yaletown and south Vancouver, including the airport, opened in 2009.

By taxi

Taxis in Vancouver are efficient and reasonably priced and their drivers generally honest. Theoretically, taxis can be hailed on the streets when the sign on the roof is lit, or picked up at taxi ranks or stands around the city, but this can often be difficult in Vancouver. Taxi services can also be ordered promptly by phone: try Black Top Ⓣ604/731-1111, Maclure's Cabs Ⓣ604/731-9211, Vancouver Taxi Ⓣ604/871-1111 or Yellow Ⓣ604/681-1111. Cabbies in Vancouver expect a 10 to 15 percent tip.

Driving

It's unneccessary to rent a car while staying in Vancouver – the transport system is inexpensive and efficient, and you can reach Victoria, Whistler and the Sunshine Coast using regular bus services. And if you're crossing to Victoria with a view to exploring Vancouver Island, you can hold off renting a car until you reach Victoria – this will save you the cost of taking the car across on the ferry, not to mention the hassle involved waiting to board at busy times. That said, if you plan to do any hiking on the city's outskirts, a car is necessary to reach many of the trailheads.

If you do drive, try and avoid bottlenecks outside the city centre (especially on the North Shore bridges) between 7 and 9am and after 3pm on weekday afternoons. Unlike other parts of Canada, drivers in Vancouver are allowed to turn right at a red light (but only once pedestrians have crossed); speed limits are usually no higher than 80–110km/h (50–65mph) outside the city, 50km/h (31mph) in the city limits, unless otherwise specified.

Among other regulations, seat belts are mandatory, you must give way to buses, and when turning left at intersections cars are expected to cross in front of their opposite number. Pedestrians have the right of way at crossings and intersections. Vancouver has numerous overhead traffic lights that may be unfamiliar to drivers from Europe, so keep your eyes peeled.

Parking is invariably metered on city streets – reckon on around $2 for 80min. On streets with free parking, park in the direction of the traffic and not closer than 6m to a stop sign or 5m to a fire hydrant. Illegally parked vehicles will be towed. Off-road, all-day or part-day parking options abound around the city: expect to pay between about $10 and $25 a day. For help, visit ⓦwww.easyparkvancouver.com.

Car rental

Car rental in Vancouver can be pricey when you take everything into account, with various taxes levied on the basic rental price.

Roadside assistance

Roadside assistance is available from the CAA – the Canadian Automobile Association (ⓣ604/293-2222 or 1-800/CAA-HELP for emergency assistance, ⓦwww.bcaa.com) – which has reciprocal agreements with the AAA and motoring groups from other countries.

You'll need to have a credit card to rent and, if you have an overseas driver's licence, an International Driver's Permit is recommended. Some car rental firms won't accept drivers under 25; others will charge a premium for younger drivers (minimum 21 years old). Note that it can often be cheaper to set up your car hire before leaving, in your country of origin. See below for contact details worldwide.

Car rental agencies

Alamo ⓦwww.alamo.com.
Apex ⓦwww.apexrentals.co.nz.
Auto Europe ⓦwww.autoeurope.com.
Avis ⓦwww.avis.com.
Budget ⓦwww.budget.com.
Dollar ⓦwww.dollar.com.
Enterprise Rent-a-Car ⓦwww.enterprise.com.
Europcar ⓦwww.europcar.com.
Europe by Car ⓦwww.europebycar.com.
Hertz ⓦwww.hertz.com.
Holiday Autos ⓦwww.holidayautos.co.uk. (part of the LastMinute.com group)
Irish Car Rentals ⓦwww.irishcarrentals.ie
National ⓦwww.nationalcar.com.
SIXT ⓦwww.sixt.com.
Thrifty ⓦwww.thrifty.com.

City tours

Vancouver offers a plethora of organized tours. First port of call for anyone considering a tour of any description should be the Touristinfo Centre (see p.35), which carries rack upon rack of pamphlets and flyers advertising a wide range of walking, bus, plane, helicopter and other tours.

Bus, cab and car tours

Gray Line (Ⓣ604/879-3363 or 1-800/667-0882, Ⓦwww.grayline.ca). City tours; although the ticket price includes pick-up and drop-off at your hotel, you will need to notify the company if you want to be picked up. The company's tours include the "Deluxe Grand City Tour" of the city's highlights (4hr 30min, $59) and a 4hr Indian Arm Luncheon tour ($56). It also offers a "Double Decker Attractions Loop Tour", a hop-on, hop-off affair with stops at over twenty attractions in the city. Tickets are valid for two days and cost $33.

Pacific Coach Lines (reservations required; Ⓣ604/662-7575 or 1-800/667-1725, Ⓦwww.pacificcoach.com). Offers a variety of generic tours similar to those of Gray Line (see above), but often at keener prices.

Landsea Tours (Ⓣ604/662-7591 or 1-800/558-4955, Ⓦwww.vancouvertours.com). Has smaller coaches thatn Gray Line or Pacific Coach Lines, namely "big-window" 24-seat buses and tours that include a City Highlights trip (3hr 30min; $69) and North Shore excursions (5hr 30min; $125).

The Vancouver Trolley Company (Ⓣ604/801-5515 or 1-888/451-5581, Ⓦwww.vancouvertrolley.com). Offers tours narrated by drivers in red mock-San Francisco trolley buses that depart every 30min from one of 29 stops around the city: the $35.25 all-day ticket allows you to get on and off at will at any of the stops. A full circuit takes 3hr.

Vancouver Nature Adventures (Ⓣ604/684-4922 or 1-800/528-3531, Ⓦwww.vancouvernatureadventures.com) is one among the many companies offering nature and wildlife tours of the Fraser River, Capilano Canyon and other locations near the city. Taxi companies such as Black Top (Ⓣ604/ 731-1111) and Yellow Cab (Ⓣ604/ 681-1111) also often give tours for up to five people: a 1hr 30min city tour costs around $70.

Finding your way in Downtown Vancouver

Most addresses in Downtown Vancouver are straightforward and easy to find. Most consist simply of a street or avenue and number (500 West Pender St), though on long streets and avenues we have added "cross" street or avenue to help you find the relevant block (500 West Pender at/near/and Seymour). Where an address has several numbers, as in 150–1450 Robson, the first figure refers to the suite number, the second to the building number.

In **Downtown**, Carrall Street marks the axis from which streets and buildings are numbered and designated to east and west. To the west, numbers increase towards Stanley Park; to the east they increase towards Commercial Drive. Thus 500 West Pender would be five blocks west of Carrall. The axis for numbering to the south is the Canada Place Pier – there's no numbering to the north, as there's only the Burrard Inlet to the north of the pier. Thus numbers increase as you head south through Downtown towards False Creek and Granville Island.

The system works in the same way **off the Downtown peninsula**, although here Ontario Street marks the axis for numbering and designation to east and west, and all east–west roads are avenues and all north–south roads are streets.

Walking tours

Walkabout Historic Vancouver (Ⓣ604/720-0006 or 439-0448, Ⓦwww.walkabouthistoricvancouver.com). Offers three basic 2hr walking tours around Downtown–Gastown and Granville Island (2 daily at 10am and 2pm; $25; private tours and times can be arranged) with the tour guides dressed in nineteenth-century costume.

Architectural Institute of BC (Ⓣ604/683-8588 ext 306, Ⓦwww.aibc.bc.ca/pub_resources/aibc_outreach/architectural_walking_tour). A choice of six excellent and inexpensive architectural walking tours (June–Aug, Tues–Sat, 1pm, $5).

Rockwood Adventures (Ⓣ604/980-7749 or Ⓣ1-888/236-6606, Ⓦwww.rockwoodadventures.com). Guided walking tours of Stanley Park, Lynn Canyon, Capilano River Canyon and the rainforest at Lighthouse Park; a tour of Bowen Island has a return by floatplane. Hotel pick-ups are available.

Chinese Cultural Centre ($5; Ⓣ604/687-7793). Guided tours of Chinatown; tours are scheduled for 11am and 1.30pm during the summer months but have to be booked ahead during the rest of the year.

Horse and carriage tours

AAA Horse & Carriage Ⓣ604/681-5115, Ⓦwww.stanleyparktours.com. Provides horse-drawn tours of Stanley Park in 20-person carriages between mid-March and mid-October; go to the information booth on Park Drive east of the Rowing Club, the starting point for the leisurely 1hr trips around the park's best-known sights (departures every 20 to 30min; from $26.99). A shuttle bus is available to the booth from ten Downtown locations.

Air and boat tours

Harbour Air Seaplanes (Ⓣ604/274-1277 or 1-800/665-0212; Ⓦwww.harbour-air.com). Operates from the waterfront terminal west of Canada Place. A total of 12 trips is available, from the 30min Panorama Tour of the city (from about $99) to half-day wilderness excursions, full-day trips to Victoria ($289) and the "Fly 'n' Dine" package ($199) to Horseshoe Bay.

West Coast Air (Ⓣ604/347-2222, Ⓦwww.westcoastair.com) offers a 30min aerial Vancouver Scenic Tour ($99) and an 85min Glacier and Alpine Lakes Tour ($269), which includes a short photo stop.

Helijet International (Ⓣ604/270-1484 or 1-800/987-4354, Ⓦwww.helijet.com). More expensive options by helicopter from Vancouver Harbour and the airport. Prices are $99 for the 8min Crown Mountain Tour, $179 for the 20min Coastal Scenic Tour and $250 for the 30min Greater Vancouver Scenic Tour.

Harbour Cruises (Ⓣ604/688-7246, Ⓦwww.boatcruises.com). Boat tours between May and October, including 75min harbour tours (generally 3 daily; $29.95), the 4hr Indian Arm Luncheon Cruise (daily at 10.30am; from $64.95) and the 3hr Sunset and Dinner Cruise (daily at 6.30pm; from $74.95) aboard an authentic paddle wheeler, the MPV Constitution: it departs from the northern foot of Denman Street in Coal Harbour by Stanley Park.

The media

Vancouver has a good selection of newspapers and magazines, featuring news and listings. The city's TV and radio offerings run the usual gamut found in major Canadian cities, ranging from the heavily commercial – and American-influenced – to more quality-oriented public broadcasting.

Newspapers

Vancouver has two local daily newspapers, the Vancouver Sun (ⓦwww.vancouversun.com) and the tabloid Province (ⓦwww.vancouverprovince.com). The Globe and Mail (ⓦwww.theglobeandmail.com), Canada's main nationwide newspaper, is better for international and Canada-wide coverage, and also has a daily BC news section and arts roundup with a BC provincial bias. The Globe's only rival is the more conservative National Post (ⓦwww.nationalpost.com). Owing to the large Asian population in Vancouver, daily editions of the Chinese Oriental Star and the Indo-Canadian Voice are also widely available.

In Victoria, the main paper is the Victoria Times Colonist (ⓦwww.timescolonist.com).

For arts listings and other comment and reviews there's the weekly Georgia Straight (ⓦwww.straight.com), published on Thursdays, 45 years old in 2012, and looking a little tired, but still the go-to choice.

Magazines

Another listings magazine to look out for if you want to know where the hip locals are shopping, eating and drinking is the Vancouver Magazine (ⓦwww.vanmag.com). Featuring a "cheap eats" section as well as extensive listings, this monthly is an excellent resource. Similar, and found in many hotels (or, occasionally, the visitor centre), is the free Where Vancouver, which also has useful maps, shopping information, and many current museum and other openings.

A few literary publications deserve special note: The Capilano Review (ⓦwww.thecapilanoreview.ca) has been going for over twenty years and is a leading voice in international arts. Prism International (ⓦwww.prism,arts.ubc.ca), published by the University of British Columbia, and Room of One's Own (ⓦwww.roommagazine.com) both publish new and established fiction writers, the latter exclusively by women.

TV and radio

Canadian TV is dominated by US programming, though the publicly subsidized Canadian Broadcasting Corporation (CBC) offers good drama and documentaries. The main local TV station is BCTV, a news and entertainment station, while Vancouver Television is a local entertainment station; cable television is commonplace, both in private homes and in the vast majority of hotel and motel rooms.

As regards radio, CBC Radio One (105.7 FM) is Vancouver's frequency for the Canadian Broadcasting Corporation, an excellent source for public affairs, news and arts programming. For just news, try CFTR (680 AM) or CFRB (1010 AM). Vancouver's urban radio station, THE BEAT (ⓦwww.thebeat.com) can be found at 94.5 FM. For the latest pop sensations, tune in to Z95.3 (95.3 FM) or FOX (99.3 FM). Classic rock is found on ROCK 101 (101 FM), and alternative sounds are on CO-OP RADIO (102.7 FM) and Xfm (104.9 FM). JR-FM (93.7 FM) does country, and for classical try CBC Radio Two (105.7 FM). The best site for sport is CKNW (98.0 FM). An excellent studio radio station featuring alternative and world artists and listings is UBC's CiTR (101.9 FM).

Travel essentials

Costs

If you're prepared to buy your own picnic lunch, stay in hostels and stick to the least expensive bars and restaurants, you should be able to get by on around Can$55/US$40/£25 per day. Staying in a good B&B, eating out in medium-range restaurants most nights and drinking often in bars, you'll go through at least Can$130/US$100/£60 per day, with the main variable being the cost of your room. On Can$200/US$150/£90 per day and upwards, you'll be able to live in relative luxury, enjoy a few city tours and eat well, though if you're planning to stay in the best hotels and to have a big night out pretty much every night, this still won't be anywhere near enough. As always, if you're travelling alone you'll spend much more on accommodation than you would in a group of two or more: most hotels do have single rooms, but they're fixed at about 65 percent (ie, not half) of the price of a double.

Restaurants don't come cheap, but costs remain manageable if you stick to the less pricey joints. A reasonable three-course meal with wine or beer can be had for around Can$25–30 per person, as long as you drink in moderation. Tipping at a restaurant is expected – usually fifteen to twenty percent – unless the service has been dire; taxi drivers expect a tip too, of the same amount. Museum admission prices are mostly in the Can$7/US$5/£3 range (though some, such as the Vancouver Art Gallery, are shockingly more expensive), but discounts of at least fifty percent are routinely available for children, seniors and students; indeed, concessionary fares and rates for teenagers, Canadian students and senior citizens are offered on all sorts of things, including public transport.

Tax and rebates

Virtually all prices in Canada – for everything from bubble gum to hotel rooms – are quoted without tax, which means that the price you see quoted is not the price you'll end up being required to pay. Across the province of British Columbia, which includes Vancouver, there's a provincial sales tax (PST) of 7 percent on most goods and services, which rises to 10 percent on hotel bills and in restaurants and bars; this is supplemented by the nationwide goods and services tax (GST), a 5 percent levy equivalent to VAT or IVA in Europe. Note the GST rebate once offered to visitors is no longer available.

Currency

Canadian currency is the dollar ($), made up of 100 cents (¢) to the dollar. Coins are issued in 1¢ (penny), 5¢ (nickel), 10¢ (dime), 25¢ (quarter), $1 and $2 denominations: the $1 coin is known as a "loonie", after the bird on one face; the newer $2 coin is less inventively named a "twoonie". Paper currency comes in $5, $10, $50, $100, $500 and $1000 denominations. Although US dollars are widely accepted, it's often on a one-for-one basis, and as the US dollar is usually worth more than its Canadian counterpart, it makes sense to exchange US currency.

Crime and personal safety

Canada has a very low crime rate in general, and while Vancouver is not the most crime-free of Canadian cities (that honour goes to Toronto), the city is very safe and largely free of violent crime. Some cases of smash-and-grab have been reported regarding cars with US licence plates and rental vehicles – travellers should avoid leaving their valuables in the car (or at least place them where they can't be seen) and park in a well-lit, central location.

Few citizens carry arms, muggings are uncommon, and street crime less commonplace than in many other major cities – though the usual cautions about poorly lit urban streets and so forth stand. Note also that the police are diligent in enforcing traffic laws.

Almost all the problems tourists encounter in Vancouver are to do with petty crime – pickpocketing and bag-snatching – rather than more serious physical confrontations. As such, it's good to be on your guard and know where your possessions are at all times.

Thieves often work in pairs and, although theft is far from commonplace, you should be aware of certain ploys. Watch out, for instance, for the "helpful" person pointing out "birdshit" (actually shaving cream or similar) on your coat, while someone else relieves you of your money; for someone inviting you to read a card or paper on the street to distract your attention; or for someone in a café moving for your drink with one hand while the other goes for your bag. If you're in a crowd of tourists, watch out for people moving in unusually close.

Sensible precautions against petty theft include carrying bags slung across your neck and not over your shoulder; not carrying anything in pockets that are easy to dip into; and having photocopies of your passport, airline ticket and driving licence, while leaving the originals in your hotel. When you're looking for a hotel room, never leave your bags unattended.

If you are robbed, you'll need to go to the police to report it, not least because your insurance company will require a police report. Remember to make a note of the report number – or, better still, ask for a copy of the statement itself. Don't expect a great deal of concern if your loss is relatively small, and don't be surprised if the process of completing forms and formalities takes ages.

Although generally you can walk around the city without fear of harassment or assault, and there are no clearly defined "no-go" areas as such, there are some rather shady locales at night – Pacific Central Station, much of Chinatown and on East Hastings especially – and visitors and women travelling alone should always be on their guard. Consequently, and especially until you are familiar with the city's layout, it's always best to err on the side of caution, particularly at night. Using public transport, even late at night, isn't usually a problem – but if in doubt take a taxi.

In the unlikely event that you are mugged, or otherwise threatened, never resist, and try to reduce your contact with the robber to a minimum; either just hand over what's wanted, or throw money in one direction and take off in the other. Afterwards go straight to the Vancouver City Police, who can be contacted at ⓣ604/717-3535. For emergencies (police, fire or ambulance), call ⓣ911.

Travellers with disabilities

Vancouver is one of the most accessible city in the world for travellers with disabilities. All public buildings are required to be wheelchair-accessible and provide suitable toilet facilities; almost all street corners have dropped kerbs/sidewalk wheelchair ramps (14,000 in total), as do the stairs at Robson Square; and most major attractions and hotels are now required to have ramps and elevators. Public transportation is accessible, with most buses equipped with wheelchair lifts and SkyTrain and SeaBus stations equipped to handle wheelchair access.

Indeed, the city's public transport system is particularly disability-friendly and publishes the Rider's Guide to Accessible Transit, available from Translink by calling ⓣ604/953-3040. More specifically, Pacific Coach Lines has accessible services between Vancouver and Victoria, as does Greyhound to Kelowna and points between. Visit ⓦwww.translink.bc.ca for general city transit information. For more general information, visit the Canadian government's first-rate site ⓦwww.accesstotravel.gc.ca.

General assistance in Vancouver

In the city, there are various organizations that can provide help and assistance for those with disabilities. The BC Paraplegic Association, 780 South West Marine Dr (ⓣ604/324-3611, ⓦwww.canparaplegic.org or www.bcpara.org), has lift-equipped vans for rent in and around the city.

BC Disability Sports (ⓣ604/737-3039, ⓦwww.disabilitysport.org) can offer details of competitive and recreational sports and facilities in the city (including riding, sailing, climbing, and track and field events); the BC

Mobility Opportunities Society (Ⓣ604/688-6464, Ⓦwww.disabilityfoundation.org) also provides sailing and other recreational activities. Note, too, that if you are camping, the BC Parks Disabled Access Pass is no longer valid.

Disabled services in Vancouver

BC Coalition of People with Disabilities Ⓣ1-800/663-1278 or 604/875-8835 (TDD). Advocacy Access Ⓣ604/872-1278, Ⓦwww.bccpd.bc.ca.
Canadian National Institute for the Blind Ⓣ1-866/659-1843, Ⓦwww.cnib.ca.
TransLink HandyDART Specially adapted door-to-door bus service for locals and visitors Ⓣ604/575-6600.
UBC Disability Resource Centre Ⓣ604/822-5844 or 604/822-9049 (TDD), Ⓦwww.students.ubc.ca/access/.
Western Institute for the Deaf and Hard of Hearing Ⓣ604/736-7391 (voice) or 604/736-2527 (TDD), Ⓦwww.widhh.ca.

Entry requirements

Citizens of the EU, non-EU Scandinavia and most Commonwealth countries, including Australia and New Zealand, travelling to Canada do not need an entry visa – just a valid passport – to stay up to six months, though the Canadian immigration officer who decides the length of your stay at the point of entry is more likely to allow you three.

United States citizens simply need proof of US citizenship (a birth certificate or a valid passport, though not a US driver's licence) and some form of photo identification. But check the latest arrangements for US citizens returning to the US – a passport may be required. If US citizens are entering Canada from another country, they must have a valid passport, naturalization certificate or green card. Permanent residents of the US should have their green card (US Resident Alien Card). Joint US–Canada programmes are available for regular travellers from the US to Canada, designed to speed up border-crossing.

All visitors to Canada have to complete a customs declaration form, which you'll be given on the plane or at the US–Canadian border. On the form you'll have to give details of where you intend to stay during your trip. If you don't know, write "touring", but be prepared to give an idea of your schedule and destinations to the immigration officer.

The Canadian immigration officers rarely refuse entry, but they may ask how much money you have and what job you do; they may also ask to see a return or onward ticket. Make sure you have proof of sufficient funds to support yourself. Travellers with criminal convictions (even those for drunk driving) should note that they may be refused entry. Ask the embassy before you go. Note also that although passing overland between the US and Canada used to be generally straightforward, there have been increasingly long delays since the September 2001 terrorist attacks on New York City and Washington, DC.

If you want to stay for more than six months or if you plan to study or work – even temporarily – you will need a visa. Contact the Canadian embassy, consulate or high commission in your country for authorization prior to departure (see below for contact details). Once inside Canada, if an extension of stay is desired, written application must be made to the nearest Canada Immigration Centre well before the expiry of the authorized visit.

The Government of Canada's "Canada International" website (Ⓦwww.canadainternational.gc.ca) contains useful information and links for anyone planning to visit, study or work in Canada. If you plan to visit or transit through the US, check what the US requirements are for nationals of your country, as they may be different from those of Canada; more information can be found at Ⓦhttp://travel.state.gov/visa_services.

Canadian high commissions, consulates and embassies

A full list of Canadian overseas representatives is available at Ⓦwww.canadainternational.gc.ca.

Canadian consulates abroad

Australia Canberra High Commission, Commonwealth Ave, Canberra, ACT 2600 Ⓣ02/6270 4000; Melbourne Consulate, Level 27, 101 Collins St, Melbourne, VIC 3000 Ⓣ03/9653 9674; Perth Consulate, 267 St George's Terrace, Third Floor, Perth, 6000 Australia Ⓣ08/9322 7930;

Sydney Consulate General, Level 5, Quay West Building, 111 Harrington St, Sydney, NSW 2000 ⓣ02/9364 3000.
Ireland Embassy, 7-8 Wilton Terrace, Dublin 2 ⓣ01/234 4000. For visa services contact the Immigration Division in London.
New Zealand Wellington High Commission, Level 11, 125 The Terrace, Wellington 6011 ⓣ04/473 9577. Auckland Consulate, Level 9, 48 Emily Place, Auckland 1010, ⓣ09/309 3690.
UK High Commission, Macdonald House (visa services), 1 Grosvenor Square, London W1K 4AB ⓣ020/7258 6600; Canada House (consular and passport enquiries), Trafalgar Square, London SW1Y 5BJ (ⓣ020/7258 6421. Also consular representation in Belfast, Cardiff and Edinburgh.
USA Embassy, 501 Pennsylvania Ave NW, Washington, DC 20001 ⓣ202/682 1740, for immigration and visas; also consulates or consulates general in 19 other US cities.

Health

Most visitors won't have any major health worries in Vancouver. Doctors and dentists can be found in the Yellow Pages (ⓦwww.yellowpages.ca), though for medical emergencies call ⓣ911. The Shopper's Drug Mart has a central pharmacy at 1125 Davie St (open 24hr; ⓣ604/669-2424).

If you plan to do a lot of hiking or other outdoor activities in the Vancouver region, you may want to take some of the typical precautions (DEET, protective clothing) against potentially disease-carrying insects, like mosquitoes, blackflies and ticks. West Nile and Lyme disease are not unknown to the area.

Insurance

The only thing worse than an accident or having something stolen on holiday is being out of pocket because of it. You'd do well to take out an insurance policy before travelling to Canada to cover against theft, loss and illness or injury, especially as Canada's generally excellent health service costs nonresidents anything from $50 to $2000 a day for hospitalization. There is no free treatment to nonresidents, but if you do have an accident, medical services will get to you quickly and charge you later.

Before paying for a new policy, however, it's worth checking whether you are already covered: some all-risks home insurance policies may cover your possessions when overseas, and many private medical schemes include cover when abroad. For residents from elsewhere in Canada, provincial health plans usually provide full cover for hospitalization, but for a visit to a physician you may need to pay up front and seek reimbursement later.

Holders of official student/teacher/youth cards in Canada and the US are entitled to meagre accident coverage and hospital inpatient benefits. Students will often find that their student health coverage extends during the vacations and for one term beyond the date of last enrolment. Some credit card companies also offer coverage if your holiday is purchased using your card; however, this type of coverage tends to be quite minimal.

Internet

Vancouver is well geared up for Internet and email access with numerous cafés. In addition, note that many of the better hotels provide email and Internet access for their guests free or at a minimal charge.

Mail

Canada Post operates branches in scores of locations, mostly as one part of a larger retail outlet, mainly pharmacies and stationery stores. The main post office is at 349 West Georgia St (ⓣ1-800/267-1177, ⓦwww.canadapost.ca) and is open Mon–Fri 8am–5.30pm. There are also postal facilities in branches of stores such as Shopper's Drug Mart. If you're posting letters to a Canadian address, always include the postcode or your mail may never get there.

Stamps can be purchased at Canada Post branches or offices as well as from automatic vending machines, the lobbies of larger hotels, airports, train stations, bus terminals and many retail outlets and newsstands. Current postal charges are 54¢ for letters and postcards up to 30g within Canada, 98¢ for the same weight to the US, and $1.65 for international mail (also up to 30g).

Maps

The Touristinfo Centre (see p.35) provides a comprehensive map of Vancouver, which, along with the maps in this guide, should be sufficient for your needs. If you're planning to use city transport, the excellent Transit Route Map & Guide is available from the infocentre as well as from stores boasting "FareDealer" stickers.

Canada's three leading map publishers – MapArt, the Vancouver-based ITMB, and Rand McNally – all have maps of Greater Vancouver, with more detailed insets for the central area. MapArt also publishes both a map and a street atlas of Vancouver and the Fraser Valley.

For more detailed mapping of the central area of the city, MapArt's Vancouver FastTrack is a handy concertina map with plans of Downtown, the central area and the region. MapEasy's plan, with its characteristic hand-drawn style, shows in addition to places of interest numerous hotels, restaurants and shops Downtown, on Granville Island and in Stanley Park. Compass's pocket-size map is a combination of two handy, if less detailed, pop-out plans.

For those planning to venture farther afield, ITMB has a contoured map of Vancouver's North Shore hiking trails at 1:50,000 and a road map of southwest British Columbia at 1:580,000. Mapping of Vancouver Island comes from ITMB at 1:400,000 with contours and hiking trials, or from Rand McNally and MapArt at 1:550,000 and 1:500,000 respectively, both with numerous street plans and the Gulf Islands. Both MapArt and Rand McNally also publish a street plan of the Vancouver Island's main town, Victoria, while ITMB has a special hiking map at 1:50,000 of the West Coast Trail in Pacific Rim National Park.

Money

Vancouver has plenty of ATMs (or ABMs – Automatic Bank Machines, as they are often known in Canadaa). Most ATMs accept a host of debit cards, including all those carrying the Cirrus, Plus or Interac coding. If in doubt, check with your bank to find out whether the card you wish to use will be accepted – and if you need a new (international) PIN. You will often be charged, however, for using ATMs in bars, clubs and shops. Credit cards can be used in ATMs too, but in this case transactions are treated as loans, with interest accruing daily from the date of withdrawal. All major credit cards, including American Express, Visa and MasterCard, are widely accepted.

If you need to change money, Vancouver's banks usually offer the best deals. Outside opening hours for banks, you might consider a bureau de change – try Thomas Cook, with several branches in the city. American Express cheques can be cashed at its Downtown office, 666 Burrard St (Mon–Fri 8.30am–5.30pm, Sat 10am–4pm, closed Sun; ⓣ604/669-2813, ⓦwww.americanexpress.ca) at the corner of Hornby and Dunsmuir streets.

At the time of writing, the rate of exchange is $2.10 to the pound sterling, $1.10 to the US dollar, $0.85 to the Australian dollar, and $0.75 to the NZ dollar. For the most up-to-date rates, check the currency converter website ⓦwww.xe.com/ucc/.

Opening hours and public holidays

Vancouver is a city for the traditional shopper, where artisan stores, cute boutiques, antiques vendors and ethnic markets still lord it over the urban mini-mall. Many places are

Public holidays

New Year's Day Jan 1
Good Friday varies; March/April
Easter Sunday varies; March/April
Easter Monday varies; March/April
Victoria Day third Monday in May
Canada Day July 1
BC Day first Monday in August
Labour Day first Monday in Sept
Thanksgiving second Monday in October
Remembrance Day Nov 11
Christmas Day Dec 25
Boxing Day Dec 26

closed on public holidays – though not the city's bars, restaurants and hotels. Public transport keeps moving on holidays, too, operating a scaled-back service. For a list of festivals and events, see p.201.

Shopping hours are fairly uniform, with most places open seven days a week: Mon–Wed and Sat 9/9.30am–6pm, Thurs & Fri 9/9.30am–9pm and Sun 10am–5/6pm. Malls have slightly longer hours, and convenience stores, like 7-11, are routinely open much longer, often 24hr. Liquor used to be on sale Mon–Sat only, but the law has been changed and it can now be purchased from government liquor stores on Sundays, too.

Post offices generally open Mon–Sat 10am–5pm. Hours at museums vary, but they are generally open daily (except Monday) from around 10/11am to 5pm or 5.30pm, with one late night a week, usually Thursday until 8pm. As for restaurants, these are usually open daily from 11/11.30am to 11pm, with or without an afternoon break from around 2.30/3pm to 5/6pm. Bars are open daily until 1am or later; dance clubs are often closed on Sunday and Monday nights – the rest of the week, they begin to get busy around 10pm and close at 2am or later.

Phones

Domestic and international telephone calls can be made with equal ease from public and private phones. Public telephones are commonplace. All are equipped for the hearing-impaired and take coins. Most also accept prepaid calling cards, as well as credit cards. Local calls cost 25¢ from a public phone, but are free on private phones (though not usually hotel phones).

When dialling any Canadian number, either local or long-distance, you must include the area code – ⓣ604 in Vancouver. Long-distance calls – to numbers beyond the area code of the telephone from which you are making the call – must be prefixed with "1". On public telephones, this "1" puts you through to the operator, who will tell you how much money you need to be connected. Thereafter, you'll be asked to shovel money in at regular intervals – so unless you're making a credit card or reverse-charge/collect call you'll need a stack of quarters (25¢ pieces).

To confuse matters, some connections within a single telephone code area are charged at the long-distance rate, and thus need the "1" prefix; a recorded message will tell you this is necessary as soon as you dial the number. To save the hassle of carrying all this change, you could consider either buying a telephone card back home or here.

As for tariffs, the cheap-rate period for calls is between 6pm and 8am during the week and all weekend. Note also that many businesses, especially hotels, have toll-free numbers (prefixed by ⓣ1-800, ⓣ1-888 or similar numbers). Some of these can be dialled only from phones in the same province, others from anywhere within Canada, and a few from anywhere in North America. Finally, remember that although most hotel rooms have phones, there is almost always an exorbitant surcharge for their use.

If you want to use your mobile phone in Vancouver, you'll need to check cellular access and call charges with your phone provider before you set out. The mobile network now covers almost all of the city and works on GSM 1900 – which means that mobiles bought in Europe need to be triband to gain cellular access.

Tourist information

Information on Vancouver is fairly easy to track down, either over the Internet or, upon arrival, at the Touristinfo Centre Downtown; maps of the city are readily available from local bookstores.

Useful phone numbers

Directory enquiries local (from private and public phones) ⓣ411; long-distance within North America from private phones ⓣ411, from public phones ⓣ1+ area code + 555-1212; international, call the operator ⓣ0.

Emergencies Police, fire and ambulance ⓣ911.

Operator (domestic and international) ⓣ0.

Phoning abroad from Vancouver To Australia: ⓣ011 + 61 + area code minus zero + number; to the Ireland: ⓣ011 + 353 + area code minus zero + number; to New Zealand: ⓣ011 + 64 + area code minus zero + number; to the UK: ⓣ011 + 44 + area code minus zero + number; to the US: ⓣ1 + area code + number.

Phoning Vancouver from abroad Dial your country's international access code, then the area code, followed by the number.

Vancouver area code ⓣ604.

Victoria area code ⓣ250.

The excellent Touristinfo Centre (mid-May to Sept daily 8am–6pm; Sept–May Mon–Sat 8.30am–5pm; ⓣ604/683-2000, 682-2222 or 1-800/663-6000 or 1-800/435-5622, ⓦwww.tourismvancouver.com) can be found almost opposite Canada Place (see p.42) in the Waterfront Centre, 200 Burrard St at the corner of Canada Place Way.

Besides offering free information on the city and much of southeastern British Columbia, the office provides foreign exchange facilities and BC TransLink (transit or public transport) tickets and information; tickets to sports and entertainment events can be purchased through a separate booth. Same-day tickets for events are also often available at a discount.

The infocentre also has one of the most comprehensive accommodation services, backed up by bulging photo albums of hotel rooms and B&Bs: the booking service is free. Smaller kiosks open in the summer (July & Aug) in a variety of locations, usually including Stanley Park and close to the Vancouver Art Gallery on the corner of West Georgia and Granville streets (daily 9.30am–5.30pm, Thurs & Fri till 9pm).

Websites

ⓦ**www.vancouver.ca** The city government's comprehensive site features links to almost everything you need, including an arts and events calendar, information on parks and gardens, and maps of walking tours.

ⓦ**www.vancouversun.com** The Vancouver Sun, the city's morning newspaper, provides news, sport and weather updates as well as film, art gallery and music listings.

ⓦ**www.straight.com** The online version of The Georgia Straight, Vancouver's free news and entertainment weekly. This is your best bet for what's happening in the city.

ⓦ**www.visitorschoice.com** This comprehensive, professional website presents events, attractions, festivals, dining, shopping and accommodation information.

ⓦ**www.canada.com/vancouver** Features the best Vancouver newspapers, local news and listings.

ⓦ**www.cbc.ca/radio** Vancouver's public radio station can be accessed live over the Internet for news and feature stories.

ⓦ**www.gayvancouver.net** Gay and gay-friendly accommodations, businesses, restaurants, nightlife, events and services.

ⓦ**www.hellobc.com** Visit this page for information on accommodation and travel ideas for trips around the province.

ⓦ**www.vcmbc.com**The Vancouver Coast and Mountains Tourism Board provides information and ideas for golfing expeditions, touring, outdoor activities and general trips out of town.

The City

The City

1

Downtown

Downtown is Vancouver's dazzling heart, home to its glittering high-rise skyscrapers and other modern architectural marvels, as well as many of the city's key shopping streets, a good deal of its prime office space, most of its big luxury hotels, one of its major galleries and its prime stretches of waterfront. The streets are also a pleasure to walk for their own sake, and some of your most enduring memories of Vancouver will probably involve turning a Downtown corner to be rewarded with a sudden and sensational view of the Pacific and the jagged peaks of the Coast Mountains.

Broadly speaking, the Downtown core is bounded by the waterfront to the north and south (Burrard Inlet and False Creek respectively), Stanley Park to the west and Gastown and Chinatown to the east. As the city has grown, however, Downtown has spread. South of the Downtown core you'll find the revitalized and funky warehouse neighbourhood of **Yaletown**, a small grid of streets attracting new small businesses, specialist stores, bars, cafés and restaurants. Most of Downtown's other peripheral areas hold little interest. Bordering Stanley Park, the upscale **West End**, for example, is pleasant but largely residential – with one or two interesting streets, such as Denman – while much of the nameless southern area outside Yaletown is nondescript at best.

Downtown Vancouver differs from many North American cities in that people both live and work here, lending the area a vibrancy and dynamism often missing in other urban centres. Neighbourhoods such as the West End and Yaletown, for example, feel like living communities, complete with markets and neighbourhood stores. In this they take their cue from Downtown's main street, and one of its chief shopping thoroughfares, **Robson Street**, a central axis crammed with restaurants and a mixture of designer stores, useful shops and late-night outlets.

The Downtown core

Downtown's other principal thoroughfares are **Burrard Street** – all smart shops, hotels and offices – and **Granville Street**, partly pedestrianized and also with plenty of shops and cinemas. Despite some efforts at rejuvenation, the latter is curiously seedy in places, especially at its southern end near the Granville Street Bridge – though even here, Yaletown and the False Creek waterfront's not-so-distant condominiums are beginning to push out the clubs, tat and nickel-and-dime stores as the ripple of gentrification spreads.

While you'll probably be tempted to explore Robson if you step onto the street on your first day in Vancouver, you're better off making your acquaintance with

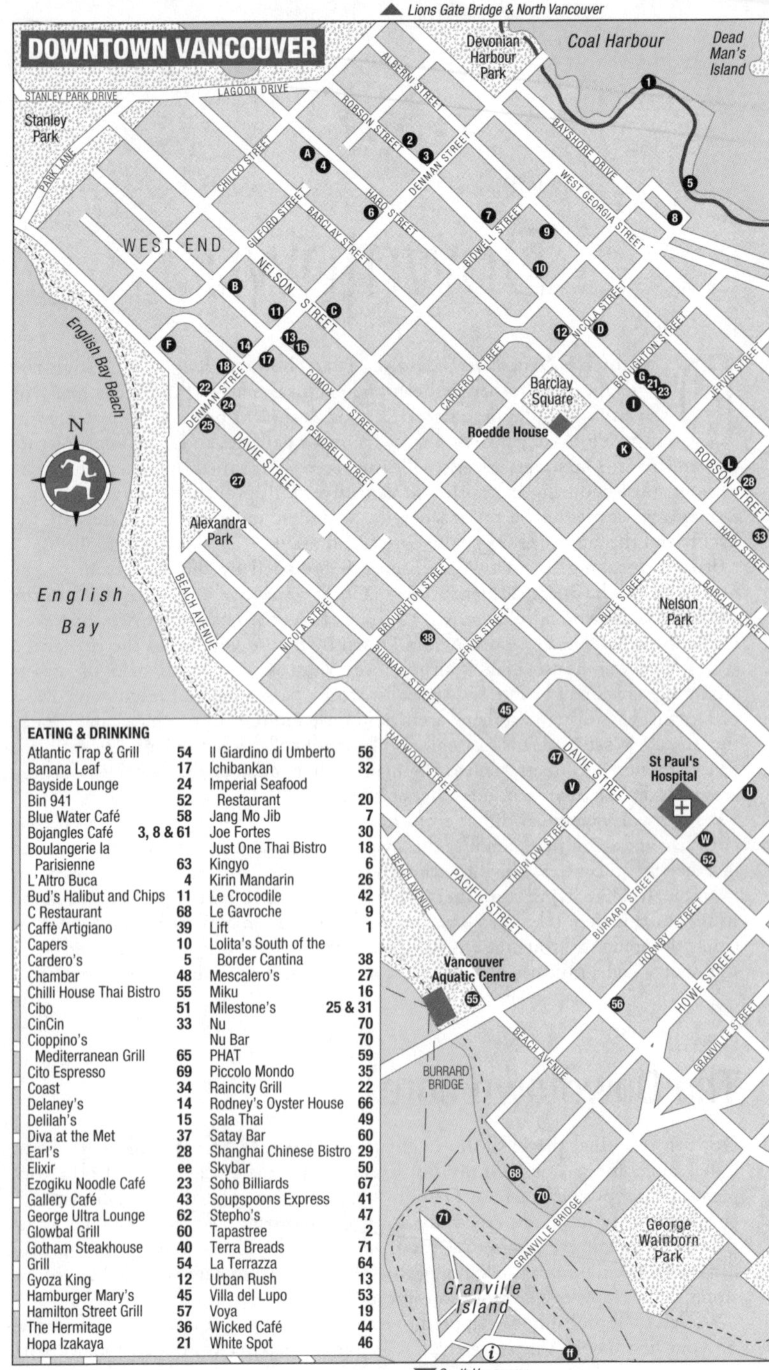
Lions Gate Bridge & North Vancouver
DOWNTOWN VANCOUVER
Devonian Harbour Park
Coal Harbour
Dead Man's Island
Stanley Park
STANLEY PARK DRIVE
LAGOON DRIVE
PARK LANE
ALBERNI STREET
ROBSON STREET
DENMAN STREET
BAYSHORE DRIVE
WEST GEORGIA STREET
CHILCO STREET
GILFORD STREET
HARO STREET
BARCLAY STREET
BIDWELL STREET
WEST END
NELSON STREET
NICOLA STREET
BROUGHTON STREET
JERVIS STREET
English Bay Beach
COMOX STREET
CARDERO STREET
Barclay Square
Roedde House
PENDRELL STREET
DAVIE STREET
N
Alexandra Park
English Bay
BEACH AVENUE
BUTE STREET
Nelson Park
BURNABY STREET
HARWOOD STREET
St Paul's Hospital
THURLOW STREET
PACIFIC STREET
BURRARD STREET
HORNBY STREET
HOWE STREET
GRANVILLE STREET
Vancouver Aquatic Centre
BURRARD BRIDGE
GRANVILLE BRIDGE
George Wainborn Park
Granville Island
South Vancouver
EATING & DRINKING
Atlantic Trap & Grill 54
Banana Leaf 17
Bayside Lounge 24
Bin 941 52
Blue Water Café 58
Bojangles Café 3, 8 & 61
Boulangerie la Parisienne 63
L'Altro Buca 4
Bud's Halibut and Chips 11
C Restaurant 68
Caffè Artigiano 39
Capers 10
Cardero's 5
Chambar 48
Chilli House Thai Bistro 55
Cibo 51
CinCin 33
Cioppino's Mediterranean Grill 65
Cito Espresso 69
Coast 34
Delaney's 14
Delilah's 15
Diva at the Met 37
Earl's 28
Elixir ee
Ezogiku Noodle Café 23
Gallery Café 43
George Ultra Lounge 62
Glowbal Grill 60
Gotham Steakhouse 40
Grill 54
Gyoza King 12
Hamburger Mary's 45
Hamilton Street Grill 57
The Hermitage 36
Hopa Izakaya 21
Il Giardino di Umberto 56
Ichibankan 32
Imperial Seafood Restaurant 20
Jang Mo Jib 7
Joe Fortes 30
Just One Thai Bistro 18
Kingyo 6
Kirin Mandarin 26
Le Crocodile 42
Le Gavroche 9
Lift 1
Lolita's South of the Border Cantina 38
Mescalero's 27
Miku 16
Milestone's 25 & 31
Nu 70
Nu Bar 70
PHAT 59
Piccolo Mondo 35
Raincity Grill 22
Rodney's Oyster House 66
Sala Thai 49
Satay Bar 60
Shanghai Chinese Bistro 29
Skybar 50
Soho Billiards 67
Soupspoons Express 41
Stepho's 47
Tapastree 2
Terra Breads 71
La Terrazza 64
Urban Rush 13
Villa del Lupo 53
Voya 19
Wicked Café 44
White Spot 46

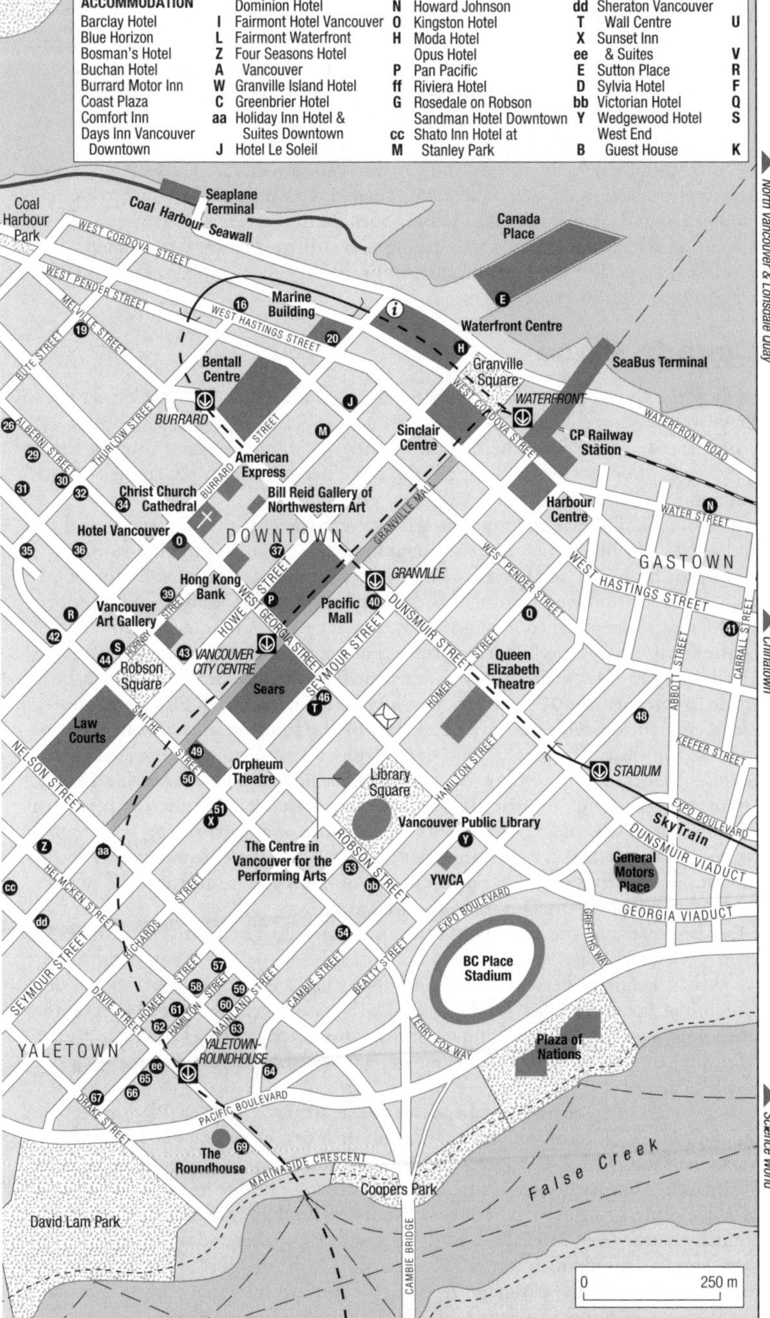
ACCOMMODATION
Barclay Hotel I
Blue Horizon L
Bosman's Hotel Z
Buchan Hotel A
Burrard Motor Inn W
Coast Plaza C
Comfort Inn aa
Days Inn Vancouver Downtown J
Dominion Hotel N
Fairmont Hotel Vancouver O
Fairmont Waterfront H
Four Seasons Hotel Vancouver P
Granville Island Hotel ff
Greenbrier Hotel G
Holiday Inn Hotel & Suites Downtown cc
Hotel Le Soleil M
Howard Johnson dd
Kingston Hotel T
Moda Hotel X
Opus Hotel ee
Pan Pacific E
Riviera Hotel D
Rosedale on Robson bb
Sandman Hotel Downtown Y
Shato Inn Hotel at Stanley Park B
Sheraton Vancouver Wall Centre U
Sunset Inn & Suites V
Sutton Place R
Sylvia Hotel F
Victorian Hotel Q
Wedgewood Hotel S
West End Guest House K
Coal Harbour Park
Seaplane Terminal
Coal Harbour Seawall
Canada Place
WEST CORDOVA STREET
WEST PENDER STREET
MELVILLE STREET
WEST HASTINGS STREET
Marine Building
Waterfront Centre
SeaBus Terminal
Granville Square
WATERFRONT
WATERFRONT ROAD
CP Railway Station
BUTE STREET
Bentall Centre
BURRARD
THURLOW STREET
ALBERNI STREET
BURRARD STREET
American Express
Sinclair Centre
Christ Church Cathedral
Bill Reid Gallery of Northwestern Art
GRANVILLE MALL
Harbour Centre
WATER STREET
Hotel Vancouver
DOWNTOWN
GASTOWN
WEST PENDER STREET
GRANVILLE
Hong Kong Bank
HOWE STREET
WEST GEORGIA STREET
Pacific Mall
DUNSMUIR STREET
Vancouver Art Gallery
HORNBY STREET
VANCOUVER CITY CENTRE
SEYMOUR STREET
Robson Square
Sears
RICHARDS STREET
Queen Elizabeth Theatre
ABBOTT STREET
CARRALL STREET
HOMER
Law Courts
SMITHE STREET
KEEFER STREET
Orpheum Theatre
Library Square
HAMILTON STREET
STADIUM
NELSON STREET
EXPO BOULEVARD
SkyTrain
Vancouver Public Library
DUNSMUIR VIADUCT
The Centre in Vancouver for the Performing Arts
ROBSON STREET
YWCA
General Motors Place
HELMCKEN STREET
EXPO BOULEVARD
GEORGIA VIADUCT
GRIFFITHS WAY
SEYMOUR STREET
CAMBIE STREET
BEATTY STREET
BC Place Stadium
DAVIE STREET
MAINLAND STREET
YALETOWN
YALETOWN-ROUNDHOUSE
TERRY FOX WAY
Plaza of Nations
PACIFIC BOULEVARD
DRAKE STREET
The Roundhouse
MARINASIDE CRESCENT
Coopers Park
False Creek
David Lam Park
CAMBIE BRIDGE
0 250 m
North Vancouver & Lonsdale Quay
Chinatown
Science World
Stamp's Landing
Spyglass Place & South Vancouver

the city at the northern end of Burrard. This is where you'll find the city's main **Touristinfo Centre** (see p.35) and **Canada Place**, a superb waterfront complex that provides a literal and visual introduction to Vancouver's past and present. Close by, you can enjoy an overview of the city from the **Harbour Centre**, a high-rise building with a panoramic viewing level. Then you might stroll up Burrard towards Robson to take in a medley of minor sights and buildings, of which the Art Deco **Marine Building** is the most compelling.

On Robson, the main cultural lure is the **Vancouver Art Gallery**, the city's principal collection of art, where the chief attractions are first-rate travelling exhibitions and the paintings of Victoria-born Emily Carr. Finally you should take a look at the development that's taking Downtown's reach farther south and southeast, especially the magnificent **public library**, a striking piece of modern architecture built in 1995.

Canada Place

Built as the Canadian pavilion for Expo '86, **Canada Place**, at 999 Canada Place Way (walkways open daily 24hr; free; Ⓣ604/775-7200, Ⓦwww.canadaplace.ca), which stands across from the main infocentre, is an architectural tour de force, housing the luxury *Pan Pacific* hotel, the city's main cruise-ship terminal, restaurants and a glitzy convention centre.

Its design, and the manner in which it juts into the port the equivalent of three and a half city blocks, is meant to suggest a ship, a nod to the vital role of the city's port both past and present. This visual allusion is reinforced by the building's most distinctive feature, the five great 27m-high Teflon-coated fabric "sails" that make up its roof, a motif continued by the vast hotel and convention centre – the "mast" – which rises above the complex. Much of the surrounding area has been, or is currently being developed, to expand the convention area to triple its current size. It's unlikely you'll want to spend much time in the hotel, bland convention centre or any other part of the interior, as the main point of interest for casual visitors is the "deck", or **walkway**, that wraps around the building. Dotted with infoboards that describe the immediate cityscape and the appropriate pages of its history, the walkway starts at an attractive **fountain** adorned with the flags of Canada's provinces and territories. It provides stunning vistas across the Burrard Inlet of North and West Vancouver, with the mountains and forest as a backdrop, and the huge green sanctuary of Stanley Park to the west on the Downtown waterfront.

Key landmarks on the mountains across the water are **The Lions**, unmistakeable twin peaks reputedly named after their resemblance to the lions designed by Sir Edwin Landseer between 1857 and 1867 that stand at the foot of Nelson's Column in London. Other versions of how the peaks were christened suggest the innocuous name was adopted and vigorously promoted by city elders to help erase from the collective memory the name given to the landmarks by early settlers – Sheila's Paps.

Even better than the mountain views is the window Canada Place offers on Vancouver's **port**, a constant buzz and hum of boats, helicopters and floatplanes. Vancouver vies with Los Angeles and New York for the title of North America's busiest port. The harbour was first used for exporting timber in 1864 in the shape of fence pickets to Australia. Today it handles around 83 million tonnes of cargo annually, turns over $40 billion in trade and processes around 3000 ships a year from almost a hundred countries. The best way to see the port at close quarters is to ride the SeaBus, the passenger ferry across Burrard Inlet that runs to Lonsdale Quay from a terminal in Waterfront SkyTrain station (see opposite).

The alternative to enjoying the view is enjoying Canada Place's **CN IMAX cinema** (screenings afternoons and evenings daily; prices start at $12; Ⓣ604/682-4629 or 682-IMAX, Ⓦwww.imax.com/Vancouver), the world's first such cinema, which contains a five-storey-high screen designed for spectacular special-format films (some 3-D) accompanied by high-powered IMAX Digital Sound. The number of films made for the format is limited, and they generally last only 45min. They often involve rock concerts, the natural world, space exploration and wildlife subjects – and are generally a waste of a good screen.

Burrard Street

After seeing Canada Place you could walk a few minutes east to explore Gastown (see p.54) or take in the handful of small sights that lie on or just off **Burrard Street**, just to the south. Many of the sights are free, in particular the Marine Building and Christ Church Cathedral. Others take a bit more time and require money up front, notably the Harbour Centre. When you've walked down Burrard you'll still be well placed for Gastown or – more pertinently if you wish to continue exploring Downtown – for Robson Street and the Vancouver Art Gallery.

Canadian Pacific Railway Station

Walk east on West Cordova one block and you'll come to the SeaBus Terminal and Waterfront SkyTrain station, both housed in the old **Canadian Pacific Railway Station** at 601 West Cordova St, a listed heritage building. It opened in 1915 as the western terminus of Canada's first transcontinental railway, a role it has long since surrendered to the drab CNR and VIA Rail terminal in the southeast part of the city.

Angel of Victory (1922), the bronze statue in front of the station, was sculpted by Coeur de Lion MacCarthy and commissioned by the Canadian Pacific Railway (CPR) as a memorial to its employees who died in World War I.

More anodyne art is displayed inside the grandiose Neoclassical building, namely romantic scenes of the Canadian Rockies you might have viewed from the railway back when it was first built: they were painted by the wife of an early CPR executive. Otherwise the interior is given over to ticket machines and a handful of very dull shops.

Harbour Centre Tower

Almost opposite the former Canadian Pacific terminus, at 555 West Hastings at Seymour and Cordova, stands the Cordova Street entrance to the very popular **Harbour Centre** (daily: May to mid-Oct 8.30am–10.30pm; mid-Oct to April 9am–9pm; The Lookout! $13; Ⓣ604/689-0421, Ⓦwww.vancouverlookout.com). Opened by the first man on the moon, Neil Armstrong, in 1977, it was the city's tallest building for a long time and known by locals as "the hamburger", after its bulging upper storeys.

On a fine day it's definitely worth paying to ride the stomach-churning, all-glass, SkyLift elevators that run up the side of the tower – 167m in a minute – to the fortieth-storey observation deck. This deck is known as "The Lookout!" and provides a glorious 360° view: free tours lasting between 25 and 45 minutes pointing out the city landmarks below are available every hour on the hour.

The deck also offers a variety of mildly interesting video and other displays, plus an expensive restaurant – eat here and the ride up is free. While the ticket to The Lookout! is rather overpriced for what it delivers, it is valid all day (remember to keep your receipt), so you can return and watch the sunset.

The Marine Building

Retrace your steps to Canada Place and turn left up Burrard Street. Almost immediately on your right, at 355 Burrard St (near the intersection with West Hastings), stands the 25-storey **Marine Building** (lobby open office hours; entrance free), which English poet and architectural critic Sir John Betjeman called the "best Art Deco office building in the world".

The enterprise was the brainchild of J.W. Hobbs, vice-president of G.A. Stimson, a Toronto-based finance company, and president of Hobbs Bros, a ship-owning concern.

Completed in 1930, this was the tallest building in the British Commonwealth for ten years after it opened. It was intended as a paean in stone to Vancouver's maritime links and designed to resemble a rocky headland, or, as local architects McCarter and Nairne rather effusively claimed, "some great marine rock rising from the sea clinging with sea flora and fauna, in sea green, flashed with gold".

The building's fascinating **facade** has featured in many a Vancouver-shot TV show or movie, its main sunburst door perfect for any film requiring a "period City Hall" shot. Across the facade is a series of stylized Art Deco **bas-reliefs** depicting old planes and various other forms of transport, complemented by a frieze of waves and other maritime motifs and settings. Such themes were radical at a time when architects were still largely preoccupied with Neoclassical and neo-Gothic conceits.

Architects and designers came up with a host of ideas for sea creatures – snails, turtles, carp, scallops, seahorses, skate – to adorn every surface. Mingled with these are motifs further emphasizing Vancouver's transport links – boats and trains (to represent the city's status as a major port and rail terminus), stained glass which highlights the exploits of Captain George Vancouver (his ship, *Discovery*, is pictured on the horizon over the main entrance, with stylized Canada geese flying overhead), and a collection of aircraft, Zeppelins, cars and famous ships such as the *Golden Hind*, *Resolution*, *Beaver* and *Empress of India*.

The maritime theme continues inside the beautiful old **lobby** in which Hobbs envisaged a 27m-long "Grand Concourse" adorned in the manner of a treasure-laden Mayan temple. A vaulted ceiling offsets blue and green tiles lit by sconces designed to resemble ships' prows. Note the inlaid zodiac floor, and the fantastic Art Deco wood-and-brass elevator doors – among the most beautiful entrances in North America.

Much of the lobby, and the building as a whole, might have been even more spectacular but for the fact that work was interrupted by the Wall Street Crash of 1929. Some of the extravagances were reined in, but Hobbs pressed on with construction, lavishing a total of $2.3 million on his dream, $1.1 million over budget. The building's opening was a failure, however, and almost everybody associated with the folly came to grief – including Hobbs. In 1933, after three years in which tenants could be found only for the first four floors, G.A. Stimson went bust, and the Marine Building was offered to the city as a town hall for $1 million. The city declined. It was eventually sold to Guinness, the Irish brewing dynasty, for $900,000, considerably less than it had cost to build.

Today, after years of moderate decline, the Marine Building has been returned to its former glory, some $20 million having been spent on restoration since the 1980s.

Christ Church Cathedral

Two blocks up Burrard Street you'll come to the Anglican **Christ Church Cathedral** (visiting hours Mon–Fri 10am–4pm; church open longer hours for services; ⓣ604/682-3848, ⓦwww.cathedral.Vancouver.bc.ca), at no. 690 (near the corner of Georgia). A neo-Gothic building begun in 1888 (making it the city's oldest church), it was completed in 1895 and is now all but hemmed in by modern skyscrapers.

The city's parish history began on December 30, 1888, when the first service was held – without a church – at 720 Granville St in what was then the town of Vancouver. In 1889, a committee was formed to collect funds for the building of a church, eventually acquiring land from the Canadian Pacific Railway through the offices of Henry John Cambie, chief engineer of the CPR's Pacific division and warden of the new church.

The church was completed in 1895 and dedicated a year later. Don't be fooled by the sandstone cladding – inside, the building has a partly wooden frame of massive Douglas fir timbers culled from local forests. Initially the building served as the parish church for the immediate area but as Vancouver grew, so did its reach, and it was made the city's cathedral in 1929.

Inside, check out the mighty **organ**, built in 1949 after an earlier Wurlitzer gave up the ghost – it was rather cobbled together from war surplus parts and bits of the old Wurlitzer. Also look for the cathedral's emblem, a Celtic cross, which is dotted around the exterior and interior, and note the three-fish motif at its heart – it acknowledges the Coast Salish and other original West Coast inhabitants.

In 1971 the building and its stunning wooden ceiling narrowly escaped demolition when the local religious authorities wanted to cash in on its site, by now a prime piece of real estate. In the face of public opposition, the building was listed as a heritage site and thus protected in 1976.

Hotel Vancouver and the Hong Kong Bank

Cathedral Place stands close to the junction of Burrard Street and **Georgia Street**, which takes its name from the Strait of Georgia between Vancouver and Vancouver Island. The junction is dominated by the unmistakeable bulk of the **Fairmont Hotel Vancouver** at 900 West Georgia St (see p.121), the city's leading traditional luxury hotel.

This is the institution's third incarnation. The first, a four-storey wooden building, was built in 1886 by the Canadian Pacific Railway, which had been given roughly 6000 acres of Downtown land in return for making Vancouver the western terminus of the first trans-Canadian railway. The second hotel on

▲ The Marine Building

the site was built in 1916 but quickly proved too modest. The present pile, designed by architects John S. Archibald and John Schofield, was begun in 1929 and completed ten years later.

You'll soon learn to recognize the hotel's distinctive green-patina copper gables, built as part of the building's mock French-château design, which are visible from many points as you walk the city. The hotel also sports finely carved stone gargoyles (said to be copies of eleventh-century originals made for a variety of French cathedrals) and a large statue of the Roman god Hermes. Drop by the lobby if you want to see more – the concierge occasionally conducts tours, currently on Saturdays at 10.30am and 1pm.

Turn east on West Georgia at this point and, across the street at the first intersection with Hornby, take a quick look in the lobby of the **Hong Kong Bank** at 885 West Georgia St, notable for a gargantuan piece of kinetic art by Alan Storey known as *The Pendulum*. At 27m in length, the hollow pendulum is one of the world's largest, weighing in at 1600kg, though the term is slightly fraudulent, as the device is helped in its 6m swing by mechanical hydraulics at its fulcrum. The rest of the lobby is given over to temporary art exhibitions.

The Bill Reid Gallery of Northwest Art

The **Bill Reid Gallery of Northwest Art** at 639 Hornby St, between Dunsmuir and West Georgia sts (Wed–Sun 11am–5pm; $10; Ⓣ604/682-3455, Ⓦwww.billreidgallery.ca), opened in 2008, primarily to celebrate the work of the eponymous Haida sculptor, carver, goldsmith and writer, who died in 1998 aged 78. It's a beautiful contemporary space, perfectly suited to Reid's clean-lined, monumental works, but also to his more delicate jewellery and smaller carvings. Around 40 of the artist's works make up the permanent collection – look out, in particular, for *Mythic Messengers*, an 8.5-metre bronze frieze – but there are also works by earlier and other aboriginal artists that place Reid's work, and that of Northwest art in general, in context. You can also watch a film of Reid at work, and there are often temporary exhibitions devoted to emerging and established artists, Canadian and American, from the Pacific Northwest. If Reid's work appeals, be sure to visit the Museum of Anthropology (see p.87), which houses one of his masterpieces.

Vancouver Art Gallery

Downtown's main museum, the **Vancouver Art Gallery** (Mon–Wed, Fri–Sun & public holidays 10am–5.30pm, Tues & Thurs 10am–9pm; $20.50; Ⓣ604/662-4700, 662-4719 recorded information, Ⓦwww.vanartgallery.bc.ca) occupies a former courthouse at 750 Hornby St at Robson. The building was completed in 1911 and converted by leading Canadian architect Arthur Erickson (see box, p.89) during the 1970s redevelopment of Robson Street and Robson Square.

When the gallery opened in 1983 it retained much of the courthouse's august grandeur, preserving its stolid stonework, Neoclassical pillars, ornate plasterwork and the glass-topped dome and rotunda. Erickson also preserved former Chief Justice Allan McEachern's courtroom (now the gallery boardroom) on account of its beautifully carved judge's bench: the room – every inch your idea of a typical North American "courtroom" – has been used in all manner of movies, most famously *The Accused*, starring Jodie Foster.

The courthouse's original architect, Francis Mawson Rattenbury, lived a life that might have provided material for any number of movies. Rattenbury, who was also responsible for the cream of Victoria's historic buildings (see p.221), retired to

England, where he enjoyed only a short period of repose before being murdered in 1935 by his wife and her teenage lover, the family chauffeur.

In many ways this story is a lot better than the gallery's art – the permanent collection comprises over 80,000 works and is valued at over $100 million, but the only part of the collection you can be sure of seeing is the Emily Carr section on the top floor. The other three floors are given over to touring shows and rotating displays from the permanent collection. Thus you can never be sure quite what you will see of the latter, which features a rather sparse international collection with some of the lesser works of Warhol and Lichtenstein, as well as Italian, Flemish and British paintings spanning the sixteenth to twentieth centuries.

In recent years, the gallery has made a determined effort to collect contemporary works – videos, sculptures, installations and, in particular, photo-based and photo-conceptual art. In the last area the gallery boasts the largest such collection in North America, including wonderful pieces by Cindy Sherman (notably her "self" portraits), Jeff Wall, Rachel Whiteread, Jenny Holzer and the magnificent monumental photographs of Andreas Gursky.

But, of course, you can't be sure you'll see these – the display spaces seem to be given over to travelling exhibits. So even if these shows are interesting – and they frequently are excellent – the very steep admission means you are taking a rather expensive chance. What redeems the place for the casual visitor are the 200 powerful works of Vancouver artist **Emily Carr** (see box, p.48). As with the permanent collection, however, not all these paintings are on display at any one time. The ones that are will inevitably display Carr's thematic and stylistic trademarks, namely a passion for the landscapes and aboriginal cultures of the Pacific Northwest.

Whether you're coming to the gallery for an exhibition or not, be sure to visit the excellent **Gallery Café** (Mon–Wed & Fri–Sat 9am–5.30pm, Thurs 9am–9pm, Sun 10am–5pm; see p.131) – the food's good, and there's a great outdoor terrace.

Southeast Downtown

Southeast Downtown is the area where the face of Vancouver is changing most dramatically. The district, bounded by Richards Street to the west, Robson Street to the north and False Creek to the south, has seen considerable residential and other building since the early 1990s, the many high-rise developments a vivid expression of Downtown's vitality and the desire of people to live close to the heart of the city. Thanks to ongoing efforts by the city council (tax breaks, improvement to infrastructure and so forth), Vancouver proper, as opposed to Greater Vancouver, has shown a net increase in population over the last fifteen years, reversing a drift of people to the suburbs (which nevertheless continue to grow at a startling rate).

Much of southeast Downtown's growth owes itself to the fact that this is really the only direction Downtown could expand – water lies to the north and south, while to the west much of the land is already taken up with the top-dollar properties of the West End.

For the time being, most of the action is on Homer and Hamilton streets, and on the False Creek waterfront, where numerous high-rise residential blocks have appeared. Things have also changed in the converted warehouse district of **Yaletown** and around the eastern end of Robson Street, where a lacklustre area that once boasted only the 1983 **BC Place Stadium** – a large and

Emily Carr

Western Canada's most celebrated painter, **Emily Carr** was born in 1871 into a prosperous Victoria family. She led an artistic life that was almost clichéd – one that was eccentric, thwarted, ridiculed, bohemian and impoverished by turn, but also one that was ultimately successful and triumphant.

Things got off to a bad start. She was orphaned at an early age, and then her remaining family tried to persuade her against an artistic career, a way of life then deemed unsuitable for a woman. Ignoring their advice, she made her own way to San Francisco's California School of Art in 1890 at the age of just 19. Unable to make ends meet there, she was forced to teach for a living, an activity she continued on her return to Victoria in 1893.

In 1899, she travelled to Ucluelet on the west coast of Vancouver Island, where she came into contact with the art and culture of the indigenous **Nuu-chah-nulth**, an experience that would influence and feature in her work for the rest of her life. After a brief sojourn in England, marked by illness as she trained at art schools, Carr returned to Victoria in 1904, where the provincial and largely hidebound world of early-twentieth-century British Columbia viewed her lifestyle as wildly eccentric or worse. She often travelled with either a dog or parrot for company, and in time acquired a menagerie that included cats, cockatoos, a white rat named Susie and a Capuchin monkey known as Woo. Carr even made pinafores for her charges to wear on walks in the park with their owner.

In 1906, Carr moved to a studio in Vancouver at 570 Granville St. A year later she travelled to Alaska and again encountered the aboriginal cultures and northern landscapes that would eventually colour her art. Four years later, still feeling her work lacked power and technique, she went to Paris, where she absorbed the lessons of the new art movements sweeping the city. Chief among these was the **Fauve** ("wild beast") school, so called because of the frenzied distortions, random patterns and bright, almost violent colours of its exponents' paintings.

Returning to Vancouver in 1911, she exhibited work from her French sojourn. The show – and another in 1913 – was panned, her work rejected as impenetrable or offensive by British Columbia's staid critics. It wasn't until the late 1920s that Carr's work began to find a receptive audience. Her change of fortune followed her encounter with the **Group of Seven** painters, a celebrated assembly of eastern Canadian artists who, like Carr, looked to the Canadian landscape for much of their inspiration.

Painting with renewed confidence, she made repeated visits to aboriginal villages and wilderness settings over the next ten years, completing some of her most accomplished work from a ramshackle caravan equipped with improvised shelters for her pets. She attained a degree of international recognition in the process – but never saw much financial gain. Carr died in 1945, secure in her status of Canada's first major female artist.

otherwise unexceptional sporting and entertainment venue – has been joined by the sensational **Vancouver Public Library** and Centre in Vancouver for the Performing Arts.

The Vancouver Public Library

Of southeast Downtown's new buildings, the most startling is the **Vancouver Public Library** (Mon–Thurs 10am–9pm, Fri–Sat 10am–6pm, also Sun noon–5pm except when the Sunday is adjacent to a public holiday; Ⓣ604/331-3603, Ⓦwww.vpl.vancouver.bc.ca) at 350 West Georgia St, built for over $100 million. When it opened in 1995, it was the most expensive public project ever sanctioned by the city; it houses more than 1.2 million books and research items, making it one of North America's largest public libraries. To the casual observer the superb terracotta-coloured structure resembles a postmodern version of the Roman Colosseum, though architect Moshe Safdie apparently – and unconvincingly – claims the similarities are unintentional. While many architects disdain it, regarding it as a vapid pastiche, locals view it with almost universal admiration.

The library and its surrounding buildings – cafés, shops, library bookstore, day-care centre and seven-storey reading area – occupy a city block known as **Library Square**, bounded by Hamilton, West Georgia, Robson and Homer streets (the main entrance is at the corner of Homer and Robson). It's well worth walking into the library and taking the escalators to the upper floors, if only to admire the views. Otherwise take a break in one of the cafés or watch the world go by from the atrium and library steps, two favoured city places in which to hang out or catch some sun.

Yaletown

The knock-on effect created by the library and the area's new residential high-rise development is spreading quickly to surrounding streets, particularly in the quarter known as **Yaletown**, a small, hip and genuinely captivating two- or three-street grid of interesting shops, cafés and restaurants centred on Homer, Hamilton and Mainland streets between Drake Street to the south and Smithe to the north. Much of the surrounding area, notably large tracts around the southern end of Homer and other streets, are still pretty dull. The same goes for the walk from central Downtown, though the new Canada Line now offers a station at the southern edge of Yaletown at Yaletown-Roundhouse.

Yaletown takes its name from the many Canadian Pacific railway workers who settled here in the 1880s, having followed the railway west from the town of Yale 180km away in interior British Columbia. At the time, it had more saloons per acre than anywhere in the world and was considered one of North America's most lawless enclaves.

Today the area is in a state of flux – much of it is still officially listed as a commercial zone, a legacy of the days when it was a warehouse and packing district. Plenty of changes are transforming the area. Upper floors have become trendy lofts and offices for funky design, advertising, media and other companies. Below, the broad, raised walkways provide the perfect stage for café terraces, while the narrow, lofty or otherwise unusual spaces of the old warehouses have been taken over by often dramatically designed restaurants and bars. There are also plenty of small specialist shops, including a disproportionately large number of kitchen and interior-design stores. It's a great place to wander day or night.

At **Yaletown Landing** on the north shore of False Creek at the foot of Davie Street, you can catch one of the small **ferries** (see p.25) that ply the waters to and from Science World (see p.76), Granville Island (see p.71) and beyond. If you are headed to Granville Island, this is a much better approach than walking across the Granville Street Bridge.

On and behind the False Creek waterfront, you'll come face to face with the most dramatic physical expression of Vancouver's dynamic development as a city. The area was once a massive railway marshalling and switching yard that was partly transformed for the world's fair known as Expo '86. After the fair finished, the land was sold to Hong Kong real-estate tycoon Li Ka Shing for next to nothing on the understanding that he would build residential properties on the site. He did not disappoint, and high-rise condominiums have been going up at the rate of two or three a year for almost twenty years.

There are no specific sights in Yaletown or the False Creek waterfront developments to the south, but as you walk between the two or head for the former's shops, cafés and restaurants it's worth taking in **The Roundhouse** on Pacific Boulevard just off Davie, a legacy of the area's railway days, when the distinctively shaped building was used to repair and turn locomotives. Today it's a community centre and showcase for local arts groups; take a look inside to appreciate the interesting space and Engine 374, the locomotive that pulled the first passenger train into Vancouver in 1887.

The West End

The **West End** of the Downtown peninsula is bordered by Stanley Park and roughly delineated on its eastern flank by Burrard and Thurlow streets. There's not an awful lot to see here, for virtually the whole area is given over to affluent residential housing. Indeed, the large number of high-rise blocks and condominiums make this one of the most densely populated areas in Canada. At the same time, the area is tranquil and predominantly traffic-free, which gives it the air of a cosmopolitan and close-knit small town – one reason, along with the proximity of the ocean and Stanley Park, so many people want to live here.

The most visible part of the area for most visitors is the portion centred on **Robson Street**, which bisects the district. It contains the bulk of the West End's shops, restaurants and – a distinctive feature – its high-rise apartment or suite hotels, many of which have been converted from former residential usage (see pp.115–128 for accommodation). Most of the action happens near its junction with Burrard, the interest and quality of shops and restaurants tailing off as you travel west.

Elsewhere, the inner grid of streets making up the West End's core contains one or two diversions you might make if you are walking west to Stanley Park, notably **Barclay Square**. None, though, is exactly compelling, and interest only really picks up on **Denman Street**, focus of a buzzing café and restaurant scene. This has been prompted partly by its status in the late Seventies and Eighties as Vancouver's first "gay village" (the West End still has a sizeable gay community) and partly by its proximity to the park-fringed **English Bay Beach**, which sees an overflow of strollers, joggers and visitors from nearby Stanley Park. It's a tremendous place to window-shop at the various specialty stores – small craft shops, galleries and delicatessens – or to wander at random, and a fine spot for lunch or a drink before or after a visit to the park.

Barclay Square and around

Barclay Square between Nicola and Broughton streets (and one block south of Robson) is a glimpse of an older West End, a one-block nineteenth-century fossil containing nine heritage homes built between about 1890 and 1910. Its centrepiece is **Roedde House Museum** (Tues–Fri 1pm–4pm, Sat noon–5pm, Sun 2am–4pm; $5; ⓣ604/684-7040, ⓦwww.roeddehouse.org) at 1415 Barclay St in the square's southeast corner, a rare piece of domestic architecture by Francis Rattenbury, the architect responsible for, among other things, the *Empress Hotel* and Parliament Buildings in Victoria (see p.221). Built in 1890 in the Queen Anne style, it has been beautifully restored to its period pomp inside and out.

Before the arrival of white settlers, the area around Barclay Square had been the home of Musqueam and Squamish peoples for thousands of years. The first foreigners – three Englishmen – arrived in the 1860s, paying $550 for virtually the whole area, though the eventual owner, as in so much of western Canada, would be the Canadian Pacific Railway, which purchased the land in the late 1880s to build top-end residential properties. The biggest houses were built close to the ocean at English Bay, but plenty of other fine properties, such as those in Barclay Square, were constructed inland. Most were created before a boom in the first decade of the twentieth century which saw the building of the *Sylvia Hotel* (see p.118), for years Vancouver's highest structure, and many streets of less prestigious homes. Less prestigious, that is, for the time. Today, houses such as those in Barclay Square and around are coveted for their rarity.

Mole Hill to English Bay Beach

The eleven Edwardian homes at **Mole Hill**, near the corner of Comox and Bute streets, would have gone the same way as the West End's other buildings but for a concerted campaign by local residents in the 1990s to preserve the area. While Barclay Square captures a slice of Vancouver in the 1890s, this enclave presents a picture of the area as it would have appeared in about 1925.

More fragments of the old city can be found on nearby **Pendrell Street** one block south. At the corner with Broughton Street, for example, at 1119 Broughton St, is the grand former home of Thomas Fee, one of the leading architects and developers during the West End boom at the beginning of the twentieth century.

Continue west on Pendrell and then turn left on Nicola and right on Davie. On the right just beyond Broughton, at 1531 Davie St, you come to **The Gabriola**, a far more enticing prospect. This was one of the West End's first big mansions, built in 1900 for a sugar magnate, B.T. Rogers, who eventually sold up when lesser residential housing nearby caused the neighbourhood's stock to fall. The house was then divided into apartments but has been a restaurant – or vacant – since 1975.

Take Cadero or Bidwell southwest to the waterfront and you come to Beach Avenue and Alexander Park, the latter part of the stretch of parkland that fringes Sunset Beach to your left as you face the water and **English Bay Beach** to your right. Just beyond the park's northern tip stands a sculpture known as **Inukshuk** facing out over English Bay, a venerable Inuit symbol traditionally used as a sign of hospitality and an aid to navigation. Continue along the bay northwards, past Denman on your right, and you'll come eventually to the fringes of Stanley Park (see p.62).

2

Gastown and Chinatown

Vancouver's Downtown core is something of a historical accident, for the city's original Victorian heart – and its modern birthplace – actually lies to the east in an area known as **Gastown**, a designated historic district just a few minutes' walk from Canada Place and the rest of Downtown. The area takes its name from "Gassy Jack" Deighton, an impossibly colourful publican whose bar – aimed at workers in a nearby lumber mill – provided the focus for a shanty village that by 1869 had been officially incorporated as the town of Granville. Fire consumed much of this original settlement in 1886 (see p.258), but the arrival of the transcontinental Canadian Pacific Railway in 1887 brought renewed prosperity to the district and with it the birth of modern Vancouver, the only major Canadian metropolis that did not begin life as a fur-trading post.

Over the course of the twentieth century, the city's Downtown focus moved west and the ghost of Gastown's boozy beginnings returned to haunt it, as its cheap hotels and warehouses became something of a skid row for junkies and alcoholics. Ironically, the area's dilapidation helped to preserve the historic buildings, for no developer would touch the place. By the 1970s, however, the city was ready to bulldoze the entire area – together with much of **Chinatown** and Vancouver's other older eastern districts. A motley assortment of hippies, heritage buffs, Chinatown businesspeople and inhabitants took to the barricades. The plans were shelved, but not before work began on one of the intended plazas and malls – Granville Square at 200 Granville St, home to one of the city's tallest buildings.

Gastown was then declared a historic site – one of two in the city (the other is Chinatown) – and an enthusiastic $1.3 million beautification programme was set in motion. Many of the venerable two-storey stone and brick Victorian buildings were restored, old frontages were retained or reinstated, and the handful of streets and alleys were cleaned up and decked in hanging baskets of flowers. However, the end product never quite became the dynamic, city-integrated spot the planners had anticipated and was for years derided by locals as little more than a tourist trap.

Today, much of Gastown has the look of a determined piece of city rejuvenation aimed at visitors – especially on **Water Street**, its main axis – and is distinguished by new cobbles, fake gas lamps, *Ye Olde English Tea Room*-type cafés, atrocious souvenir shops and a generally overpolished patina. At the same time, interesting cafés, galleries (notably those devoted to aboriginal art and crafts: see p.171) and

Jack Deighton

Gastown owes its existence to **Captain John "Gassy Jack" Deighton**, a retired English sailor and riverboat pilot who arrived in Vancouver – then little more than a clearing in the woods – on September 29, 1867. He paddled ashore in a canoe accompanied by his aboriginal wife, mother-in-law, mother-in-law's cousin Big William (brought along to do the paddling), a mangy yellow dog, two chairs, two chickens, $6 in cash and a barrel of whisky.

Born in Hull, England, in 1830, Deighton became a sailor on British and then American ships, apparently making the switch because the food was better and more plentiful on US vessels. He later became a river pilot on the Fraser River, eventually opening a saloon in New Westminster – now a suburb of southern Vancouver – serving the prospectors travelling to the Cariboo region in the British Columbia interior during the Gold Rush of 1862.

His labours there, however, came to an abrupt end after a squabble with his American partner. Deighton had left the friend in charge of the saloon while he was travelling, and in his absence the friend laid on a spectacular Fourth of July celebration, sinking most of the saloon's profits into gunpowder, rockets, firecrackers and an extraordinary quantity of booze on the house. Deighton returned to find himself ruined.

Moving north, he quickly sniffed new entrepreneurial possibilities on the shores of Burrard Inlet, which was home to Hasting Mill. Workers at the mill could earn up to $1000 a month – an immense sum – and yet had virtually nothing to spend it on, certainly not liquor. The nearest drink was twenty miles away.

Deighton, so the story goes, promised the lumbermen drinks on the house if they helped him build a bar. Within 24 hours the new **Globe Saloon** was doing a roaring trade. A second bar followed, accompanied by a village of shacks that was soon christened **Gassy's Town**, partly after Deighton's tendency to "gas" and partly because of his repeated tendency to get heavily "gassed", or drunk.

In 1870, Royal Engineers surveyed the nine buildings making up the ramshackle quarter, a prelude to the incorporation of the site as the town of Granville. The survey and its projected new roads left Deighton's bar stranded in the middle of a street, leading him to buy Granville's first official lot for $65. Here, at the southwest corner of Water and Carrall, he built another saloon, a two-storey affair known as the **Deighton Hotel** with bar, billiard room, bedrooms and terrace. The point where the two streets met became known as Gastown, with Deighton its self-proclaimed mayor.

Gassy Jack died in 1875, aged just 44 – his dying words were apparently a curse aimed at a barking dog – and was toasted at his funeral with drinks whose cost came to $165, a substantial sum at the time. The Deighton Hotel, for its part, would vanish in the great fire of 1886.

Today, Gassy Jack is remembered by a statue at Gastown's heart in **Maple Tree Square** (see p.56), supposedly on, or close to, the site of the original Globe Saloon. Vancouver's unlikely "founder", appropriately enough, is shown perched atop a whisky barrel.

restaurants have made themselves felt, and though there's not an awful lot to see or do, the area's certainly worth a stroll for its better cafés, lively Sunday crowds and occasional points of interest such as a police museum and characterful old alleys.

Gastown's more drab peripheral streets merge almost seamlessly into **Chinatown**, a no less shabby looking area, but one that's redeemed by its obvious sense of community – this is very much a Chinese enclave – and the sights, smells and interest of its colourful streets, markets and cultural attractions. After Gastown, it's also the second of the city's two designated historic districts. The main sight here is the **Dr Sun Yat-Sen Garden**, a traditional Chinese Ming Dynasty garden, but you'll have as much fun simply wandering the streets, shopping for Chinese goods or eating in the many authentic restaurants. A word of warning, however: Chinatown and its environs have a definite edge, especially at night, and you don't want to encounter any of its more unsavoury characters. More details are given below.

Gastown

Gastown is a small, self-contained area that hinges on **Water Street**, so named because it stood on Vancouver's waterfront before land reclamation, the railway and new port facilities edged it farther inland. Most of the area's shops, restaurants, cafés and points of interest lie on or just off the street, although as gentrification and redevelopment take hold, so Gastown's prettier core is spreading east along Powell and Alexander streets.

At Water Street's eastern end lies **Maple Tree Square**, close to the site of Gassy Jack's original bars. Away from Water Street to the east, Gastown's immediate vicinity contains one odd little attraction – a **police museum** – and a handful of appealing old streets and good bars, cafés and restaurants (see pp.133–147 for details), plus a smattering of commercial galleries of aboriginal and other contemporary art (see p.171).

South and east of Gastown lies a far, far seedier area altogether, a down-at-heel crisscross of streets that has yet to benefit from either gentrification or the improving effects of big city-funded renovation projects. Action is promised, but at present it's a grim sight – derelict buildings, boarded-up shops and battered streets; the domain of addicts, pimps, prostitutes and the homeless. It is strongly recommended that you avoid this area after dark – and specifically the area near the junction of Main Street and East Hastings Street – and preferably during the day as well, when you should consider a bus or taxi to take you to Chinatown. Most **crime** in these parts is drug-related, although it is certainly not as prevalent or violent as in some North American cities. During the day, when more people are about, however, the worst you can expect is the usual hassle from street people for spare change.

Start your tour of Gastown just east of the Waterfront SkyTrain and SeaBus terminal at the corner of Water, Cordova and Richards streets. This is an easy walk from Downtown, but **buses** #4, #7, #8, #10, #16 and #20 from Granville or Burrard will drop you on or close to the junction, which leaves you well placed to explore Water Street, Gastown's main artery.

Water Street

First stop along **Water Street** is **The Landing**, a period building at no. 375, constructed in two parts – western (1908) and eastern (1913). Originally

Tours of Gastown

To explore Gastown and parts of Downtown with a guide, join one of the regular **guided walks** around the area with Walkabout Historic Vancouver (tours start daily at 10am and 2pm; $25 per person; for more information and details of departure points, call ⓣ604/720-0006 or 439-0448, ⓦwww.walkabouthistoricvancouver.com). In addition to a Chinatown and Gastown tour, the company offers a Downtown-Gastown and Granville Island tour (see p.28) and a Downtown-Gastown tour. All routes are wheelchair-accessible.

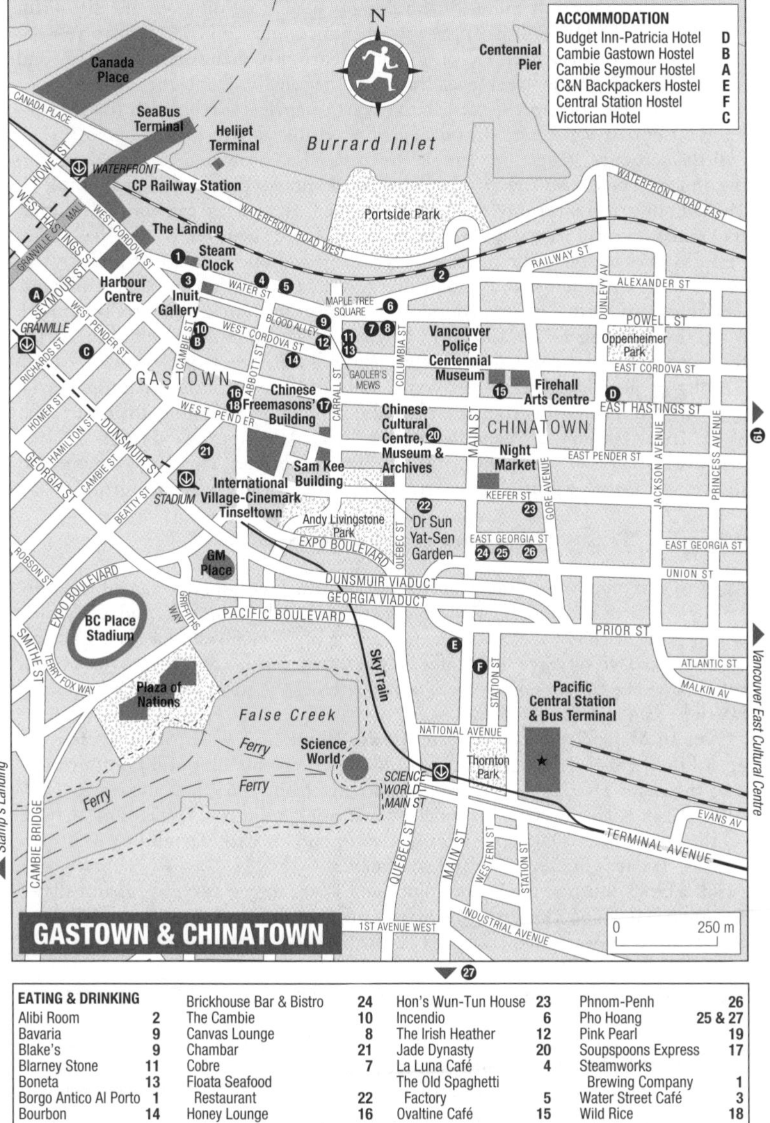

known as the Kelly Douglas Building, it was built by Frank Douglas and Robert Kelly, who started a trading business in 1896. Two years later they grew rich supplying prospectors headed for the Yukon goldfields during the Klondike Gold Rush. The building was partly constructed using gold-rush receipts, serving as a warehouse and head office until 1946. Restored in 1988, it is now a small upscale mall with around 25 stores, and it's worth stopping here to enjoy the harbour views.

Among the more intriguing establishments here is an office of the **BC Film Commission** (Ⓣ604/660-2732, Ⓦwww.bcfilmcommission.com), where you can obtain details of films and TV programmes currently being shot in and around Vancouver. Note the steel rods running diagonally from the ground-floor windows to the top storey, part of the defence against earthquakes (it's a little-known fact that Vancouver sits on an area of seismic activity).

At the corner of Water and Cambie streets stands Gastown's main crowd-pleaser, the much-hyped, two-tonne **steam-powered clock**, the world's first. Built in 1977, it's invariably surrounded by tourists armed with cocked cameras, all awaiting the miniature Big Ben's quarter-hourly toots and whistles or the bellowing performances on the hour that seem to presage imminent explosion. The steam comes from an underground system that was used to heat surrounding buildings. The clock was created by Ray Saunders, one of several figures immortalized in the **Magasin Building** at 322 Water St, where each of the column capitals of the facade features a bronze head of a figure connected with the history of Gastown.

Along or just off Water Street you'll find not only a considerable number of souvenir shops and other tourist tat but also genuinely interesting diversions such as the **Inuit Gallery of Vancouver** (Mon–Sat 10am–6pm; Ⓣ604/688-7323 or 1-888/615-8399, Ⓦwww.inuit.com), at 206 Cambie St. This large commercial showcase features expensive Inuit sculpture, jewellery and other art forms.

Maple Tree Square and around

At its eastern end Water Street opens into **Maple Tree Square**, named – unsurprisingly – after a maple tree that grew here, and under which it's said Granville's worthies sat in 1885 to settle on the new name of "Vancouver" for their growing metropolis. Two or three little cafés on the square make a good place for a break before turning tail or taking a cab east – a block or so beyond here begin the Hastings' badlands (see opposite).

Close to Maple Tree Square is the **Byrnes Block** at 2 Water St, built after the great fire in 1886. This is Vancouver's oldest heritage building still on its original site; the older Hasting Mill store, which dates from 1865, was moved to 1575 Alma Rd in Kitsilano. One of the city's first brick buildings, it stands on the site of the two-storey Deighton House, the second of Jack Deighton's Gastown saloons. Today it houses a café and apartments.

Half a block south of the Byrnes Block and Water Street, two tiny, quaint alleys, **Trounce Alley** and **Gaoler's Mews**, run off Carrall Street into Blood Alley (no one seems to know how this last alley came by its evocative name).

The Vancouver Police Centennial Museum

From Blood Alley, cross Carrall Street, then follow East Cordova Street to the **Vancouver Police Centennial Museum** (Mon–Sat 9am–5pm, closed Sun & public holidays, shorter hours possible in winter; $7; Ⓣ604/665-3346, Ⓦwww.vancouverpolicemuseum.ca) at no. 240. Note – do not approach on East Hastings, which is a decidedly seedy and unpleasant street. East Cordova, though close by and parallel, is better. A bizarre and fascinating little museum, it is inexpensive, easily seen and leaves you well placed for a short (two-block) walk south to the centre of Chinatown. The museum is housed in the city's old Coroner's Court Building and takes its name from the fact that it was established in 1986 to celebrate the centenary of the Vancouver police force.

The building has its own place in Vancouver folklore, not least because it was here that the actor **Errol Flynn** was brought after he died in Vancouver in

1959. Flynn arrived in the city in October 1959 with his best acting days well behind him. With him was his "personal assistant", a 17-year-old blonde not known for her secretarial skills. Within two days Flynn had dropped dead in his rented West End apartment.

The body was brought to the Coroner's Court, where the pathologist conducting the autopsy is said to have removed a piece of Flynn's penis and placed it in formaldehyde to keep as a souvenir. The horrified chief coroner is said to have pulled rank and reattached the missing piece to the corpse with sticky tape. The body was then dispatched to Los Angeles for burial. This was not the end of the story, however, for it emerged that somewhere between the West End and the morgue, a key to a Swiss safety-deposit box that Flynn wore round his neck had disappeared. When Flynn's lawyers opened the box three years later, the stock certificates and half a million dollars in cash they had expected to find were nowhere to be seen.

The **autopsy room** is still there, together with a suitably macabre selection of mangled and preserved body parts arranged around the walls. Other rooms worth seeing include the forensics lab, a police cell and a radio room, while a variety of thematic displays deal with notorious local criminals, weapons seized from criminals, crime-scene reconstructions, gambling, uniforms, counterfeit money and a sizeable collection of firearms. Finally, the museum's "Cop Shoppe" has an interesting line in police-related gifts and souvenirs.

To get to the museum by public transport, take buses #8, #10, #16, #20 along Hastings Street to Main, then walk one block north to East Cordova.

Chinatown

A city apart, Vancouver's vibrant **Chinatown** is clustered mainly on East Pender Street from Abbott to Gore and on Keefer Street from Main to Gore (buses #8, #10, #16, #20 and #50). Vancouver's 100,000-plus Chinese, the vast majority of whom live in the area, make up one of the largest Chinese communities outside the Far East – on a par with those of New York and San Francisco – and are the city's oldest and largest ethnic group after the British-descended majority. Many crossed the Pacific in 1858 to join the Fraser Valley Gold Rush; others followed under contract to help build the Canadian Pacific Railway. Most stayed, and found themselves treated appallingly (see box, p.58), seeking safety and familiarity in a ghetto of their own, where clan associations and societies helped build the distinctive houses of recessed balconies and ornamental roofs that have made the area a protected historic site.

Unlike gimmicky Gastown, Chinatown is all genuine – shops, hotels, markets, tiny restaurants and dim alleys vie for attention amidst an incessant hustle of jammed pavements and the buzz of Chinese conversation. Virtually every building replicates an Eastern model without a trace of self-consciousness, and written Chinese characters are far more prevalent than English ones. The district brings you face to face with Vancouver's multiculturalism and helps explain why wealthy Hong Kong immigrants – who can afford to relocate – continue to be attracted to the city. There's an edge to Chinatown, however, especially at night, and though central districts are fine, lone tourists are better off avoiding Hastings and the backstreets.

Apart from the obvious culinary temptations – and it is the district's restaurants that bring most locals and visitors here – Chinatown's main points of reference are its **shops and markets**. One of the best markets is the open-air **night market** at Main and Keefer streets (May–Sept Fri–Sun 6pm–midnight), a cornucopia of sights, smells and sounds that seem all the more vivid as darkness falls. Interesting shops can be found across the district, with stores boasting fearsome butchery displays and such edibles as live eels, flattened ducks, "hundred-year-old" eggs and other stuff you'll be happy not to identify. Keefer Street stands out as **bakery** row, with lots of tempting stickies on offer like moon cakes and *bao*, steamed buns with a meat or sweet-bean filling.

British Columbia and the Chinese

Canada, and British Columbia in particular, owes a huge debt to the Asian labour and initiative that helped build the country. But for a province and city that now justly pride themselves on their multicultural élan, Vancouver and BC's past treatment of its Chinese immigrants makes for shabby reading.

The first large wave of immigrants arrived on Canada's west coast in 1858, lured by the discovery of gold in the British Columbia interior. Another major migration followed in the early 1880s – some 11,000 arrived between 1881 and 1885 alone – when Chinese labourers were needed to help **build the Canadian Pacific Railway**. They were paid a dollar a day, half of what white workers were paid. It's estimated that three Chinese died for every kilometre of track built in labour-intensive sections such as the Fraser Canyon in central British Columbia.

In Vancouver, a handful of Chinese arrivals formed a small settlement in **Saltwater City** – their name for Vancouver. After the great **fire** that swept Vancouver in 1886, the Chinese were enlisted to help rebuild the young city and were leased sixty hectares (about 148 acres) of forest rent-free for ten years on the condition they clear and farm the land. Within a year, some ninety Chinese were living and working on and around Dupont (now Carrall) and Westminster (now Main) streets.

Elsewhere in British Columbia, the Chinese remained in the region once the railway – the main source of employment – had been completed. Thereafter they began to compete with local European-born and American workers for jobs in the burgeoning sawmills, lumber camps, mines and canneries. In the mid-1880s, for example, some 1500 of the estimated 2000 miners in British Columbia were Chinese. Crucially, they were prepared – or could be persuaded – to work for less than white workers.

Prejudice, violence and discrimination were the consequence. In Vancouver, this was made manifest when Chinese settlements on Dupont Street, along with shacks and tents on False Creek, were burned in **anti-Chinese riots in 1887**. A labour boycott was also effected, the railway being the only employer allowed to exempt itself from the ban on Chinese labour. This was accompanied by an official boycott of businesses that traded with the Chinese – such businesses were daubed with black crosses.

A more permanent expression of prejudice came soon after with the formation of the **Asiatic Exclusion League**, a racist organization that as late as 1907 was able to attract a crowd of 30,000 to an anti-Chinese parade on Cambie Street. Such leagues would survive almost to the middle of the twentieth century. Japanese and other Asian immigrants could expect the same welcome.

Given the pattern of prejudice, it is no wonder that Chinatown developed as a self-contained enclave. Several generations would pass before the barriers came down. In 1947 the Chinese, for example, were finally granted citizenship and legal rights. Fresh antipathy emerged among some Vancouver locals as recently as the mid-1990s, however, when an influx of wealthy Hong Kong immigrants – who left Hong Kong because they feared the consequences of the British handover of the city to the Chinese in 1997 – sent property prices soaring (prices have since calmed down).

Today, while Vancouver's Chinatown still remains a distinctive Chinese enclave, there is no sense that it is also a ghetto. Most second-, third- and fourth-generation Canadians of Chinese ethnic origin are now fully integrated into the life and fabric of the city – and live in many different areas – something that seems only fitting given Vancouver's pivotal role in the increasingly important and interlinked markets of the Pacific Rim.

▲ Dr Sun Yat-Sen Garden

More specific targets might include the Ten Ren Tea and Ginseng Company on the corner of Keefer and Main, which has a vast range of teas, many promising cures for a variety of ailments (free tastings). In a similar vein, it's worth dropping into one of the local **herbalists**, such as Tung Fong Hung Medicine Company at 536 Main St at East Pender St to browse amongst their panaceas: snakeskins, reindeer antlers, buffalo tongues, dried seahorses and bears' testicles are all available if you're feeling under the weather. Ming Wo, at 23 East Pender, is a fantastic cookware shop, with probably every utensil ever devised, while China West, at 41 East Pender, is packed with slippers, jackets, pens, cheap toys and the like. A star among the **supermarkets** is the T & T at 179 Keefer St and Abbott, which has an extraordinary range of produce and is particularly distinguished, if that is the word, by its bizarre assortment of (live) seafood, among other things. For other shops in Chinatown, see p.174.

The Sam Kee Building and around

Most visitors to Chinatown flock dutifully to the 1913 **Sam Kee Building**, two blocks west of Main and one north of Keefer at the corner of Carrall and East Pender; at just 1.8m across, it's often claimed to be the world's narrowest building. The story goes that in 1912 the city authorities forcibly bought most of Sam Kee's land to widen Pender Street but refused to compensate him for one tiny strip that wasn't required for the new street. Kee's neighbour had hopes of buying the strip for next to nothing but Kee decided to spite the neighbour and the authorities by constructing this slip of a building. Customers at his general store had to be served through the windows.

Behind the building is the sombre **Shanghai Alley**, once a den of shops, restaurants, flophouses, public baths and worse – today it just looks rather forlorn. Opposite, at 1 West Pender, the **Chinese Freemasons' Building** is a structure whose conservative Victorian appearance on Carrall says much about certain Chinese arrivals' determination to fit in with the prevailing Anglo-Saxon majority.

Note, though, the building's Pender flank, which has fine examples of Cantonese recessed balconies. Dr Sun Yat-Sen (see below) sought shelter in the building for months in 1911, hiding from agents of the Qing (or Manchu) Dynasty he would eventually help overthrow.

Dr Sun Yat-Sen Garden

Chinatown's chief cultural attraction is the small **Dr Sun Yat-Sen Garden** at 578 Carrall St near Pender (May to mid-June daily 10am–6pm, mid-June to Aug daily 9.30am–7pm, Sept daily 10am–6pm, Oct daily 10am–4.30pm, Nov–April Tues–Sun 10am–4.30pm; $10; ⓣ604/662-3207, ⓦwww.vancouverchinesegarden.com).

This was the first authentic, full-scale classical Chinese garden built outside China and still the only such garden in the western hemisphere. Named after the founder of the first Chinese Republic (see below), who was a frequent visitor to Vancouver, the park was created for Expo '86 and cost $5.3 million, $500,000 of which came from the People's Republic – along with 52 artisans and 950 crates of materials. The latter included everything from limestone rocks from Taihu – whose jagged shapes are prized for this sort of garden – to the countless tiny pebbles that make up the intricately patterned courtyard pavements.

The whole design is based on classical gardens developed in the city of Suzhou during the Ming Dynasty (1368–1644). China's horticultural emissaries, following traditional methods that didn't allow use of a single power tool, spent thirteen months in Vancouver replicating one such garden. To achieve a subtle balance of yin and yang – small and large, soft and hard, flowing and immobile, light and dark – the gardeners juxtaposed, among other things, large and small stones and rock with running water.

Throughout the garden, every stone, pine tree and flower was placed with thought for its mystical and symbolic qualities. Groupings were designed to give areas a special mood and unique character, and to reinforce the seasonal and cyclical nature of the garden.

Serenity, above all, was prized in Suzhou Ming gardens, which were originally designed by Taoist poets to encourage contemplation and inspiration. They always

Dr Sun Yat-Sen in Vancouver

Dr Sun Yat-Sen was born in what is now Zhongshan in Guangdong province, China, in 1886. Despite being raised in a peasant family, he was sent at an early age to live with his elder brother in Hawaii, where he was exposed to a Western education. Eventually he became a doctor, but he abandoned his career to further the cause of democracy in his native country, then under the autocratic control of the Qing (Manchu) Dynasty. The first Chinese leader of a political movement not to come from the gentry, he travelled around the world to raise money for political change, making visits for this purpose to Vancouver in 1897, 1910 and 1911.

It was during the last of these that the city's Chinese community made its most significant contribution to revolutionary coffers. Sun Yat-Sen received the support of the Cheekungtong, a group of prominent Chinese freemasons. The men mortgaged their lodgings and other buildings to provide money for the cause, raising $35,000 in all – the cash financed an abortive revolution in 1911 near Guangzhou, six months before the successful overthrow of the Qing (Manchu) Dynasty. To this day, a memorial at Huang Hua Kang lists the names of prominent Chinese-Canadian benefactors and communities from the period. Sun Yat-Sen became first president of the Republic of China a year later but quickly relinquished the post to concentrate his efforts on the country's economic transformation. Following his early death in 1925 from liver cancer, he was given the honorary name Kuo Fu, or Father of the Country.

contained four principal elements in harmony – water, rocks, plants and architecture – and, by combining elements from the natural landscape such as rivers, lakes and trees in a small space, sought to concentrate the life force, or *qi*, which infuses them.

Free 45-minute **guided tours** are given on the half-hour and explain other elements of the Taoist philosophy behind the carefully placed elements. At first glance the garden seems a touch small and austere, and the impression isn't helped by a preponderance of sponsors' nameplates and the glimpses of the road, pub and high-rise building outside the walls. After a time, though, chances are you'll find the garden working its calm and peaceful spell. Note that there are numerous exhibitions and events held in and around the garden throughout the year, including walking tours of Chinatown (currently Wed at 1.30pm; $10; call ⓣ604/662-3207 to register and purchase advance tickets).

Chinese Cultural Centre Museum & Archives

Alongside the entrance to the gardens at 555 Columbia St, the 1998 **Chinese Cultural Centre Museum & Archives** (Tues–Sun 9am–5.30pm; $3; ⓣ604/658-8880, ⓦwww.cccvan.com) is Chinatown's community focus. It is also a sponsor of the Chinese New Year festivities, fifteen days of processions, theatrical performances and other cultural events (ⓣ604/687-6021, ⓦwww.bcchinesenewyear.com for more information). It's an ugly building, the gate aside, but it hosts changing exhibitions and its museum – the first of its kind – is dedicated to Chinese-Canadian history and culture, including a section designed to offer insights into the role of Chinese-Canadian soldiers who fought during World War I and World War II. Guided tours of the museum are available ($5). You can also attend 45min workshops ($5 each) in t'ai chi, painting, knotting, calligraphy and Chinese music. Lunch is available for between about $5 and $10.

Next to the gardens and centre lies the small and slightly threadbare **Dr Sun Yat-Sen Park** (free), which, though less worked than the Dr Sun Yat-Sen Garden, is still a pleasant place to take time out from Chinatown. Hours are the same as for the garden, and there's an alternative entrance on Columbia Street and Keefer.

3

Stanley Park

One of the world's finest urban spaces, **Stanley Park** crowns the tip of the Downtown peninsula. It is a huge green heart of woodland, temperate rainforest, marshes, beaches and untamed landscapes that provides a link to the not-so-distant days when Vancouver was little more than a clearing in the west-coast wilderness. At 988 acres, it's one of the largest urban parks in North America – some twenty percent larger than New York's Central Park. Though there have been homophobic attacks on gays in some areas at night, the park is generally exceedingly safe, and receives an estimated eight million visitors a year – though it's worth stressing that only the outer edge is developed for recreational use. Much of the park's interior, by contrast, is nearly impenetrable scrub and forest that, while home to lots of wildlife – including herons, coyotes, eagles, owls and more – is visited by relatively few people and crisscrossed by just a handful of trails (most of them well-maintained gravel paths), producing a wonderful escape for those prepared to explore beyond the park's margins. A powerful storm in 2006 damaged parts of the park, though the 3000 trees damaged or destroyed represented a tiny fraction of the park's half million trees.

Ocean surrounds the park on three sides, ensuring some superb views from the road (Stanley Park Drive) and the deservedly popular 10.5km cycleway and pedestrian **Seawall Promenade** that trace its perimeter. Also around the fringes – and particularly along the park's southern edge, the area closest to Downtown – are plenty of more conventional urban park trappings: lawns, flowerbeds, rose gardens, tennis courts, children's playgrounds, a miniature railway, pitch-and-putt golf and lots of open, wooded or flower-decorated spaces where you can picnic, snooze or watch the world go by.

Best of all, the park has three good beaches: **English Bay Beach**, ranged along Beach Avenue; **Second Beach**, to the north, which also features a shallow swimming pool; and **Third Beach**, farther north still, the least crowded of the three and the one with the best views of West Vancouver and the mountains. English Bay, at the southern end of Denman Street, is the most readily accessible from Downtown and is particularly easy to visit after seeing the park. Away from

Park information

The city's Touristinfo Centre at 200 Burrard St at Canada Place Way (see p.36) has **information** on park tours, trails and so forth. In the park there is an interpretive centre near Brockton Point and a nearby information kiosk about 500m from the start of the Seawall near the West Georgia Street entrance. For further information on the park, contact the Vancouver Board of Parks & Recreation (Ⓦwww.vancouver.ca).

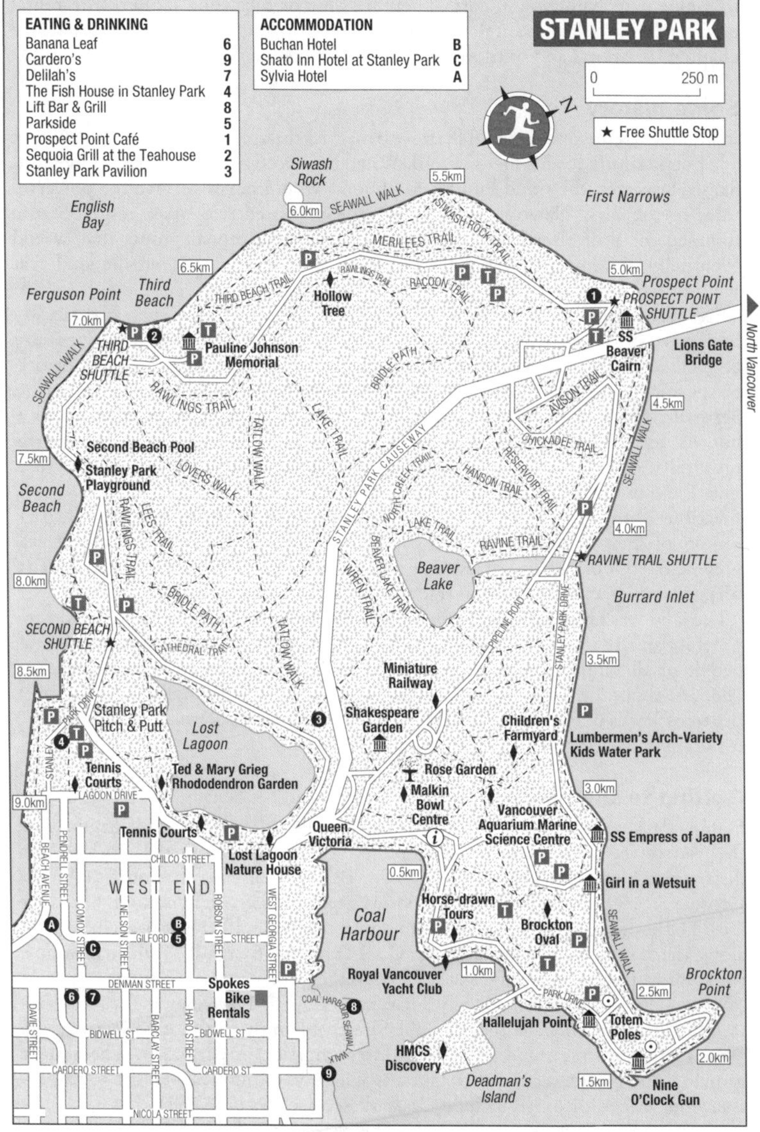

the park's many natural delights, the main attraction is the highly popular **Vancouver Aquarium Marine Science Centre**, Canada's largest aquarium.

A neat **itinerary** for a half-day or so in the park and surrounding area – namely English Bay Beach and Denman Street a couple of blocks east of the park – would be to walk or take the bus to the park and stroll, cycle or skate all or part of the Seawall. It's between 8.8km and 10.5km if you do the whole thing, depending on precisely where you start and finish, so factor this in if you want to tackle it in whole or in part. There's a slew of bike- and Rollerblade-rental places nearby (see opposite). For more on what you can do in the park, see chapter 16, Sports and outdoor activities.

Some history

In 1865, entrepreneur Edward Stamp earmarked the area that is now Stanley Park as a potential site for his first sawmill. When he voiced his plans to the indigenous Salish, however, they told him his log booms would never survive the powerful tides in the First Narrows waters near the proposed site. As a result, Stamp founded his mill elsewhere, and with it one of the nodal points that would eventually develop into Vancouver. Loggers thus largely ignored the land that would become Stanley Park.

The rest of the peninsula now occupied by Vancouver, however, had already been partially logged in the 1860s. However, in 1886 the newly formed city council – showing typical Canadian foresight and an admirable sense of priorities – moved to make what had by then become a military reserve into a permanent park. Impetus for the move came from the Canadian Pacific Railway, but its motives were not entirely philanthropic. The company hoped the proximity of the park would improve the value of its properties in the West End – and it was not disappointed.

Various Musqueam, Salish and other native villages had been situated in the park – most of their inhabitants moved peacefully to North Vancouver – and several present-day hiking paths correspond to old aboriginal trails. Otherwise, the city was preserving an almost virgin tract of wilderness.

The land was saved for posterity in the name of Lord Stanley, Canada's governor general from 1888 to 1893, who dedicated the park "to the use and enjoyment of people of all colours, creeds and customs for all time". It was officially opened in 1888. At about the same time, and with equally admirable foresight, the Vancouver Board of Parks & Recreation was created, a body now responsible for almost 200 parks covering 3158 acres of the city.

Getting to the park

Stanley Park is a simple **walk** from most of Downtown – allow about 15min from the Vancouver Art Gallery – and a pretty lengthy one from the city's eastern districts such as Gastown and Chinatown. Beach Avenue to the south and West Georgia Street to the north are the obvious approaches if you're on foot, but as the Coal Harbour waterfront development continues apace, the most peaceful walk is along the waterfront promenade, the **Coal Harbour Seawall Walk**, which now runs almost unbroken from Canada Place to the park.

While development immediately adjacent to Canada Place may make it difficult to pick up the promenade there for the foreseeable future, it's easy to access from West Cordova Street, and from Coal Harbour Park in particular. There are a growing number of cafés and restaurants where you can break up the journey – stand-out places for lunch include *Cardero's* (see reviews on p.151).

If you want to save your walking for the park, take a **taxi** or Stanley Park **bus** #19 from the corner of Burrard and Pender streets Downtown to the so-called Stanley Park Loop just inside the park by Lost Lagoon. Other buses which travel close to the park are the #6, which runs through the south side of Downtown along Davie and Beach Avenue (look for "Beach" on the front of the bus and get off at the corner of Davie and Beach Avenue); and the #5 ("Robson"), which runs along Robson to the corner of Robson and Denman Street.

Note that driving a **car** here can be foolish, especially at weekends, when parking is just about impossible. If you do drive, remember that traffic is one-way around the park, which means you have to use the park's West Georgia Street, or northern, entrance. Parking meters are dotted around the park, both on the roads and in dedicated parking areas: most take credit cards if you don't have the right change.

Getting around the park

Walking round the Seawall Promenade – a distance of between 8.8 and 10.5km depending on where you start – takes about two hours at a fairly brisk pace. If you want to rent a bike, go to the corner of Denman and West Georgia streets, where there's a cluster of **bike rental** outlets. Spokes, 1798 West Georgia St (daily 9am–dusk; ⓣ604/688-5141, ⓦwww.vancouverbikerental.com), is a big, busy place that's been in business since 1938 (from $6.67 an hour for a wide variety of bikes, including children's bikes and tandems with child trailers). You need to leave ID, and a cash, Visa, Amex or MasterCard deposit. Helmets, which are compulsory in BC, and locks are included in the rental.

If this place looks too frenetic you might walk a few metres up the street to the smaller Bikes 'n' Blades (ⓣ604/602-9899), which also rents **in-line skates**. Directly opposite at 745 Denman St is another rental outlet, Bayshore Bicycle & Rollerblade Rentals (daily 9am–dusk; mountain bikes from $6 an hour, $16.80 for four hours; ⓣ604/688-2453, ⓦwww.bayshorebikerentals.ca). From Denman it's just a minute's pedalling to the park, but watch out for the traffic on the busy intersections off West Georgia and by the park entrance.

If you don't want to walk, cycle or skate, there's the free Stanley Park Shuttle **bus service**, which runs every 12 to 15 minutes in summer only (late June to late Sept daily 10am–6.30pm; ⓣ604/257-8400). At the time of writing its future funding is in question: check with the visitor centre for current services, if any. The green and gold gas-powered, old-fashioned-looking bus (contracted from the Vancouver Trolley Company) makes fourteen stops at the most popular sights around the park, starting from the car park at the Miniature Railway. You can transfer to the service from the #19 Translink service from West Pender via West Georgia Street. Another alternative is to take a **horse-drawn tour** of the park; see p.28 for details.

Note that drivers on Stanley Park Drive and cyclists on the Seawall Promenade must follow a **counter-clockwise route**. Walkers can obviously go in either direction, but if you insist on a clockwise approach you'll being going against the flow of both cyclists and many other walkers. For this reason the account of the park below follows a counter-clockwise route starting at the foot of West Georgia by the Stanley Park Loop and Lost Lagoon.

Around the Seawall

Stanley Park, especially on a busy Sunday, offers a good idea of what it means to live in Vancouver – blessed with great scenery at their doorstep, residents here have a passion for the outdoors and for making the most of it by walking, biking, jogging or in-line skating around the **Seawall**. The wall was conceived in 1917 as a precaution against erosion and took almost sixty years to complete. Granite boulders had to be cut and trimmed on the beach to manageable 45kg blocks and then hauled to the wall.

If you're walking, biking or taking the shuttle bus around the wall, there are any number of minor diversions en route, not to mention a couple of good places for snacks and a couple of exceptional **restaurants** for lunch or dinner. The Seawall path is clearly divided, with lanes for cyclists and pedestrians, but keep an eye out anyway: if you're cycling, be sure to observe various speed restrictions and to follow the instructions to dismount at blind corners and other indicated points.

▲ Along the Seawall Promenade

From Lost Lagoon to Hallelujah Point

The first thing you see in the park is **Lost Lagoon**, a lake that started life as a tidal inlet and part of Coal Harbour. Its water all but disappeared at low tide, a process exacerbated when a causeway replaced the bridge over the inlet in 1916. By 1929, the area was cut off from the sea and had become a natural freshwater lake. In 1938 it was declared a wildlife sanctuary and the park board began to scatter seeds regularly to encourage birds. Walk its pretty waterfront path to admire the dozens of waterfowl species – including geese, several varieties of duck and a handful of rare trumpeter swans – that inhabit its shoreline.

The city side of the lagoon boasts the **Lost Lagoon Nature House** (July to early Sept Tues–Sun 10am–6pm, rest of the year Sat & Sun 9.30am–4.30pm; free; ⓣ604/257-8544), which offers displays on the park and the lagoon's flora and fauna; animals that live in the area ranging from birds to racoons, beavers, coyotes, bald eagles and squirrels. You may also catch a glimpse of the odd skunk, or at least smell one. Vancouver's Ecology Society (ⓣ604/257-8544, ⓦwww.stanleyparkecology.ca) runs **guided walks** from the centre, usually on a Sunday ($5), and organizes a variety of other free or inexpensive activities, most aimed at children.

A few steps inland from the lagoon are the **Malkin Bowl**, an arena used for outdoor performances in summer (see p.203), and the **Rose Garden** and **Shakespeare Garden**, two of the park's horticultural highlights. The site was originally home to the park board's greenhouses; they have since been moved, but the board still grows all the flowers – around 350,000 a year - used in the city's parks and gardens. Late spring and summer here sees hundreds of mostly old rose varieties and clematis in bloom (275 rose varieties in all, and 3000 individual bushes), while swathes of annuals bring colour to the beds later in the year. If you're keen on **gardens**, make a point of seeing the **Ted and Mary Greig Rhododendron Garden** around the pitch-and-putt golf course, at its best in mid- to late May, and the annual summer carpets of bedding plants at Prospect Point (see p.68).

The Seawall path brings you to a parking area and **information booth**, a source of maps and the starting point for horse-drawn tours of the park (see p.29). Curving to the right you'll pass the private Royal Vancouver Yacht Club premises, while ahead, jutting into Coal Harbour and linked to the park by a narrow causeway, is **Deadman's Island**. This probably takes its name from an ancient Salish burial ground on the site, but it has also been an aboriginal battleground, a lumber camp, a squatters' village and a quarantine station during the city's smallpox epidemic between 1888 and 1890. The military took it over in World War II for "temporary" use but has yet to return it.

Continuing east, you come to **Hallelujah Point**, so called because the Salvation Army once held revival meetings here. On the seaward side of the path nearby is the 1894 **Nine O'Clock Gun**, which for many years was fired nightly at 9pm, partly, it's said, to help ships' captains set their chronometers and partly to indicate the curfew that once marked the end of the day's fishing. It still performs at 9pm every day.

From Brockton Point to Prospect Point

The tip of **Brockton Point** represents the park's most easterly point, a belvedere for the port and the Lions Gate Bridge that appears to your left. The point was once the site of a pioneer graveyard, and it was here that one of the young city's first lumber magnates, Edward Stamp, cleared a site in 1865 for a sawmill. The proposed mill was moved farther east (to the site of present-day Gastown) when Stamp discovered the currents of the Burrard Inlet here were too powerful to allow the creation of log booms.

Walk west around the point past the unexceptional Brockton Point Lighthouse (closed to the public) and you'll pass the **Chehalis Monument**, a memorial to the nine people killed nearby when a tugboat was struck by the liner *Princess of Victoria* in 1906. Moving on, you can't miss that most English of sights, a cricket pitch – a monument to Vancouver's powerful early links with Britain – nor a crop of **totem poles** created by the Haida, Kwakiutl and other aboriginal peoples. The totems form part of an aborted 1889 scheme to recreate an aboriginal village on the site. Look out for the carving of the woman with full lips and arms outstretched apparently in an embrace, a favourite backdrop for newlyweds having their photographs taken – they are presumably unaware that the totem represents the legendary "crazy bear woman who comes down from the mountains to steal children". As for other totem-pole icons, the whale represents the lordship of the sea, the eagle the kingdom of the air, the wolf the genius of the land, and the frog the transitional link between land and water. For further information, visit the **Brockton Visitor Centre** (daily; May, June & Sept 9am–6pm; July & Aug 9am–8pm; rest of the year 9am–4pm) which also has refreshments and toilets.

Almost 1km from Brockton Point you pass a bronze statue on a rock called **Girl in a Wetsuit** (1972). It looks like a modern reinterpretation of Copenhagen's *Little Mermaid*, but the sculptor, Elek Imredy, maintains no connection at all was intended with the Danish statue. At the junction about 200m beyond, turn left on Avison Way and you'll come to the **aquarium** (see p.69), while a little beyond Avison Way, the Hummingbird Trail strikes south if you want to curtail your walk.

Stay with the Seawall, however, and beyond the Avison Way junction just inland you find **Lumberman's Arch**, a large arch of timber from vast Douglas firs erected in 1952 to honour logging workers. Formerly the site of a Salish village, Khawaykhway, wiped out by the smallpox outbreak in 1888, its meadow surroundings are a favourite for families and those seeking a siesta. There's a refreshment stand here plus the **Variety Kids Water Park** (daily May–Sept; free), a small but fun collection of ankle-deep pools, artificial geysers and other watery features for smaller children (note that the facility is unsupervised).

If you head a little farther into the park you'll come to the Miniature Railway and **Children's Farmyard** (Easter to late Sep daily 11am–4pm, Oct–Easter weekends only plus Christmas week and evenings in Oct, weather permitting,

11am–4pm; $6, under 12 $3; ⓣ604/257-8530), where children can admire animals. This partly replaces the park's zoo, closed in 1993.

Also aimed at children, the **Miniature Railway** (same hours as Children's Farmyard except late June to early Sept, daily 10.30am–5pm; $6, under 12 $3; ⓣ604/257-8531) about 200m to the northwest appears equally popular with adults. It's estimated that the mini-locomotives, one of which is a copy of a Canadian Pacific steam engine, carry as many passengers annually as all the Alaska-bound cruise ships combined. The trains run on a circuit through towering cedars and Douglas firs, a particularly good trip if you're in the city during October and the first week or so of November, when the railway turns into the **Hallowe'en Ghost Train**, a nocturnal ride (6–10pm; $10 adults, $6 children under 12; includes entry to Farmyard) through the woods, specially illuminated for the occasion. Order tickets in advance through Ticketmaster (ⓣ604/280-4444, ⓦwww.ticketmaster.ca).

A similar lighted display takes place in winter, when the park board presents **Bright Nights** (early Dec to early Jan, except Christmas Day daily 3–10pm; adults $8, children $5), when more than 750,000 lights transform the park.

Back on the waterfront promenade, it's a little over 1km to the **Lions Gate Bridge**, roughly the halfway point on the Seawall. You could also walk here from the railway along Pipeline Road, enlivening this less attractive route by taking the short self-guided nature trail around Beaver Lake en route. Just beyond the bridge, a short detour from the main Seawall route cuts to **Prospect Point**, a 60m-high basalt cliff and wonderful viewpoint that's home to the *Prospect Point Café* (ⓣ604/669-2737) – good for coffee and a snack – public toilets, a colony of nesting cormorants and a cairn to the Hudson's Bay Company's SS *Beaver*, the first ship to travel the entire west coast of North America. If you want a break from the waterfront walk, you can get on the Siwash Rock Trail from close to Prospect Point; it runs high above the Seawall to Third Beach (see below).

From Siwash Rock to Ferguson Point

One kilometre west of Prospect Point lies **Siwash Rock**, an offshore outcrop that has defied the weather for centuries. The rock has given rise to numerous native legends; the best known concerns a Squamish soon-to-be father named Skalish (or Skalsh) who decided to swim in **English Bay** until the waters made him free of physical and spiritual blemishes (the idea being that his newborn child should also thus start life free of stain). So impressed were the gods – Q'uas, the "transforming" god, in particular – by this selflessness that they turned him into the rock as a reward. Less romantically, the rock also served as a World War II battery site and searchlight position.

A popular summer barbecue spot among the locals, and a favourite place to settle down to watch the sunset, **Third Beach** lies 800m south along the Seawall, yet if you wish to cut back, about 100m before the beach Tatlow Walk cuts through the park to Lost Lagoon. Third Beach itself is quieter than the other English Bay beaches. It has lifeguards in summer from 11.30am to dusk. The celebrated Hollow Tree, the stump of a colossal cedar, can be found just inland at the northern end of the beach, while on the path from the beach is a gargantuan cedar more than 1000 years old that is thought to be one of the world's oldest (and largest) trees.

Continuing along the Seawall from Third Beach brings you to **Ferguson Point**, home to the good though often busy *Sequoia Grill at the Teahouse*, public toilets and a memorial cairn and fountain.

Second Beach to English Bay

Another kilometre or so beyond the point brings you to the start of **Second Beach**. Although people do swim in the sea here and at Third Beach, most bathers prefer the large **swimming pool** (ⓣ604/257-8370 or 257-8371) next to Second

Beach, generally open Victoria Day (third Mon in May) to Labour Day (early Sept). It costs $5.15 to swim here. Off-season, or in windy weather, this can be an exposed and wind-chilled spot, so dress appropriately. Alongside the pool is the children's **Stanley Park Playground**, which has two play structures, one for older and one for younger children.

While most people cut short their tour and head back to Lost Lagoon via Lagoon Drive or the parallel trails (see map, p.63), the Seawall continues south for a little under 1km to Beach Avenue, passing another excellent restaurant, *The Fish House* (see p.144). Just south of Lagoon Drive is a corner of the park that contains, among other things, the pitch-and-putt golf course, putting greens, formal gardens and seventeen free public tennis courts (first-come, first-served, but reservations possible on six pay courts May–Aug; $11.70 per hr; call ⓣ604/605-8224). There is an additional bank of four free courts just below South Lagoon Drive near the Lost Lagoon Nature House.

From here you can continue back towards West Georgia Street and your starting point or continue along the waterfront and **English Bay Beach**, another great stretch of beach bordered with a park and Beach Avenue to the rear. This in turn gives way to Sunset Beach and its eponymous park, a slightly less appealing stretch of open waterfront. If you're following this route, it's best to peel off the beach early and wander down either Denman or Davie streets, both lined with interesting shops and cafés. Buses serve both streets; Davie, if you follow it all the way, will take you to Yaletown (see p.49).

Vancouver Aquarium Marine Science Centre

The **Vancouver Aquarium Marine Science Centre** (daily: late June to early Sept 9.30am–7pm; early Sept to late June 9.30am–5pm; $19.95; ⓣ604/659-3474, ⓦwww.vanaqua.org; prepaid tickets can be obtained by calling ⓣ604/659-3552 or from ⓔprograms@vanaqua.org) at 845 Avison Way is Stanley Park's most popular destination. The aquarium ranks among North America's largest, and with over a million visitors a year is the most visited sight in Canada west of Toronto's CN Tower. It contains around sixty thousand living exhibits representing some six hundred different species.

Like the park zoo before it – now closed – the complex has been targeted by animal rights campaigners for its treatment of beluga whales and performing dolphins, not to mention cooped-up seals and otters. The whales are huge draws, but you can't help but feel they should really be in the sea, despite all the hoopla surrounding their $14 million marine-mammal area – it is shamefully small for the animals concerned. You should also be aware that the open-air site becomes extremely crowded, as do the underground display areas. Arrive early.

There are several key areas to visit. The **Arctic Canada** section in the Jean MacMillan Southern Arctic Gallery spotlights the fragile world of the Canadian north – everything from cod to beluga whales – and offers a chance to see whales face to face through glass and hear the sounds of whales, walruses, seals and other creatures in this icy domain.

Special exhibits are devoted to Lancaster Sound off Baffin Island, an area whose position in the high Arctic is belied by the surprising richness of its marine life. The H.R. MacMillan Gallery here has an interesting **Whalelink** section devoted to current research into orca or killer whales. All round the aquarium, visitors can watch research sessions in progress as well as feeding and "play" sessions with marine animals.

The **Pacific Canada habitats** of the Sandwell North Pacific Gallery perform a similar role for otters, beavers and other creatures of the waters of Vancouver, the Georgia Strait, Vancouver Island and the rest of British Columbia. Other warm parts of the Pacific are examined in the MacMillan Tropical Gallery, with specimens such as sharks, sea turtles and coral-reef fish from Micronesia, Indonesia and the Philippines. From here you enter the domain of the **Amazon Rainforest**, a tremendous area that displays the bountiful vegetation, fishes, iguanas, three-toed sloths, poisonous tree frogs and other creatures of the rainforest in a climate-controlled environment: check out the hourly "rainstorms". Giant cockroaches and massive, hairy tarantulas are also often on view. Closer to home, the **BC Waters Gallery** and **Ducks Unlimited Wetlands** displays are fairly self-explanatory – they're also fascinating, if less striking than the rainforest exhibits.

There's a café at the aquarium, the *Upstream Café*, if you need a reviving drink or snack, and **guided tours** behind the scenes: call, visit the website or enquire at the ticket office for details of tours, including 45min Trainer Tours, where you learn what it takes to be an animal trainer; Animal Encounters, face-to-face encounters with beluga whales (reservations ⓣ604/659-3552 or 1-800/931-1186); and sleepovers, where you get to see the attractions after everyone else has gone home.

4

Granville Island

One of Vancouver's most compelling sights, **Granville Island** is the city's most enticing "people's place" – one of the titles it likes for itself. It's a joy to visit for its own sake and for the pleasure of milling around busy cafés, scouring market stalls piled with exotic goods, watching street performers, shopping in small specialist craft stores and galleries, eating a Sunday brunch looking out over the ocean or enjoying a nightcap. As you would expect, the whole place is hugely popular – around 10.5 million people come here every year. While a morning is long enough to wander the island and browse the shops, market and galleries, you could easily spend longer, or, given the ease with which you can visit from Downtown and elsewhere, come back for a second visit another day

Technically a peninsula rather than an island, Granville Island sits on False Creek – the arm of water that marks the southern edge of the Downtown peninsula – and lies half-hidden beneath the superstructure of the Granville Street Bridge, which links Downtown to the city's southern suburbs. The word *island* in this context conjures up the wrong idea, for this is no green and bucolic retreat in a city setting, but rather a deliberately jumbled collection of shops, restaurants and other businesses juxtaposed with a marina, open spaces, the odd houseboat, an art school and light-industrial units, whose faint – and deliberately retained – whiff of warehouse squalor means the place never runs the risk of being quaint or pretentious.

The constant buzz of activity and variety of things – and people – to look at make it a tremendous and easygoing place to wander, and a superb place to shop, in particular for food – the endless stalls in the large, covered food hall here constitute one of North America's great markets. Most locals and visitors alike come during the day, especially at the weekend, but the restaurants and bars and the Arts Club Theatre, a performance space with bar and lounge (see p.152), are enough to keep the place alive at night.

East of the island at the other end of False Creek, and easily reached by ferry, is **Science World**, distinguished by a striking geodesic dome which forms a prominent part of the city skyline, but whose science-related displays are somewhat disappointing.

Some history

Granville Island began as little more than marsh and a couple of seaweed-laden sandbanks in False Creek, an area favoured by Vancouver's original Squamish inhabitants as winter fishing grounds. It came to the attention of white settlers in 1889, when a bridge was built linking the north and south shores of False Creek. First up were three contractors who circled the sandbars with stakes, intending to build a sawmill. They were soon seen off by the Canadian Pacific Railway – which got a court order backing up its claim to the land – an action which would result

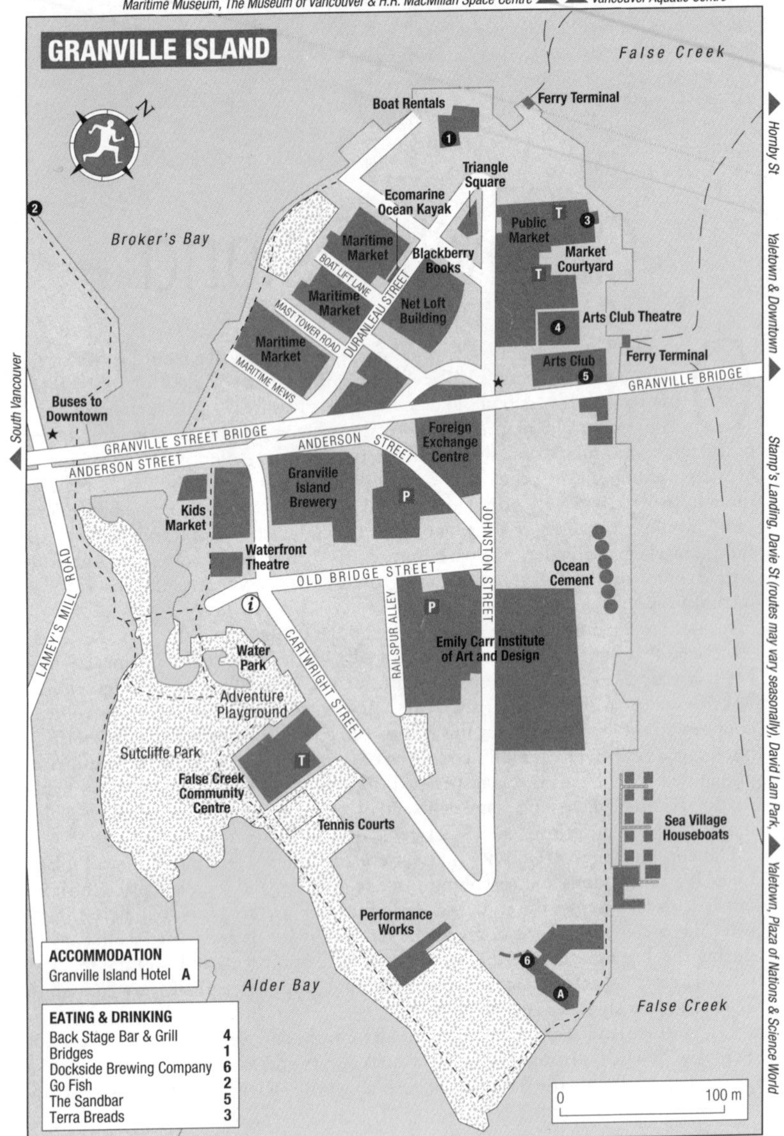

in years of squabbles over water and foreshore rights between the CPR, the provincial government, the city council, local businesspeople and the federal fishing and marine ministries.

All interested parties came up with their own plans, including one by the CPR for a colossal railway station and another for a $10 million port. In 1915 the new harbour commission pulled rank and paid the federal government $1 for the land and then spent $300,000 running railway tracks and a wooden road to the south shore of False Creek. The 760,000 cubic metres of slurry were dredged from the sea bed and poured into a wooden stockade around the mudflats.

The reclaimed swampland opened in 1916 as Industrial Island, an area with 80 lots just 3m above sea level. It quickly prospered as an ironworks and shipbuilding centre, businesses having been attracted by virtue of its proximity to the ocean and to local sawmills and rail yards. In 1930, 1200 people worked on the site, a figure that grew during World War II, when, as the city's industrial fulcrum, it turned to the production of anti-torpedo nets, minesweeping ropes and other maritime-related war materials.

Dredging operations gradually filled in the area to the south of the island, effectively making it a peninsula rather than an island. The same operations were actually part of a never-realized five-stage plan to fill the whole of False Creek, a project which would have changed the face of the city for the worse by robbing Vancouver of Granville Island and the False Creek waterfront. Many industrial tenants then moved out, anxious to find cheaper land and keen to take advantage of the new possibilities offered by road haulage.

By the 1960s virtually all business and trade had moved on, further spurred on by the loss to fire of Wright's Ropes and Pacific Bolts, hitherto among the island's industrial mainstays. Soon after, the island's yards were abandoned, and the place then quickly became a rat-infested dumping ground for the city's rubbish.

Fortunately, in 1972, the federal government agreed to bankroll a $25 million redevelopment programme that retained some of the old false-fronted buildings, tin-shack homes, seawall and rail sidings. Most of the renovation and new construction work had been finished by 1979 – and, despite years of doomsaying from

False Creek ferries

Ferries serving Granville Island and other points on False Creek are by two rival companies: Aquabus (ⓣ604/689-5858, ⓦwww.theaquabus.com) and False Creek Ferries (ⓣ604/684-7781, ⓦwww.granvilleislandferries.bc.ca). Both provide a useful and very frequent service year-round daily between about 7am and 10.30pm (8.30pm in winter). Aquabus runs boats in a continuous loop from the foot of Hornby Street Downtown to Granville Island and from Granville Island to Vanier Park and its museums, docking just below the Maritime Museum (see p.81) – the fare is $3 for each journey. Aquabus also runs ferries between Granville Island and Stamp's Landing, Spyglass Place and the Yaletown dock by the road loop at the eastern foot of Davie Street (all $4). Ferry trips from the Plaza of Nations and Science World to Granville Island cost $6.

False Creek Ferries runs boats between Granville Island and the Vancouver Aquatic Centre at the foot of Thurlow Street at the northern end of the Burrard Bridge ($3) and between Granville Island and the Maritime Museum in Vanier Park ($4). The company also operates ferries to Granville Island from Yaletown ($4) and from Stamp's Landing ($4) on the south side of False Creek en route from Science World ($6). A day pass covering all False Creek Ferries routes is $14.

Passengers buy **tickets** on board with both companies. Note that many of the Vanier Park and Science World services run daily only in summer: in the off season (generally from Oct to mid-May) the services are restricted to weekends. Departures are between every 5 and 30 minutes, depending on the day (they are more frequent at weekends) and destination: Granville Island services to and from the Vancouver Aquatic Centre are most frequent; those to and from Yaletown and Science World the least frequent.

You could also board one of the company's narrated "mini-cruises" (daily every 30min 8.25am–9.10pm, 25min, $7; weekends & public holidays 9.25am–7.10pm, 40min, $10).

politicians and city inhabitants alike, was immediately successful in attracting businesses and people. Work continues unobtrusively to this day, financed entirely by profits from the island, which employs 2500 people and is totally self-supporting.

Getting to Granville Island

The most direct approach to Granville Island is to take **bus** #50 (the "False Creek South" service) from Gastown or Granville Street: this drops you just a few steps from the entrance to the island and runs daily until around 12.30am. The walk south along Granville Street from Downtown and across the Granville Street Bridge might look like the obvious approach, but it's deceptively long, not terribly attractive and probably only worthwhile on a fine day when you need the exercise. Alternatively and more fun, tiny bathtub-size private **ferries** run to Granville Island from a variety of points along False Creek (see box, p.25).

Island practicalities

Granville Island is easy to negotiate, despite an ad hoc arrangement of "streets" – the passages amidst the jumble of industrial units, waterfront and other buildings hardly conform to the normal notion of a street – and public spaces designed to preserve a dynamic and open-plan feel. There's a good **infocentre** at 1592 Johnston St (daily 9am–6pm; ⓣ604/666-5784, ⓦwww.granvilleisland.com) for island-related information, including maps. A **currency exchange** facility is located in the same building, as well as displays on the island's history, a direct-call phone for taxis, a change machine for parking (though you'd be well advised not to come by car) and ATMs on the wall outside. Public toilets stand adjacent.

Note that many of the island's shops and businesses are closed on Mondays, and that if you want a **bus back** to Downtown you should *not* take the #51 from the stop opposite the infocentre – it goes in the wrong direction. Instead, walk out of the island complex's unmissable single road entrance underneath the bridge, and at the junction the #50 stop is immediately on your right; this bus goes Downtown.

▲ Al fresco dining on Granville Island

The island has plenty of cafés and takeaway food stalls, as well as a couple of larger bar-restaurants. Details of where to eat and drink can be found on pp.133–147 and p.152.

The island

Granville Island does not lend itself easily to any sort of set itinerary – the whole idea of the place is that it is unfocused and designed to encourage wandering. This said, there is one must-see target – the **market** in the Public Market Building – but the chances are you'll have the most fun simply walking around the various galleries and specialist craft or book shops, grabbing a drink at one of the bars or cafés, and buying a picnic from the market to eat outdoors on the waterfront. A list of the island's best shops and galleries can be found below and on pp.171–183.

In addition to various commercial art galleries and craft outlets (everything from weaving to jewellery) – several of which are collected in the **Net Loft Building** (daily 10am–7pm) to the west of the market – you may also be able to catch an occasional temporary art exhibition at the **Emily Carr Institute of Art and Design**, 1299 Johnston St (Ⓣ604/844-3800), an art school near the south of the island.

The Granville Island Brewery

One of the first buildings you'll see if you walk to the island from the bus stop under the girders of the Granville Street Bridge is the **Granville Island Brewery**, 1441 Cartwright St (store daily 10am–8pm; tours daily at noon, 2pm & 4pm; $9.75; Ⓣ604/687-2739, Ⓦwww.gib.ca), a small concern that, despite having no formal pub, offers guided tours that include tastings of its fine, additive-free beers. Note that tour times change seasonally, so call first to check the latest details. There's also a shop here where you can buy souvenirs, a selection of leading British Columbia wines, and the brewery's own beer – try the light, easy-to-drink Gastown Amber Ale or the stronger Scottish Ale and Brockton Black, both dark beers with a rich, malty taste.

If you want to drink these beers in a more conducive setting, you can order them at most of the island's bars and restaurants. The brewery is part of a long tradition of brewing and beer-drinking locally, it being claimed that Captain George Vancouver was the first white to brew beer here, when he used fresh spruce needles and molasses as the basis for a beer aimed to combat scurvy among his crew.

Tucked away before the brewery on the same side of the street is the excellent **Kids Market**, a collection of shops, cafés and activities aimed at children (see p.186). The children-only Water Park lies nearby.

The Granville Island Public Market

Far broader in its appeal than the Granville Island Museums, and a dominant feature amongst the maze of shops, galleries and businesses, the **Granville Island Public Market** (daily 9am–7pm) is the island's undisputed highlight. On summer weekends, it's packed with people and a phalanx of buskers. The quality and variety of **food** is staggering, and the endless groaning stalls of fruit, fish, vegetables, cakes, meat, cheese and other more exotic and gourmet foods are augmented by dozens of counters and cafés selling ready-made snacks and potential picnic ingredients.

If you can eat it or drink it, it's probably here; everything from fudge (visit Old Worlde Fudge), doughnuts (Lee's) and turkey (Turkey Stop) to tortillas (La Tortilleria), Belgian chocolate (Brussels Chocolates) and the inevitable muffins (Muffin Granny). Old favourites include the Stock Market, crammed with home-made stocks and meals, and the Salmon Shop, where you can buy some of the finest salmon in Canada, which is to say in the world. There is also a wide variety of takeaway outlets. Parks, patios and walkways nearby provide lively areas to eat and take everything in. The only drawbacks here are the sheer number of people on busy days and the foul flocks of pigeons, seagulls and other birds that assault you for food. Pick up a free **pamphlet**, *The Fresh Sheet*, which is full of details about the market, recipes and forthcoming events.

Science World

Science World (Mon–Fri 10am–5pm, Sat & Sun 10am–6pm; Science World $19.75, OMNIMAX $10 for single feature, second feature currently Fri & Sat evening $5; combination tickets $24.75 for Science World entry and one OMNIMAX film; ⓣ604/443-7440 or 443-7443 recorded 24-hour line, ⓦwww.scienceworld.bc.ca) at 1455 Québec St and Terminal Avenue is one of Vancouver's most distinctive buildings. Its Buckminster Fuller–designed geodesic dome is one of the main structural survivors of the city's Expo '86 world fair. The museum it now houses, however, is something of a disappointment, at least for adults. Probably only children, at whom the place is largely aimed, will be satisfied by the various hands-on displays, which include the opportunity to make thunderous amounts of noise on electronic instruments and drum machines.

Several major galleries deal with all manner of natural history and science-related themes, and several daily demonstrations are held to help explain the science of water, fire and air. Activities include the chance to search for gold, crawl through a beaver lodge, wander a vast maze, see the workings of a beehive and play a tune by walking on a giant synthesizer.

These displays are supplemented by regular touring exhibitions. Be warned that the place becomes very busy, especially on rainy days and before about 2pm during the school year, when vast parties of schoolchildren run riot. There's a gift shop and good-value *White Spot Triple O* restaurant-café if you need a retail or refreshment break.

The best things here if you're an adult are the building itself – at least its striking external appearance – and the chance to catch a special-format movie on the vast screen of the **OMNIMAX Cinema** near the top of the dome. As with all these giant screens, however, the number and variety of films adapted for the format is fairly limited – typically rock concerts and natural history features.

The easiest way to get here is by taking the **SkyTrain** to Main Street–Science World. Although relatively close to Chinatown, the museum is not easily reached from there – the roads are busy and the walk is grim – and the place is difficult to fit into a coherent itinerary. It's far more fun to see it as part of a **boat trip** (see p.25), including it with Granville Island on a longer itinerary that also takes you to Kitsilano and Kits Beach and to the nearby museums of Vanier Park (see pp.79–82), which can be reached either by ferry or by walking from Granville Island along the False Creek seawall.

5

South Vancouver

South of Granville Island and False Creek you enter a part of Vancouver that looks and feels very different from the city's core. Gone, for the most part, are the skyscrapers and glorious views of Downtown; in their place are streets, buildings and panoramas of far less architectural or visual impact – low-rise residential housing, malls and the other staples of suburbia. Save for one or two distinctive sights, this could be just about any suburb of any city in North America.

Much of this part of **South Vancouver** (or, as it is sometimes confusingly called, the West Side) you can ignore completely, notably the long run of undistinguished residential districts that stretch towards the airport, New Westminster and the Fraser River. Points of interest include **Vanier Park**, a big area of grass and trees that's noteworthy as the home to all but one of the city's main museums – the **Museum of Vancouver**, the **Vancouver Maritime Museum** and the **H.R. MacMillan Space Centre**: the last also contains the city's planetarium and observatory.

To the west lies the **Kitsilano** district (better known as Kits), in its day something of a hippie enclave but now a leafy and pleasantly gentrified residential area with a good beach and public swimming pool, funky cafés, restaurants, galleries and interesting stores. Farther south are **Queen Elizabeth Park** and **VanDusen Botanical Garden**, green spaces that enliven the sprawl of the area's suburbs, and – to the west – the prosperous suburbs of Point Grey and Shaughnessy and the University of British Columbia (UBC) and its surroundings (see p.86). However, you're as likely to visit this area for its **beaches** as its sights, which stretch around much of the peninsula's northern shore from the busy but appealing Kits Beach in the east to the laid-back clothing-optional Wreck Beach on the western fringe of the UBC campus (see p.93).

You could easily incorporate a visit to the area's museums with a trip to Granville Island, taking the **ferry** from False Creek and the island – it docks just below the Maritime Museum. Coming from Downtown, take the #22 Macdonald **bus** south from anywhere on Burrard or West Pender – get off at the first stop after the bridge and walk west a short distance on Cornwall Street and take the first right north on Chester Street to the park and museums. Parts of southern Vancouver have also benefited from the arrival of SkyTrain's new **Canada Line**, with King Edward station, in particular, useful for visits to Queen Elizabeth Park and the VanDusen Botanical Garden.

Alternatively, walk or cycle the Seawall from Granville Island to Vanier Park and the rest of Kits. Don't tackle too much, however – certainly not the UBC and its Museum of Anthropology (see p.87), which you'll probably want to keep for another day.

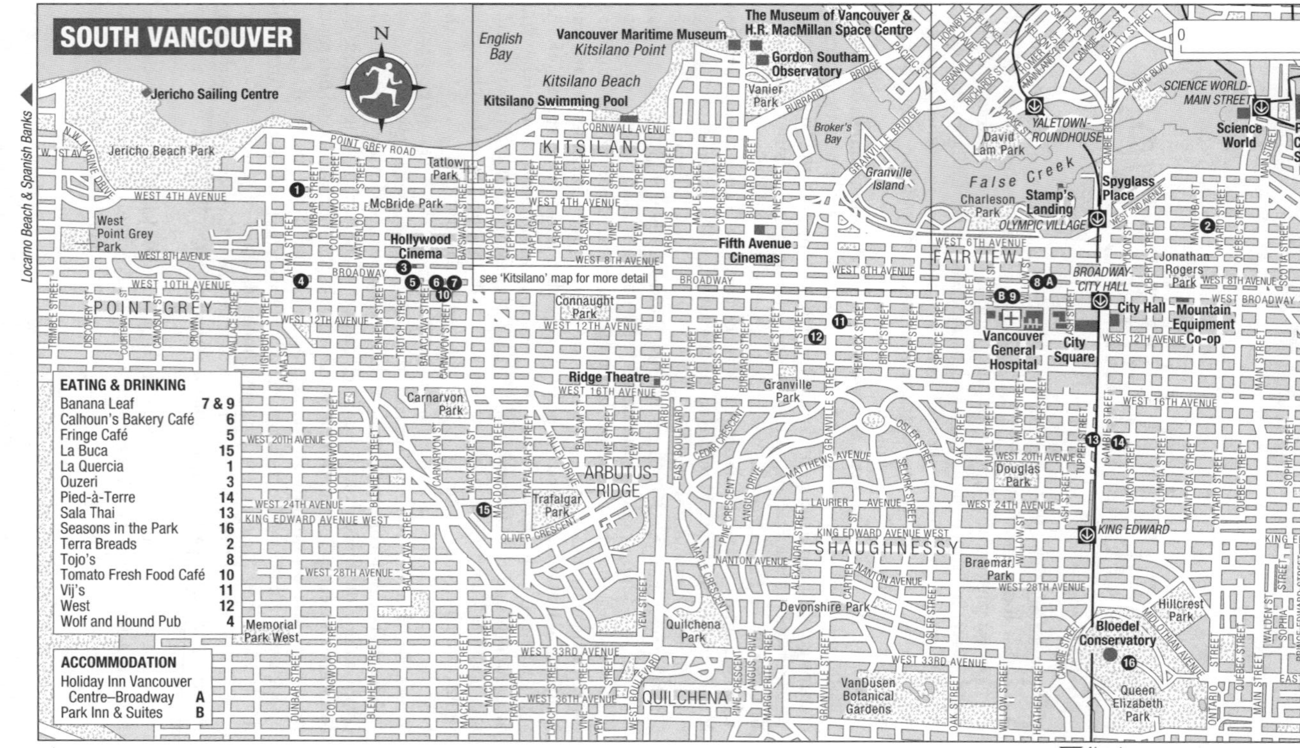
SOUTH VANCOUVER
N
0 1 km
EATING & DRINKING
Banana Leaf 7 & 9
Calhoun's Bakery Café 6
Fringe Café 5
La Buca 15
La Quercia 1
Ouzeri 3
Pied-à-Terre 14
Sala Thai 13
Seasons in the Park 16
Terra Breads 2
Tojo's 8
Tomato Fresh Food Café 10
Vij's 11
West 12
Wolf and Hound Pub 4
ACCOMMODATION
Holiday Inn Vancouver Centre–Broadway A
Park Inn & Suites B
see 'Kitsilano' map for more detail
Locarno Beach & Spanish Banks
Airport
English Bay
Jericho Sailing Centre
Jericho Beach Park
West Point Grey Park
Vancouver Maritime Museum
Kitsilano Point
Kitsilano Beach
Kitsilano Swimming Pool
The Museum of Vancouver & H.R. MacMillan Space Centre
Gordon Southam Observatory
Vanier Park
Broker's Bay
Granville Island
False Creek
David Lam Park
Charleson Park
Stamp's Landing
Spyglass Place
Science World
Pacific Central Station
SCIENCE WORLD-MAIN STREET
YALETOWN-ROUNDHOUSE
OLYMPIC VILLAGE
BROADWAY-CITY HALL
KING EDWARD
Tatlow Park
McBride Park
Hollywood Cinema
Fifth Avenue Cinemas
Connaught Park
Ridge Theatre
Granville Park
Carnarvon Park
Trafalgar Park
Memorial Park West
Quilchena Park
Devonshire Park
VanDusen Botanical Gardens
Douglas Park
Braemar Park
Jonathan Rogers Park
City Hall
Mountain Equipment Co-op
Vancouver General Hospital
City Square
Hillcrest Park
Bloedel Conservatory
Queen Elizabeth Park
KITSILANO
POINT GREY
FAIRVIEW
ARBUTUS RIDGE
SHAUGHNESSY
QUILCHENA
POINT GREY ROAD
WEST 4TH AVENUE
WEST 8TH AVENUE
BROADWAY
WEST 10TH AVENUE
WEST 12TH AVENUE
WEST 16TH AVENUE
WEST 20TH AVENUE
WEST 24TH AVENUE
KING EDWARD AVENUE WEST
KING EDWARD AV EAST
WEST 28TH AVENUE
WEST 33RD AVENUE
EAST 33RD AVENUE
WEST 36TH AVENUE
CORNWALL AVENUE
N.W. MARINE DRIVE
W. 1ST AV
KINGSWAY
GRANVILLE BRIDGE
BURRARD BRIDGE
CAMBIE BRIDGE
PACIFIC BLVD
MAIN STREET
CAMBIE STREET
GRANVILLE STREET
OAK STREET
ARBUTUS STREET
DUNBAR STREET
ALMA STREET
MACDONALD STREET
BURRARD STREET
MATTHEWS AVENUE
OSLER STREET
MIDLOTHIAN AVENUE
VALLEY DRIVE
OLIVER CRESCENT
MAPLE CRESCENT
EAST BOULEVARD
NANTON AVENUE

Vanier Park

Vanier Park sits on the waterfront at the west end of the Burrard Bridge, close to the residential and entertainment centres of West 4th Avenue and Kitsilano. Named after Georges Vanier, Canada's popular governor-general between 1959 and 1967, the park itself is unremarkable, with large areas of open grass and few trees (and so offers little shade on a hot day), and is not worth visiting for its own sake unless you want some fresh air and a bit of beach without trekking all the way to Kits or Jericho. Its main role is to provide a setting for two of Vancouver's main museums – the Museum Vancouver and of Vancouver Maritime Museum – and the planetarium and other exhibits of the H.R. MacMillan Space Centre. It also hosts occasional festivals, including Bard on the Beach and the Vancouver International Children's Festival (see p.202).

South Vancouver's beaches

Some of the most tempting parts of South Vancouver are its beaches, in particular **Kitsilano Beach,** or "Kits Beach". Named – like the district behind it – after Chief Khahtsahlanough (or Khahtsahlano), a Squamish chieftain of a band who once owned the area, it is edged by Cornwall Avenue west from Arbutus Street as far as Trafalgar Street. You can walk here on the coast path from Vanier Park and the Vancouver and Maritime museums (about 30min) or, from Downtown, take a #22 bus southbound on Burrard Street.

Kits is the hippest and busiest of the city's beaches, especially popular with the university volleyball and rippling-torso crowd, as well as the more well-heeled locals. Families also come here, though, to take advantage of the warm and safe swimming area, while sunbathers can take up a position on the grass to the rear. There's a tremendous range of cafés and takeaway food outlets on Cornwall Avenue and, to a slightly lesser extent, Yew Street. The best place for food and drink near the beach is the *Watermark* restaurant, with a glass-fronted dining room upstairs and less expensive concessions below.

At the western end of Kits Beach, at Yew and Cornwall streets, you'll find one of the world's largest outdoor **saltwater pools** (late May to mid-June Mon–Fri noon–8.45pm, Sat & Sun 10am–8.45pm, mid-June to early Sept Mon–Fri 7am–8.45pm, Sat & Sun 10am–8.45pm, rest of Sept Mon–Fri 7am–7.15pm, Sat & Sun 10am–7.15pm; $5.15; ⓣ604/731-0011). It's Vancouver's most popular outdoor heated pool and easily reached if you're on the beach already by walking along the beachfront promenade. The shoreline path linking Kits Beach with other points east and west is a lovely place to take an evening stroll, ride a bike or simply sit on a bench and watch the street life. Follow the path all the way east and it takes you to Granville Island by way of Vanier Park and the museums. The bars and restaurants of Kits fuel something of a party spirit on the beach, and there's always plenty going on.

Jericho Beach, west of Kits and handy for those staying in the youth hostel, is a touch quieter and serves as a hangout for the windsurfing crowd. Still farther west, Jericho blurs into **Locarno Beach** and **Spanish Banks**, progressively less crowded and the start of a fringe of sand and parkland that continues round to the University of British Columbia (UBC) campus. Locals rate Spanish Banks the most relaxed of the city's beaches, while Locarno is one of its most spectacular, especially at low tide, when the sand seems to stretch forever. Bikers and walkers use the dirt track above Locarno, beyond which a broad sward of grass with picnic tables and benches runs to the road.

At low tide the more athletically inclined could walk all the way round to UBC (others can take the bus), where the famous clothing-optional Wreck Beach (see p.93) lies just off the campus area below NW Marine Drive.

Explorepass

The **Explorepass** ($30) is available for single entry to the Vancouver Museum, the Maritime Museum and the Science Centre. Entry to the three sights need not be on the same day. The pass is available from the Vancouver Touristinfo Centre (see p.36) or from participating sights. For more information, visit ⓦwww.vanierpark.com/explorepass.

The Museum of Vancouver

Founded in 1894, the **Museum of Vancouver** (July & Aug daily 10am–5pm, Thurs also 5–8pm, rest of the year Tues, Wed, Fri–Sun 10am–5pm; $11; ⓣ604/736-4431, ⓦwww.museumofvancouver.ca) in Vanier Park is Canada's largest civic museum. The museum's purpose is to trace the history of the city and the lower British Columbian mainland. Its flying saucer-shaped building dates from 1968, and is a nod to the conical cedar-bark hats of the Haida and other aboriginal peoples, the area's earliest inhabitants. The strange fountain outside recalls the crab-like animal of native legend that guards the entrance to the city's harbour. By neat coincidence, it also evokes the astrological sign corresponding to July 1, Canada's birthday.

Though it's the main point of interest at Vanier Park, the museum is not as captivating as you'd expect. It claims to hold 300,000 exhibits, but it's hard to know where they could all be, and a visit needn't take more than an hour or so.

As it is, the museum features a patchy assortment of baskets, tools, clothes and miscellaneous artefacts of aboriginal peoples – including a huge whaling canoe, the only example of such a vessel in a museum – covering the 8000 years of aboriginal history before the arrival of white settlers. After this, the main collection weaves in and out of Vancouver's history up to World War I, full of offbeat and occasionally memorable insights if you have the patience to read the accompanying briefs.

Among the best are the accounts of the often extraordinary exploits of early explorers, notably Simon Fraser (see p.256); the displays spotlighting forestry and the lumber industry; and the immigration section, which re-creates what it felt like to travel in steerage, the cheapest class in the transatlantic boats that brought settlers to North America from Europe. The chronological displays devoted to the twentieth century are disappointing – most of the exhibits here, such as furniture and kitchen utensils, would look more at home in an antique shop. Again, this may well change when the museum has undergone its refurbishment.

The H.R. MacMillan Space Centre

The **H.R. MacMillan Space Centre**, also known as the Pacific Space Centre (Tues–Sun 10am–5pm; evening laser shows Thurs–Sun at varying times; Space Centre $15, additional Virtual Voyage rides $7; evening laser show $10.75; ⓣ604/738-7827, ⓦwww.spacecentre.ca), incorporates the MacMillan Planetarium and a range of space-related displays and shows. Like the Museum of Vancouver, with which it shares a building, it lies in Vanier Park and can be accessed at 1100 Chestnut St or from the small ferry landing in the park.

Its main draws are its star shows – the standard planetarium fare – and very loud, very brash evening laser and music extravaganzas. These are held in the H.R. MacMillan Star Theatre – there's an extra charge for the evening shows, but the star shows (held several times daily, usually in the afternoon) are free with general admission. The evening shows are very popular, so arrive in good time or make reservations.

Many of the centre's exhibits are high-tech and hands-on, especially in the Cosmic Courtyard, where interactive displays allow you to battle an alien, design a spaceship, guide a lunar robot or plan a voyage to Mars. Many displays also involve lots of impressive computer and other audiovisual effects, notably the Virtual Voyages Simulator, a flight simulator that gives you a sense of the motion you might encounter during space travel and other journeys. Rides on the simulator last about 5 minutes (entrance is included with admission) and involve experiences ranging from colliding with a comet to taking trips on a roller coaster or to other planets. The **Gordon Southam Observatory**, the small domed building close to the Space Centre, has a telescope that is usually available for public stargazing on clear Saturday nights (call the Space Centre or ⓣ604/738-2855 for current times; donation); astronomers are on hand to show you the ropes and help you position your camera for a "Shoot the Moon" photography session of the heavens.

The Vancouver Maritime Museum

After the space-age look and high-tech displays of the Space Centre, the rather dated appearance of the **Vancouver Maritime Museum** (May–Sept daily 10am–5pm, Oct–April Tues–Sat 10am–5pm, Sun noon–5pm; $10; ⓣ604/257-8300, ⓦwww.vancouvermaritimemuseum.com) is likely to come as a disappointing jolt. That said, the museum is a great place to bring children and will appeal if you have any feeling at all for ships and the sea. It is also close to the waterfront and the Heritage Harbour jetty, used by ferries to and from Granville Island and the rest of False Creek (see p.25). It's not too big, so there's no danger of museum fatigue if you're finishing the day here after seeing Vanier Park's other two museums.

The collection itself features such treasures as original charts from George Vancouver's ships, lovely early photographs evoking late nineteenth-century Vancouver, and a vivid reconstruction of a tugboat bridge. Much of the rest of the presentation, however, doesn't quite do justice to the status of the city as one

▲ Heritage Harbour

The St Roch and the Northwest Passage

The Maritime Museum's star turn is the *St Roch*, a **Royal Canadian Mounted Police schooner** celebrated as the first craft to make a single-season traverse of the fabled **Northwest Passage** around the American continent. This route continues to exert a romantic allure – and, in the wake of oil discoveries in the far north, an increasingly economic attraction as well. Crossed in its entirety fewer than fifty times, it is the world's most severe maritime challenge, involving a voyage from north of Baffin Island west of Greenland to the Beaufort Sea above Alaska. Some 50,000 icebergs constantly line the eastern approaches and thick pack ice covers the route for nine months of the year, with temperatures rising above freezing only in July and August. Perpetual darkness reigns for four months of the year, and thick fog and blizzards can obscure visibility for the remaining eight months. Even with modern technology navigation is almost impossible: a magnetic compass is useless as the magnetic north lies in the passage, and a gyro compass is unreliable at high latitudes; little is known of Arctic tides and currents; sonar is confused by submerged ice; and the featureless tundra of the Arctic islands provides the only few points of visual or radar reference.

John Cabot can hardly have been happy with his order from Henry VII in **1497** to blaze the northwest trail, the first recorded instance of such an attempt. The elusive passage subsequently excited the imagination of the world's greatest adventurers, including **Sir Francis Drake**, **Jacques Cartier**, **Sir Martin Frobisher**, **James Cook** and **Henry Hudson.**

Details of a possible route were pieced together over the centuries, though many paid with their lives in the process, most famously **Sir John Franklin**, who vanished into the ice with 129 men in 1845. Norwegian **Roald Amundsen** achieved the **first sea crossing** in 1906, following a three-year voyage. Then came the successful *St Roch* voyage, led by a Canadian Mountie, **Henry Larsen**, in 1944. More recently, huge icebreakers have explored the potential of cracking a commercial route through the ice mainly for the export of oil from the Alaskan and new Beaufort fields and for the exploitation of minerals in Canada's Arctic north.

of the world's leading ports, with the exception of the wonderfully renovated 1928 *St Roch*, the first vessel to navigate the famed Northwest Passage in a single season (see box above) and to circumnavigate North America; a beautiful craft, it now sits in its own wing of the museum, where it can be viewed by guided tour only (tours run roughly every 30min).

Special summer shows and exhibitions spice things up a little, especially for children, as do the Pirates' Cove and Children's Maritime Discovery Centre, full of computers for interactive games and education, model ships, telescopes trained on ships in the harbour and a store of seafaring costumes for dressing up.

Note that there are plans to create a National Maritime Centre on the Lonsdale waterfront in North Vancouver, and although it's unlikely the Maritime Museum will be relocated, some of its exhibits may find their way to any new centre. See the museum's website for the latest information.

Kitsilano

The district of **Kitsilano** was named by the Canadian Pacific Railway, which – inevitably – had acquired most of the local land by the last decade of the nineteenth century. It half-heartedly acknowledged the area's previous aboriginal owners by adapting the name of Khahtsahlanough (or Khahtsahlano) in 1904, after a former chief of the aboriginal village, Sun'ahk, which stood on the site until its inhabitants were "dispersed" in 1901. The district runs roughly west from Burrard to Alma Street, and south from the waterfront to 16th Avenue.

Kits has long been a desirable place to live, with its attractive 1920s houses and well-built apartment blocks. Attracting hippies and other counterculture types in the 1960s, it became Vancouver's equivalent of Notting Hill or Haight-Ashbury.

Today's younger hipsters head for Yaletown, or the more gritty environs of Main Street and Commercial Drive to the east, while the more moneyed set, or grown-rich hippies, has moved west to Point Grey and south to the Shaughnessy neighbourhoods. But Kits is still hugely popular, thanks to the pleasant laid-back atmosphere that has survived from times past, and to an extremely healthy arts, culture and nightlife scene – the area has a number of good cafés, bars and restaurants as well as interesting stores and galleries. These are mostly on or near the main streets, especially West Fourth Avenue, the backstreets beyond being largely residential. Classic survivors (or good copies) from the good old days, and still worth a visit, include the *Naam* restaurant (see p.142) and *Sophie's Cosmic Café* (see p.132).

Kits Beach, the most popular of the city's beaches, epitomizes the district's young, reasonably moneyed and relaxed feel. There's little in the way of local accommodation, save for one or two B&Bs and a good hostel (see p.127), though if you do stay here bear in mind the 10min bus or cab journey to Downtown.

South Vancouver's parks and gardens

South Vancouver's mostly residential suburban spaces south of Kits and Vanier Park have next to nothing to see and, were it not for the presence of two of the city's major greenspaces, would be an area you would probably only visit in passing. **Queen Elizabeth Park** is the larger of the two spaces, and while lacking the ocean-fringed setting of Stanley Park and the wilderness of the North Shore's provincial parks, still attracts some six million visitors a year. The **VanDusen Botanical Garden** is smaller and, as its name suggests, has a more focused horticultural ambition than its near neighbour, but ranks as one of the continent's finest botanical gardens.

Queen Elizabeth Park

Queen Elizabeth Park (Bloedel Floral Conservatory open April to early Sept Mon–Fri 9am–8pm, Sat & Sun 10am–9pm, rest of the year daily 10am–5pm; park free, conservatory $4.80; Ⓣ604/257-8584 or 257-8570, Ⓦwww.city.vancouver.bc.ca/parks) lies between Cambie and Ontario streets and West 29th and West 37th avenues. It barely holds its own with Stanley Park – but then few parks do – yet still merits a visit if you're in this part of the city and relish the idea of a spacious, pretty and well-landscaped garden.

Its big draw is the **Bloedel Floral Conservatory**, an indoor space at 33rd Avenue at Cambie Street that replicates the climate, flora and some of the fauna of desert, subtropical and rainforest habitats. The Floral Conservatory commands a 360-degree view of the city and features 500 varieties of exotic plants and fifty species of birds. You'll also find many of the trappings of an urban park, including tennis courts, pitch-and-putt golf, lawn bowling, a roller-hockey court, a basketball area and the Nat Bailey Stadium, a fine place to watch the city's Vancouver

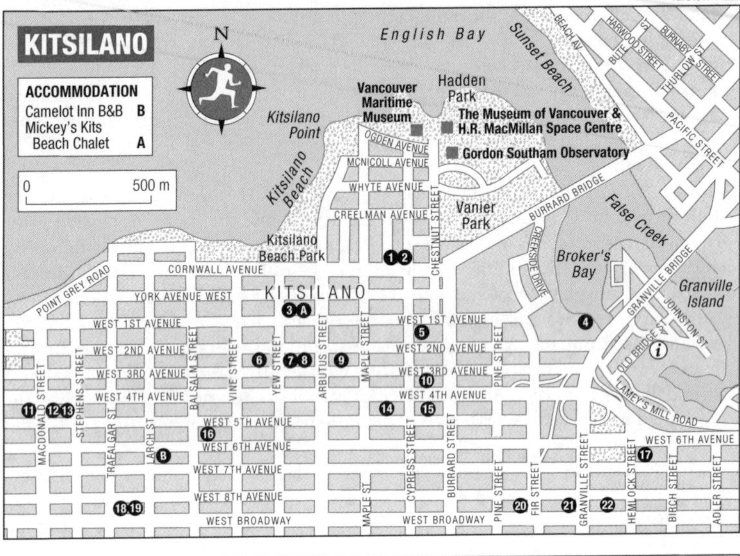

EATING & DRINKING

Akbar's Own	20	Darby's Pub	11	Lumière	19	Terra Breads	16
Bin 942	21	Epicurean	5	Mistral	18	Topanga Café	12
Bishop's	7	Flying Wedge	2	The Naam	13	Trattoria Italian Kitchen	15
Bistro Pastis	8	Fuel	14	PHAT	10	Wicked Café	17
Capers	6	Go Fish	4	Planet Veg	1		
Cru	22	King's Head	3	Sophie's Cosmic Café	9		

Canadians baseball team play (see p.199): the stadium is on the east side of the park at Ontario Street and 29th Avenue.

At 136 acres, Queen Elizabeth Park is Vancouver's third-largest green space. It sits on the panoramic **Little Mountain**, the stump of an old volcano and the highest point on the south side of the city (153m). A winding road spirals gently up its slopes, passing through an arboretum en route to the summit. On the eastern slopes you'll find examples of virtually every native British Columbian tree and shrub. The summit is partly taken up by two former quarries, originally used for building Vancouver's roads and by the Canadian Pacific Railway during the construction of the transcontinental railway at the end of the nineteenth century. The CPR offered the quarries to the city's parks department in 1919 but the city didn't accept the dubious gift until ten years later, by which time it was an eyesore and derelict.

Both of these were reworked and landscaped after 1930 as the **Quarry Gardens**, vast rock gardens filled with flowers and shrubs, and dotted with ponds, fountains and tinkling waterfalls. Don't be surprised at weekends if you have to thread your way through wedding parties waiting to be photographed – it's not unknown for numerous pairs of newlyweds and friends to be here smiling for the camera in high season.

The quarries form part of the park's varied history, the area having started life in the 1870s as a timber camp. It then served as a dairy farm and Chinese vegetable garden before the quarries were worked in the first years of the twentieth century to provide stone for the large number of roads then being built in a nascent Vancouver. The site's transformation into a park was completed on the occasion of a visit by Britain's King George VI and Queen Elizabeth in 1939.

Bus #15 gets you here: it runs the length of Cambie from Pender Street Downtown. Or take the new Canada Line **SkyTrain** to King Edward station.

Bloedel Floral Conservatory

At the top of Little Mountain, the **Bloedel Floral Conservatory**, a 43m-diameter dome made up of 1500 Plexiglas bubbles, presents a wonderful medley of sights, sounds and smells as you walk from the heat and humidity of a rainforest through subtropical habitats to end up in the dry heat of near desert. The bulk of the money ($1.25 million) required to build the dome came from the lumber industrialist Prentice Bloedel – ironically, given the timber industry's effect on the British Columbian landscape elsewhere.

Around 500 species of plants from across the globe are collected within the structure, together with about 100 free-flying birds (around fifty species in all), among them numerous noisy and vividly coloured parrots.

Close to the conservatory, and a pretty place to **eat** lunch or dinner, is the *Seasons* restaurant, West 33rd Ave and Cambie (Ⓣ604/874-8008 or 1-800/632-9422), where virtually every table has a view over the gardens to the city beyond. It's especially popular for brunch at weekends, and three fireplaces allow for outdoor eating on the terrace year-round.

VanDusen Botanical Garden

Anyone with even remotely green fingers should visit the 54-acre **VanDusen Botanical Garden** (daily: June–Aug 9am–9pm; March & Oct 10am–5pm; April 10am–6pm; May 10am–8pm; Sept 10am–7pm; Nov–Feb 10am–4pm; $8.85, Oct–March $6.50; Ⓣ604/878-9274, Ⓦwww.vandusengarden.org) at 5251 Oak St, which is that rarest of things – a former golf course that became a piece of useful landscape. *Horticulture* magazine rates it – deservedly – as one of the world's top-ten botanical gardens, though the UBC Botanical Garden (see p.92) also has its fans. It's easily seen, especially if you're also visiting Queen Elizabeth Park, as it lies on Oak Street at the corner of 37th Avenue, just a few blocks west of its larger neighbour. If you're coming from Downtown, take **bus** #17, which runs down Hemlock or the Canada Line **SkyTrain** to King Edward.

The garden was a CPR-owned mess of bush and tree stumps in 1910, when it was leased to the Shaughnessy Golf Club, which remained in residence until 1960. It opened as a garden in 1975 and features many thousands of trees, shrubs and plants from around the world, all of which are well labelled, making the tranquil walkways and shrubberies an education as well as a pleasure. Like other gardens in Vancouver, the storms of winter 2006 damaged the grounds, resulting in the loss of 412 trees and around 150 shrubs, though much of the cosmetic damage has long been repaired.

Various parts of the gardens are themed – there's a Rose Garden, Lake Garden and Rhododendron Walk, for example – but the trees and flower beds are designed so that there's something worthwhile to see every month of the year. One of the most popular areas, at least among children, is the **Elizabethan Hedge Maze**, made up of around a thousand pyramid cedars – each is only 1.5m high so that adults can keep track of their children's progress, or lack of it, from a grassy knoll nearby.

Events are held in the garden throughout the year, among them a major Flower and Garden Show, usually in the first week of June, and the Christmas Festival of Lights, when thousands of tiny lights illuminate the gardens (for more information, see chapter 18, Festivals and events).

6

The University of British Columbia

Though the University of British Columbia (UBC) might seem an unlikely point of interest, its world-class Museum of Anthropology is by far the best of the city's museums and galleries. The museum is devoted largely to the art and culture of the aboriginal peoples of the Pacific Northwest coast, highlighted by a sensational collection of totem poles and large-scale carved works.

Home to some 37,000 students, the vast campus is 13km from the city centre, and is located on the western edge of a large peninsula fringed by English Bay. Given the time you'll need to devote to reaching the site – allow at least 30min by bus, car or taxi from Downtown (see below for details) – it's well worth taking in some of the other sights on and around the campus. If time is short, you should see two fine gardens – the beautiful UBC **Botanical Garden** and smaller Japanese-style **Nitobe Memorial Garden**. On a longer trip, you might want to come prepared for a spell on popular **Wreck Beach**, a stretch of sand infamous for its clothing-optional policy on sunbathing. If that doesn't appeal, you can swim in more decorous surroundings at the UBC Aquatic Centre (see p.198).

If you have transport, or have cycled to the campus, then you might also want to explore the **University Endowment Lands**. This huge area includes the campus but is also a domain of large tracts of forest and semi-wilderness. Much the same can be said of the countryside southeast of the Lands, a protected area known as **Pacific Spirit Regional Park**, created in 1988 and almost twice the size of Stanley Park. Note that you *will* need transport to access these – you can't come to the UBC campus and easily walk to, or explore, the park or the Endowment Lands.

Getting to the UBC and the Museum of Anthropology

To get to the **UBC** and the **Museum of Anthropology** by **bus** from Downtown, catch any 'UBC' bus (notably the #4) south from Granville Street and stay on until the end of the line, the "University Loop", near the centre of the campus.

To reach the museum, turn right from the bus stop, walk along the tree-lined East Mall for about ten minutes, then turn left on NW Marine Drive and walk until you see the museum building signposted on the right (about another 5min).

To get here by **car**, the easiest route is to drive west along Fourth Avenue – which becomes Chancellor Boulevard and then NW Marine Drive – until you reach the campus. Watch on the right for a sign indicating the museum car park.

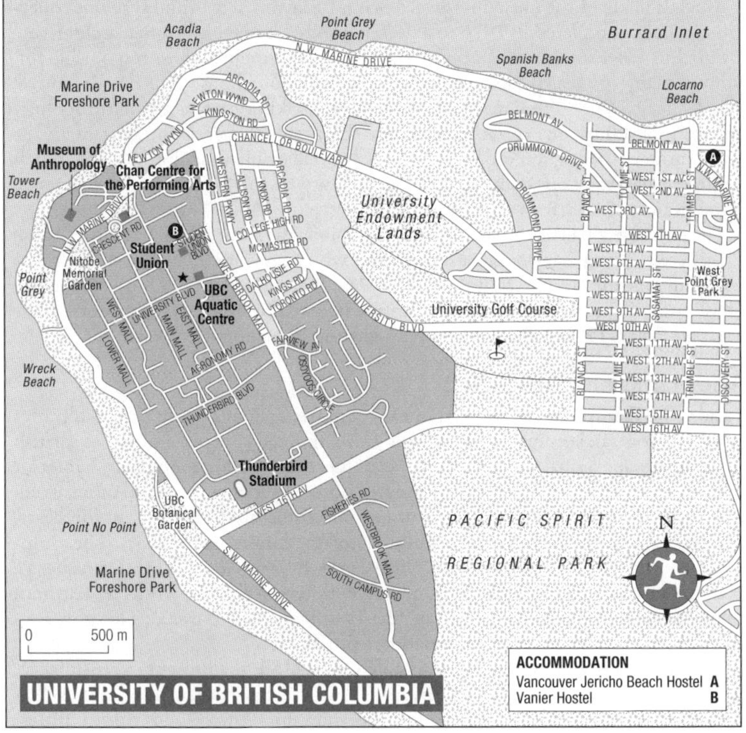

Note that there is a free shuttle **bus**, the C20, around the campus from Student Union Boulevard, taking in the museum, Wreck Beach (see p.93) and Nitobe and Botanical gardens.

The Museum of Anthropology

The superlative **Museum of Anthropology** (mid-May to mid-Oct daily except Tues 10am–5pm, Tues 10am–9pm; mid Oct to mid-May Tues 11am–9pm, Wed–Sun 10am–5pm; $10, Tues 5–9pm $6; ⓣ604/822-5087, ⓦwww.moa.ubc.ca) at 6393 NW Marine Drive is devoted to the art and culture of the aboriginal peoples of the Pacific Northwest, and the Haida in particular. Its collection of carvings, totem poles and artefacts is unequalled in North America, and the superb modern galleries also feature artefacts from other aboriginal cultures. Not the least of the museum's attractions is its architectural élan, the building's modern and uncluttered appearance providing a perfect setting for its often ancient, strange and shamanistic works of art.

The university began its ethnographical collection – which now numbers 535,000 objects in its entirety – in 1927, but a museum to store them only started life in the late 1940s as an ad hoc arrangement in the basement of the university's main library. The present building was made possible by a grant from the federal government in 1971 to mark the centenary of British Columbia's entry into the Canadian Confederation. Today, it is Canada's largest teaching museum, and was renovated and enlarged in time for the 2010 Winter Olympics.

Much is made of the museum's award-winning layout, a cool and spacious collection of halls completed in 1976 to a design inspired by Haida beamed architecture by Arthur Erickson (see box opposite), the eminent architect also responsible for, among many other projects, converting the city's courthouse into the Vancouver Art Gallery. While the Great Hall is the most striking part of the anthropology museum building, one of its architectural highlights comes at the start, with the vast entrance doors, carved in 1976 by four aboriginal sculptors. The reliefs represent narrative episodes from the mythology of the Skeena Valley aboriginal peoples in central British Columbia.

The entrance is flanked by cedar panels that mimic the shape of the traditional Salish "bent boxes", simple rectangular cedar boxes with heavy lids. Standing at the top of the stairs outside are two figures in red cedar. *Ancestor Figure* (1997) by Musqueam artist Susan Point holds a "fisher", a creature believed to have healing powers, while *Welcome Figure* (1984) is the work of Nuu-chah-nulth sculptor Joe David.

The Ramp and Great Hall

Inside, the **Ramp**, or walkway from the entrance, contains many large sculptures removed for safekeeping in the 1950s from the cedar plank houses of British Columbia's aboriginal peoples. Some were decorative and stood against interior and exterior walls; others served as massive posts to support roofs and other structural beams. Sculptures from houses of coastal peoples usually represent forebears, or powerful figures linked with the history of the houses' inhabitants. The sculptures are arranged geographically, with works by the Coast Salish (Musqueam, Saanich and Tsartlip) on both sides and, lower down on the left, works by northern peoples such as the Haida, Gitxsan (or Tsimshian) and Nisga'a. The gorgeous blanket here is a Musqueam work dating from 1997.

Still more outstanding is the remarkable **Great Hall**, the museum's centrepiece, a vast, airy space inspired by aboriginal post-and-beam cedar longhouses that makes a perfect artificial setting for the museum's thirty-odd **totem poles**. (Conservation concerns prohibit displaying them outdoors, where they often belong.) Though the exhibits themselves have very little by way of information,

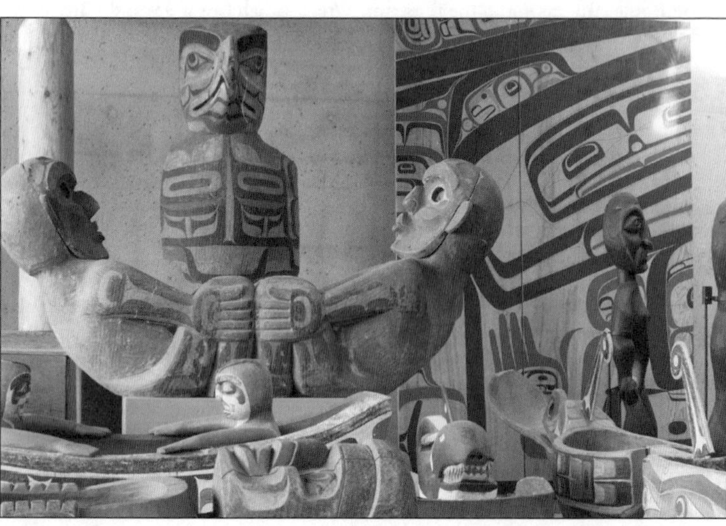

▲ The Museum of Anthropology

Arthur Erickson

Barcelona has Gaudí; Rome, Bernini and London, Sir Christopher Wren. Vancouver has **Arthur Charles Erickson** (1924–2009), born in the city, an iconoclast and modernist whose work in and around the city has influenced its appearance more than any other architect, living or dead. Among his major public projects were the Provincial Law Courts, Robson Square, the Vancouver Art Gallery and the Museum of Anthropology. Farther afield his works include the Canadian Embassy in Washington DC, California Plaza in Los Angeles, the San Diego Convention Center, the Napp Laboratories in Cambridge, England, and City Hall in Fresno, California.

Erickson's career took off in 1963, when he won a competition to design Vancouver's Simon Fraser University. For inspiration he turned to the hill towns of central Italy and the Acropolis in Athens, where hills are a frame for and an organic part of the town or monument they are supporting. The result – with its innovative use of material, especially concrete (Erickson has been called the "**poet of concrete**"), crisp angles and uncompromising penchant for the linear– was considered a triumph. Today the vast campus area spreads in a sequence of angular, low-rise buildings that fold into the contours of the mountains.

More projects followed, notably the **Museum of Anthropology** at the University of British Columbia (see p.87), designed to house the totems and other artefacts of the Pacific Northwest aboriginal peoples. Again Erickson was determined to retain or evoke the natural setting in which such artefacts, especially the totems, would originally have been found. He used large areas of glass, then added subtle lighting to reproduce the effect of natural light and shadow. Ramps and suddenly revealed interior vistas were used to satisfy another of Erickson's concerns, namely how one moves around a building. "Most of my concepts have to do with how one moves," he said of the museum, "and since the site is sloped, I felt the whole movement should be down one long ramp, with more and more revealed, until the whole space burst open with a view of the sea."

Erickson's career was something of a rollercoaster, financial problems in the 1990s having brought his practice to its knees and forced him from his home. This experience, among others, led him to turn to Vancouver's deprived eastern margins, where his conversion of the old Portland Hotel was part of a plan to create subsidized housing and a linked collection of community buildings and services. Before his death, however, his star and his practice were once again in the ascendant, with work on renovation of the Museum of Anthropology and other city centre projects.

there is an information desk near the entrance, along with sourcebooks with photographic and written essays on Pacific Northwest aboriginal art and culture.

From the Great Hall, enormous 15m-high windows look out to the **museum grounds** where there are more totem poles and a collection of nineteenth-century **Haida buildings** (constructed in 1962), complete with family dwellings, mortuary house and longhouses built along the traditional north-south axis. Even the plants and grasses are those that would have been indigenous to a village of this type. The totem poles are memorial and mortuary poles and date from 1951 to the present: the most recent was raised in 2000. You're free to wander around the grounds, something that's worth doing as much for the fabulous views of the ocean and distant mountains as for the exhibits.

Most of the poles and monolithic carvings, indoors and out, are taken from the coastal peoples of the Haida (see box, p.91), Salish, Tsimshian and Kwakiutl (see p.261), all of whom have shared cultural elements. Scholars really don't know terribly much about the arcane mythology behind the carvings, but the best guess is that the many different animals correspond to different clans or the creatures after which the clans were named.

The rest of the collection

The museum's third main component is the **50th Anniversary Gallery** (gallery 3), created in 1999 to celebrate the museum's 50th anniversary. Its aim is to highlight the diversity and scope of Northwest Coast aboriginal art, past and present, which it does by combining beautiful examples of contemporary art in a variety of media – wood, textiles, semi-precious stones and so forth - with a range of high-tech interactive displays and computer links.

One of the museum's great virtues is that few of its major displays are hidden away in basements or back rooms; instead they're displayed in the new *Multiversity Galleries*, opened in January, 2010, close to the Great Hall. In all, the collection boasts some 35,000 objects of cultural and archeological note – and most are open to scrutiny. More delicate items such as fabrics and works on paper are not displayed, though many are brought out of safekeeping for occasional exhibitions in the various of the galleries.

Most of the permanent collection revolves around Canadian Pacific cultures, but the Inuit and Far North exhibits are also outstanding. So, too, are the jewellery, masks and baskets of Northwest aboriginal peoples in the new galleries, all strikingly delicate compared to the blunter and more monumental carvings of the Great Hall. Look out especially for the argillite sculptures of animals and other items, made from a jet-black slate found only on British Columbia's Haida Gwaii, or Queen Charlotte Islands.

The **African** and **Asian** collections are also pretty comprehensive, but they appear as something of an afterthought alongside the more interesting indigenous artefacts. Rounding off the smaller galleries are a technically minded archeological section and a three-gallery wing built to house the **Koerner Collection**, a rather incongruous assortment of six hundred European ceramics, dating from the fifteenth century onwards and donated by a private collector.

The Raven and the First Men

The museum saves its best single sculpture for last. **The Raven and the First Men** is a modern sculpture designed by the celebrated Haida artist Bill Reid (1920–1998). Housed in a separate rotunda, it's the museum's pride and joy and has achieved almost cult status in the city, where you'll see it on any number of posters and postcards. Carved from a 4.5-tonne block of yellow cedar (made of 106 laminated timbers), the work took over three years to complete and required the almost continuous labours of five assistants.

As beautiful as the work is, however, its rotunda setting makes it seem oddly out of place – almost like a corporate display. The sculpture depicts the Haida legend of human evolution with stunning virtuosity, depicting figures squirming from a half-open clamshell, overseen by an enormous and stern-faced raven, the "trickster" of Haida myth who tempted humanity from its birthplace. According to the legend, life began when the raven flew from the heavens to find the earth blanketed in snow. The bird stole the sun from the gods and forged the rivers, oceans, forests and animals. It then found a clamshell on a beach and coaxed five men from it with the promise of peace and prosperity. Eventually, it told them where they might find women.

Nitobe Memorial Garden

There are various very minor sights dotted around the museum, but they amount to nothing of genuine interest. For the exception, turn right out the front entrance and a 5min walk brings you to the **Nitobe Memorial Garden** (daily April–Oct 9am–5pm; call for winter hours; $6 or $12 with the UBC

The Haida

The **Haida** are widely considered to have the most highly developed culture and sophisticated art tradition of British Columbia's aboriginal peoples. Extending from the Haida Gwaii (Queen Charlotte Islands) to south Alaska, their lands included major stands of red cedar, the raw material for their huge dug-out **canoes**, intricate **carvings** and refined **architecture**. Though renowned as traders and artists, the Haida were also feared **warriors**, paddling into rival villages and returning with canoes laden with goods, slaves and the severed heads of anyone who had tried to resist. Thanks to their skill on the open sea, they've been called the Vikings of the Pacific Northwest. This success at warfare was due, in part, to their use of wooden-slat armour, which included protective face vizors and helmets topped with terrifying images.

Socially the Haida divided themselves into two main groups, the **Eagles** and the **Ravens**, which were further divided into hereditary kin groups named after their original village location. Marriage within each major group, or *moiety*, was considered incestuous, so Eagles would always seek Raven mates and vice versa. Furthermore, descent was traced through the **female line**, which meant that a chief could not pass his property on to his sons because they would belong to a different *moiety* – instead his inheritance passed to his sister's sons.

Haida **villages** were an impressive sight, their vast cedar-plank houses dominated by 15m **totem poles** displaying the kin group's unique animal crest or other mythical creatures. Entrance to each house was through the gaping mouth of a massive carved figure; inside, supporting posts were carved into the forms of the crest animals, and most household objects were similarly decorative. Equal elaboration attended the many Haida ceremonies, one of the most important of which was the **mortuary potlatch**, serving as a memorial service to a dead chief and as the validation of the heir's right to succession. The dead individual was laid atop a carved pole near the village entrance, past which the visiting chiefs would walk wearing robes of finely patterned mountain-goat wool and immense headdresses fringed with long sea-lion whiskers and ermine skins. A hollow at the top of each headdress was filled with eagle feathers, which floated down onto the witnesses as the chiefs sedately danced.

After **European contact** the Haida population was devastated by smallpox and other epidemics. In 1787, there were around 8000 Haida scattered across the archipelago. Their numbers were then reduced from around 6000 in 1835 to 588 by 1915. Consequently they were forced to abandon their traditional villages and today gather largely at two sites on the Haida Gwaii. At other locations the homes and totem poles fell into disrepair, and only at **Sgan Gwaii**, a remote village at the southern tip of the Haida Gwaii, has an attempt been made to preserve an original Haida settlement; the village is now a UNESCO World Heritage Site.

These days the Haida number around 2000 and are highly regarded in the North American art world; the late Bill Reid is among the tribe's best-known figures, and scores of other Haida craftspeople produce carvings and jewellery for the tourist market. Artists also play a powerful role in the Haida Gwaii's social, political and cultural life, having been vocal in the formation of the Gwaii Haanas National Park Reserve and the protection of other important aboriginal sites of historical and cultural significance.

Botanical Garden; ⓣ604/822-6038, ⓦwww.nitobe.org), a small Japanese garden near Gate 4, Memorial Road, off West Mall that is good for a few minutes of peace and floral admiration.

Begun some forty years ago, it was created to honour Inazo Nitobe (1862–1933), who strove to improve trans-Pacific relations, and it is considered the world's most authentic Japanese garden outside Japan – despite its use of many non-Japanese species. The garden is full of gently curving paths, trickling streams and waterfalls, as well as numerous rocks, trees and shrubs placed with precision and according to the balanced principles of yin and yang. It comprises both the **Tea Garden**, whose arrangement is designed to inspire peaceful introspection, and the **Stroll Garden**, whose design follows the shape of the Milky Way and symbolizes a journey through life from youth to old age.

UBC Botanical Garden

Almost directly opposite the Nitobe Garden, at 16th Ave and 6804 SW Marine Drive, lies the larger **UBC Botanical Garden** (Mon–Fri 9am–5pm, Sat & Sun 9.30am–5.30pm; $8; Ⓣ604/822-4208, Ⓦwww.ubcbotanicalgarden.org), established in 1916 and Canada's oldest botanical garden. It claims some 10,000 species of plants, shrubs and trees and consists of eight separate gardens – Alpine, Arbour, Asian, British Columbian Native, Contemporary, Food, Perennial Border and Physic. Horticultural experts rate this as better than the VanDusen Botanical Garden (see p.85) because its layout is more subtle and its displays better-organized: non-experts will find both gardens equally attractive. Also on site is the **Botanical Garden Centre**, with a shop that has one of the city's best selections of gardening books and implements, as well as some of the rarer or more unusual plants and shrubs from the garden.

The Gardens

Non-gardeners will probably be most interested in the obviously impressive swathes of shrubs and stands of vast trees in the **David C. Lam Asian Garden**. Surrounded by second-growth fir, cedar and hemlock, this, the largest of the gardens, is home to 400 varieties of rhododendrons – more than any other Canadian garden and best seen in May. It also features roses, flowering vines, magnolias, hydrangeas and floral rarities such as blue Himalayan poppy and giant Himalayan lily.

The **Physic Garden** is a re-created sixteenth-century monastic herb garden, and though there are some macabre poisonous plants here, most of the flora are actually medicinal. Many of the plants were taken from the similar Chelsea Physic Garden in London, which in turn collected plants from Britain's Tudor and medieval periods. Plants include foxgloves, which provide the heart remedies digitoxin and digoxin, and periwinkle, used in the treatment of leukaemia. Interpretive panels provide information about these and other plants, including those used to treat "violent blood" or "angry snake bite", those used to make teas, and those grown to be strewn on the floor and in rooms to sweeten the often fetid air of medieval interiors.

The sloping **British Columbia Native Garden** shelters some 3500 plants and flowers found across British Columbia in a variety of bog, marsh and other habitats – everything from coastal rainforest species to the flora of the arid semi-desert of the interior. The smaller **E.H. Lohbrunner Alpine Garden** manages to coax rare alpine varieties from five continents to grow at a level some 2000m below their preferred altitude, while the **Food Garden** produces a cornucopia of fruit and vegetables in a remarkably restricted area. It has some intriguing rarities – check out the strange, apple-like espalier fruit, for example; the entire crop is donated to charity.

It's well worth taking one of the guided **tours** to spot things you might otherwise miss: they generally run once daily a couple of times a week; call the garden for latest details. Note that if you visit the botanical garden in winter you won't be disappointed, for there's even a special Winter Garden full of plants and shrubs adapted to seasonal cold.

Wreck Beach

Wreck Beach, about 1km south of the Nitobe garden, is well known in Vancouver mainly because it's a pristine patch of sand where, in summer, you can strip off as many clothes as you like. In the past, the nakedness was a touch half-hearted and sporadic, and invited a fair amount of prudish tut-tutting. These days, the nudity is pretty much accepted but not expected – wear as much or as little as you wish. The beach, part of a larger 7.8-kilometre beach reaching round the UBC promontory, becomes fairly crowded and commercialized in summer, but there are plenty of driftwood logs and fallen tree trunks on the sand which allow you to lay claim to a private patch of sand.

The beach's reputation shouldn't hide the fact that it's also a very beautiful and broad strand, edged by the ocean on one side (with many shallow and often warm pools) and bordered by lofty trees on three other flanks. It's also well looked after, thanks to the Wreck Beach Preservation Society (Ⓦwww .wreckbeach.org), which, among other things, organizes beach events and prevents the commercial side of things from getting out of hand. This means occasionally reining in the many food-sellers, body-painters, beach-casino operators and the like, though attitudes to all and sundry are pretty relaxed. For more on **nudism** in Vancouver, incidentally, visit Ⓦwww.vantan.ca.

Access is from SW Marine Drive near Gate 6 at the foot of University Boulevard. The beach can be a little tricky to find, but plenty of well-worn tracks, including trails #3, #4 and #6, lead down the steep slopes above the beach, and just about any student on the campus will be able to point you in the right direction. On a busy summer day, you won't be able to miss the access, for parked cars are jammed bumper to bumper on SW Marine Drive above the trails to the beach.

Trail #4 leads down to Tower Beach to the north of Wreck Beach from Gate 4 a short distance south of the anthropology museum and before the Nitobe Memorial Garden. The best of the Wreck Beach sand is below trail #6. You'll find the trailhead just beyond the garden heading away from the museum. To the south of this is the North Arm breakwater, separating the beach from log-booming grounds farther to the south and east. The trailhead for #7, further round SW Marine Drive still, at the junction, leads to the Old Wreck Beach Trail, which runs south and west round the peninsula to the uncommercialized section of the beach.

Pacific Spirit Regional Park

If you're out at the university and wish to hike or mountain bike in quiet, if not terribly spectacular, surroundings, take advantage of the **University Endowment Lands** and **Pacific Spirit Regional Park**, the latter on the east side of the campus. A huge tract of wild parkland – larger than Stanley Park, but visited by relatively few people – the non-campus part of the Endowment Lands boasts 48km of trails and offers the chance to spot wildlife such as blacktail deer, otters, foxes and bald eagles. Best of all, there are few signs of human presence – no benches or snack bars, just the occasional signpost. The area was heavily logged at the start of the twentieth century, but much of the forest has regenerated.

Much the same goes for Pacific Spirit Regional Park, the largest green space in the city, which until 1989 formed part of the Endowment Lands. The area offers a combination of forest, foreshore and other natural habitats and has 53km of walking, cycling, jogging and equestrian trails, most of them pretty flat. All the trails are well marked and signposted, so there's little chance of getting lost. If you do wander off-track, three major roads bisect the park to provide points of reference; park wardens also patrol the area. Note that after conflict between hikers and bikers (the park is especially popular with the latter), various trails have been set aside for hiking only, with 35km of mixed-use trails and 18km just for walkers.

If you have time to walk just one trail, plump for the **Swordfern Trail** (trail #24) in the park's southwest corner. It runs through typical British Columbia fir and cedar forest and starts from SW Marine Drive opposite the parking area and Simon Fraser Monument, the latter a memorial to the explorer who sailed down the river that bears his name in 1808. A trail from the road on the same side as the monument drops steeply through ancient forest towards the Fraser for views of the gargantuan log booms on the river – the largest such booms in Canada.

While you really need transport to access much of the park – or to give yourself a choice of trails – you can get close to the park with public transport by taking the #4 or #10 **bus** towards the UBC (see p.86) and getting off at Blanca Street and West 16th Avenue, close to the park's main access points and 400m from the **Park Centre** (Mon–Fri 8am–4pm; ⓣ604/224-5739 or 432-6350) at 4915 West 16th Ave. The centre has trail maps and provides information on some of the park's key habitats, most notably the **Camosun Bog**, a rare wetland with its own distinctive flora and fauna: it's accessed by boardwalk from Camosun Street and West 19th Avenue.

7

North Vancouver

North Vancouver – or North Van, as it's generally known – embraces most of the mountains, forests and residential districts that you see as you gaze across the Burrard Inlet from Vancouver's Downtown peninsula. The area contains some compelling sights, but the journey to North Van itself – especially by SeaBus catamaran – is almost as alluring as anything you'll see when you get there, thanks to the mesmerizing views of the Downtown skyline and teeming port, a side of the city that's otherwise easily missed.

If you've no time or heart for longer trips to North Van, then you should at least make this crossing, spending an hour or so at Lonsdale Quay before catching the SeaBus back to Downtown. Lonsdale Quay is the SeaBus terminal on the north shore, home to a fine food and general market that is well worth seeing but suffers by comparison with the even more impressive market on Granville Island.

Most of North Van is residential – the population of the incorporated city and district is about 48,000 – as is neighbouring **West Vancouver** (West Van), which has a population of around 43,000 and despite its name also lies north of the Downtown peninsula. West Van is the name given to the district roughly west of the Capilano River, an area whose cosseted citizens boast the highest per capita income in Canada. North Van's eastern limit is the vast inlet of Indian Arm. Together they make up the so-called **North Shore**.

Few people cross the Burrard Inlet to view these leafy suburbs, however; the real reason to make the crossing is to sample North Vancouver's outstanding areas of natural beauty – Lynn Canyon Park, Grouse Mountain, the Capilano River and its environs, Mount Seymour Provincial Park, Cypress Provincial Park, Lighthouse Park and the Lower Seymour Conservation Reserve.

All the above parks offer fine **hiking** possibilities in summer, as well as **skiing** and winter activities on a range of good trails (see individual entries for some suggestions). However, for a straightforward and dramatic taste of the scenery – or if you have time for only one excursion – then you should make for **Grouse Mountain**, where a cable car whisks you to over 1200m for some superb views of the city and the surrounding area. Your best bet if you have more time and wish to hike is Mount Seymour, which is the closest park to Downtown if you want wild scenery. It is also easily accessible, thanks to the road that runs partway up the mountain. If you're really keen to make the most of the area's natural beauty, stay on the North Shore, where there is a handful of bed and breakfast options, some close to the major parks (see p.124).

North Vancouver's most advertised sight is the Capilano Suspension Bridge, a commercialized and overrated affair – it's a busy footbridge across a gorge – which you might catch on your return from Grouse Mountain. You might also ignore it completely in favour of the scenery – and an interesting salmon hatchery – elsewhere on the Capilano River. For the best seascapes close to Vancouver, make

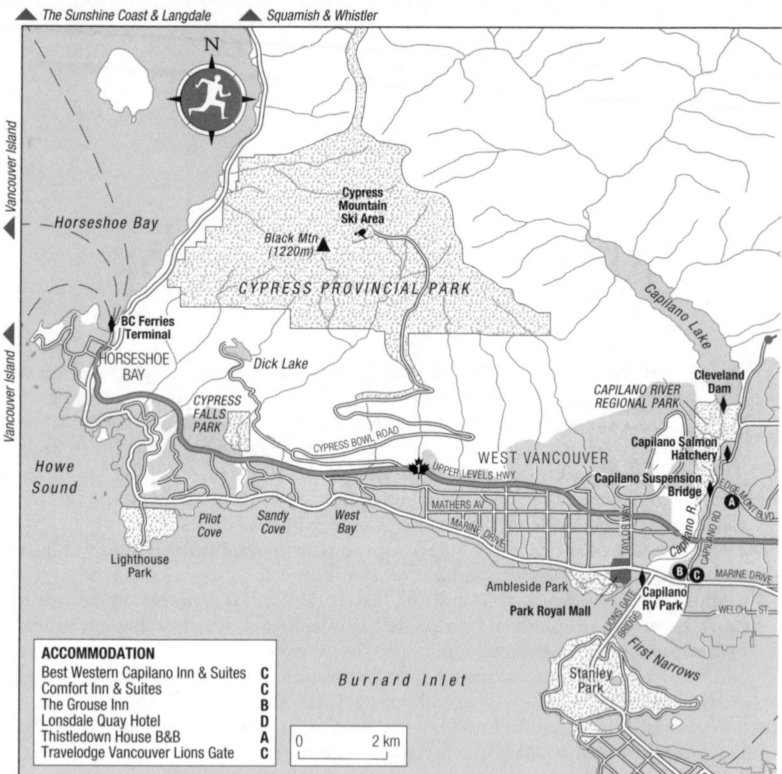

the longer trip to **Lighthouse Park** on the western tip of the North Shore, full of trails, sea views and magnificent virgin forest.

Vancouver's Touristinfo Centre (see p.36) has plenty of information and accommodation listings for North Van, but you might also want to consult the area's own infocentre at 102–124 West 1st St, North Vancouver (Mon–Fri 9am–5pm; ⓣ604/987-4488, ⓦwww.nvchamber.bc.ca). Two smaller infocentres – one at the bottom of Lonsdale Road by the Lonsdale Quay (ⓣ604/984-8588) and the other at the junction of Marine Drive and Capilano Road (ⓣ604/980-5332) – are open from mid-May to early September daily 9am to 5pm.

Some history

As with Downtown, North Vancouver's modern history has its roots in the lumber industry. While the Downtown area can be traced to the creation of Edward Stamp's Hasting Mill in 1865 (see p.258), the North Shore took shape around the Pioneer Mills, located around 6km east of the present Lions Gate Bridge, which began operation three years earlier. The earliest transportation across the Burrard Inlet, aboriginal canoes aside, was provided in 1866 by a rowing boat operated by Jack Thomas, a gravel merchant, who, for a small toll, rowed mill workers to and from Gassy Jack Deighton's saloons (see p.53).

In 1873 Thomas settled in what today is West Vancouver, becoming the North Shore's first permanent white resident. With him was his aboriginal wife, Row'i'a,

the granddaughter of Chief Ki'ep'i'lan'o, after whom the Capilano River and other city streets and landmarks are named.

Over the next 25 years, residents of what would become today's Downtown began to cross to the North Shore to picnic – in summer, tents would stretch along much of Burrard Inlet shoreline – or to walk or ski on Grouse Mountain. They were helped by the inauguration of a regular ferry service to North Van in 1900 and to West Van in 1909. The construction of summer cottages and a few homes followed, but for the most part the area remained the domain of logging, fish canning and other industries. All this changed after about 1938, when the opening of the Lions Gate Bridge provided the spur for the development of the North Shore as a residential alternative to Downtown and the New Westminster suburbs.

Getting to North Vancouver

The **SeaBus** from Downtown is the best and most practical approach to North Vancouver (see p.25) if you are using public transport. Most of the places covered in this chapter are then accessible by bus or taxi from the bus terminal alongside the dock at Lonsdale Quay (see p.98). Remember that if you come to North Van by SeaBus, you can take advantage of your ticket's 90-minute validity for onward bus journeys from Lonsdale Quay – long enough to get you to most of the destinations in this chapter.

If you don't cross the Burrard Inlet by boat, there are two other approaches by **bus**, **bike** or **car** from Downtown and the south shore of the Burrard Inlet: one is via the Lions Gate Bridge to the west, the other via the Iron Workers Memorial Second Narrows Bridge well to the east. Note that both are busy during rush hours and at weekends. The Lions Gate crossing leaves you well placed for trips to Grouse Mountain, the Capilano River and Canyon, and Cypress Provincial Park and Lighthouse Park. The Second Narrows crossing is more convenient for Mount Seymour Provincial Park.

Buses across the Lions Gate Bridge are a mixture of TransLink and blue West Van buses. The latter are run by a different company but accept TransLink tickets. TransLink buses that cross the bridge include the #240, #246, #250, #251, #252 and #257; the most convenient are the #240 and #246, both of which you can catch from stops Downtown on West Georgia Street. West Van services from Downtown include the blue #241, #247, #253, #254 and #258. Almost immediately across the bridge is a major bus interchange, **Park Royal**, named after the adjoining shopping centre. Note that delays are common on the Lions Gate Bridge, especially during rush hour.

Fewer buses cross the Second Narrows Bridge – the alternatives are the TransLink #28 and #210 or blue West Van #211, #214, #290 and #292. Almost immediately across this bridge is the third of North Van's major bus interchanges, **Phibbs Exchange**, which you'll need to use only if you're heading for Mount Seymour.

Lonsdale Quay

Lonsdale Quay is the North Van terminus for the SeaBus catamarans that cross the Burrard Inlet from the Waterfront Station terminal Downtown (see p.43). As you alight from the boat, the bus terminal is immediately in front of you – buses (#226, #228, #229, #230, #236, #239, #242, #246) to all points leave from the bays here. The **Lonsdale Quay Market**, 123 Carrie Cates Court (retail outlets 10am–7pm, market 9am–7pm; restaurants have longer hours; Ⓣ604/985-6261, Ⓦwww.lonsdalequay.com) – which to all intents and purposes *is* Lonsdale Quay – lies a few seconds' walk to the right.

The quay, and the market in particular, was developed in the mid-1980s as part of an attempt to regenerate the area, prompted by the introduction of the SeaBus service and the success of the Granville Island market on the southern edge of Downtown. Development continues apace, the latest significant addition to the quay being the smart *Lonsdale Quay Hotel* (see p.124) directly above the market.

While not as vibrant as its Granville Island equivalent, the Lonsdale Quay Market is still an appealing place, with around eighty shops and stalls arranged over two levels – the first level is devoted mainly to fresh and cooked food, the second to small speciality shops. If you're travelling with children, you might want to make a beeline for **Kids' Alley** on level 2, which features children's clothes stores, toys and other shops aimed at children.

The market also has great fresh fruit and vegetable stalls and numerous takeaway food counters selling a wide range of ethnic fast foods, mainly Far Eastern noodle and stir-fry stands, as well as other snack foods. The wooden promenades here are wonderful places to have a picnic or grab a coffee as you look out over the port, tugs and moored fishing boats towards the Downtown skyline. It's hard to see how these views can be improved, but if you want to escape the boardwalks for grass and trees, make for the small **waterfront park** just to the west of the bus terminal.

You'll find further shops and eating places on **Lonsdale Avenue**, North Van's key commercial thoroughfare, which strikes northeast from the quay, but there's little or nothing here to compare with what you'll find in the market.

Grouse Mountain

Named by hikers in 1894 who stumbled across a blue grouse (a type of bird), **Grouse Mountain**, 6400 Nancy Greene Way (daily 9am–10pm; cable-car tickets $37.95 return; ⓣ604/980-9311 or 984-0661, ⓦwww.grousemountain.com), now lures well over a million visitors a year. This deserved popularity owes itself to the views and the Swiss-built **cable-car ride** that runs from the base station, which is 290m above sea level, to close to the mountain's 1250m summit. The eight-minute ride on North America's largest cable cars (each carries 100 people) is exhilarating, and the views of Vancouver and its surroundings at the top are sublime. Note that the expensive ticket includes the ride plus most attractions on the mountain, including a wildlife refuge, lumberjack 'sports', chairlift and bird of prey displays.

You might also come here towards dusk to see the city's lights twinkle into life, or, better still, book a table at *The Observatory* at the summit, easily Vancouver's most panoramic restaurant. You'll be in good company – the restaurant, in a previous incarnation, was where one-time Canadian prime minister Pierre Trudeau brought the future Mrs Margaret Trudeau on their first date. Less formal dining is possible in the *Altitudes Bistro*. Admission to the cable car is complimentary with advance dinner reservations; restaurants can be contacted through the general Grouse Mountain phone and website listed above.

The mountain rises above the Capilano River 12km from central Vancouver and some way to the north of the Capilano Suspension Bridge, Salmon Hatchery and Capilano River trails, so it's a good idea to combine some or all of these sights with a trip to the mountain. In summer it's also worth arriving early as queues build up fairly quickly. If you take one of the first cable cars, you could be up and down the mountain in a couple of hours – there's not a huge amount to do at the summit – and then have time left to devote to the Capilano River, Lighthouse Park or Downtown. If you're in Vancouver in winter, then the mountain offers plenty in the way of skiing, boarding and other activities (see box, p.101).

▲ Grouse Mountain cable

To get directly to the base station from Lonsdale Quay, take the special #236 Grouse Mountain–Pemberton Heights **bus** from the depot by the SeaBus terminal: the service usually departs from Bay 8. You can also take a #246 Highland bus from Bay 7 and change to the #232 Grouse Mountain at Edgemont Village or take the #232 from Phibbs Exchange. If you're coming by **car** from Downtown, follow West Georgia Street through Stanley Park and cross the Lions Gate Bridge. Take the North Vancouver exit to Marine Drive, then turn left and follow Capilano Road for 5km. There's free parking in the gravel lot adjacent to the base station, but places go quickly.

The summit

Grouse Mountain's twin cable cars make up North America's longest aerial tramway and provide an exciting, if expensive, way of getting up and down the mountain. It's possible to walk up on the aptly named **Grouse Grind Trail** from the trailhead by the chalet at the base station, but it's not a great hike – a huge grind of a climb in a short distance (an ascent of 853m over 2.9km), with little by way of views. If you do fancy the challenge, be sure to use insect repellent. Allow one and a half hours if you're fit, two hours if you're not; the record for the ascent is 27 minutes and 18 seconds.

It's far easier, of course, to settle instead into the almost inevitable queue for the ticket office to the cable car; be sure to get here early. After eight minutes in the car (there are departures every 15min) and two stomach-churning lurches over the tramway's twin towers, you reach the summit (or – at 1128m – as close to it as the tramway can manage), which, with its restaurants and tourist paraphernalia, is anything but wild. The **views**, though, are stunning, stretching across the city as far as the San Juan Islands 160km away in Washington State.

Have a quick look at the **interpretive centre** off to the right when you leave the cable car. A 25min film, *Born to Fly*, on the history of Grouse Mountain, an eagle's-eye view of southwestern British Columbia, is shown in the **Theatre in the Sky** downstairs (every half-hour in summer, hourly in winter; admission included in your cable-car ticket). There are also a couple of cafés and a smarter restaurant if you need fortifying after your ascent. The first of the cafés, *Altitudes Bistro*, has panoramic views and serves contemporary West Coast food, but it fills up quickly; otherwise try the more formal *Observatory* restaurant. Ask at the interpretive centre, or the small information desk just beyond the centre, about easy **guided walks** (summer daily 11am–5pm): the Tribute to the Forest (30min) leaves on the hour, the similar Walk in the Woods (35min) every hour on the half-hour.

Walk up the paved paths away from the centre for about five minutes – you can't get lost – and you come to the site of the 45-minute "Lumberjack Shows" (three times daily at noon, 2.30pm and 4.30pm; free), involving various crowd-pleasing sawing and wood-chopping demonstrations. Just beyond this is the **Scenic Chairlift** (also included in your ticket; daily June–Oct 11am–8pm), which judders upwards for another eight minutes to the mountain's actual summit: views of the city and Fraser Delta are even better, only slightly spoilt by the worn paths and buildings immediately below you.

Another attraction on the mountain is the Refuge for Endangered Wildlife, with several **grizzly bears** that were found as orphaned cubs (their mother had probably been shot by hunters). In an ideal world, the bears would not need to be taken in, and a certain amount of controversy raged for a while, but none would have survived long in the wild – and once used to humans, any return to the wild is almost impossible. Today, most locals seem rather pleased to know the bears are there, and the animals have a generous amount of space in which to live. A big

Winter on Grouse Mountain

Grouse Mountain is a favourite for people wanting to **ski** or **snowboard** after work, and its brightly illuminated slopes and dozen or so runs are a North Vancouver landmark on winter evenings. The mountain has attracted locals since the early twentieth century, but in those days a skiing round-trip was a three-day affair. The first chalet appeared in 1926 soon after a toll road was cleared to the mountain: a double chairlift – North America's first – was built in 1949. Since then, the facilities have continued to improve – 2000 saw the introduction of the $4.3 million Screaming Eagle, Vancouver's first high-speed quad chair.

The mountain is especially good for beginners or those learning to ski. The Snow School offers two-hour drop-in **lessons** (Mon–Fri at noon, Sat–Sun & public holidays 9.45am, noon & 2.15pm; single session $40, $81 with lift, $72 with rental and $113 with lift and rental) as well as ski and snowboarding packages. Separate skill-improvement and adult- and women-only four-session courses ($143, or $319 for lesson, lift and rental) are also available. Register with Guest Services at the base station at least an hour before the start of a session or at Alpine Guest Services on the main floor of the chalet thirty minutes prior. Cross-country skiing is also available on groomed and patrolled trails.

The resort's vertical drop is 384m and the base elevation 274m. Terrain is 30 percent novice, 50 percent intermediate and 20 percent expert. There are 25 runs (including three green, fourteen blue and six black diamond), the longest of which stretches for 2.4km: 13 runs are available at night and for snowboarding. Lifts include two aerial trams, one high-speed quad, three double chairs, two T-bars and two rope tows. There's also a 100m half-pipe for snowboarders.

A **day pass** currently costs $50 from 9am to 10pm ($40 after 4pm) and allows you to ride the cable car and gives unlimited skiing or snowboarding. Five- and ten-day passes and season passes are available for $200, $400 and $750 respectively. Rental costs are $40 for skis or snowboards ($50 for high-performance equipment) and $25 for a suit. Skates ($5), snowshoes ($25), helmets ($5) and so forth are also available. Book online or call ⓣ604/980-9311 for rentals. If you're not skiing or boarding, consider a sleigh ride (every 15 minutes from the base station), snowshoe tour (there are six snowshoe trails totalling 12.8km) or skating on a huge pond at the summit.

Call ⓣ604/980-9311 or 984-0661 or visit the website (ⓦwww.grousemountain.com) for more **information** and regular snow, lift, run and weather reports.

electric fence stops them from entertaining any thoughts of an escape. Down at the cable-car station at the base of the mountain there is also a wolf enclosure.

Check with the office at the lower cable-car base station or the upper terminal chalet for details of long **hikes** – many are down below rather than up at the summit proper. The best stroll is to **Blue Grouse Lake**, a pretty lake north of the skyride (15min); the Goat Ridge Trail is for experienced hikers. More rugged paths lead into the mountains of the West Coast Range, but for these you'll need maps (see p.207).

The Capilano River

The lively little **Capilano River** rises in the mountains of the North Shore and empties into the Pacific 32km later just west of the Lions Gate Bridge. In the last 10km or so before it runs into the ocean, it boasts a range of natural sights and other attractions, most of which lie within a narrow strip of protected park on either side of the river and its gorge. To make best use of your time, visit the sights on the way back from Grouse Mountain, either by walking or jumping off the #236 bus on the run back from the cable car's base station.

From north to south the sights are the Cleveland Dam, Salmon Hatchery and Capilano Suspension Bridge. Farther south lies Ambleside Park, a popular recreational spot alongside the point at which the river enters the sea. Although the park is linked by trails to the sights farther north, it's more easily seen from the shoreline road approaches to the east.

Much of the river is protected by the **Capilano River Regional Park** (daily: May–Labour Day 8am–9pm, rest of the year 8am–5pm or dusk, whichever is later; ⓣ604/224-5739, ⓦwww.metrovancouver.org/services/parks), founded in 1926 after large-scale commercial logging ceased in North Van. Most of the key sights within the park are linked by 26km of well-kept **trails**, including the major **Capilano Pacific Trail**, on or near the river; they are also easily accessed from the road running parallel to the river on its eastern side – note that it starts as Capilano Road at its southern end, then becomes Nancy Greene Way towards Grouse Mountain. If you drive, be sure to hop out and walk some of the park's trails – the misty rainforest scenery, crashing river, cliffs and huge stands of timber are superb. Note that **no cycling is allowed on the park's trails**, only on the commuter cycling trail from West Van and North Van, which passes over the gravel road on top of the dam.

The Cleveland Dam

The **Cleveland Dam** divides Capilano Lake from the river and sits at the northern edge of the river park about 1km south of the Grouse Mountain base station. From the parking area, toilets and picnic area off Nancy Greene Way you can walk across the top of the 195m-wide dam, built in 1954, and look down on Capilano Lake, the source of 40 percent of Vancouver and the Lower Mainland's (the city's hinterlands) drinking water – 17 billion gallons of water are stored and 100 million gallons released daily. The views also embrace forested slopes and surrounding peaks, including the two Lion mountains – named after their shapes – whose distinctive profiles you'll have seen from Downtown and elsewhere; they're the highest points on the North Shore range of the Coast Mountains, with **West Lion** reaching 1646m and **East Lion** topping 1599m.

A signboard map of local **trails** is located near the parking area: a good bet is the short **Giant Fir Trail**, which leads to what is probably the park's largest tree – a 500-year-old monster some 61m high and 2.4m in diameter. To access the trail, cross the dam and take the trail down the west side of the river. After about ten minutes' walk you come to a fork and a sign for the Great Fir Trail on your left. Continue past the eponymous fir and you reach another fork. Turn left and you come to the **Second Canyon Viewing Deck**, which offers a great view of the Cleveland Dam from below; take the right fork and after a couple of minutes' walk the Cable Pool Bridge will take you across the river for a quick route to the salmon hatchery; for a longer way round from this point (allow an extra 30 minutes) you could follow the Coho Loop Trail, crossing the river on the Pipeline Bridge before looping back upriver to the hatchery. If you want to loop back to the dam's car park, take the signed trail back up the hill and along the east bank from the hatchery. Allow an hour for the round-trip hike from dam to hatchery and back.

Capilano Salmon Hatchery

The Capilano River's modern **salmon hatchery** (daily: June–Aug 8am–8pm, May & Sept 8am–7pm, April & Oct 8am–4.45pm, Nov–March 8am–4pm; free; ⓣ604/666-1790 between 8am and 4pm, ⓦwww-heb.pac.dfo-mpo.gc.ca), a federally run operation, is designed to help salmon spawn and thus replenish declining stocks. It's quickly reached by trail from the Cleveland Dam or a 1km side road (or the Pipeline Trail) from the signed main entrance off Capilano Road. This access road comes about 200m after the busy roadside entrance to the Capilano Suspension Bridge. If you're coming on the bus up the hill from Vancouver, ring the bell for the stop after the Bridge.

Life started to become difficult for salmon on the Capilano River in 1889, when the river was partially dammed. It became critical in 1954, when the completion of the Cleveland Dam not only blocked the route of coho and steelhead salmon returning to spawn in the river's headwaters but also destroyed 95 percent of the salmon's spawning territory and 75 percent of their rearing territory. To help the fish, the city authorities built a concrete weir and fish ladder that collected returning salmon on their way upstream. The fish were then transferred to tanks and carried above the dam to be released. This addressed the problems of the returning salmon but not those of young salmon going the other way, which suffered predictably high losses as they plunged over the Cleveland Dam.

As stocks continued to decline, the city decided the only solution was to build a hatchery that would rear and release salmon *below* the dam. Work began in 1969 and was completed two years later at a cost of $3 million. Chinook salmon were also introduced, part of an attempt to create a self-sustaining run of this prized sport fish. The hatchery was the first of many similar schemes across the province.

It now nurtures a colossal number of fish a year, releasing 525,000 coho "smolts", or young fish, into the river, along with 600,000 Chinook and 15,000 steelhead. Some idea of the travails of the fish can be gained from the number of returning salmon – just 14,000 coho, 740 Chinook and thirty steelhead annually. The hatchery also conducts important scientific work, largely through the tagging of fish, thus allowing it to trace migration and ocean-survival patterns, and provides ladders up the riverbed for those spawning salmon still doomed to head upstream.

You can view these ladders and, in season, catch a close-up glimpse of the salmon through indoor glass panels. You can also observe salmon at various stages of their development in eye-level tanks. There's always something to see, but some seasons are more exciting than others: coho and steelhead adults start to return to the river in **June**, when you can see them "running" and watch the daily emptying of "traps" for the returning adults and the transport of coho adults above the dam. **Autumn** sees the continued return of coho and steelhead (until Dec) and the arrival of Chinook adults (Sept–Dec), along with the tagging of smaller fish and the transfer of small "fry" to rearing troughs. **Winter** is quieter for large-fish activity, but you can still view the rearing activities of the centre. In **spring**, the "winter-run" steelhead adults ride the river until May and the smolts of all three salmon types are released.

The low, simple building is well designed and the information plaques on the work of the hatchery are interesting, but it's a prime stop on city coach tours, so the place can often be packed in the middle of the day. The scenic area below the hatchery – a lovely stretch of river and forest – is worth exploring, especially the pretty Dog's Leg Pool (1km), which is along a swirling reach of the Capilano River. Walk along the river trails for just a few minutes and you can enjoy pretty scenery away from the hatchery crowds.

Capilano Suspension Bridge

The Capilano River's most publicized attraction is the inexplicably popular 137m-long **suspension bridge** (daily: mid-May to Aug 8.30am–8pm, early May & Sept to mid-Oct 9am–7.30pm, late Oct & mid-March to mid-April 9am–6pm, late April 9am–6.30pm, Nov to mid-March 9am–5pm; $28.95; Ⓣ604/985-7474, Ⓦwww.capbridge.com). Its main claim to fame, and one that attracts more than

800,000 visitors a year, is that it is the world's longest pedestrian suspension bridge, dangling 70m above the vertiginous Capilano Gorge.

The first bridge here – a ramshackle affair of hemp rope and cedar planks – was built in 1889 by a local landowner, the Scottish civil engineer **George Grant Mackay**, to access his holdings across the gorge. Mackay was also a city park commissioner and active in ensuring that Stanley Park, among other green spaces, was preserved for posterity. He also bought and sold land on the British Columbia mainland and founded the now large and prosperous fruit-growing town of Vernon in the Okanagan region in central southern British Columbia. His bridge's swaying and precarious construction – its creaking caused local aboriginal peoples to nickname it the "laughing bridge" – attracted thrill-seekers, making this Vancouver's oldest "attraction", though the present structure – which looks similar but is far more robust – dates from 1956. Celebrities who have made the crossing include Marilyn Monroe, Katharine Hepburn, the Rolling Stones, Walter Cronkite and Margaret Thatcher – the last so enjoyed the experience that she did it twice.

Although part of the park, the footbridge is privately run as a moneymaking venture – something which rather counts against it, especially when you can have much the same sort of gorge, forest and river scenery free of charge up the road. Stick to the paths elsewhere in the park, therefore, and avoid the pedestrian toll, which buys you a walk across the bridge (scenic as far as it goes, but hardly hair-raising), miscellaneous tours, forestry exhibits and trails, the inevitable gift shop and café, a totem park and a visit to an aboriginal carving centre; frankly none of this is particularly interesting. Furthermore, if you want the suspension bridge experience – which, after all, amounts to little more than a view – there's one you can cross free in Lynn Canyon to the east (see opposite).

Capilano Pacific Trail

The trail from the Cleveland Dam south past the hatchery and suspension bridge forms part of the scenic **Capilano Pacific Trail**, which you can, if you want a long (and rewarding) walk, follow for virtually the whole length of the river south of the dam (about 7km) to its mouth near Ambleside Park in West Van (see opposite). Various loops and river crossings en route allow you to make circular routes – up one bank and down the other – if you don't want to walk the whole thing. Note that lower down the trail passes through less arresting residential districts, but in its upper reaches it runs through glorious forest habitats and along the river, which crashes over a tumble of rocks in a rush of white water.

Among the most interesting intersecting or branch trails is the Rabbit Lane Trail (4km return) close to the park's northern entrance near the dam, once used by the Capilano Timber Company to haul lumber – hence its gentle grades. Farther south, the short secondary trail to **Ranger Pool**, though steep in places, is well worth a detour, thanks to the density of the evergreen cover, the profusion of ferns and the sheer peace and quiet of the forest.

Farther south still, close to the coast and Hwy 1, you might access the park and its trails from Keith Road, east off Taylor Way. There's a trailhead here for the Capilano Pacific Trail signed by the Greater Vancouver Regional District (GVRD). The trail leaves the river for a while here and follows Keith Road for a distance, looking more like a country lane than a city road, despite its proximity to the Upper Levels Highway Bridge.

Ambleside Park

The Capilano Pacific Trail's conclusion (or start) is **Ambleside Park**, which runs west of the Capilano River's mouth as far as 13th Street. This is one of the North Shore's most popular parks, a magnet for strollers, joggers, dog-walkers and those who simply want to sit back and enjoy the buzz of marine activity offshore as well as the views of the Lions Gate Bridge and across the Burrard Inlet to Stanley Park. There's a long sandy beach (with calm water, despite the tidal currents farther offshore), duck pond, playground, pitch and putt golf and one of the old ferry buildings from the early days of white involvement with the North Shore. People often come here at dusk in the summer, especially on Saturdays, when many of the cruise ships leave port – the ships and twinkling lights of the city make a great spectacle. You're also likely to see plenty of fishermen from the Capilano Indian Reserve, on whose land the park stands.

Lynn Canyon Park

For a quick taste of backwoods Vancouver, visit the 618-acre **Lynn Canyon Park** (spring & autumn 7am–7pm, summer 7am–9pm, winter 7am–dusk; free), a quiet, forested area between the Capilano River to the west and Mount Seymour to the east. It has a modest ravine and suspension bridge that, unlike the more popular Capilano Suspension Bridge, you don't have to pay to cross. Several easy walks of up to ninety minutes take you through fine scenery – cliffs, rapids, waterfalls and the 80m-high suspension bridge over Lynn Creek – all just a twenty-minute car or bus ride from Lonsdale Quay.

Before entering the gorge, it's worth popping into the **Ecology Centre** in the park at 3663 Park Rd, off Peters Road (daily: June–Sept 10am–5pm; Oct–May Mon–Fri 10am–5pm, Sat & Sun noon–4pm; donation suggested; Ⓣ604/981-3103 or 987-5922, Ⓦwww.dnv.org/ecology), a friendly and informative interpretive centre where you can pick up maps and pamphlets on the park's trails and its many small mammals and other wildlife. You'll also learn about the area's ninety-year-old, second-growth forest – that is, forest that has grown after the virgin first-growth forest had been logged. Most of the original forest was gone by the early twentieth century, but in places around the park you can still see the stumps of gargantuan first-growth trees. The size of the second-growth trees and lush undergrowth provides a vivid illustration of the sheer fecundity of temperate rainforest and the benign effects of 150cm of rain a year for almost a century. Equally gripping are some of the forest's creatures, notably the aptly named banana slug, which can reach a length of 25cm from gorging on dead vegetation.

To reach the park, take bus #228 from Lonsdale Quay to its penultimate stop at Peters Road, from where it's a signposted ten-minute walk to the gorge; alternatively, take the less frequent #229 Westlynn bus from Lonsdale Quay, which drops you about five minutes closer. If you're approaching by car from the south, take the Lynn Valley or Mountain Highway exit from Hwy 1 (the roads intersect near the park) and from Lynn Valley Road turn right onto Peters Road.

Trails in Lynn Canyon Park

The Ecology Centre often offers guided walks in the summer (July–Aug daily at 2pm), but you can just as easily follow the park's handful of **trails** yourself. The most popular walk is the easy **Thirty-Foot Pool Trail**, a 15min stroll from the parking lot up the east side of the canyon and over the suspension bridge. It's a fairly level walk the short distance to and after the bridge, with a set of steepish steps near the end. The 40min **Twin Falls Trail** is a longer loop that starts at the suspension bridge. Once across, take the boardwalk east, turning right at the fork and following signs to Twin Falls. Cross the wooden bridge, climb the steps out of the canyon and in the clearing at the top take the Centennial Trail north (following the fence) back to the car park. You can also hike part of the **Baden-Powell Trail**, a long-distance path from Horseshoe Bay to the west that runs through several North Shore parks (p.111). Its Lynn Canyon section takes about 75 minutes to trek and follows Lynn Creek on its west bank.

Trails from Lynn Canyon Park also feed into trail systems in other parks, notably **Lynn Headwaters Regional Park**, a large protected area with tougher trails into the Coast Mountains, and the Lower Seymour Conservation Reserve, which borders Lynn Canyon Park on its northeast edge. The latter can be reached from a trail beyond the Thirty-Foot Pool by way of Lillooet Road, which marks the boundary between the reserve and the park.

The Lower Seymour Conservation Reserve

Just northeast of Lynn Canyon Park lies the 14,000-acre **Lower Seymour Conservation Reserve**, a large area of temperate second-growth rainforest, river flood plain and alpine meadows in a spectacular glacier-carved valley containing the Seymour River, which bisects the reserve from north to south. The reserve was formally known (and is occasionally still referred to) as the Seymour Demonstration Forest (open year-round daily 8am–dusk, until 9pm in summer; ⓣ604/990-0483, ⓦwww.metrovancouver.org/services/parks) and is bordered to the west by Lynn Headwaters Regional Park and to the east by Mount Seymour Provincial Park (see opposite). For years it was mostly off limits, having first been ruthlessly logged and then inaccessible until 1987 because its valuable watershed provided much of Vancouver's drinking water. Today most of it is open to the public. At the river's and park's northern limit is the **Seymour Dam**, approached by the **Seymour Mainline Road**, a 12km paved road (bikers and walkers only at weekends) that shadows the river to its west and strikes off from the gatehouse near the reserve's southern limit.

The gatehouse is situated at the northern end of Lillooet Road; if you're coming by public transport, you need to take the #229 Lynn Valley bus to Dempsey Road and Lynn Valley Road. To reach the gatehouse it's a ten-minute walk over Lynn Creek via the bridge on Rice Lake Road. By car, take exit 22 from Hwy 1 at the north end of the Ironworkers' Memorial Second Narrows Bridge. A large green GVRD sign at the intersection guides you towards the reserve past Capilano College and a cemetery.

The Mainline Road is a great favourite with bikers and in-line skaters (normally only the first 2km are open for recreational use on weekdays), but it is just one of myriad biking and hiking trails (40km in all) that strike off into the forest from the gatehouse and points along the road. From the car park it's 2.2km one-way to the Seymour River, where you can pick up the **Twin Bridges Trail** (7km return) south or the more appealing, winding **Fisherman's Trail** north to Mid-Valley Bridge (5km one-way); return on the Mainline Road. For a short stroll, follow the 400m **Forest Ecology Loop Trail** from the car park, which emerges at Rice Lake before looping back. Generally, the trails here offer rather less variety than those in parks to the east and west; the river itself, though, and the easier trails will be a hit with children. Free organized tours with forestry officials run most summer weekends: call the above number for details.

Twin Bridges, Riverside, Fisherman's and other hiking trails are also open to **mountain bikers**, along with a range of other trails that run beyond the reserve's borders. The trails here are some of the best in the region for bikers, partly because they can be challenging and partly because the forestry work here keeps much undergrowth in check and the trails clear: there is also little snow cover at lower elevations in winter.

Mount Seymour Provincial Park

Mount Seymour Provincial Park (always open; free) is the largest – at 8668 acres – and most easterly of the North Shore's provincial parks close to Downtown. It is also the wildest, and the one – with Cypress Provincial Park (see p.109) – that most closely resembles the rugged, high mountain environments of the British Columbia interior. It protects the summit of the eponymous mountain as well as much of its lower slopes and hinterland. To get here by **bus**, take the #239 from Lonsdale Quay to Phibbs Exchange and then the #215 to the Mount Seymour Parkway-Indian River bus stop (1hr), from which point you'll have to walk up the 13km **Mount Seymour Road** to the heart of the park.

The park dates from 1936 and is named after Frederick Seymour, governor of British Columbia from 1864 to 1869. Because of its height, the park straddles two bio- and geo-climatic zones – the coastal western hemlock and mountain hemlock zones. Below the 1000m mark you'll see old-growth Douglas firs and vast, beautiful western red cedars, mixed with lesser coniferous and deciduous trees. Above this height the forest comprises mainly mountain hemlock, yellow cedar and amabilis fir, with high alpine meadows swathed in wildflowers in spring. You may well see coyotes and deer close to the road, while in the backcountry cougars, black bears and bobcats are not unknown. Start eating a picnic and you're almost guaranteed a visit from a Canada jay, identified by its bright colouring and raucous call. Other indigenous birds include Stellar's jay (British Columbia's official bird), grouse, siskin, kinglet and – during autumn migrations – several types of hawk.

For further **information** on the park, call ⓣ604/924-2200, visit ⓦwww.env.gov.bc.ca/bcparks or ask at the city's Touristinfo Centre for the blue *BC Parks* pamphlet on the park. Among other things, the pamphlet has a good **map** that makes sense of the park's trails and their various links and permutations.

Mount Seymour Road

Mount Seymour Road climbs from the park headquarters at the junction with Indian River Road to over 1000m, ending at a car park and the trailheads for several upper-mountain trails (see p.108). En route it also passes four or five trailheads for lower and shorter (and generally less spectacular) trails, all explained and mapped on various infoboards at points up the road. The first of these is the **Old Buck Trail** (2.3km to junction with the Baden-Powell Trail; 2hr, 670m elevation gain), which leaves from near the park entrance across the road from the gatehouse. This shadows the Mount Seymour Road for just over 1km and then picks up an old logging road before meeting and crossing the Baden-Powell Trail (see p.111); from there the trail heads north to cross the approach road higher up and continues as the Upper Old Buck Trail-Perimeter, which rejoins the road higher up still.

As an alternative to taking the Old Buck Trail, keep following Mount Seymour Road to the **Vancouver Picnic Area** (about midway up the road), a popular spot in summer. There are toilets here, picnic tables and a park information shelter, plus the trailhead for the 750m **Mushroom Parking Lot Trail** (15min), little more than a stroll into the woods, and the Old Buck Access Trail, an easy 1km path (allow 30min) that runs east almost level to meet the Old Buck Trail coming up from the south.

Two kilometres beyond this picnic area you come to the popular viewpoint at **Deep Cove Lookout** – views are superb along much of the road, but they're especially good here, where signboards identify the city and other more distant landmarks below. Deep Cove Lookout offers trailhead access to some higher trails via the **Perimeter Trail** (1.5km, 45min, 240m elevation gain to Goldie

Lake and connection to Goldie Lake Loop, see below) and Upper Old Buck Trail. Continue just under 2km and on a sharp bend is the trailhead for the **Old Cabin Trail** (430m, 1hr 45min, 240m elevation gain), a connector trail which runs east to join the Perimeter Trail coming up from the south and the onward trail to Goldie Lake. Just a few hundred metres on is the end of the road, where you'll find a car park, toilets, picnic tables, a park kiosk and info boards on the various trails that start here.

Trails in Mount Seymour Provincial Park

Several major trails from the parking area at the top of the road in the park proper are manageable in a day, but be aware that rain or fog can suddenly appear, while snow lingers as late as June. You must be properly equipped.

Among the easiest hikes is the **Goldie Lake Loop** (2km, minimal elevation gain), a half-hour stroll that starts behind the First Aid station and heads east through a forest of hemlock, cedar and the park's oldest trees, Douglas firs, before returning to the First Aid station. About 500m along this trail, you can branch off onto the **Flower Lake Loop** (1.5km, 45min, 150m elevation gain), a path that leads through subalpine bog and pond habitats that offer a good chance of seeing several bird species.

Of similar length but with little climbing is the **First Lake Loop–Dog Mountain Trail**, which begins west of the chairlift and pushes though thick old-growth fir forest to First Lake (1km, 30min, minimal elevation gain). Here you meet the trail junctions for Dog Mountain or Mount Seymour – follow the trail west to the former (2km one-way, 40min, minimal elevation gain) for fine **views** of Vancouver and the Seymour River Valley.

The **Mount Seymour Trail** itself (4km **round-trip**, 2hr, 450m elevation gain) is the park's busiest, starting near the north end of the car park before traversing Brockton Point and First and Second Pump peaks. The reward for a fairly stiff climb is a panorama from Mount Seymour (1455m) that on clear days extends over the city to the Gulf Islands. Also popular is the **Mystery Lake Trail**

Winter on Mount Seymour

Mount Seymour (ⓣ604/986-2261 for Guest Services, 718-7771 for Snow Line, ⓦwww.mountseymour.com) has a developed skiing, snowboarding and **winter activities** programme. It has the city's highest base elevation in the car park at the top of Mount Seymour Road, and its 22 runs (the longest is 2.4km) are accessed by three chairlifts and a tow. The vertical rise is 330m, and the terrain divides into 40 percent novice, 40 percent intermediate and 20 percent advanced. Average snowfall is 300cm, or about half of Cypress Mountain's (see p.110) and a third of Whistler's (see p.244).

Shuttle services (ⓣ604/718-7771 for information) run here daily in winter from various points on the North Shore, notably Lonsdale Quay and Phibbs Exchange. Skiing and other activities are available at night until 10pm. Lift passes cost $42 from 9.30am until 5pm (from 8.30am at weekends and holidays) and $33 after 5pm. The mountain has excellent equipment rental and ski-school outlets: a full set of ski or snowboard gear costs $40 ($35 after 4pm), with a suit $24, jacket $15.50, pants $12 and helmet $8.

While the activities are franchised to a private operator, the provincial government's BC Parks puts out two backcountry ski trails from the car park and park kiosk, where you'll also find the latest snow and avalanche reports (the latter are a real hazard). The **Mount Seymour Backcountry Access** runs 7km to the saddle between First and Second Pump peaks (allow 3hr return on skis, 4hr on snowshoes). The easier First Lake Trail loops out to the lake (with virtually no elevation gain) and picks up the Mount Seymour Trail for the return to the car park (1hr return on skis, 2hr on snowshoes).

(1.5km one-way, 45min, 180m elevation gain), which leads from the parking area straight into a forest of fir, hemlock and cedar, reaching Mystery Lake (good for a cooling swim in summer) via an occasionally rocky route that shadows a ski lift with relatively few gaps in the trees for views. You can return the same way or curve east around the lake and follow well-signed trails that either run up the mountain or drop more directly back to the parking area.

The wildest and most demanding hike for serious walkers is the **Elsay Lake Trail** (7km one-way, allow a full day, 500m elevation gain), which follows the Mount Seymour Trail until the divide just east of First Pump Peak, about 1km from Mount Seymour. From here it runs along an intermittently marked trail to the forest- and mountain-circled Elsay Lake, where there is a rough backcountry shelter. There is no loop return – the homeward leg retraces your outbound route. You are allowed to **camp** here and elsewhere north of Brockton Point within the normal park regulations – in essence, leave no trace and light no fires. Bring your own water as no potable water is provided anywhere.

Cypress Provincial Park

Cypress Provincial Park (always open; free) is the most westerly of the big parks that partially cover the dramatic mountains and forest visible from Vancouver's Downtown. It's also among British Columbia's most visited day-use parks and probably the most popular of the North Shore's protected areas. This has to do not only with its scenic diversity, but also with its wilderness. The 7443-acre park divides into northern and southern sections joined by a narrow corridor of land. The southern section (first designated in 1975) has road access in the shape of the **Cyprus Access Road** (or Cypress Parkway), some developed facilities, accessible trails and lots of rugged backcountry. The northern section (protected in 1982) is considerably wilder and can be approached only via the 29km Howe Sound Crest Trail (see p.111) from the southern section or by tracks from Hwy 99 and Howe Sound to the west.

To get here you really need a car or bike: the heart of the park, main car park, Alpine ski and principal trailheads in the southern section are at **Cypress Bowl** at the end of the access road, 15km north of exit #8 off Hwy 1-99 (the Upper Levels Hwy) at Cypress Bowl Road. Note that as you follow the road you'll pass a turn after 13km to the right for the **Hollyburn** Nordic skiing area, only really relevant if you are here in winter or wish to tackle one or both of the long distance trails that start from this area. To get within striking distance using public transport, take the #253 Caulfield/Park Royal **bus** or the #257 Horseshoe Bay Express bus from the Park Royal interchange. The Cypress Access Road, the main approach, has great **views** over the city and as far as Mount Baker in Washington State.

Though there's nowhere to stay in the park in summer, backcountry **camping** is allowed in the park's northern section, at some higher elevations above the Nordic and Alpine ski areas in the south, and along the Howe Sound Crest Trail, where there are four preferred sites: the plateau above Enchantment Lake (11km from Cypress Bowl), Magnesia Meadows (14.5km), Brunswick Lake (19km) and Deeks Lake (22km from Cypress Bowl). Campfires are not permitted and there are no facilities.

Trails in Cypress Provincial Park

Cypress Provincial Park's five major (and many minor) trails can be rugged and muddy, but they're always well marked, and even just a few minutes from the parking area you can feel that you are in the depths of the great outdoors. Follow any of these walks and you'll soon see how the park came by its name, which is taken from the huge old yellow cypress trees that proliferate here. Trails depart

Winter in Cypress Provincial Park

Cypress Provincial Park has two closely linked **ski and snowboard areas** – the Alpine skiing area at Cypress Bowl (☎604/926-5612, ⓦwww.cypressmountain.com) and the Nordic ski area at Hollyburn (☎604/922-0825) just to the southwest. There are a total of 52 runs. The vertical rise is 512m, while cross-country ski trails total 16km, including 5km set aside for night skiing. The Nordic area also has dedicated snowshoe trails and special tobogganing areas. There is a licensed lounge and café on site.

Full-day lift **passes** cost $56.19 ($16.98 for cross-country passes, $12.63 for snow tubing, $23.18 for snowshoeing), with discounted night ($44.76 after 5pm, $36.19 after 7pm) and season passes ($259) also available. Ski or snowboard sets cost $41.59 to rent ($47.79 for a performance kit), helmet $6.60, boots $17.54 and suit $26.55. Drop-in lessons cost $50 for two hours ($85 with lift pass, $118 with pass and rental) and are held weekdays at 11.30am and 7.30pm, weekends 10.30am, 1.30pm and 3.30pm.

If you don't have **transport**, Cypress Mountain Sports, 510 and 518 Park Royal St, West Van, runs a shuttle (☎604/878-9229) several times daily in season from Lonsdale Quay, Horseshoe Bay and the Caulfield and Park Royal shopping centres. The same company also provides equipment, rental and repair services, and guided snowshoe treks of the area.

The ski operation is franchised by the provincial government to a private operator, but BC Parks marks three winter **backcountry trails**: the Hollyburn Hikers' Access Trail (5km return to Hollyburn Mountain summit), from the BC Parks kiosk in the Nordic ski area; the Black Mountain Plateau Winter Trail (7km round-trip, marked to summit of Black Mountain), which starts 50m from the BC Parks kiosk at Cypress Bowl; and – from the same starting point – the Bowen Lookout Winter Trail (3km round-trip), which runs through the Yew Lake meadows. Obtain a free pass from the Cypress Mountain ticket office for access.

either from the parking area at the top of the access road or from the Hollyburn Nordic ski area lower down the same road. In addition there are two much longer trails that cut through the park: the Howe Sound Crest Trail and Baden-Powell Trail (see opposite).

The best short trails are those that kick off from the top of the access road in Cypress, starting with the easiest, the **Yew Lake Trail** (2km round-trip, 45min, minimal elevation gain), a self-guided interpretive trail that is wheelchair-accessible. It runs northwest from the car park through subalpine meadows and past the lake and has an additional short loop through a stand of old-growth forest. Almost equally easy, the **Black Mountain Loop** (2.5km round-trip, 45min, 100m elevation gain) also passes through subalpine meadows and skirts several small mountain lakes on the plateau southwest of Cypress Bowl, with short side trails to viewpoints over Yew Lake and the city. The more arduous **Cabin Lake Trail** (1km plus 7km round-trip, 3hr, 275m elevation gain) requires taking the Baden-Powell Trail for 2.7km from the Cypress Bowl car park, connecting with the Cabin Lake Trail itself on Black Mountain (1220m). This trail passes several small lakes and the Yew Lake Lookout before rejoining the Baden-Powell Trail for the return to Cypress Bowl.

One of the two main trails from the Nordic ski area, the **Four Lakes Loop**, also makes use of a segment of the Baden-Powell Trail. It starts at the BC Parks information kiosk at the Hollyburn Mountain Nordic ski area car park. Follow the Burfield Trail to the Baden-Powell Trail (100m past First Lake) and then follow this for 500m to pick up the West Lake and then Blue Gentian trails. At Blue

Gentian Lake take the Lost Lake Trail past Lost Lake to the Brother's Creek Trail for a return to Blue Gentian Lake. From here take the Blue Gentian Trail west for 300m back to the Baden-Powell Trail. The total loop is 7.2km via Brother's Creek (including 1km to First Lake, 1.7km to West Lake, 2.1km to Blue Lake and 3.2km to Lost Lake).

The second trail from the Nordic ski area is the more ambitious **Hollyburn Peak Trail** (8km round-trip, 3–4hr, elevation gain 400m), which takes you to the top of Hollyburn Mountain (1325m) to the north for some sensational views – though the trail follows the rather dull power-line road before picking up the Baden-Powell Trail and last 1.3km of the Hollyburn Peak Trail.

Long-distance trails

The **Howe Sound Crest Trail** is a great choice for experienced hikers who want to do a little more than simple day hikes but aren't equipped or prepared for multi-day treks into the backcountry. That said, you will need decent equipment (tent, stove, sleeping bag, boots and so forth) to tackle the 29km of this trail (see p.181 for rental details). The trail starts at Cypress Bowl and follows the narrow corridor of protected land to Cypress Park's northern section, passing the Lions Peaks and wonderfully named Mount Unnecessary. It then descends to Hwy 99 just south of Porteau Cove Provincial Park and north of Horseshoe Bay. The trail is rugged and easily lost in parts, especially in bad weather, and is not recommended to inexperienced hikers beyond Bowen Lookout (and should not be attempted at all beyond this point in winter).

An even more challenging track, the **Baden-Powell Trail** is longer – at 42km – and, in running west to east across the length of the North Shore, goes against the grain of the landscape, being forced to drop into and climb out of the many north-south valleys and creeks that run south to the coast. It is a trail that most casual visitors will tackle in the small sections that bisect some of the North Shore's protected areas, notably Cypress Park and Mount Seymour provincial parks. This said, given the proximity of North and West Van, you could easily arrange to walk the trail, spend the night in hotels or bed and breakfast accommodation and return the following day.

The trail was begun in 1967 as one of British Columbia's centenary projects and completed in 1971. Its western trailhead is just 2.5km southwest of Cypress Provincial Park in the car park at the north end of Eagle Ridge Drive, just off Hwy 1 (about 1km south of Horseshoe Bay). Buses will drop you nearby if you want to tackle this **first section of trail**: the distance from the trailhead to Cypress Bowl is 8.5km, with an elevation gain of 1014m (allow 5–6hr). The walk the other way – predominantly downhill – is clearly much easier. Alternatively, walk the section east from Cypress Bowl, a 9.5km trail with a 470m elevation change (more down than up). This will bring you out on Craigmohr Drive in residential West Van.

Lighthouse Park

The 185-acre **Lighthouse Park** (always open; free) lies just west of Cypress Provincial Park on Beacon Lane, off Marine Drive, and offers a seascape and forest semi-wilderness at the extreme western tip of the North Shore, 8km from the Lions Gate Bridge. It was initially established in 1881 as a lighthouse reserve. Getting here by public transport is easy – the West Van #250 **bus** makes the journey all the way from West Georgia Street in Downtown to a few moments' walk from the park entrance.

Smooth granite rocks and low cliffs line the park's shore, backed by huge Douglas firs up to 1500 years old, some of the best – and most accessible – virgin forest in southern British Columbia. It's the last vestige of first-growth forest in or near the city: it's sobering to think that the entire region once looked something like this. You'll also see arbutus, identified by its smooth but often peeling orange bark – it's Canada's only native broadleaf evergreen. The rocks make fine sun beds, though the water out here is colder than around the city beaches. It's also a great place to bring a picnic.

If you want to walk, there are around 13km of trails. A signboard at the car park shows the paths, including the two easy trails to the 1912 Point Atkinson **lighthouse** itself – you can take one out and the other back, a return trip of about 5km which involves about two hours' walking, less for keen walkers. Although the park has its secluded corners (no camping allowed), it can be disconcertingly busy during summer weekends. For more **information** on the park, contact the city's Touristinfo Centre or call ⓣ604/925-7200 or 925-7000.

Listings

Listings

8 Accommodation

Vancouver has plenty of central accommodation in all price brackets. At the top end are world-class Downtown hotels such as the venerable *Hotel Vancouver* and *Four Seasons*, and glittering high-rise palaces that command magnificent views of the mountains and Downtown waterfront. Mid-range and inexpensive options rarely boast such panoramic positions, but it's still possible to find good central choices with plenty of character and quality for under $150.

The widest **choice** in all categories can be found in **central Downtown**, the most pleasant and practical base for exploring the city, so unless your budget is extremely tight there's really no reason to stay in any other location. As a result, our listings are arranged primarily by **price** rather than location, though we have also given the best choices in some of the city's more peripheral districts.

That said, if you want to explore Downtown, there are few persuasive reasons for staying in North or West Vancouver, for example, where there is only a handful of hotels and bed and breakfast options, or in any location south of Granville Island or False Creek, unless you're headed for the youth hostel in Kitsilano.

Possible reasons for staying **outside the Downtown** core are if you wish to be close to the airport or a ferry terminal for an early getaway, want the peace and quiet offered by some of the excellent bed and breakfast options out of town, or are on a very tight budget, as there are plenty of cheap motels on the various strips in the city's northern, southern and eastern suburbs – Capilano Road in North Vancouver and along Kingsway south of Downtown are key locations. Bear in mind, though, that Downtown hostels and the excellent YWCA offer rates to match all but the cheapest (and dowdiest) out-of-town motels; you simply have to plan and book ahead.

And if you want peace and quiet but still wish to be central, you might plump for one of the smattering of hotels in the quieter and more residential **West End**, the area adjacent to Stanley Park, as even here you're still effectively in Downtown.

A central location doesn't necessarily mean high **prices**: there are excellent inexpensive or mid-range options – but you'll have to book ahead to secure a room in such places in midsummer. If you get stuck, there are two free reservations services to help out (see p.116).

In the **budget bracket**, you'd be well advised to steer clear of the area east of Downtown between **Gastown and Chinatown**. On the face of it this district has a large number of inexpensive hotels, but most are flophouses of a dinginess and unpleasantness that make them options of absolute last resort. These areas are also not particularly safe at night, and the backstreets should be avoided at all times. There is a rash of especially dreadful places on Hastings Street a few blocks either side of Main Street: don't be tempted into these on any account. Gastown itself has a couple of honourable exceptions, but these are often housed above a bar where live bands and late-night drinking may keep you awake till the small hours.

Again, if you really need to stick to the rock-bottom price bracket, you're better off in the **hostels** (see p.126), the **YWCA** or one of the marginally less dodgy hotels north of the Granville Street Bridge, still in part a tame but tacky red-light area but increasingly part of the gentrification process that is spreading from Yaletown.

Vancouver has three good **Hostelling International hostels**, plus a handful of other reasonable, privately run hostels. Relatively low-price accommodation is also available in summer at the University of British Columbia's Vanier Hostel, though the campus is a long way from Downtown, and many of the rooms go to convention visitors. If you're in the city for a longer period, check out the small ads in the *Vancouver Sun* newspaper for details of rooms and apartments to rent.

Surprisingly for a place so close to the great outdoors, Vancouver is not a camper's city – the majority of the in-city **campsites** are for RVs only and will turn you away if you've got only a tent. We've listed the few places that won't.

Out of season, hotels in all categories offer reductions, and you can reckon on thirty percent discounts on the prices below. Many hotels will also offer discounted weekly rates in both high and low season. Remember, too, that the prices below are for doubles, though even the smartest hotels will introduce an extra bed into a double room at very little extra cost if there are three of you. As another way of saving money, or if you intend to be in the city for some time, it's also worth noting that many hotels have kitchenettes or fully fitted kitchens if you want to cook for yourself.

Accommodation services

Vancouver is a busy city between June and September, and you should book rooms weeks, preferably months, ahead, especially if you hope to stay at one of the better-known bargains. If you leave it until the last minute, have trouble tracking down a room, arrive in the city without a bed, or simply wish to browse accommodation in advance, the Vancouver Touristinfo Centre (Ⓣ604/683-2000, Ⓦwww.tourismvancouver.com) offers a free accommodation reservation service and extensive online listings.

Bed and breakfasts

Vancouver has a host of **bed and breakfast options**, but very few are cheap – expect to pay $95-plus for a double – or central enough to make useful bases for sightseeing. However, if you choose well, you can have access to beaches, gardens, barbecues and as little or as much privacy as you want. Watch out for places in Downtown that describe themselves as B&Bs; in most cases these are just small hotels – they're often very nice, but rooms can cost as much as or more than those in Downtown hotels in the mid-range and expensive price brackets.

Bed and breakfast accommodations tend to close and open from year to year, so it's safest to book a room through a reservation agency that knows which ones are still around. However, most agencies offer phone services only and require two days' notice – fine if you're planning ahead, but not much use if you need to find a place on arrival. In the latter case it's best to visit the city's main infocentre at the foot of Burrard Street (see p.36), where you can browse through folders containing details and pictures of dozens of bed and breakfast options and use the centre's accommodation service. In either case, make sure you know exactly where your B&B is located and how far you'll have to travel to see the sights.

If you need to use an **agency**, the following have accommodation throughout the city and in Victoria, the Gulf Islands and beyond: Best Canadian Bed & Breakfasts (Ⓦwww.bedsandbreakfasts.ca), www.bcsbestbnbs.com and www.wcbbbcanada.com).

Accommodation prices

All **accommodation prices** in this chapter are in Canadian dollar rates unless otherwise specified. Prices are for the least expensive double room in each establishment in high season, excluding special offers. Note, however, that many hotels in all categories have frequent off-season, weekly or weekend offers and that virtually all will introduce a third bed into a double room for only a few dollars. Many hotels will also allow children under a certain age – usually 12 years – to sleep free if they share their parents' room. Always enquire about deals.

Note, too, that room prices are quoted without BC's eight percent **provincial hotel tax** levied on hotels and other establishments with more than four rooms and added to your bill when you check out. The federal five percent **goods and services tax** (GST) is also levied: refunds for visitors are no longer available.

Also invaluable is the official Super Natural British Columbia reservation service (Ⓣ1-800/435-5662 or 604/435-5622 within Greater Vancouver and 250/387-1642 outside North America; Ⓦwww.hellobc.com), which has access to a large database of rooms and can sometimes offer better last-minute rates than those listed by the hotels themselves.

Downtown hotels

Hotels are dotted across Vancouver's **Downtown** peninsula, so wherever you stay you won't be more than a few minutes' walk or a short bus or taxi ride from the main sights. The quietest and most peripheral places lie in the **West End**, which, despite their distance from the main core, have the advantage of being close to the beaches and green spaces of Stanley Park. East of here, **Robson Street** houses several hotels, many of them former high-rise apartment blocks that have been converted into big, bland but serviceable mid-price accommodation. These are reasonably convenient for both Stanley Park and the Downtown shops and galleries without being especially close – relatively speaking – to either. There are also hotels in all categories at the heart of the peninsula, with a great choice of upmarket options on or close to the waterfront.

On the area's southern and eastern fringes – **Gastown** and **Granville Island** – there are only a handful of hotels, but as gentrification takes hold, the old flophouses on the southern end of Granville and Howe streets are being converted by the mid-market hotel chains into functional places to stay.

Inexpensive

Budget Inn-Patricia Hotel 403 East Hastings St at Dunlevy Ⓣ604/255-4301 or 1-888/926-1017, Ⓕ254-7154, Ⓦwww.budgetpathotel.bc.ca. This 92-room hotel is well known among backpackers and budget travellers, and is widely advertised across Vancouver. However, the six-storey building is located a long way from Downtown in the heart of Chinatown (certainly too far to walk comfortably). This is an exciting or grim location, depending on your point of view, though some feel distinctly unsafe in the area and you wouldn't want to walk the surrounding streets in the small hours. The hotel itself is clean, well run, in relatively good condition, and the best of the many generally awful places in this district. Rooms are available in several price categories, and rates include a good breakfast at a nearby café. Free parking is available. $79–135

Buchan Hotel 1906 Haro St at Robson and Denman Ⓣ604/685-5354 or 1-800/668-6654, Ⓕ685-5367, Ⓦwww.buchanhotel.com. Some of the 61 rooms in this 1926 three-storey building are smallish, and only half boast private bathrooms, but all are clean and priced accordingly (there's a $60 range from top to bottom for rooms of differing standards here). Try for rooms on the east side, which are brighter and overlook a small park, or the four "executive" front-corner rooms, which are well furnished and the best in the house. On a quiet tree-lined West End street, the hotel is not convenient for walking to Downtown; pick-up and drop-off for the airport shuttle (see p.23) is a 5min walk away. Facilities include a laundry room and in-house bike and ski storage, and rooms have TVs but no phones. Children under 12 stay free in their parents' room. $79–135

Burrard Inn 1100 Burrard St near Helmcken ⓣ604/681-2331 or 1-800/663-0366, ⓕ681-9753, ⓦwww. burrardinn.com. A pleasantly dated motel with standard fittings: 18 of the 70 rooms have kitchen facilities for self-catering (you'll pay an extra $5–10 for these), making this a good bet for families; some rooms look onto a charming garden courtyard. The general location isn't as convenient as some Downtown hotels, but you are still just four blocks from Robson St and from Yaletown to the east. Rooms have phones and TVs; other facilities include a restaurant and free parking. $89–139

Kingston Hotel 757 Richards St at Robson ⓣ604/684-9024 or 1-888/713-3304, ⓕ684-9917, ⓦwww.kingstonhotelvancouver .com. One of Vancouver's best-known bargains, the Kingston is well run, clean, safe and handily situated on the eastern edge of Downtown. Its well-decorated interior successfully affects the warm and comfortable look and feel of a European-style hotel, though its 52 rooms are fairly small and standard in appearance. Nine have private bathrooms and TVs, while the rest have a phone (no TV), washbasin and share good bathrooms at the end of each corridor. There's also a coin laundry and a modest but free breakfast to start the day. Off-street parking is available half a block away from $10 a day. With the *Sylvia*, this is by far the best accommodation at its price in the city. Book well ahead. $75–175

Moda Hotel 900 Seymour St ⓣ604/683-4251 or 1-877/683-5522, ⓕ683-0611, ⓦwww .modahotel.ca. Not far from the *Kingston* (see above), the former dowdy *Dufferin* was gutted in 2006, a glamorous 57-room boutique hotel emerging from the debris. It's not the best location, but not bad either, and this is a chic place to stay, made better by the excellent restaurant on site (see *Cibo Trattoria* review, p.139). $169–239

Sylvia Hotel 1154 Gilford St ⓣ604/681-9321, ⓕ682-3551, ⓦwww.sylviahotel .com. Located in a 1912 greystone, the *Sylvia* is an ivy-covered local landmark that was one of the city's first hotels and earliest high-rise buildings (some rooms are in a low-rise annexe added in the mid-1980s). It stands on English Bay virtually on the beach two blocks from Stanley Park, and its snug bar, quiet, friendly service, restaurant (with outdoor terrace for summer dining), old-world charm and sea views make it one of Vancouver's best places to stay in its price range. It's also a perennially popular place, making reservations for one of its 120 rooms essential. The lobby raises expectations – great stained-glass windows, plump chairs, red carpets and marble staircase – not fulfilled by the rooms, which are mostly relatively plain and come in seven different types (this guide's price code covers only a handful of the very cheapest available: most are more expensive), all with private bathrooms and, in the 23 suites (which are big enough for families), kitchen facilities. Angle for one of the more expensive south-or southwest-facing rooms – they have the best views of English Bay and the sunset. Low-season rates are available between October and May. $145–180

Victorian Hotel 514 Homer St at Pender ⓣ604/681-6369 or 1-877/681-6369, ⓦwww .victorianhotel.ca. The family-run *Victorian* is situated about as far east as you'd want to be but remains within easy walking distance of Gastown and the rest of Downtown. It was built in 1898 as one of the city's first guesthouses and has been carefully restored: many of its rooms have high ceilings, hardwood floors, elegant bathrooms and period features such as original fireplaces and mouldings. Prices for double rooms vary by up to $60, depending on whether they have private bathrooms and/or kitchenettes. All rooms have phones and small TVs; continental breakfast is included. $99–159

Moderate

Barclay Hotel 1348 Robson St at Jervis ⓣ604/688-8850, ⓕ688-2534, ⓦwww .barclayhotel.com. This is one of the nicer of several hotels at the north end of Robson (see also the *Greenbrier* and *Robsonstrasse* below), about halfway between Stanley Park and the Vancouver

Art Gallery. It features 90 rooms in several price categories (low-season rates are available) and a rather chintzy French rustic ambience in places. Given its rooms and facilities, which include a/c, a restaurant and a lounge, it's something of a bargain. $75–135

Blue Horizon 1225 Robson St at Bute ⓣ604/688-1411 or 1-800/663-1333, ⓕ688-4461, ⓦwww.bluehorizonhotel.com. This is not in the same league as some of the costlier places on this stretch of Robson, and feels more like a motel than a hotel, albeit one that's located in a 31-storey 1960s high-rise. Its 214 a/c rooms are spacious and were renovated in 2000 to give them a neat, contemporary look (though bathrooms are relatively small). All are on corners, with large windows and small balconies; the "Superior" rooms on the 15th floor and above offer great views (indeed, superior to those of its more expensive rivals). You can specify a nonsmoking room or request to stay on a "Green Floor", where rooms have energy-saving lighting, recycling bins, low-flow showers and other features that have earned the *Blue Horizon* a Green Hotel award. There's an indoor pool, sauna, Jacuzzi, outdoor café on Robson St, in-house bistro and Shenanigan's sports bar-lounge and nightclub. $149–359

Bosman's Hotel 1060 Howe St between Nelson and Helmcken ⓣ604/682-3171 or 1-888/267-6267, ⓦwww.bosmanshotel.com. Though it doesn't offer too many frills, this is a well-located hotel with free parking and a restaurant and lounge just two blocks from Robson. It has 102 modern, a/c rooms (all with TVs) at a range of prices, but some look on to Howe, one of the city's busier streets, so even with double-glazing, traffic may be an issue here. There is, however, an outdoor swimming pool for use in summer. $99–139

Coast Plaza Hotel & Suites 1763 Comox St at Denman ⓣ604/688-7711 or 1-800/663-1144, ⓕ688-5934. ⓦwww.coasthotels.com. The main appeal of this popular 35-storey, 269-room hotel is its West End location just steps from the beach, the Seawall and the buzz of Denman St. It was originally built as apartments above the Denman Place Mall; now guests of the hotel can use the Denman Fitness Centre and rather claustrophobic basement pool there free of charge. Though it's not the value it once was, the comfortable, if slightly dated, rooms have balconies and are spacious, especially if you go for the one- and two-bedroom suites (some with kitchens), and the English Bay views are exceptional. The hotel is popular with a wide range of clients, from tour parties to film crews and jobbing actors. There's a free shuttle to Downtown. $199–479.

Comfort Inn Downtown Vancouver 654 Nelson St ⓣ604/605-4333 or 1-888/605-5333, ⓕ605-4334, ⓦwww.comfortinndowntown.com. There have been lodgings of sorts in this heritage building for years, but thanks to a retro-inspired refit, complete with lots of black-and-white photographs and 1950s neon, this boutique hotel now has a hip and stylish look. Rooms all come with high-speed Internet access, voicemail and a/c. The room price includes a continental breakfast in *Doolin's Irish Pub,* and a pass to clubs owned by the same management. The location is convenient for the restaurant and clubs of both Yaletown and the lower end of Granville St. $99–239

Days Inn Vancouver Downtown 921 West Pender St at Burrard ⓣ604/681-4335 or 1-877/681-4335, ⓦwww.daysinnvancouver.com. Something of a city institution, this old 85-room, seven-storey building in the financial district in the heart of Downtown has plenty of character and lots of original Art Deco touches. Rooms are a/c but relatively plain for the price, and ten have showers only, rather than showers and baths. Ask for a room away from the busy street, preferably one with harbour views. Facilities include restaurant, bar and valet parking ($10), and low-season deals are available from November to April. $159–259

Greenbrier Hotel 1393 Robson St at Broughton ⓣ604/683-4558 or 1-888/355-5888, ⓕ669-3109. ⓦwww.greenbrierhotel.com. The *Greenbrier* stands on a pleasant city block between Stanley Park and the heart of Downtown. Though the building's nothing great to look at, the interior of this former apartment block has been nicely transformed into a variety of 33 one-bed and family suites with neat, modern decor and the option of fully equipped kitchens. Many rooms have sea and mountain views, and there's free parking, but Robson is busy day and night, so this isn't the most tranquil of locations. $99–249.

Holiday Inn Hotel & Suites Downtown **1110 Howe St between Davie and Helmcken ⓣ604/684-2151 or 1-800/663-9151 in the US & Canada or 1-800/465-4329 worldwide, ⓕ684-4736, ⓦwww.holidayinnvancouverdowntown.com.** The "Downtown" in the name is rather misleading, for while this large 245-room hotel is reasonably central, it actually stands at the Granville Island end of Howe St. Unlike some of the dingier hotels nearby, this is a classy place, with lots of facilities, including sauna, pool and kids' activity centre, plus rooms with kitchenettes for self-catering. Yet at this price – there is an extraordinary $230 range between top and bottom rates for doubles – there are also plenty of alternatives elsewhere. $219–499

Howard Johnson Hotel Downtown **1176 Granville St ⓣ604/688-8701 or 1-888/654-6336, ⓕ688-8335, ⓦwww.hojovancouver.com.** Every year the tawdry southern reaches of Granville St become just a little more amenable, and this renovated hotel is part of the ongoing process. Transcending the standard bland Howard Johnson norm, the 110 rooms over five floors are surprisingly stylish, with straightforward furnishings: they're also nicer and more spacious than those of the competing *Ramada* nearby. One-bedroom suites with sofabeds have kitchens and are ideal for families, but while safe, this is still hardly the nicest part of town. $99–279

Riviera Hotel **431 Robson St at Nicola ⓣ604/685-1301 or 1-888/699-5222, ⓦwww.rivieraonrobson.com.** More towards the Stanley Park rather than the Vancouver Art Gallery end of Robson, the *Riviera* started life in the 1960s as an apartment building but has been converted into a hotel with thirteen large studios and 28 two-room (one-bedroom) suites. All have well-equipped kitchens and balconies, with great harbour and mountain views from the rear (north-facing) side of the building. Free parking and weekly, monthly and low-season rates are available. $98–288

Robsonstrasse Hotel & Suites **1394 Robson St at Broughton ⓣ604/687-1674 or 1-888/667-8877, ⓕ685-7808, ⓦwww.robsonstrassehotel.com.** Like the nearby *Greenbriar*, this hotel, midway between Stanley Park and the centre of Downtown, has a variety of double rooms and suites with kitchenettes at a wide range of prices. It's also a/c, and offers free parking and a guest laundry. $104–254

Sandman Hotel Downtown **180 West Georgia St at Homer ⓣ604/681-2211 or 1-800/726-3626, ⓕ681-8009, ⓦwww.sandman.ca.** This 302-room hotel is the flagship of a reliable mid-price chain with hotels all over western Canada, and is reasonably well placed at the eastern edge of Downtown. The rooms are bland but comfortable in the manner of chain hotels and are well equipped and rather spacious: all have a/c and some have kitchenettes. Underground parking is available, and guests have access to an indoor swimming pool, whirlpool and health club. The ground floor hosts the popular *Shark Club Bar & Grill* (see p.150). Low-season rates are available. $159–239

Shato Inn Hotel **1825 Comox St between Denman and Gilford ⓣ604/681-8920.** A quiet, family-run place convenient to Stanley Park and the beach, the *Shato* is a good choice if you can't get into the *Sylvia* a block away. All rooms have phones and TVs, and some have balconies and/or kitchen units. Underground parking is available and rates are lower off season. $100–165

Sunset Inn & Suites **1111 Burnaby St at Thurlow ⓣ604/688-2474 or 1-800/786-1997, ⓕ669-3340, ⓦwww.sunsetinn.com.** This is one of the better modern high-rise apartment hotels on the fringes of the West End and a good spot for a longer stay. It has fifty spacious studios and one-bedrooms in all, renovated in 2007, each with a balcony (though views are nothing special): most have recently been updated. Facilities include a laundry, free parking, exercise room and quiet location close to shops. Downtown is a 10min walk away. Low-season and weekly rates are available. $169–599

West End Guest House **1362 Haro St near Jervis ⓣ604/681-2889 or 1-888/546-3327, ⓕ688-8812, ⓦwww.westendguesthouse.com.** This wonderful, small and carefully restored 1906 guesthouse lies in a quiet area despite being just a block from Robson. The Victorian feel is completely realized, right down to the gramophone in the old-time parlour, a lovely collection of old photographs of the city and the sherry and iced tea available in the afternoon. The eight bright, very attractive rooms (lots of antiques and your own stuffed animal) have private bathrooms and touches you'd expect in a luxury hotel – notably terry bathrobes, feather mattresses and your own slippers. Book well in advance. Full breakfast included and free loan of bikes. No smoking. $210–275

Expensive

The Fairmont Hotel Vancouver 900 West Georgia St at Burrard ⓣ604/684-3131 or 1-800/441-1414, ⓕ662-1929, ⓦwww.fairmont.com. This venerable but thoroughly renovated 1939 hotel is Vancouver's most famous and prestigious hotel and the one to go for if money's no object and you want more traditional old-world style than some of Vancouver's other world-class hotels offer, a Downtown location, and all the refinements (spa, fitness centre, pool and so on) and attention to detail you'd expect in a hotel of this calibre. $329–2,249

The Fairmont Waterfront 900 Canada Place Way ⓣ604/691-1991 or 1-800/441-1414, ⓦwww.fairmont.com. A more modern but equally illustrious alternative to the staid *Fairmont Hotel Vancouver* (see above), this is a fabulous 489-room, multistorey affair on the dazzling Downtown waterfront. The location is unbeatable, especially if you have a room with a view, and everything about the place speaks of style and good taste. As in the *Vancouver*, the open-to-the-lobby restaurant and bar is a good place to eat or drink even if you're not staying here. Guests can use the health centre or third-floor heated outdoor pool, fringed by a herb garden whose produce is used in the hotel's restaurant, distinguished by huge floor-to-ceiling windows looking out over Coal Harbour. From $329

Four Seasons 791 West Georgia St at Howe ⓣ604/689-9333, 1-800/268-6282 in Canada, 1-800/332-3442 in US, ⓦwww.fourseasons.com. A Four Seasons hotel rarely disappoints, and Vancouver's is no exception. The location is perfectly central, located a block from Robson and the Vancouver Art Gallery, and the 385 rooms occupy a 28-storey high-rise building above the Pacific Centre mall. Rooms are enormous, the service immaculate, and the public spaces stunning, none more so than the covered Garden Terrace, complete with lots of greenery, waterfalls and a superlative Inuit tapestry. If you're staying or not, you should definitely think about sampling the buffet breakfast, served on this terrace – it's one of the best in the city (from $13). Similarly, the hotel's main restaurant is widely considered among the city's elite and is open to all. From $350

▲ Fairmont Hotel Vancouver bar

Granville Island Hotel 1253 Johnson St ⓣ604/683-7373 or 1-800/663-1840 in Canada & the US ⓕ683-3061, ⓦwww.granvilleislandhotel.com. If you stay at this modern and recently expanded hotel on the eastern edge of Granville Island, you'll be at the heart of one of the city's trendiest and most enjoyable little enclaves. Though not as luxurious as the *Pan Pacific* and the *Fairmont* hotels, you will still pay a premium for the location and spectacular waterfront setting, as well as for oversized bathtubs, health club, tennis courts and microwaves. $215–265

Hotel Le Soleil 567 Hornby St at West Pender ⓣ604/632-3000 or 1-877/632-3030, ⓕ632-3001, ⓦwww.hotellesoleil.com. Le Soleil is a luxury "boutique" hotel with 119 rooms (all suites, but for ten doubles) done up in a style reminiscent of a fussy 19th-century French country house rather than the sleek contemporary model favoured by most hotels of this ilk, notably the *Opus,* which is a better bet if you also favour that look (see review below). The extravagant lobby, with its chandeliers, sumptuous carpets and glittering vaulted ceiling, sets the tone. The rooms follow suit, with rich fabrics, Biedermeier-style furniture and brightly coloured wallpapers. The marble-bedecked bathrooms are especially impressive, but the windowless living rooms of some suites can be gloomy – check what you're getting. While the rooms may not be to all tastes – and the *Wedgewood* (see opposite) might be a better bet if you want this sort of hotel – the service is hard to fault and the location is excellent for shopping and sightseeing – though Hornby does not quite have the cachet of Burrard or Howe nearby. Access to the YWCA alongside is available to residents. Rooms from $275.

Opus Hotel 322 Davie St ⓣ604/642-6787 or 1-866/642-6787, ⓕ685-8690, ⓦwww.opushotel.com. Opened in August 2002 to a lot of hype (which continues to this day), the *Opus* is a stylish, contemporary place to stay that lives up to Yaletown's hip reputation. Outside, it's just another seven-storey former warehouse, but inside the designers have got to work with the bold, if predictable, palette of colours and materials (mosaic, marble, expensive fabrics) that seems to be required of most modern city boutique hotels. The 96 rooms are equally fetching – expensive linens, firm beds, CD players, big windows and bathrooms you'd more than happily install at home. For the best views, ask for an upper south-facing room. Bear in mind, though, that this location is not the best for sightseeing. From $339

Pan Pacific 300–999 Canada Place ⓣ604/662-1-8111 or 800/663-1515 in Canada, 800/937-1515 in the US, ⓦwww.panpacific.com. If you walk around Canada Place and wonder what happens in the magnificent white high-rise that looms above the complex's famous "sails", then wonder no more, for it's occupied by the Pan Pacific, the most expensive and spectacularly situated of Vancouver's modern luxury hotels. It also gets the highest, Five Diamond ranking from the AAA; the only other Five Diamond hotel in Vancouver is the Sutton Place Hotel. An eight-storey atrium and lobby set the tone, with vast, twelve-metre picture windows that look out over the harbour. All 504 rooms enjoy great views (the hotel rooms start on the building's eighth floor), and those whose numbers end in 10 and 20 have sweeping panoramas from their bathrooms as well. Service and facilities are impeccable, and the heated outdoor pool and health centre are state-of-the-art; some rooms, though, are small compared with those in the Four Seasons and Fairmont hotels. From $319

▲ Atrium of The Pan Pacific Centre

Rosedale on Robson Suite Hotel 838 Hamilton St at Robson ⓣ604/689-8033 or 1-800/661-8870, ⓕ689-4426, ⓦwww.rosedaleonrobson.com. The Rosedale's 1990s exterior and already dated lobby may not have the architectural élan of the dramatic main library building opposite, but the location is convenient and the prices, though not the lowest, are a good value if you're travelling as a group or a family. There are designated family suites (with toy boxes and bunk beds for smaller kids), and the one- and two-bedroom suites have extra pull-out beds and kitchenettes. The indoor pool is excellent. The hotel has 203 rooms but is popular with tour groups, so book early and check the website for deals at well below posted rates. $180–350

Sheraton Vancouver Wall Centre 1088 Burrard St at Helmcken ⓣ604/331-1000 or 1-800/663-9255, ⓕ893-7121, ⓦwww.sheratonwallcentre.com. There's nothing understated about this hotel just south of Robson Square: part of the Wall Centre – two tall black-glass shrouded skyscrapers completed in 2001 and now a distinctive feature of the skyline – it has 733 rooms, virtually all of which have views, though they are unfortunately compromised by the fact that the tinted glass of the (unopenable) windows adds a sunglass hue to the panorama. The rooms are pleasant, none too big, contemporary in an obvious way – the usual signature blonde wood – and have decent bathrooms. But this is a chain hotel, albeit a spectacular one (the lobby and Roman courtyard are particularly gargantuan), and the preponderance of tour groups, plus the sheer size, makes for an anonymous stay. But if this is what you want, along with an up-to-the-minute spa, pool and health club, then the Sheraton does the job as well as any. $239–499

Sutton Place 845 Burrard St between Robson and Smithe ⓣ604/682-5511 or 1-800/961-7555, ⓕ682-5513, ⓦwww.suttonplace.com. Having opened in 1986, Sutton Place stole a march on some of its luxury rivals, and for years has been the hotel of choice for visiting celebrities. Though its bland, almost tasteless exterior hardly holds out the promise of a stylish world-class hotel, a renovation in 2004 has kept its 397 spacious rooms up to the mark, with the full set of de rigueur facilities (including WiFi, DVDs and flat-screen TV in all rooms), and a tasteful, European-style décor that is traditional rather than groundbreaking. There's a good pool, a well-equipped gym and the new Vida Wellness Spa. $220–450

Wedgewood Hotel & Spa 845 Hornby St at Robson ⓣ604/689-7777 or 1-800/663-0666, ⓕ608-5348, ⓦwww.wedgewoodhotel.com. This is a classy and sophisticated boutique hotel: the 85 rooms are spacious and romantic (some have fireplaces), the service is first class, and the location across from the Vancouver Art Gallery and Law Courts is as central as you please (but ask for rooms looking at the gallery – rear-facing rooms are second-best). The rooms are also elegant and expensively furnished (bathrooms are a wow), and the personal touch of Greek-born proprietor Eleni Skalbania, whose independent ownership accounts for much of the hotel's success, has made it a favourite of visiting stars, dignitaries in the know and judges and lawyers attending sessions in the nearby courts. Patrons and locals alike also make a beeline for the hotel's equally lauded and cosy *Bacchus* bar and restaurant, where afternoon tea or, a little later, a perfect Martini, hit the spot nicely. From $350

The North Shore

The North Shore embraces **North Vancouver** – the area across the Burrard Inlet opposite the Downtown peninsula – and **West Vancouver**, the mix of residential and open country along Marine Drive and the Trans-Canada Highway (Hwy 1) towards Lighthouse Park and Horseshoe Bay. Accommodation – and there isn't much – is concentrated mostly in the former, as the moneyed enclaves of West Vancouver, which has some of the country's most expensive real estate, are hardly conducive to the notion of hotels and motels.

There is no point staying here if you want to get to grips with Downtown, even if you have a car, as traffic across the Lions Gate Bridge – the only vehicular access – is often bad. This said, there are several reasonably priced **motels** in the area, mostly just over the Lions Gate Bridge on or close to the junction of Capilano Road and Marine Drive. If you are using public transport, then you'll need to use either buses (which will also have to run the gauntlet of traffic on the bridge) or the SeaBus, a lovely crossing, but one whose novelty will wear off after several trips.

The main reasons you may want to be on the North Shore are to access the BC Ferries terminal at **Horseshoe Bay** easily or to be more handily placed for the hikes and other outdoor activities afforded by Grouse Mountain and the Capilano River, Mount Seymour and Lynn Canyon parks. If this is your intention, there are some delightful **bed and breakfast** options close to the parks.

The city's reservation services (see p.116) can also help out here, but North Vancouver has its own **visitor centre** at 102–124 West 1st St (Mon–Fri 9am–5pm; ⓣ604/987-4488, ⓦwww.nvchamber.bc.ca) with information on the area's accommodation. Two smaller offices are open from mid-May to early September daily 9am to 5pm at the bottom of Lonsdale Road by the Lonsdale Quay (ⓣ604/984-8588) and at the junction of Marine Drive and Capilano Road (ⓣ604/980-5332).

Inexpensive

Comfort Inn & Suites 1748 Capilano Rd ⓣ604/988-3181 or 1-888/988-3181, ⓦwww.vancouvercomfort.com. Take the Capilano Road exit (Exit 14) off Hwy 1 for this motel, which offers a variety of one- and two-bedroom suites, some with kitchens (for an extra $10). Facilities include an outdoor pool, Jacuzzi and laundry, and low-season rates are available $119–289.

Travelodge Vancouver Lions Gate 2060 Marine Drive ⓣ604/985-5311 or 1-800/578-7878, ⓦwww.lionsgatetravelodge.com. Noise can be a problem at this standard chain motel, given its busy (but convenient) position between the Lions Gate Bridge and Capilano Road. In its favour is the fact that it was refurbished in 2002, the rooms are a/c, there's an outdoor pool, and rates are reasonable. $99–159

Moderate

Best Western Capilano Inn & Suites 1634 Capilano Rd ⓣ604/987-8185 or 1-800/644-4227, ⓦwww.bestwesterncapilano.com. Virtually on the junction of Marine Drive and Capilano Road, this is one of several chain motels just east of the Lions Gate Bridge. There are standard rooms and rooms with kitchenettes for an additional $20, as well as laundry, restaurant and outdoor summer pool. $119–249

The Grouse Inn 1633 Capilano Drive ⓣ604/988-7101 or 1-800/779-7888, ⓦwww.grouseinn.com. *The Grouse Inn* is located close to Downtown road links – one block east of the Lions Gate Bridge and one block south of Hwy 1 at Exit 14. Choose among 80 regular or superior rooms and one- or two-bedroom kitchen suites (the kitchens cost an extra $29). Rates include a continental breakfast and drop in low season. Among the facilities are a/c, free parking, a heated pool and a children's playground. $109–289

Thistledown House B&B 3910 Capilano Rd ⓣ604/986-7173 or 1-888/633-7173, ⓦwww.thistle-down.com. This 1920 heritage building lies immediately east of the Capilano River park (just north of Edgemont Blvd) and en route for Grouse Mountain, offering easy access to trails. En-suite rooms are tastefully restored and furnished with antiques, and there are lovely gardens; room rate includes a full breakfast and afternoon tea. Rooms are all nonsmoking; low-season rates are available. $149–295

Expensive

Lonsdale Quay Hotel 123 Carrie Cates Court ⓣ604/986-6111 or 1-800/836-6111, ⓦwww.lonsdalequayhotel.com. What you pay for the simple but tastefully appointed rooms here will get you smarter accommodation in Downtown, but you are paying for a location right on the Lonsdale Quay waterfront (which results in fabulous harbour views) and above the quay's superb market (see p.98): escalators from the market itself lead you to the hotel reception on the third floor. The hotel is bright and modern and effects the usual design conceits and trimmings of the "boutique" property, including Internet access and spa, as well as offering bike hire and two restaurants. $150–500

South Vancouver

Whereas the North Shore has its obvious scenic attractions, it's hard to see any appeal in the accommodation found in the broad sweep of suburbs that make up South Vancouver. Prices are no keener than Downtown, though roads are less prone to congestion than the Lions Gate Bridge approach from the North Shore – and you also have the option of the SkyTrain, which bisects the area from Downtown to New Westminster.

With the honourable exception of the odd guesthouse near Kits Beach, many of the lodgings here are motels, most notably the Holiday Inn and Ramada properties on West Broadway near Oak and the cluster on Kingsway southeast of the intersection with Victoria Drive. Listed below are the cheapest options on Kingsway – price being the only real reason for being on this busy thoroughfare – but there's also a substantial array here of more expensive Best Western, Days Inn and other chain options. We have also given an option close to the Tsawwassen ferry terminal in case you need to catch an early ferry.

Inexpensive

2400 Motel 2400 Kingsway ⓣ604/434-2464 or 1-888/833-2400, ⓕ430-1045, ⓦwww.2400motel.com. These 65 basic motel bungalow units lie on Kingsway between 33rd Ave East and Nanaimo/Slocan. Family suites and rooms with kitchenettes are available, and there's free parking, with plenty of buses to Downtown from the doorstep. $89–199

City Centre Motor Hotel 2111 Main St ⓣ604/876-7166 or 1-800/707-2489, ⓦwww.citycentermotorhotel.com. Ignore the "city centre" bit, because this standard motel is nowhere close: rather, it's on busy Main St (between East 5th Ave and East 6th Ave), 10min walk from the Science World–Main St SkyTrain station to the north. Rooms are a/c, there's plenty of free parking, and rates are very competitive, but that's about it. $60–85

Howard Johnson Plaza Hotel 395 Kingsway ⓣ604/872-5252 or 1-800/663-5713, ⓦwww.howardjohnsonvancouver.com. If you are going to be on Kingsway, you may want to opt for this, the nearest of this busy road's hotels to Downtown. The 96 rooms are smallish, but they are a/c, some have excellent city views, all have phones, there's free parking and a continental breakfast is included in the room rate. $119–149

Mickey's Kits Beach Chalet 2142 West 1st Ave at Yew St ⓣ604/739-3342 or 1-888/739-3342, ⓦwww.mickeysbandb.com. The Jericho Beach youth hostel aside (see p.127), there's a surprising shortage of places to stay in the laid-back Kits district. This is the nicest of a limited choice: it has three quiet, private (nonsmoking) rooms with the option of en-suite or shared bathrooms, plus TV, Web access and self-serve continental breakfast, and all just two blocks from the beach. $135–175.

Moderate

Coast Tsawwassen Inn 1665 56th St, Delta ⓣ604/943-8221 or 1-800/663-1141, ⓦwww.tsawwasseninn.com. The main appeal of this chain hotel is its location off Hwy 17 just 5km northeast of the BC Ferries' terminal at

Airport hotels

There are several choices close to the **airport**, though given the easy links to Downtown (see p.23), it's hard to see how you could get stuck either on arrival or be so pushed for time on departure that you would have to check into one of these often soulless retreats. However, there are exceptions, as evidenced in the listings below, as well as frequent bargains and last-minute deals, so if you are using an airport hotel, shop around.

Fairmont Vancouver Airport ⓣ604/207-5200 or 1-800/441-1414, ⓦwww.fairmont.com. There is no doubt where you want to be before or after flying if money is no object, and that's this luxurious and hugely convenient hotel, whose 392 extraordinary soundproof rooms are in the airport complex itself (access is via a walkway at the far end of the US departure hall). If you've ever thought that staying in an airport hotel was a waste of time, this place will make you think again. Everything hi-tech than can be crammed into a room has been crammed here, and everything has been designed to soothe the jet-lagged or harassed air traveller. Prices start at $199, but you'll almost certainly end up paying more unless you check in during low season. The hotel is especially popular during the skiing season, when many people travelling long haul wisely spend a night here at the end of a trip before journeying to or from Whistler. From $199

Delta Vancouver Airport 3500 Cessna Drive, Richmond ⓣ604/278-1241 or 1-800/268-1133, ⓕ276-1975, ⓦwww.deltavancouverairport.com or www.deltahotels.com. Next choice, from the point of location, is this big 415-room hotel, 2km from the airport. The river setting is nicer than many an urban setting and the rooms were overhauled in 2002. There's a regular airport shuttle. $179–279

Tsawwassen. Rates include a continental breakfast and among the facilities are a heated indoor pool, hot tub, sauna and restaurant. $134–264

Holiday Inn Vancouver Centre–Broadway 711 Broadway West at Heather ⓣ604/879-0511 or 1-800/HOLIDAY, ⓦwww.hivancouver.com. It is hard to know why you would want to pay $149 and upwards for a double room in a big chain hotel outside Downtown, but if you want the security of knowing what to expect, this will do the job, with good chain-hotel rooms, and lots of in-room and public facilities (indoor pool, sauna and a choice of restaurants). The best rooms have city, ocean and mountain views. $149–264

Park Inn & Suites 898 Broadway West ⓣ604/872-8661, ⓦwww.parkinn.com/vancouver. The 118 rooms of this chain hotel are on the busy stretch of Broadway north of Vancouver's city hospital. Rates are more competitive than some of its neighbours, but otherwise facilities and rooms are what you would expect of a good mid-range chain. $125–185

Hostels

Cambie Gastown Hostel 310 Cambie St at Cordova ⓣ604/684-6466 or 1-877/395-5335, ⓦwww.cambiehostels.com. The 1897 *Cambie* is a private hostel located in Vancouver's oldest hotel and pub just off Gastown's main streets, and has a much nicer and more central position than many of the city's hostels. Beds are arranged in two-, four- or six-bed bunkrooms, and there are laundry, luggage-storage and bike-storage (but no cooking) facilities. There's a deservedly popular and inexpensive bar-grill with a good patio downstairs, so aim for beds away from this area if you want a relatively peaceful night's sleep. No curfew. From $27 per person in a dorm room; private double or quad rooms $60 per person. Weekly rates available.

Cambie Seymour Hostel 515 Seymour St at West Pender ⓣ604/684-7757 or 1-866/623-8496, ⓦwww.cambiehostels.com. This is the second, newer, calmer and more central of the *Cambie*'s stable of hostels (there's a third on Vancouver Island). Like the Gastown location (see above), the management has made an effort to ensure that rooms in this heritage building are pleasant, secure and well kept, and provide laundry, storage, Internet and food and drink. No curfew. Doubles in a bunk room cost $27 per person ($24 Oct–April) and $58 per person in a double bed ($52 off-season).

Central Station Hostel 1038 Main St ⓣ604/681-9118, 682-2441 or 1-800/434-6060, ⓦwww.cnnbackpackers.com. This hostel is in a location that can most kindly be described as edgy. Each of the very basic 104 rooms (renovated when the hostel opened) comes with sink, fridge and TV, and there's Internet access and an inexpensive restaurant and bar (with pool and darts) on site. Dorm beds $20 ($25 mid-June to Sept) or $120 ($150) weekly, singles/doubles $50/55 ($310 weekly).

C&N Backpackers Hostel 927 Main St ⓣ604/682-2441 or 1-888/434-6060, ⓦwww.cnnbackpackers.com. This hostel is a well-known backpackers' retreat that, despite renovation and new management, is still not exactly dazzling and its location on the eastern edge of Downtown is hardly the best. Indeed, it is so far from anything but the Pacific Central Station and bus depot – which is 150m away – that it's hard to see why anyone aside from those who come in on a late bus should want to stay here. Lots of people, do, though. No curfew. Same rates as *Central Station Hostel* (see above).

SameSun Hostel 1018 Granville St at Nelson ⓣ604/682-8226 or 1-877/562-2783, ⓕ682-8240, ⓦwww.samesun.com. *SameSun* has followed up the success of other hostels across Canada with a zippy, bright hostel in Vancouver, although its chosen location on Granville St – while central and away from the worst of this street's tawdriness – is not the quietest in the city. The hostel has 250 beds in two- and four-bed rooms and offers a free shuttle from the bus–train station, secure lockers, modern kitchen and common area, games room and Internet access. No curfew. From $25 per person; doubles from $65.

Vancouver Central Hostel (HI) 1025 Granville St ⓣ604/685-5335 or 1-888/203-8333, ⓦwww.hihostels.ca. Vancouver's newest and smartest HI hostel on busy Granville St is a far cry from the humble days of hostelling. It offers 214 beds in private double rooms with TV and en-suite bathrooms, four-bed dorms and a/c in most rooms. Family rooms are also available. Facilities include a kitchen, pub, reading lounge and shuttle runs to the other city HI hostels and the Pacific Central Station. Check-in is at noon and check-out 11am. Private doubles for members are $62 ($80 April, May & Oct; $85 June–Sept) and $70 ($88/93) for non-members.

Vancouver Downtown Hostel (HI) 1114 Burnaby St at Thurlow ⓣ604/684-4565 or 1-888/203-4302, ⓕ684-4540, ⓦwww.hihostels.ca. The second of the city's two central HI hostels is located in a former nunnery and health-care centre in the city's West End. There are 223 beds split up between shared and private rooms (maximum of four per room). Bike rental and storage as well as laundry facilities, kitchen, Internet access and storage lockers are available. A free shuttle (look for the blue HI logo) operates between this and the other city HI hostels and the Pacific Central railway and bus terminal; if you don't see the shuttle, call the hostel to find when the next one is due. No curfew. Check-in 24 hours a day; check out by 11am. Reservations are essential. Beds cost $26 ($29 April, May & Oct; $31.50 June–Sept) for members $31 for non-members ($33/35.50)), private doubles $62/80/85 for members, $85/88/93 for non-members.

Vancouver Jericho Beach Hostel (HI) 1515 Discovery St off NW Marine Drive ⓣ604/224-3208 or 1-888/203-4852, ⓕ224-4852, ⓦwww.hihostels.ca. Canada's biggest Hostelling International youth hostel has a superb and safe position surrounded by lawns next to Jericho Beach south of the city. The 286-bed hostel – a former barracks – fills up quickly, occasionally leading to a three-day limit in summer. There are dorm beds and ten private rooms (sleep up to six), which go quickly, with reductions for members and free bunks occasionally offered in return for a couple of hours' work. Family rooms are available. Facilities include kitchen, licensed café (April–Oct), bike rental and storage, storage lockers, Internet access and an excellent cafeteria. There is no curfew, but a "quiet time" is encouraged between 11pm and 7am. Check-in 24 hours a day. Dorm beds cost $22 ($26 July & Aug) for members, $26 ($30) for non-members. Doubles are $63 ($76 July & Aug) for members, $71 ($84) for non-members.

▲ Jericho Beach Hostel

Vanier Hostel University of British Columbia (UBC) 5961 Student Union Blvd ⓣ604/822-1000, ⓕ822-1001, ⓦwww.conferences.ubc.ca. This hostel is on the UBC campus, which means it's a long way from Downtown (see p.86 for transport details) but close to the Museum of Anthropology and trails and sights such as Wreck Beach (see p.93). As substantial bonuses, you get clean, safe accommodation (bed linen included), TV lounge, laundry, an Internet kiosk in the lobby, affordable campus food outlets and pubs and access to the University's fitness facilities, tennis courts and indoor and outdoor pools. Open early May to late Aug only. No curfew. Additional discounts are available for HI and ISIC cardholders on the room rates that start at around $25 single, $50 double.

YWCA Hotel-Residence 733 Beatty St between West Georgia and Robson ⓣ604/895-5830 or 1-800/663-1424, ⓕ681-2550, ⓦwww.ywcahotel.com. Vancouver's excellent Y offers the best inexpensive accommodation in the city. It was purpose-built in 1995 in a handy east Downtown location close to the central library. The nearest SkyTrain station is Stadium, a 5min walk. Top-value rooms (especially for small groups) are spread over eleven floors with a choice of private, shared or hall bathrooms. There are no dorm beds. TVs come with most rooms, plus there are sports and cooking facilities, Internet access, lounges, a/c, laundry rooms as well as a cheap cafeteria and rooms with mini-kitchens. Open to men, women, couples and families. Check-in is 3pm, check-out by 11am. Rates for the various configurations of rooms come in two bands: A (June–Oct), B (rest of the year). Singles cost $68/61 in the two bands; doubles $82/70 with shared bathroom or $125/84 with private bathroom. Four-person rooms (two double beds) are also available from $142/94, plus $10 for each additional adult.

Campsites

In a city famed for its natural beauty and opportunities for outdoor activities, it's something of a disappointment – and a municipal failing – that not only are there no public or private campsites in or near the city centre, but also that among the handful of sites that do exist further out none could be described as particularly memorable. To pitch a tent or hook up an RV you'll have to head to North Vancouver or to the suburbs of Richmond and Burnaby, neither of which are places you'd choose to camp.

Burnaby Cariboo RV Park 8765 Cariboo Place, Burnaby ⓣ604/420-1722, ⓕ420-4782, ⓦwww.bcrvpark.com. This 237-pitch site about 16km east of the city centre has luxurious facilities (indoor pool, Jacuzzi, laundry, free showers and convenience store) and a separate tenting area away from the RVs (for which there are full hook-up facilities). Take the Gaglardi Way exit (#37) from Hwy 1, turn right at the traffic light, then immediately left. The next right is Cariboo Place. Open year-round. Tent sites $36.50, RV sites $31.50–55.

Capilano RV Park 295 Tomahawk Ave, North Vancouver ⓣ604/987-4722, ⓕ987-2015, ⓦwww.capilanorvpark.com. This is a pretty unattractive place – think car park rather than verdant pastures – but it is the city's most central site for trailers and tents, located beneath the north foot of the Lions Gate Bridge and a short walk from the Park Royal Shopping Centre: take the Capilano Rd South or Hwy 99 exit off the Lions Gate Bridge. There are full RV facilities and hook-ups, plus swimming pool, free showers, washrooms and laundry, ice and water. Reservations (with deposit) essential June to Aug. $30–45 per site.

Park Canada Recreational Vehicles Inn 4799 Hwy 17, Delta ⓣ604/943-5811 or 1-877/943-0685, ⓦwww.parkcanada.com. Convenient for the Tsawwassen ferry terminal to the southwest, this 145-pitch site has partial and three-way hook-ups for RVs and – despite the name – some separate tent sites. There are free showers, washrooms, laundry facilities, a heated pool and a grocery store, and, if this is your thing, the site's right next to a waterslide and golf course. Tent sites $27.50, RV sites $33.50.

9

Eating

Vancouver locals eat out more than the residents of any other city in Canada: once you've been here for a few hours, it's easy to see why. The number and variety of restaurants is intoxicating, as is the range of European, Asian and Pacific Rim cooking (see p.130 & *Eating out* colour section). Furthermore, the quality of the restaurants and the food they serve is generally exceptional, thanks to a demanding public and a plethora of superb natural ingredients. Most types of cuisine are available at prices that span the spectrum from budget to blowout, but costs are generally lower than in other major cities: if you want to eat well, you'll be spoilt for choice – and won't have to spend a fortune.

The city's immigration history makes this a melting pot of different ethnic cuisines. **Chinese**, **Italian** and **Japanese** have high profiles, along with **French**, **Greek** and other European imports. **Vietnamese** and **Thai** are more recent arrivals, and these often provide the best starting point – cafés and the inevitable fast-food chains aside – if you're on a tight budget.

For a city on the Pacific, specialist **seafood restaurants** are relatively thin on the ground, but those that exist are of high quality and often remarkably cheap. Seafood of some sort, however, crops up on most menus – salmon, a major fish in BC waters, is ubiquitous in all its forms and tastes entirely different from the mostly farmed variety available in Europe. **Vegetarians** are well served by one or two specialist places and will find an excellent choice of dishes in most "mainstream" restaurants.

Inexpensive options are provided by the countless **cafés** near the beaches, in parks, along Downtown streets and on Granville Island. Many sell light meals as well as coffee and snacks. **Little Italy**, the area around Commercial Drive (between Venables and Broadway), has always been good for cheap cafés and restaurants – though none so good as to merit a special journey – but as new waves of immigrants fill the area, Little Italy is increasingly dividing into "Little Vietnam", "Little Nicaragua" and so forth. Yaletown and the heavily residential **West End** – notably around Denman and Davie streets, Vancouver's "gay village" – also boast a selection of interesting cafés.

As far as **location** is concerned, restaurants are spread around the city but are naturally more densely packed **Downtown** and sparser in North and West Vancouver. Downtown is especially thick with top-drawer establishments and fast-food outlets. You'll eat well in several places in **South Vancouver**, but here the question is whether the blander, often suburban setting and the distance from where you're likely to be staying make the journey worthwhile. Places in **Gastown** are generally tourist-oriented, with some notable exceptions, in marked contrast to **Chinatown**'s bewildering array of genuine and reasonably priced options.

Farther afield, the former warehouse district of **Yaletown**, is a key eating and nightlife area. Good cafés and restaurants line 4th Avenue in **Kitsilano** and

Pacific Rim cuisine

Although many Vancouver restaurants still specialize in cuisine from a single region, an increasing number across the ethnic divides are subscribing to the notion of **fusion cuisine** – variously described as "West Coast", "Canadian" or "Pacific Rim" – a (not always successful) cross-cultural approach to cooking that is trendy all over but particularly popular in a city with such a rich multi-ethnic mix. Italian is often the base cuisine – pastas, chicken dishes and so forth are common to a host of Vancouver restaurants – to which might be added ingredients, flavours or cooking techniques more commonly associated with Chinese and other Far Eastern cooking. Some of the wilder experiments of the late 1990s, however, have generally given way to cooking that is a little more restrained.

Note that the term *Canadian cuisine* does not always indicate fusion cuisine – in many parts of Canada it stands for pasta (again), steaks, chicken, salmon, burgers and the other safe North American staples. In Vancouver, however, it can also be applied to dishes that borrow from **aboriginal traditions**, such as alder-smoked salmon, venison, grilled oysters, clam fritters and other more exotic dishes.

neighbouring West Broadway, though these require something of a special effort if you're based in or around Downtown – try them for lunch, perhaps, if you're at the beach or visiting the nearby Vanier Park museum complex.

If you do go upmarket, don't feel inhibited by the need to dress up: Vancouver is a typically relaxed West Coast sort of city, and casual but neat will suffice in all but the stuffiest hotel or business-oriented restaurants.

If you're coming from Europe, note that the term *entrée* in North America refers not to a starter or appetizer but to the main course. **Lunch** is generally served from about noon to 1 or 2pm, while **dinner** is served from 6.30pm until 10 or 11pm, a little later in summer. **Smoking** in restaurants is prohibited – the bylaw is strictly enforced.

Cafés, chains and light meals

Vancouver takes its coffee seriously, even by North American standards. Indeed, actress and comedian Bette Midler remarked in one performance in the city that she had "never seen so much coffee in all my life". The global conglomerates are ubiquitous, but there's no need to patronize them – small, individual places abound.

High-quality and healthy "fast-food" options have also proliferated in the last couple of years, with high-quality **small chains** to the fore. *Cactus Club Café*, with around 15 outlets in and around the city, is highly recommended for its sexy dining rooms and good, grown-up West Coast food – chunky burgers, Portobello fajitas, perfect salads – as are the long-established *White Spot*, *Burgoo* and *Soupspoons* for soup, salads and other light meals. All offer good value and are ideal for families travelling with children.

Cafés come and go quickly, but on any stroll round **Granville Island** or **Yaletown** you'll be guaranteed to find good, inexpensive food and snacks – and, invariably, the chance to enjoy them outside in sunny weather. Note that cafés in the *Waves Coffee* and *Blenz* chains have **WiFi**.

If you want to supplement café options with picnic supplies, good sources of **take-away food** include branches of the *Capers Whole Foods Market* organic supermarket (see review below) and two excellent small bakery-café chains: *Cobs Breads* and *Terra Breads* (see p.132).

Bavaria 203 Carrall St, Gastown ⓣ604/687-4047. A simple, small and no-frills place with a couple of tables outside on Maple Tree Square almost in front of Gassy Jack's statue. Its inexpensive all-day breakfast is great value. Open Mon–Sat 7am–7pm, Sun hours vary.

Blake's 221 Carrall St, Gastown ⓣ604/899-3354. One of several relaxed places on this short Gastown stretch of Carrall St to drop by for a coffee, sandwich or snack and the chance to while away an hour writing a postcard or reading the newspaper. Open Mon–Sat 7am–8pm, Sun 8am–7pm.

Bojangles Café 785 Denman St at Robson St, West End ⓣ604/687-3622, ⓦwww.bojanglescafe.com. This West End institution is a little smarter than most cafés on a street full of small places to grab a coffee or snack. Lunches are well priced, with the "deluxe" sandwiches particularly good value. There's a small, sunny patio for outside eating and drinking. Open Mon–Fri 6.30am–9.30pm, Sat & Sun 6.30am–10pm. Also now on the waterfront en route for Stanley Park from Downtown at 1506 Coal Harbour Quay at Nicola St and in Yaletown at 1089-1097 Marinaside Crescent.

Boulangerie la Parisienne 1076 Mainland St, Yaletown ⓣ604/684-2499, ⓦwww.boulangerieparisienne.com. A café and bakery with a striking and very pretty all-blue interior that – true to its name – opens up French-style onto the pavement in summer. Open daily 7am–9pm.

Caffè Artigiano 763 Hornby St at Robson St, Downtown ⓣ604/696-9222, ⓦwww.caffeartigiano.com. Across from the Vancouver Art Gallery, this café serves the best coffee in town. You can also choose from a full crop of croissants and other pastries, plus grilled sandwiches and light pasta dishes – though quality here is not on the level of the coffee. There is an older, less cosy branch at 1101 West Pender St on the corner of Thurlow (Mon–Fri 6am–5pm, Sat 6.30am–4pm): other locations farther afield include 740 West Hastings St, 574 Granville St at Dunsmuir St, and 2154 West 41st St. The Hornby St branch is open Mon–Fri 6.30am–9.30pm, Sat 7am–9.30pm & Sun 7am–8pm.

Capers Whole Food Markets 1675 Robson St, Downtown ⓣ604/687-5288, ⓦwww.wholefoodsmarket.com/capers. Capers is a three-branch local chain (but part of the larger multinational Whole Food chain) of pristine supermarkets selling natural and organic foods, many of which can be bought as sandwiches and snacks in the on-site cafés. The Robson St branch is open Mon–Sat 8am–10pm and Sun 8am–9pm. There are also branches at 2285 West 4th Ave (daily 8am–10pm; ⓣ604/739-6676) and 3277 Cambie St (daily 8am–10pm, ⓣ604/909-2988).

Delaney's 1105 Denman St at Nelson St, West End ⓣ604/662-3344. A landmark café on this busy street, with a buzzy atmosphere and coffees, cakes and light meals to eat in or take away. Open daily 6.30am–11pm.

Epicurean 1898 West 1st Ave at the corner of Cypress Ave, Kitsilano ⓣ604/731-5370, ⓦwww.epicureancaffe.com. A wonderful Italian deli in Kits that has a few tables inside (and outside in good weather). Have a coffee any time, along with pastries, or a savoury snack, panini or light meal from the deli counter. Eat in or take away. Success downstairs has spawned a restaurant and lounge upstairs (Tues–Sun 5.30–11pm) with similarly successful Italian food. Deli and café open daily 8am–11pm.

Flying Wedge 3499 Cambie St, Downtown ⓣ604/874-8284, ⓦwww.flyingwedge.com. If you want good, cheap pizza, this is the place: thin-crust pizza by the slice (but no alcohol) and takeaway at various outlets, including the Waterfront Centre, 27–200 Burrard St, Downtown ⓣ604/681-1122; Library Square, 207–345 Robson, Downtown ⓣ604/698-7078 (lunch only); the Royal Centre, 244–1055 West Georgia St, Downtown ⓣ604/681-1233; 1059 Denman St, West End ⓣ604/689-9700; and 1937 Cornwall Ave, Kitsilano ⓣ604/732-8840. Open daily 10.30am–10.30pm.

Gallery Café 750 Hornby St (Vancouver Art Gallery), Downtown ⓣ604/688-2233. Relaxed, stylish and pleasantly arty place at the heart of Downtown for coffee, good lunches and healthy, high-quality snack food and light meals (especially good desserts); also has a popular summer patio. Open Mon–Wed & Fri–Sat 9am–5.30pm, Thurs 9am–9pm, Sun 10am–5pm.

Hamburger Mary's 1202 Davie St and Bute St, West End ⓣ604/687-1293, ⓦwww.hamburgermarys.ca. These may well be the best burgers in the city (though by no means the cheapest), but there are plenty of other things on the menu. Lots of people end the evening for a snack at this former West End diner, which sets up outside tables when the weather is fine. Open Mon–Thurs 8am–3am, Fri & Sat 8am–4am, Sun 8am–2am.

Joe's Café 1150 Commercial Drive at Williams, East Vancouver ⓣ604/255-1046, ⓦwww.joescafebar.com. Way out east, but an absolutely authentic café if you are in this part of town, full of happily coexisting elderly locals, lesbian activists, newly arrived immigrants, artists, would-be intellectuals and other neighbourhood characters. Daily 7.30am–10pm or later.

La Luna Café 117 Water St, Gastown ⓣ604/687-5862. One of only a couple of places for coffee, muffins and snacks on Gastown's main street that has the character – helped by a warm and welcoming, yellow-painted interior – to raise it above the usual tourist-oriented cafés in this part of the city. Open Mon–Fri 7.30am–5pm (7pm in summer), Sat & Sun 10am–5pm.

Ovaltine Café 251 East Hastings St, Chinatown ⓣ604/685-7021. Beyond Main St and up the hill from The Only Café, which it resembles, this is a classic diner that's been around for over half a century. It's easily recognizable by the distinctive neon sign outside. Open Mon–Fri 7am–9.30pm, Sat–Sun 8.30am–9.30pm.

PHAT 1055 Mainland St at Nelson St, Yaletown ⓣ604/684-6239, ⓦwww.phatdeli.com. Jewish deli sandwiches, soups and all-day breakfasts, with a second Kits branch at 1859 West 4th Ave ⓣ604/737-7428. Stands for "Pretty Hot and Tasty" – though be warned that the food can come with a touch of attitude from staff. Open Mon–Fri 7am–5pm, Sat 8am–5pm, Sun 9am–4pm.

Prospect Point Café Stanley Park ⓣ604/669-2737, ⓦwww.prospectpoint.ca. Midway round the Stanley Park Seawall, with great views of the ocean, this café has a large walk- or bike-by clientele, so it can become busy, especially at weekends. But as a target for inexpensive refreshment in Stanley Park it's perfect. Daily 9am–8pm.

Sophie's Cosmic Café 2095 West 4th Ave at Arbutus St, South Vancouver ⓣ604/732-6810, ⓦwww.sophiescosmiccafe.com. This 1950s-style diner is a Kits institution, packed for weekend breakfast and weekday lunch (expect a wait unless you arrive early). It is renowned for its vast, spicy burgers, mussels, milkshakes, good vegetarian options and whopping breakfasts. Some may find its self-conscious kitsch a little too contrived. Mon–Thurs 8am–9pm, Fri–Sun 8am–9pm or later.

Soupspoons Express 555 West Hastings St at Carrall St, Gastown ⓣ604/689-9798, ⓦwww.soupspoons.com. The Joinville family came to Vancouver from Paris and brought a slew of great soup recipes with them, now sold at a small chain of deli-style soup bars. About ten daily specials (all made on the premises) are available, along with pastries and panini, focaccia and croque monsieurs. Daily 8am–6pm.

Stanley Park Pavilion 610 Pipeline Rd near the Malkin Bowl, Stanley Park ⓣ604/602-3088, ⓦwww.stanleyparkpavilion.com. A predictable but perfectly pleasant park café in a period building from 1911; the self-service outlet here serves cakes, teas, coffees, burgers, salads and other light meals and snacks. It's much closer to the park entrance than the *Prospect Point Café* (see above) and so a good place for a break if you're not intending to walk too far. Open daily 10am–6pm.

Terra Breads Granville Island Public Market ⓣ604/685-3102, ⓦwww.terrabreads.com. Tremendous rustic, grainy and fresh-baked breads are the speciality here, with black olive, rosemary, focaccia, cheese, onion, rye, raisin, grape, pine nut and other variations available. You can also pick up the odd accompaniment and sandwich to combine with a drink from elsewhere. Open daily 9am–7pm. There are other branches, including one in Kitsilano at 2380 West 4th Ave at Balsam St (Mon–Fri 7am–7pm, Sat & Sun 7am–6.30pm), plus the latest outlet at 53 West 5th Ave at Ontario St (Mon–Fri 7am–6pm, Sat 8am–5pm).

Urban Rush 1040 Denman St at Comox, West End ⓣ604/685-2996. Locals love to moan about the slow service, but the food in this deli-café is among the best – and best-looking – in the city. Great for people-watching. Open daily 7am–10pm (later in summer).

Wicked Café 861 Hornby St at Smithe St, Downtown ⓣ604/569-5480, ⓦwww.wickedcafe.ca. Fairtrade coffee and good-value snacks at the heart of Downtown by the Wedgewood Hotel, or in a second outlet in tiny premises a couple of blocks south of Granville Island at 1399 West 4th Ave ⓣ604/733-9425. Both open daily 7am–7pm.

Restaurants

In the listings that follow, restaurants are grouped by **cuisine**. Most are located in central Downtown, but there are also several well-defined dining and nightlife areas outside the Downtown core. In the West End, you'll find plenty to choose from on Denman and Davie streets, while Yaletown is full of often smart and style-conscious places. In more laid-back Kitsilano, the traffic from the beach has given rise to a plethora of casual dining options – pasta places, cafés and pubs – on the stretch of Yew Street between Cornwall and Second avenues. Commercial Drive way out east is an emerging area, but this is a long way to go for what is likely to be more a bohemian than a purely gastronomic experience. To find the exact location of a restaurant listed, note which part of town it's in (neighbourhoods are included with each street address) and then consult the relevant chapter map.

As for **price**, we've given an indication of what you can expect to pay for a main course (often called an *entrée* in Canada), which means anything from a plate of pasta or a pizza to a steak, salad or fish dish. Bear in mind that portions are often pretty generous, so if you can limit yourself to a main course, salad and glass of wine, you can happily eat in places that might normally be beyond your budget. Bear in mind, too, that you'll often enjoy the same dishes at lunch as at dinner for considerably less money.

Wine will push prices up a little, being generally rather overpriced, especially if you opt for French or New World wines. Reckon on at least $25 for a bottle of wine in a restaurant, much more if you want something reasonably good or interesting. See the colour insert for more wine.

Alcohol is expensive in Canada – don't be surprised if the drink portion of your bill comes to more than the cost of the food.

Taxes may be included in the price, but **service** rarely is, and you should definitely **tip** at least fifteen percent – unless the meal and service dictate otherwise.

Chinese

Floata Seafood Restaurant 400–180 Keefer St, Chinatown ⓣ604/602-0368, ⓦwww.floata.com. You can eat dim sum (see box, p.135) in many Vancouver Chinese restaurants, but one of the most popular places to indulge is Floata, currently Canada's largest Chinese restaurant. It has over 1000 covers, but the vast area is divided into smaller "rooms" with moveable partitions, helping create a slightly more intimate feel. Despite its size – the main dining area is nearly the length of a city block – the restaurant is not easy to find: it's on the third floor of a mall close to the Dr Sun Yat-Sen Garden. Dim sum is popular – and cheap – at lunch; choose from the dumpling-laden carts being wheeled around by countless waitresses and expect to pay only $4 to $7.50 per dish. In the evening, menu items become more adventurous and expensive: set

Brunch

While **brunch** is not the institution in Vancouver it is in some North American cities, Sundays here are as potentially lazy as elsewhere, and the combination of fine settings – views of mountains, park and forest – and relaxed places to eat makes the late-morning weekend meal an attractive proposition. Granville Island is an obvious location – but is busy at weekends, as are restaurants and cafés in Kits and Stanley Park. To be sure of a table, book ahead.

Recommended places that serve and specialize in brunch include the *Alibi Room* (see p.151), *Blue Water Café* (see p.143), *Bridges* (see p.145), *Cardero's* (see p.151), *Milestones* (see p.146), *Naam* (see p.143), *Seasons in the Park* (see p.147) and *Sophie's Cosmic Café* (see opposite).

menus can be a good option here. Open daily 7.30am–10pm.

Hon's Wun-Tun House 108–268 Keefer St at Gore St, Chinatown ⓣ604/688-0871, ⓦwww.hons.ca. This canteen-like Cantonese spot started life more than twenty years ago as an inexpensive, basic and popular place known for its "pot stickers" (fried meat-filled dumplings), home-made noodles (go for those with shrimp, meat or dumplings or the spicy oyster, ginger and green onion) and ninety-odd soups (including fish ball and pig's feet). Success spawned other branches and a slight smartening-up when the original place moved from Main Street, but the queues, good food, long menus (over 300 items) and low prices (only around $6–12 for a main course) remain unchanged. It's invariably packed and hectic, but the service is efficient. Dim sum is available, and there's a separate vegetarian menu. Also at 1339 Robson St and three other outlets. Open Mon–Thurs & Sun 11am–11pm, Fri & Sat 11am–midnight.

Imperial Chinese Seafood Restaurant 355 Burrard St, Downtown ⓣ604/688-8191, ⓦwww.imperialrest.com. A grand and opulent spot with seats for 300 in the old Marine Building that serves fine, but pricey, Cantonese food (good dim sum, fresh egg noodles, delicious lobster in black bean sauce, pan-fried black cod and more) and looks nothing like the standard Chinese restaurant: the long dining room has white walls, smart royal-blue carpet and crisp white table linen; windows run down one side, offering good city views. Open Mon–Fri 11am–10.30pm, Sat & Sun 10.30am–10.30pm.

Kirin Mandarin 1166 Alberni St near Bute, Downtown ⓣ604/682-8833, ⓦwww.kirinrestaurants.com. This was among the first of the city's smart Chinese restaurants when it opened in 1987, with a big business clientele and elegant, postmodern decor – green pastel walls, pink table linen and lots of black lacquer – that put it a world away from the more traditional and basic canteens of old-fashioned Chinatown. The service is excellent, and the superior food covers several Chinese regions, including Cantonese (good scallops in black-bean sauce) and Szechuan (try the hot chilli fish). Prices are high (mains $15 and up), but you're repaid with good food and great views of the mountains. Open daily 11am–2.30pm, 5–10.30pm.

Pink Pearl 1132 East Hastings St near Glen Drive, Chinatown ⓣ604/253-4316, ⓦwww.pinkpearl.com. This Vancouver institution (in business over a quarter of a century) is a big, fun, bustling and old-fashioned place with an unpretentious and highly authentic feel – with *Sun Sui Wah* (see below), it's the best Chinese food in the city – but it's in a dingy part of town and ten blocks east of the main part of Chinatown. Expect to rub shoulders with Chinese families (and big wedding parties at weekends) and to eat your meal amidst considerable activity: service is brisk, unsmiling yet efficient. Main courses range from about $12 to $25, but dim sum will cost just $3 to $7 a shot. The food has a Cantonese slant, strong on seafood and great for dim sum (served daily): good bets are clams in black-bean sauce, spicy prawns, and other fish and seafood options (crab, shrimp, scallops, oysters, rock cod and more) scooped from big glass tanks near the entrance. Open Mon–Thurs, Sun 9am–10pm, Fri–Sat 9am–11pm.

Shanghai Chinese Bistro 1124 Alberni St, Downtown ⓣ604/683-8222. A modern-looking but less ostentatious and more reasonably priced alternative to the *Imperial* if you want to eat Chinese Downtown. The handmade noodles are a must – there's also a daily noodle-making demonstration for the curious. Dim sum is available, but fresh seafood is the speciality, with main courses at around $20. Open Sun–Thurs 11.30am–11pm, Fri–Sat 11.30am–midnight.

Sun Sui Wah 3888 Main St, East Vancouver ⓣ604/872-8822, ⓦwww.sunsuiwah.com. This elegant and sophisticated restaurant has won deserved rave reviews, especially for its seafood, with numerous regular dishes and special catches of the day (pick from the tank or order from the menu if you are squeamish). Main dishes start at around $12, but prices for the more exotic offerings can be three or four times this figure. Dim sum is available (also with a seafood emphasis), as are meat and vegetarian options, but when all's said and done, this place is about seafood. There's a more outlying branch in the suburb of Richmond at 102 Alderbridge Place, 4940 No. 3 Road (ⓣ604/273-8208). Open daily for dim sum 10am–3pm and dinner 5–10.30pm.

Dim sum

Dim sum means "small heart" or "to touch the heart" and is a type of daytime Chinese snack, similar in many ways to brunch in the West. It originated in Canton, where most dishes are lightly cooked – steaming being the favoured method – and subtly flavoured. While there are more than 2000 dim sum dishes, most Vancouver restaurants offer a selection of around 150, including the ever-popular shrimp and pork dumplings, turnip cake, deep-fried sesame balls and steamed pork buns.

Jasmine tea or the strong black Chinese *bo lay* is usually brought to your table once you sit down. This is followed by a succession of carts piled with small plates and bamboo baskets of hot food, sometimes with savoury dishes on top, sweet below. Simply point to the dish you want; the waiter or waitress will mark your choices each time on a bill that stays at your table until the end of the meal.

Dim sum is served in most Chinese restaurants daily from about 10am to 2pm; lunch and Sundays are the busiest times. Be prepared for large crowds and big, gaudily decorated restaurants, featuring red and gold in most decorative schemes – colours chosen for their lucky associations. Best of all, dim sum is a cheap way of eating – you shouldn't spend more than about $10.

Wild Rice 117 West Pender St, Downtown ⓣ604/642-2882, ⓦwww.wildricevancouver.com. A western take on Chinese food from a former chef at Bin 941 (see p.142), with dishes and ingredients from across China refined and reworked for Canadian consumption. Go for the bite-size tasters or platters to share and don't worry too much about cost – this is generally high-quality food at a reasonable price. Main dishes (from around $15 upwards) might include wild boar with jasmine rice and plantain, rabbit wontons, winter melon salad or crispy fried duck, while desserts include warm rice pudding with chocolate and ginger. There is a good, short wine list and a choice of teas and martinis. Open Sun–Thurs 5pm–midnight, Fri 5.30pm–midnight or later, Sat 5pm–1am.

French and Belgian

Bistro Pastis 2153 West 4th Ave at Arbutus, Kitsilano ⓣ604/731-5020, ⓦwww.bistropastis.com. A romantic bistro with a genuinely Parisian look and feel. Sit at the bar for drinks and then take a table alongside or in the cosy alcove to the rear. The menu is short and to the point, with typical and well-cooked bistro staples – onion soup, *moules marinières*, coq au vin, les Saint Jacques (scallops), a quiche of the day and steak tartare. Only the highish prices lack the bistro ring of authenticity: mains are around $25, for example, but you can often have a starter size for $12 or so. The wine list is long, with many wines by the glass. Open Tues–Fri 11.30am–2pm, Sat–Sun 11am–2pm; also Tues–Sun 5.30–10.30pm.

Chambar 562 Beatty St near Dunsmuir, Downtown ⓣ604/879-7119, ⓦwww.chambar.com. Although this Belgian restaurant is a little lost, stranded east of the Downtown core, its husband-and-wife team, Nico and Karri Scheurman, quickly established *Chambar*'s high reputation after its opening in 2004. The Moroccan-tinged menu is brief, but the dishes are all generally reliable and come arranged as *petits plats*, or smaller dishes (at $9–15), or more substantial *grosses pieces* ($18–25). The classic Belgian *moules frites* are around $20, but far more exotic food is always on offer – pork chops with cherry compote, for example, or braised lamb shanks with cinnamon. Puddings are delicious, and there are 25 varieties of Belgian beer to wash down the food. Open daily 6pm–midnight.

Cru 1459 West Broadway Seymour St at Granville St, South Vancouver ⓣ604/677-4111, ⓦwww.cru.ca. A small, fairly smart and highly regarded spot a few blocks south of Vanier Park and the museums. Chef Alana Peckham is known for his tapas-like small plates ($9–16), which allow you to sample plenty of the sophisticated French regional cooking. The popular fixed-price menu ($42) is a good way to make the most of what the kitchen has to offer. Lots of good wines by the glass, too. Open Mon–Fri 11.30am–2pm, Sat & Sun 11.30am–2pm & 5.30–10.30pm or later.

Cioppino's Mediterranean Grill & Enoteca 1133 Hamilton St, Yaletown ⓣ604/688-7466, ⓦwww.cioppinosyaletown.com. It's hard to categorize this inviting restaurant – the name comes from San Francisco's cioppino, or fish stew, but some food is French-influenced, other Italian – and perhaps the best thing to do is sample a little of almost everything with the tasting menu. Suffice it to say, the warm cherrywood interior makes it an attractive choice if you are in this part of town. High rollers and visiting celebrities often show up here, but the atmosphere is relaxed enough to keep things informal. If the food seems too expensive (reckon $20 to $45 for main courses), make for the Cioppino wine bar next door for a drink instead. Open Mon–Fri noon–2.30pm & 5.30–11pm; Sat 5.30–11pm.

Elixir in the Opus Hotel, 350 Davie St near Richards, Yaletown ⓣ604/642-0577, ⓦwww.elixirvancouver.ca. A French brasserie may not be the type of restaurant you'd expect in a hotel as self-consciously funky as the *Opus*, but true to style the designers have gone to town and the three dining spaces here are suitably off kilter: there's a kitschy velvet room with red banquettes and dark-wood panelling; a lighter garden room suited to breakfast; and a flanking dining area that has more of a conventional Left Bank bistro feel. All three are linked by a horseshoe-shaped bar and feature the same French menu, which is far better than the showy dining rooms might lead you to expect, with classics such as onion soup, steaks, hearty duck and lentils, plus adventurous salads; main courses cost from about $16 to $35, *petit plats* – mini versions of the main-course dishes, available until 12.30am – run $7 and up. Elixir tends to attract the beautiful people, so dress up if you want to fit in. Open Mon–Sat 6.30am–2am, Sun 6.30am–midnight.

Le Crocodile 100–909 Burrard St, entrance on Smithe St, Downtown ⓣ604/669-4298, ⓦwww.lecrocodilerestaurant.com. This plush, upmarket French-Alsace bistro has been in business since 1983 and rivals Bishop's (see p.145) for the title of the city's best restaurant. Best overall or not, it is certainly the city's best French restaurant, a whisker ahead of *Lumière* (see opposite), some of whose chefs trained under Michel Jacob, *Le Crocodile's* driving force. The punchy decor – bright yellow walls – conjures up a suitable Parisian feel, while the menu offers something for traditionalists and adventurers alike – anything from classic *steak tartare*, onion tarte, Dover sole and calf's liver to more outré dishes involving non-Gallic staples of the Pacific Rim. A memorable meal is guaranteed – but check your credit limit first: mains cost from around $20 to $40 or more. Open Mon–Sat 11.30am–2pm, 5.30–10pm.

Le Gavroche 1616 Alberni St near Bidwell, Downtown ⓣ604/685-3924, ⓦwww.legavroche.ca. *Le Crocodile* and *Lumière* may take the culinary plaudits, but this top French restaurant (with a West Coast twist) is not far behind. Founded in 1979, it's a formal but amiable place located in an old West End townhouse, and while the food is consistently excellent – with particularly fine sea bass with white beans or veal tenderloin with lobster sauce – it's the highly romantic setting that really sets this place apart. The dining room is wonderfully cosy thanks to dark-painted walls and a big open fireplace, grand mirrors and old paintings. Expect to pay from $25 for main courses à la carte, or go for three- or four-course daily set menus from $50. Open daily from 5.30pm.

The Hermitage 115–1025 Robson St near Thurlow, Downtown ⓣ604/689-3237, ⓦwww.thehermitagevancouver.com. Warm brick walls, a big fireplace, crisp linen, antique furnishing, French-speaking waiters and a courtyard setting give this central and very highly rated Downtown restaurant a cosy, almost European feel. The chef-patron here, Hervé Martin, once cooked for King Leopold of Belgium. Among the many dishes, the onion soup, when available, is unbeatable. If a simple soup sounds too plain, you can also go for classic French food such as confit de canard or chicken breasts with a tarragon cream sauce, well priced at between $15 and $20–30. Open Mon–Fri 11.30am–2.15pm & 5.30–10.30pm, Sat & Sun 5.30–10.30pm.

Lumière 2551 West Broadway near Trafalgar St, South Vancouver ⓣ604/739-8185, ⓦwww.lumiere.ca. This is in the first rank of Canadian restaurants (and part of the Daniel Boulud group), the original head chef Rob Feenie having garnered international awards aplenty over the past decade. Cooking here is "contemporary French", a bit lighter and with more Asian nuances than you might expect to find at its rivals (see opposite), but no less pricey. A good option is to take one of the two set-price tasting menus offered each evening; one vegetarian, the other meat, fish and fowl. Visitors based in Downtown will need to take a cab here: you'll also need to book, for the simple, tasteful dining room accommodates just fifty diners. Open Wed–Sun 5.30–11pm.

Pied-à-Terre 3369 Cambie St at 19th Ave, South Vancouver ⓣ604/873-3131, ⓦwww.pied-a-terre-bistro.ca. This is an excellent mid-range, informal French bistro, with just 34 covers, run by Andrey Durbach, also responsible for the equally impressive La Buca (see p.138). The three set lunch menus at $21 are great value, and in the evening, when dining à la carte, you can sample French classics such as home-made terrines ($8.50) and beef shortrib bourguignon ($23.50). Open Mon–Fri noon–2.30pm, 5–10.30pm, Sat 5–10.30pm, Sun 5–9.30pm.

Greek

Ouzeri 3189 West Broadway at Trutch St, South Vancouver ⓣ604/739-9378, ⓦwww.ouzeri.ca. A friendly and fairly priced restaurant on a part of the strip with several other good restaurants and cafés: not too far from the hostel or beach in Kitsilano. You'll find all the Greek standards here, but the vegetable moussaka is a standout, as are the chicken livers and the prawns with ouzo and mushrooms. Open Tues–Sat 11.30am–3.30pm & 4.30–11pm, Mon & Sun 4.30–10pm.

Stepho's 1124 Davie St between Thurlow and Bute, West End ⓣ604/683-2555. This central restaurant has been here forever, and its simple interior, fine food, big portions, low prices and efficient service have made it very popular – expect a queue, though the wait is usually no more than 15min even at busy times. The daily specials are always a good bet (go for the baby back ribs if they are available): on the regular menu, the avgolemono soup (a chicken broth with lemon and egg) is tasty, as are staples such as chicken, lamb or beef pitta (with fries and tzatziki garlic sauce) and meat brochettes (souvlaki) accompanied by potatoes, rice pilaf or Greek salad. It's great value, with main courses from about $5 to $10. Open daily 11am–11.30pm.

Indian and Southeast Asian

Akbar's Own 1905 West Broadway at Fir St, Kitsilano ⓣ604/736-8180. Not as fancy as Vij's, say (see below), but a good, no-nonsense Indian restaurant on a quiet stretch of Broadway. Traditional Mughlai and Kashmiri specialities include shrimp pakora ($8) delicately fried in chickpea flour, and chicken tikka butter marsala ($11). Open Mon–Fri 11.30am–2pm, Mon–Sat 5–10pm.

Banana Leaf 1096 Denman St near Pendrell, West End ⓣ604/683-3333, ⓦwww.bananaleaf-vancouver.com. *Banana Leaf's* Denman St location means it has a lot of competition from other restaurants, but none can challenge it on its unique Malaysian cuisine. The small dining room, all dark, tropical woods, sets the authentic tone. Food might include classics such as *gado gado* (salad with a spicy peanut sauce) and *mee goreng* (fried noodles with egg) as well as more inventive local dishes such as a mango and okra salad. For most of these dishes you'll pay between $7 and $15. Fried banana with ice cream – *pisang goreng* – is the must-have pudding. Open Mon–Thurs 11.30am–3pm & 5–10pm, Fri & Sat 11.30am–11pm. There are now more recent outlets on Broadway (820 West Broadway at Willow St) and in Kits (3005 West Broadway at Carnarvon St) in South Vancouver.

Chilli House Thai Bistro 1018 Beach Ave, West End ⓣ604/685-8989, ⓦwww.thaihouse.com. A peaceful and authentic atmosphere prevails at this restaurant, thanks in large part to the exemplary and charming service. The ocean views from the patio terrace are also a major plus. The curries are delicious, as are the stir-fries and *tom yum goong* (a spicy prawn and mushroom soup), but the house speciality is Thai barbecue (meats, fish, seafood – all marinated and grilled and served with tangy peanut sauce). Main courses from around $10. Open daily 11am–10.30pm.

Phnom-Penh 244 East Georgia St near Gore, Chinatown ⓣ604/682-5777. Excellent Vietnamese and Cambodian cuisine (the menu is divided between the two), with some Chinese dishes, is served in this friendly, family-oriented restaurant. The decor features subdued lighting, images of Angkor, the Cambodian capital, and Khmer dolls. Seafood is a strength, with a renowned spicy garlic crab, plus delicious garlic and pepper prawns (in season). Also try the *bank xeo*, a Vietnamese pancake filled with prawns and bean sprouts. The hot and sour soup and deep-fried garlic squid are other dishes that guarantee regular lunchtime queues. Most mains come in at between $5 and $10. Open daily 10am–10pm.

Pho Hoang 3610 Main St at 20th Ave, Chinatown ⓣ604/874-0810; 238 East Georgia St, Chinatown ⓣ604/682-5666. The Pho Hoang on Main St was the first and is still perhaps the friendliest of the many Vietnamese *pho* (beef soup) restaurants now springing up all over the city. Choose from thirty soup varieties with herbs, chillis and lime at plate-side as added seasoning. Open for breakfast, lunch and dinner. The more recent Chinatown branch is right by Phnom-Penh (see above). Mains cost from around $8.

Sala Thai 102-888 Burrard St at Smithe St, Downtown ⓣ604/683-7999, ⓦwww.salathai.ca. Visiting celebrities and even members of the Thai royal family have patronised the elegant Downtown branch of *Sala Thai*, drawn by the best and most authentic Thai food in town. Stars notwithstanding, it is excellent value, especially at lunch or if you go for the daily specials. Standout dishes include *som tum* salad (green papaya, chillies and lime) at $8.99 and *gaeng pa-nang* (sautéed tiger prawns, scallops, coconut, kaffir lime leaves and a hot red curry) at $9.99. Open daily 11.30am–10pm. Food is the same at the more homely outlet at 3364 Cambie St at 18th Ave in South Vancouver (same hours except Sat & Sun, dinner only 5–10pm).

Simply Thai 1211 Hamilton St at Davie, Yaletown ⓣ604/642-0123, ⓦwww.simplythairestaurant.com. This plain, modern but inviting Yaletown restaurant is packed at lunch and dinner, thanks to the keen prices (dishes from around $9 to $25) as well as the good and very authentic food – the chefs are all from Bangkok. Open Mon–Fri 11.30am–3pm & 5–11pm, Sat 5–11pm.

Urban Thai Bistro 1119 Hamilton St, Yaletown ⓣ604/408-7788, ⓦwww.thaihouse.com. A few steps from *Simply Thai*, *Thai Urban Bistro* also offers good, basic Thai food at low prices in a simple setting – but it's likely to be less crowded. Mains cost from about $8. Open daily 11am–10.30pm.

Vij's 1480 West 11th Ave at Granville St, South Vancouver ⓣ604/736-6664, ⓦwww.vijs.ca. *Vij's* East Indian cooking has deservedly won just about every award going in Vancouver for Best Ethnic Cuisine. During his visit to Vancouver, the UK celebrity chef Jamie Oliver said the meal he ate here was the best he'd had in Canada. You can't make reservations – you simply line up with other hopefuls and enjoy the free tea and poppadoms while you wait. The menus change roughly monthly but rarely let go of old faithfuls such as curried-vegetable rice pilaf with cilantro cream sauce and Indian lentils with naan and yoghurt-mint sauce. The vegetarian options are excellent, and prices moderate – mains cost between about $15 and $25. The restaurant is open for dinner only, but next door, at no. 1488, the co-owned *Rangoli* (ⓣ604/736-5711, ⓦwww.vijsrangoli.com; daily 11am–8pm), a simple, stripped-down place with a few tables, offers lunch and takeaway versions of the same dishes from about $7. To get here from Downtown, take buses #8, #10 or #98. Open daily 5.30–10pm.

Italian

Borgo Antico 'Al Porto' 321 Water St, Gastown ⓣ604/683-8376, ⓦwww.alporto.ca. Gastown needs more restaurants like this: good Italian food, fair mid-range prices, especially at lunch (pastas and piazzas at $12, soups and salads around $6.50, mains $16–20), and a delightful and characterful dining room in a restored warehouse, with stone walls and wooden beams, and a bold, but warm colour scheme. Open Mon–Fri 11.30am–10.30pm, Sat & Sun 5.30–10.30pm.

La Buca 1906 4025 Macdonald St at West 24th Ave, South Vancouver ⓣ604/730-6988, ⓦwww.labuca.ca. It's a fair way to come from Downtown, but plenty of city foodies do, so if you're in Kits it's well worth booking to be sure of a table at this small neighbourhood Italian, currently one of the best informal *trattorias* in the city. Menus are seasonal – you might eat pea and mint *agnolotti* in summer, a rich *osso bucco* in winter. Year-round, be sure to try the *panna cotta* for pudding. Starters are $12, primi $13–19 and mains $27.50. Open Sun–Thurs 5–9.30pm, Fri & Sat 5–10pm. A newer, more central offshoot, *L'Altro Buca*, has opened in the West End at 1906 Haro St ⓣ604/688-6912.

Cibo Trattoria 900 Seymour St at Smithe St, Downtown ⓣ604/602-9570, ⓦwww.cibotrattoria.com. Cibo is attached to the modish Moda hotel (see p.118), formerly the dowdy *Dufferin*, and the rather stark, contemporary dining room is all of a part with the hotel's trendy, boutique-style makeover. The food, though, is not at all showy, but proper Italian rural cooking, thanks to the guiding hand early on of British chef, Neil Taylor, formerly of London's excellent *River Café*. Dishes might include classics such as calves' liver with *pancetta* and beef carpaccio with watercress. Pasta courses cost from $11–15, mains from $18. Open from 5pm Mon–Sat.

CinCin 1154 Robson St (upstairs) near Thurlow, Downtown ⓣ604/688-7338, ⓦwww.cincin.net. An excellent Downtown option with a stylish, buzzy setting of ochre-coloured walls, low lighting, long bar, open kitchen, lots of greenery and faux Renaissance statues. Plenty of fashion, politics, arts and media luminaries frequent the place, but it's never precious or showy. The refined Italian food merits the highish prices and includes top-grade home-made pastas, pizzas and desserts. Some of the best dishes, notably chicken and game, are cooked over the alderwood-fired open grill. Expect to pay from $18 for main courses. Service is first rate, and the restaurant also boasts an outstanding (if rather expensive) wine list, with plenty of wines by the glass. In summer, try to book an outside table on the terrace. Open daily from 5pm.

Il Giardino di Umberto 1382 Hornby St near Pacific Blvd, Downtown ⓣ604/669-2422, ⓦwww.umberto.com. Decent food with a pasta and game bias is served in this Vancouver institution, opened in 1973 by Umberto Menghi, who went on to own, at one point, 17 restaurants. Diners tend to be trendy and casually smart thirty-somethings, and the atmosphere in the villa-like dining room on the fringes of Yaletown is often animated, despite the muted Mediterranean-style surroundings (think burnt sienna-coloured walls, wooden beams). Some of the food is far more exotic than you'd ever find in Italy (reindeer loin, stuffed pheasant breast, ostrich in wild berry sauce). Prices, too, are higher than you'd find for this food in the home country – main courses are from around $15 to $35 and over. Weekend reservations are essential – this is something of a place to "be seen" – especially if you want to dine on the nice vine-trailed terrace. Open Mon–Fri 11.30am–3pm & 6–11.30pm, Sat 6–11.30pm.

Incendio 103 Columbia St near Alexander, Gastown ⓣ604/688-8694, ⓦwww.incendio.ca. This vividly painted pizzeria is in a heritage building decorated with funky local art just a block east of Maple Tree Square, so its location is not as downbeat or as far off the beaten track as some places closer to Chinatown. At the same time, it's hidden just enough to escape the attention of the crowds rampaging through central Gastown. It features excellent wood-fired thin-crust pizzas (over 20 varieties), calzone, good salads and a range of well-made and inventive pastas such as fettuccine with capers and a tomato and lime-butter sauce. Pizzas and main courses start at around $10. A second branch has opened in Kits at 2118 Burrard St (ⓣ604/736-2220). Gastown location open Mon–Thurs 10am–3pm & 5–10pm, Fri 10am–3pm & 5–11pm, Sat 5–11pm, Sun 4.30–10pm.

La Quercia 3689 West 4th Ave, Kitsilano ⓣ604/676-1007, ⓦwww.laquercia.ca. Made a splash when it opened in 2008, thanks to its almost faultless Northern Italian food: risottos, in particular, are superb, but the pastas are also first-rate. Starters are perhaps even better – try the beef with rocket, pine nuts and Parmesan. The only problem is size – there are just 30 covers, so be sure to book. Starters come in at $11, primi (pastas and so forth) from $12 to $17, and mains $23. Open Tues–Sun 5–10pm.

Saveur 850 Thurlow St at Smithe, Downtown ⓣ604/688-1633, ⓦwww.saveurrestaurant.com. A nicely restrained dining room, just off Robson St, that's not as formal as the austere red-brick facade may suggest. In the past the space housed a good Italian restaurant (Piccolo Mondo), and although the new chef-owners, husband and wife Stephane and Natalie Mayer, have brought a far stronger French flavour to the food, there are still plenty of Italian-influenced dishes. Starters might include a light salad such as roasted pepper, mozzarella, sugar snap peas, fennel and pine nuts, while mains (all between $14 and $19) include the likes of spaghettini with smoked black cod, capers and a cream dill sauce. The clientele are expense-account types at lunch and smooching couples in the evenings taking advantage of the elegant, quiet and low-lit romantic setting. Open Mon–Fri 11.30am–2pm & 6–10pm, Sat 6–10pm.

The Old Spaghetti Factory 55 Water St, Gastown ⓣ604/684-1288, ⓦwww.oldspaghettifactory.ca. Part of a small Canadian chain since 1970 and hardly *alta cucina*, but a reliable standby if you're in Gastown and better than the tourist trap it appears from the outside, with its spacious 1920s-style Tiffany interior and a good range of pastas, chicken and other meat and fish dishes. It's also a very good place to go with children, as prices are low, there's plenty of room, the atmosphere is informal and the simple Italian food is likely to appeal. Best of all, there's a selection of half-size and half-price dishes for kids. Open Mon–Thurs 11am–10pm, Fri & Sat 11am–11pm, Sun 11am–9pm.

La Terrazza 1088 Cambie St at Nelson St, Yaletown ⓣ604/899-4449, ⓦwww.laterrazza.ca. Many in Vancouver think *La Terrazza's* home-made pasta is the best in town, but then it should be at around $20 a serving. Mains, if anything, are even better, but again, they come at a price: a dish like roasted rack of lamb with mustard and toasted couscous, for example, costs $38, though there are cheaper options. A long wine list, and the fine terrace for al fresco dining that gives the restaurant its name, may help take your mind off the prices. Open daily from 5pm.

Trattoria Italian Kitchen 1850 West 4th Ave at Burrard St, Kitsilano ⓣ604/732-1441, ⓦwww.trattoriakitchen.ca. A big hit in Kits since it opened in 2008, thanks to a striking and buzzy contemporary interior, casual atmosphere, and prices that rarely go above the $15 mark for individual dishes. Food, too, of course, is a draw, and here things are kept simple, with decent, well-prepared basics such as penne arrabiata, pizzas and bruschetta. Open Mon–Fri 11.30am to midnight, Sat & Sun 10.30am to midnight.

Voya at the Loden 1177 Melville St at ⓣ604/639-8692, ⓦwww.voya-restaurant.com. The sumptuous 80-seat dining room at *Voya*, with its chandeliers, deep booths and backlit bar, perfectly matches the luxurious boutique hotel in which it is situated. Dress up if you're coming here, and be prepared to pay around $30 for main courses. At the same time, also be prepared for what is currently some of the best food in the city, with Italian influences informing dishes, but with plenty of sophisticated French and Asian touches. Open Sun–Thurs 5pm–midnight, Fri & Sat 5pm–2am.

Japanese and Korean

Ezogiku Noodle Café 1329 Robson St at Jervis, Downtown ⓣ604/685-8608. This 70-seat Japanese ramen noodle house (with sister outlets in Tokyo and Honolulu) is a perfect place for quick, good food Downtown. The queues may look off-putting, but the turn over's speedy. Cash only and no alcohol. Mains from $6. Also at 270 Robson St. Open daily 11am–9.45pm; 270 Robson, same hours except closed Sun.

Gyoza King 1508 Robson St near Nicola, Downtown ⓣ604/669-8278. Fight through groups of homesick Japanese students and visitors to enjoy the great comfort food (there is very little sushi here), casual atmosphere and funky, dark-walled interior of this excellent-value Downtown spot. Sit at the bar, the low front table or the higher Western-style tables and choose, tapas-style, from more than 20 types of gyoza – succulent fried dumplings with a variety of fillings (the vegetable and spinach are great) with a soy dipping sauce. Or go for noodle and robust *o-den* soups, good-value specials or *katsu-don* (breaded pork chop with rice), chased down with one of many choices of beer. If you can't follow what is going on, or understand the menu, ask the waiters – they are helpful and courteous. Main courses cost from $8 to $18. Open Mon–Thurs 5.30pm–1am, Fri 5.30pm–1.30am, Sat 6pm–1.30am, Sun 6–11.30pm.

Hapa Izakaya 1479 Robson St near Broughton, Downtown ⓣ604/689-4272, ⓦwww.hapaizakaya.com. The archetypal, and most popular *izakaya* restaurant in Vancouver (see box opposite). Small, individual dishes and low prices are the lure, along with a boisterous, busy and entertaining atmosphere. There are sushi-like raw fish options (fresh tuna with chopped spring onions and garlic bread, for example), as well as tasty hot pots and other meat dishes. For sheer drama, try the seared mackerel, where the searing is done at your table with a blowtorch. Mains cost from about $8 to $12, and the long hours mean you can eat

Izakaya

When it comes to Japanese food, sushi's crown is being challenged, at least in Vancouver, where links across the Pacific ensure the rapid take-up of most culinary trends. **Izakaya** is the latest thing – the word means "eat-drink place" and here it refers to an informal and inexpensive establishment serving a variety of small Japanese dishes (and sometimes Korean and Chinese ones as well), rather in the manner of sushi, tapas or dim sum. The food may be traditional or may include Western-influenced inventions such as asparagus wrapped in bacon or deep-fried chicken. Izakaya restaurants are usually small, diner-type places, with open kitchens and beer and sake the main liquid accompaniments to the food. The other defining quality is noise. The entire staff may greet anyone walking over the threshold with a bellowed *irashimase*, or "welcome". Waiters will call out orders, chefs will acknowledge them and the maitre d' will keep all and sundry informed of any number of details – from what's on the menu to the size of the queue outside. Izakayas started life as places for students to eat and drink, so prices are always keen (main courses shouldn't cost more than $8). Few accept reservations, though service and turnover are brisk and accommodating. *Hapa Izakaya* on Robson Street (see opposite) is one of the most popular, but also check out *Guu* (838 Thurlow St and other locations) and the Korean *E-Hwa* (1578 Robson St at Cardero St).

and drink (sake, Martinis, wine) late. Open Sun–Thurs 5.30pm–midnight, Fri & Sat 5.30pm–1am.

Kingyo 871 Denman St at Haro St, West End ⓣ604/608-1677, ⓦwww.kingyo-izakaya.com. A fun, friendly and briskly efficient bar-restaurant, with genuine Japanese look and feel – the stylish dining room is all stone walls and lacquered wood – with a lively-to-a-fault atmosphere and a wide menu of small tasting plates from $6 (or three types of sashimi for $15). Daily 5.30pm to midnight.

Ichibankan 770 Thurlow St at Robson, Downtown ⓣ604/682-6262. You can't argue with the credentials of a place that's been turning out no-nonsense sushi (plus tempura and teriyaki) for over twenty years – and at very decent prices (less than $15 for mains). The basement dining room, decked out in striking red and black, is handy for Robson St shoppers and stollers – you can either eat inside at a table or the sushi bar or buy food to take out. Open Mon–Thurs 11am–10.30pm, Fri & Sat 11am–11pm, Sun 11.30am–10pm.

Jang Mo Jib 1719 Robson St at Bidwell St, Downtown ⓣ604/642-0712. Great Korean comfort food in simple surroundings at keen prices (from $5), including pan-fried gook mahn doo (dumplings by any other name), japchae (sweet-potato noodles with sesame, Shiitake mushrooms, spinach and thinly sliced beef). Open Mon–Fri 10am–2pm, Sat 8am–5pm, Sun 8am–2pm.

Miku 1055 West Hastings St at Thurlow St ⓣ604/568-3900, ⓦwww.mikurestaurant.com. Vancouver is always quick to pick up Japanese dining trends, and sleek Miku was the first place in the city to serve Aburi sushi – flame-seared fish served as sashimi or nigiri-style with rice and adventurous sauces and condiments. Yellowtail tuna is a winner here, marinated in soy and sprinkled with spring onion and sea salt. Prices are middling: roll and oshi sushi costs around $12–15. Open Mon–Fri 11.30am–2.30pm & 5–10pm, Sat & Sun 5–10pm (weekday opening June–Sept 11.30am–10pm, Sat & Sun noon to 10pm).

Tojo's 202–777 West Broadway at Willow St, South Vancouver ⓣ604/872-8050, ⓦwww.tojos.com. Some of the best Japanese food in the city, which makes it a shame that the deceptively modest-looking sushi bar is some way from Downtown and situated on the first floor of an office building (though it has pretty views over False Creek, and in good weather you can dine outdoors). Worth the journey, however – anything on the menu involving tuna is superb, but you should sample some of the many more unusual items (such as shrimp dumplings with hot mustard sauce) or standards such as lobster claws, crab and herring roe. This is sushi close to perfection, but at prices that make sure you savour every mouthful – mains cost from about $15 to $30 and sushi from $8 to $30. Tasting menus (*omakase*) are available from $50 to $100 – you tell the waiter how much you're prepared to spend and then sit back to enjoy. You'll probably need to book at least a week in advance. Open Mon–Sat 5–10pm.

Spanish and Mexican

Bin 941 941 Davie St near Hornby, West End ⓣ604/683-1246, ⓦwww.bin941.com. It's not surprising that no one seems to have a bad word for *Bin 941*, or for its sister outlet, *Bin 942*, at 1521 West Broadway in South Vancouver (ⓣ734-9421). Both are tiny, on the slightly crazy side of funky, and packed long and late with people drawn by the up-tempo bars (the West Broadway location is marginally more subdued) and some of the city's best bite-size food. The menu's "tapatizers" include great hand-cut Yukon Gold potato fries, jumbo scallops, tiger-prawn tournedos, crab cakes, charred bok choy and many more. Puddings are less impressive. You'll pay around $10 to $15 for main dishes, prices having crept up with the place's continued popularity. Be warned, though: it's cramped and noisy (the owner is a former heavy-metal singer) – but fun. Open daily 5pm–2am.

Cobre 52 Powell St at Seymour St at Carrell St, Gastown ⓣ604/669-2396, ⓦwww.cobrerestaurant.com. Fabulous new opening in Gastown that achieves the authentic look, feel – and food – of a Latino tapas restaurant. The innovative menu dabbles in dishes from Cuba, Spain, Mexico and South America – you might eat Peruvian potato salad and pipian rojo ($13) or homegrown BC sablefish with mole Amarillo and calabaza verde ($15). Good Chilean and Argentine wines, though cocktails are the thing here, as this is a great place for drinks as well as food. Open daily from 5pm until late.

Lolita's South of the Border Cantina 1326 Davie St near Jervis, West End ⓣ604/696-9996, ⓦwww.lolitasrestaurant.com. One glance from outside at the boldly coloured dining room here gives you a pretty good idea of what to expect inside: a rather self-conscious but fun, funky and friendly neighbourhood café-restaurant that requires no dressing up, offers filling and unfancy Mexican (and other) food, and prices (from $8 for mains) that aren't going to hurt your pocket. That said, it's stranded in a pretty residential part of town, and you're unlikely to be passing by unless you're cruising the length of Davie St. If you are, though, it's a good place for a snack, light meal or invigorating late-night beer or tequila cocktail. Open Mon–Thurs 4.30pm–2am, Fri–Sun 3pm–2am.

Tapastree 1829 Robson St between Denman and Gilford, West End ⓣ604/606-4680, ⓦwww.tapastree.org. Vancouver's tapas craze of the 1990s has faded, but the best Spanish bars and restaurants (see also *La Bodega* on p.150) are still great places for inexpensive food and a relaxed early evening or wind-down late night. *Tapastree* has a vast choice of tapas from $7 to $15 whose inspiration goes way beyond Spain – look for pork ribs with Chinese barbecue sauce, Asian seafood salad, lamb with sun-dried tomatoes and Gorgonzola, and Japanese aubergine with pesto. Late in the evening patrons are likely to include chefs from other restaurants who have just got off their shift – so you know the quality's got to be good. Open Sun–Thurs 5.30–10.30pm, Fri & Sat 5.30–11.30pm.

Topanga Café 2904 West 4th Ave near Macdonald St, South Vancouver ⓣ604/733-3713, ⓦwww.topangacafe.com. A small but extremely popular Cal-Mex restaurant that's become a Vancouver institution. Prices are fair (mains from $10 to $12) and helpings large, a combination that has drawn hungry diners here for over twenty years and makes it a good place for people travelling with children. There are just forty seats, so arrive before 6pm or after 8pm to avoid the longest queues. Open Mon–Sat 11.30am–10pm.

Vegetarian

Jade Dynasty 137 East Pender St, Chinatown ⓣ604/683-8816. A Chinatown staple formerly known as the Buddhist Vegetarian Restaurant. The name may have changed, but the menu (and the rather dowdy décor) hasn't – it's crammed with plenty of inexpensive items (mains from around $7), set meals and a broad choice of dishes, including all-day dim sum. Open Mon 9am–4pm, Tues–Sun 9am–9pm.

The Naam 2724 West 4th Ave near Stephens St, South Vancouver ⓣ604/738-7151, ⓦwww.thenaam.com. Founded in 1968, this is the oldest and most popular health-food and vegetarian restaurant in the city. The ambience is comfortable and friendly – as you'd expect from a place with hippie-era origins – with live folk and other music as well as outside eating some evenings. The food can be uneven, but it's never dull or expensive – you can fill up here from as little as $5. Open daily 24hr.

Planet Veg 1941 Cornwall Ave, South Vancouver ⓣ604/734-1001, ⓦwww.planetvegrestaurant.com. There's limited inside seating at this mostly Indian fast-food and vegetarian restaurant, but most Kitsilano patrons avail themselves of the takeout option (good for a picnic at nearby Kits Beach and park), with dishes at $6 to $11. Open daily: March–Aug 11am–10pm, Sept–Feb 11am–8pm.

Steaks and seafood

Blue Water Café & Raw Bar 1095 Hamilton St at Helmcken St, Yaletown ⓣ604/688-8078, ⓦwww.bluewatercafe.net. Since opening in late 2000, this big, buzzing restaurant has remained one of Yaletown's most popular fixtures, thanks to the super-fresh sushi, fish and seafood (or pasta and other dishes with fish and seafood) and to the attractive terrace and long interior, the latter a dark, comfortable space of exposed beams and brick originally used as ballast in 1890s ships. There's an open kitchen for the fish and seafood staples (great halibut dishes, BC sablefish or salmon with pumpkin-seed gnocchi), plus the semi-circular raw bar for sushi, sashimi, ceviche, caviar and other treats. (There's also an ice bar where you can indulge in chilled vodkas and freshly squeezed fruit juices.) The service is amiable and unstuffy, the wine list first-rate and the quality is excellent. Prices for main courses are high – from about $25 – stick to the raw bar if you're on a budget. Open daily 5–11pm (bar 5pm–1am).

Coast 1054 Alberni St between Burrard and Thurlow sts, Downtown ⓣ604/685-5010, ⓦwww.coastrestaurant.ca. Opened in May 2004 by the owners of the *Glowbal Grill* (see p.146), *Coast* became a star of the booming Yaletown dining scene before moving to the heart of Downtown. The fish and seafood here comes not just from the coast of BC but from various coasts of the world – it's all divinely cooked and presented but at rather eye-watering prices ($25–40 for fish). Thus you might be offered swordfish from New Zealand, Indian Ocean tiger prawns, Alaska king crab gnocchi or "Liverpool-style" fish and chips – though it is doubtful fish and chips in Liverpool have ever been served with wild rice barley cake, lobster ragout and roasted Roma tomatoes.

▲ Blue Water Café & Raw Bar, Yaletown

A good choice of simply grilled fish is always available, along with a handful of meat dishes. Open Mon–Fri 11am to midnight, Sat & Sun 4pm to midnight.

C Restaurant 2–1600 Howe St near Beach Ave, Yaletown ⓣ604/681-1164, ⓦwww.crestaurant.com. *The Fish House in Stanley Park* (see below) is *C*'s only serious rival for the title of Vancouver's best fish and seafood restaurant – some go further and claim *C Restaurant* is the best fish restaurant in Canada, and has been since it opened in 1997. The lengthy menu, which shows plenty of Southeast Asian influences, might include a choice from the "raw bar" – say a tartare trio of scallop, wasabi salmon and smoked chilli tuna – and fish such as Alaskan Arctic char. All ingredients are impeccably chosen and come from sustainable sources. The taster of starters might include salmon gravlax cured in Saskatoon-berry tea, grilled garlic squid, abalone tempura and artichoke carpaccio – though the Skeena River sockeye terrine is unbeatable. Main courses might feature Maui hai tuna sashimi with 50-year-old balsamic vinegar or octopus-bacon-wrapped diver scallops with seared Québec fois gras. Sometimes, though, it can be best to eschew the fancier offerings, in which over-elaborate or powerful sauces can mask the delicacy of the fish, and go for more straightforward dishes. For a full insight into the chef's culinary powers, order the six-course tasting menu, but be prepared to part with $98. Otherwise, main courses start at around $20 at lunch, $30 to $40 at dinner. Views from the dining room are almost as good as the food. Daily 5–10pm.

The Fish House in Stanley Park 8901 Stanley Park Drive at Lagoon Drive ⓣ604/681-7275 or 877/681-7275, ⓦwww.fishhousestanleypark.com. The leafy setting is pretty, the restaurant is housed in an attractive white-clapboard building, and the seafood is among the city's best. Inside, the three club-like dining rooms are painted in rich greens and whites offset by lots of dark wood. Indulge yourself at the oyster bar; order any available fish baked, broiled, steamed or grilled; or check out the daily specials. Obvious choices such as fish cakes don't disappoint, but here it pays to be more adventurous: how about prawns flambéed with ouzo or ahi tuna with green-pepper sauce or – as one of several excellent vegetable accompaniments – red cabbage with fennel and buttermilk mash? Puddings are also superb: coconut cream pie is a particular winner. Excellent wine list. Mains here cost from around $20, but you can spend a lot less and enjoy the setting if you just indulge in afternoon tea (daily– –4pm) during a Stanley Park stroll. Open for lunch and dinner Mon–Fri 11.30am–2pm & 4–10pm, Sat & Sun 11am–2pm & 4–10pm.

Go Fish 1505 West Ave near Creekside Drive, South Vancouver ⓣ604/730-5040. Fish doesn't need to be fancy, as the frequent queues for this glorified fish-and-chip shack on the seawall promenade between Granville Island and Vanier Park prove. Fish comes fresh daily from boats docking at the nearby jetty, is given a coating of batter, fried or grilled, and then offered neat, with chips, salads and/or slaw, in a sandwich or with tacos. You won't spend more than about $15, usually less. When the day's catch is gone, that's it: the place closes. Open daily from 11.30am to about 6.30pm.

Gotham Steakhouse 615 Seymour St at Dunsmuir St, ⓣ604/605-8282, ⓦwww.gothamsteakhouse.com. This is the city's best steakhouse – the one visiting movie stars and captains of industry frequent – but the style and swank, not to mention the steaks, come at quite a price: 24oz ribeye costs $50 and prime rib around $40. If you want perfect steak served in style, though, this is the place: the cocktail bar is also impressive. Open daily from 5pm; cocktail bar Mon–Fri 4pm to close, Sat & Sun 5pm to close.

Hamilton Street Grill 1009 Hamilton St at Nelson St, Yaletown ⓣ604/331-1511, ⓦwww.hamiltonstreetgrill.com. An excellent wine list (with regular bargain specials), nice patio and top-quality meat have made this one of the city's best new steakhouses, far less formal than Gotham (see above), and with prices that are keener than those of rival operations (a whopping 20oz New York steak is $38; grilled sirloin $22). Seafood (8oz of king crab, $16) and braises are also first-rate; garlic mash makes a great side order, and to round off, try the home-made gingerbread pudding. Open Tues–Fri 11.30am–2.30pm & from 5pm, Sat–Mon from 5pm.

Joe Fortes Seafood and Chop House 777 Thurlow St near Robson, Downtown ⓣ604/669-1940, ⓦwww.joefortes.ca. This long-established oyster bar-cum-chophouse and seafood restaurant (named after the Caribbean seaman who became English Bay's first lifeguard) is something of a city institution, noted as a hip place for high-spirited singles, among others, and the great bar (drinks and oysters) upstairs on the year-round (heated) roof garden and terrace. The restaurant plays it straight food-wise: ample portions of fish and seafood (none from farmed stock) presented simply and without contemporary frills – the trio of grilled fish (choose from several types) is always a winner. There are many varieties of oysters available, all as fresh as you like, as well. Mains cost from around $20. The atmosphere is lively and casual, the saloon-style decor heavy on the mahogany and stained glass. Open daily 11am–11pm.

Rodney's Oyster House 1228 Hamilton St, Yaletown ⓣ604/609-0080, ⓦwww.rohvan.com. Not one of the most up-front Yaletown locations – it's tucked away in a relatively quiet dead-end street – but if you're after oysters, this fishing-shack lookalike is the place. "The lemon, the oyster and your lips are all that's required" is the pitch here. Expect up to eighteen varieties, from locally harvested bivalves to exotic Japanese kumamotos, all laid out on ice and priced from about $1.50 to $3.50 each. You can also get chowder and other types of fresh seafood, notably Louisiana wild white shrimp and tremendous Fundy scallops – main courses cost from $15 to $25. Or grab an appetizer and Martini in the adjoining *Mermaid Lounge*. Open Mon–Sat 11am–11pm, Sun 3–10pm.

The Sandbar 1535 Johnston St, Granville Island ⓣ604/669-9030, ⓦwww.vancouverdine.com/sandbar. This is a good and informal place to escape the bustle of Granville Island, with a good rooftop waterfront bar (lively on Fri and Sat evenings), an open kitchen and a main dining room. The food is mainly fish and seafood, but there are other West Coast dishes, as well as an enormous choice of wines. The quality is only middling, but the prices are fair (mains from $11), the atmosphere is easygoing, and the nautical setting (lots of wood) works well, if you like that sort of thing. This is a child-friendly lunch place, rather than a smoochy spot for refined evening meals. Open Sun–Thurs 11.30am–10pm, Fri–Sat 11.30am–11pm.

Contemporary and West Coast cuisine

Bishop's 2183 West 4th St near Yew, South Vancouver ⓣ604/738-2025, ⓦwww.bishopsonline.com. In the 25 years of its existence, Bishop's has consistently ranked as one of Vancouver's best restaurants. Although there's a frequent film-star and VIP presence, everyone gets a warm welcome – often from the Welsh-born owner himself, John Bishop. The light and refined "contemporary home cooking" – Italy meets the Pacific Rim – commands high prices but is worth it. Menus change three or four times a year according to season: if in doubt, the daily special is invariably a winner. All ingredients are organic and locally grown. The dining room is all of an understated piece – candlelight, appealing paintings, Pacific Northwest wood sculpture, white linen and a soundtrack of easy-on-the-ear jazz. It's worth dressing up a little. Of course, none of this comes cheap – main courses range from about $35 to $40. Booking days (sometimes weeks) ahead is essential. Open Mon–Sat 5.30–11pm, Sun 5.30–10pm.

Boneta 1 West Cordova St at Carrall St, ⓣ604/684-1844, ⓦwww. boneta.ca. Boneta ticks plenty of boxes: it's in a convenient Gastown location that has a burgeoning dining scene (including the highly-rated *Irish Heather*: see p.152); its large, open-concept dining room is airy and informal; it has a patio; a good wine list; and a short to-the-point (and not overly expensive) menu of hot and cold main courses from $13 to $29. It's also a welcoming place for a drink, with contemporary cocktails from $10. Open Mon–Sat 5.30pm to midnight.

Bridges 1696 Duranleau St, Granville Island ⓣ604/687-4400, ⓦwww.bridgesrestaurant.com. This unmissable big yellow building has a restaurant upstairs; a pub and informal bistro (the best option) on the ground floor, with a large outdoor deck; plus a smarter dining room on the second level. It's a reliable and very popular choice on Granville Island for a drink, snack (good nachos) or fuller meal of predictable pasta, fish and meat options. Main courses in the bistro cost from $13 to $22 and from $25 to $45 in the dining room (fixed-price menu at $40). Bistro open daily 11am–11pm; bar Mon–Sat 11am–1am, Sun 11am–midnight; dining room daily 5.30–10pm.

Delilah's 1789 Comox St near Denman, West End ⓣ604/687-3424, ⓦwww.delilahs.ca. With a name like Delilah's you somehow know you're in for a little bit of kitsch, and the glamorous, if slightly camp interior doesn't disappoint. First task here is to order one of the Martinis for which the place is famous, and which doubtless contribute to the cheerful, buzzy atmosphere that prevails. Then perhaps dip into the tapas menu, with dishes such as house-cured elk carpaccio that have almost certainly never appeared on a Spanish menu (tapas from $8). Delilah's has been around for over 20 years and has always been fun, but the food has recently picked up, and the mostly traditional (occasionally French-influenced) main courses (from $22) such as grilled beef tenderloin with foie gras butter and fresh horseradish are well worth trying. Open Tues–Wed 5–11pm, Thurs–Sat 5pm–1am.

Diva at the Met in the Metropolitan Hotel, 645 Howe St near Dunsmuir, Downtown ⓣ604/602-7788, ⓦwww.metropolitan.com. *Diva* has carved out a character completely separate from the hotel with which it's associated (a vast glass wall separates restaurant and hotel). The food is not what it was in its heyday, and chefs have come and gone, but at its best it's punchy and imaginative (with particularly good fish and seafood) and the dining rooms (dubious paintings aside) are modern and clean-lined. The popular tasting menu is the best way to sample the food, albeit at some of Vancouver's highest prices – mains cost from about $25 at dinner, but just $12 at lunch. It's a big-money, slightly showy sort of place, so dress accordingly if you don't want to stand out. Open daily 6.30am–1am.

Earl's 1185 Robson St at Bute, Downtown ⓣ604/669-0020, ⓦwww.earls.ca. This is a good choice if you don't want to mess around scouring Downtown for somewhere to eat. The mid-priced (mains from about $10 to $20), high-quality, often innovative food (sourced from farms in the Fraser Valley near Vancouver) is as eclectic as you please – everything from North American burgers to Far Eastern stir-fry and all points in between – and is served in a big, buzzy, open and casual-to-a-fault dining area. You can eat on the outside terrace in summer. Open daily 11.30am–1am.

Glowbal Grill & Satay Bar 1079 Mainland St near Helmcken, Yaletown ⓣ604/602-0835, ⓦwww.glowbalgrill.com. This is the perfect place to catch up on the hip dining and easy-living ethos of Vancouver and of Yaletown in particular – not to mention a great spot to sample the classic fusion of Asian and West Coast cuisines that characterizes so much of the city's cooking. The simple, clean-lined, modernist-inspired dining room is divided between a long raised bar and semi-isolated tables with banquettes below. An open kitchen, satay bar and lots of illuminated cubes add to the dashing, vibrant air of the place. Food can be fused to a fault, with cuisines such as Italian and Japanese coming together in dishes such as spaghetti with truffles and Kobe meatballs ($24), but there are also reasonably straight-ahead steaks, fish and mainstream Italian dishes, with mains from $18 to $35 for lobster. Around twenty wines by the glass are available, but a better place to drink at leisure or to enjoy smaller, lighter meals is the more recently opened Afterglow lounge, with suitably funky music and inventive cocktails. Both open daily 11.30am to midnight.

Lift 333 Menchions Mews, on the Coal Harbour waterfront behind the Westin Bayshore Resort, West End–Stanley Park ⓣ604/689-5438, ⓦwww.liftbarandgrill.com. You have to hope this place continues to prosper, because it cost someone $8 million to build. The omens are good. For a start, the position is divine: part of the gleaming new waterfront taking shape just east of Stanley Park, it has a super-modern and design-conscious interior – complete with vast glass walls – as well as city, harbour and mountain views that are enough on their own to guarantee that the crowds will continue to flock here (be sure to book). The food and service had an uneven start, but things have settled down, and the tuna, steak, salmon and other West Coast staples – with the inevitable sophisticated twists – are now quite good. Prices are high – with mains from around $25 – but you can go for smaller portions (between a starter and a main) to keep costs down, or simply come here for a drink – the rooftop patio on a clear day is a fine place to be. Open Mon–Fri 11.30am to midnight, Sat & Sun 11am to midnight (Sun brunch until 2.30pm).

Milestone's 1145 Robson St, Downtown ⓣ604/682-4477; 1210 Denman St, West End ⓣ604/662-3431; 1109 Hamilton St at Helmcken, Yaletown ⓣ604/684-9112; ⓦwww.milestonesrestaurants.com. These three popular mid-market chain restaurants serve cheap drinks and standard but well-prepared and occasionally innovative North American food (especially good breakfasts) in very generous portions at the heart of Downtown (fast and noisy), in Yaletown and at the English Bay Beach end of Denman St (both more laid-back). Pastas and similarly simple mains cost about $15, steaks and fish from $19. Open Mon–Wed 10.30am–10pm, Thurs 10.30am–11pm, Fri 10.30am–midnight, Sat 9.30am–midnight, Sun 9.30am–10pm.

Nu 1661 Granville St, Downtown, near Granville Island ⓣ604/646-4668, ⓦwww.whatisnu.com. Its name isn't meant to suggest "new" – *nu* is French for "naked. It is under the same management as the *C Restaurant*, though here the "naked", or unadorned, approach makes for decidedly lighter and simpler fare, with easy-to-eat finger food and classic West Coast meat and fish staples from around $18 for a main course. The dining room has a vaguely nautical, cruise-ship theme – appropriately enough, given its location on the north shore of False Creek opposite Granville Island. Open Mon–Fri 11am–1am, Sat 10.30am–1am, Sun 10.30am–midnight.

Raincity Grill 1193 Denman St near Davie, West End ⓣ604/685-7337, ⓦwww.raincitygrill.com. A long, low-ceilinged, candlelit dining room and a position near Davie St overlooking English Bay make for a romantic dining experience, but it is the food and wine, both derived mostly from British Columbian and Pacific Northwest ingredients (more than 100 varieties of Northwest and Californian wines by the glass are available), which are the main attractions here – as you'd expect from a place which has managed to prosper since 1990 and has connections with the outstanding *C* and *Nu* restaurants (see p.143 and opposite). The restaurant pioneered the Pacific Rim approach to cuisine now almost ubiquitous in Vancouver as well as the penchant for seasonal and locally sourced produce. The regional menu changes regularly, but you can always be sure to find seafood, game and poultry (most of it organic) and at least four vegetarian options. Main courses start at about $20, but the seasonal tasting menus (from $48) are excellent value. Each dish comes with a suggestion for wine (and the wine list is one of the city's best, with over 100 wines by the glass. Open Mon–Fri 5–10pm, Sat & Sun 10.30am–2pm & 5–10pm.

Seasons in the Park in Queen Elizabeth Park, Cambie at West 33rd Ave, South Vancouver ⓣ604/874-8008 or 1-800/632-9422, ⓦwww.vancouverdine.com/seasons. A pretty and panoramic position – at the heart of one of Vancouver's most popular parks – is almost enough to recommend this restaurant, but the food is as good as the romantic setting: certainly good enough for former presidents Yeltsin and Clinton, who both dined here. The menu always features fine fresh fish, seafood and local wines, but you'll also encounter dishes such as chicken breast stuffed with ricotta and pancetta in a port jus, a sun-dried tomato tart with Stilton, and some cracking puddings. Expect to pay between $18 and $35 for main dishes. Open daily 11.30am–2.30pm & 5.30–10pm (opens 10.30am on Sun).

The Teahouse Restaurant Ferguson Point, Stanley Park ⓣ604/669-3281 or 1-800/280-9893, ⓦwww.vancouverdine.com/teahouse. A very pretty and romantic spot on the west side of Stanley Park with an ocean view and outside dining. The building started in 1928 as a barracks but evolved into a large English-style cottage. It has become less twee under its current owners, who also number *Cardero's*, *Seasons* and *The Sandbar* (all reviewed on these pages) in their Vancouver portfolio. The revamped terrace is an obvious place for lunch or brunch during a walk or ride round the park. The food embraces entirely predictable West Coast and French–Italian staples (seafood and steaks, pastas, small-plate selections of Asian-influenced starters), with main courses costing from around $23 to $37. Truth be told, the food is not quite as good as the sea views, but this is still a fine spot for a drink and light meal while watching the sun go down over the ocean. Book a table on the terrace a day or so in advance. Open Mon–Sat 11.30am–9.45pm, Sun 10.30am–9.45pm (small plates menu only daily 2.30–4.30pm).

Tomato Fresh Food Café 2486 Bayswater St at Broadway, South Vancouver ⓣ604/874-6020, ⓦwww.tomatofreshfoodcafe.com. This busy place serves good, simple food, with a fresh, health-conscious bias, and has become more accessible since moving to a central Kits location in 2007. Eat in or take away, with main courses from $20, less between 3 and 5pm, when a reduced afternoon menu is available. Open daily 9am–10pm.

Water Street Café 300 Water St, Gastown ⓣ604/689-2832. This is one of the café-restaurants of choice if you wind up in Gastown – it's located just across the street from the famous steam clock. The dining rooms (one downstairs, two upstairs) are pretty and relaxed, but in summer try to book an outside table. The menu at lunch and dinner is short and well planned, with a bias towards modern, Italian-influenced. Pasta mains cost from $14, more ambitious dishes around the $20 mark. Open daily 10am–10.30pm or later.

West 2881 Granville St near West 13th Ave, South Vancouver ⓣ604/738-8938, ⓦwww.westrestaurant.com. Year after year, *West* challenges *Bishop's* and *Lumière* for the title of Vancouver's best restaurant. It's owned by the same people who run *CinCin* and the *Blue Water Café* (and *Araxi* in Whistler), excellent restaurants all, and it's to them that credit goes for the smart but never stuffy dining room and the attention to detail. The restaurant's credo – "True to our region, true to the seasons" – is a shorthand way of saying what most of the city's West Coast and many other restaurants are saying: that the emphasis is on exceptional, locally sourced ingredients. Main courses are $30 to $45, but high prices bring consistently high-quality food, with menus changing three or four times a week. Indulge in one of the three tasting menus (either $89 or $98) for a full taste of what this exceptional restaurant can offer. Open Mon–Sat 11.30am–11pm, Sun 5.30–11pm.

10

Drinking

Vancouver has a reasonable assortment of **places to drink**, many a cut above the functional dives and sham pubs found in much of the rest of British Columbia. Most are in the same areas as the major concentrations of restaurants (see p.129), particularly **Yaletown**, the revitalized **Gastown** area and other **Downtown** locations. There's also a surge of places in east Vancouver, on and around parts of Main Street and, especially, Commercial Drive, though these are in grittier parts of the city and not convenient if you're staying in or close to Downtown.

The distinctions between bars, lounges, cafés, restaurants and nightclubs – not to mention hotel bars and lounges – can be considerably blurred, and the out-and-out pubs or bars that you might find in the US or European capitals are comparatively rare here: generally it is table, not bar service, unlike the UK (leave a tip: at least $1 a drink, 15 per cent on a round) and all drinking establishments in Vancouver must serve food in some form, though the city's arcane licensing laws were overhauled in April 2002 and places can now legally stay open until 3am, or later, notably on the entertainment "strip" on Granville Street around Davie and Smithe (as opposed to midnight or earlier in years past).

Canadian beer

By and large, **Canadian beers** are unremarkable, designed to quench your thirst rather than satisfy your palate. Expect to pay around $6 for a large glass, plus 10 per cent liquor tax and 5 per cent GST. Almost everywhere in Vancouver bars, ice-cold, light, fizzy beers rule the roost. Notable exceptions are provided by small microbreweries or brewpubs, but the market is still dominated by the two largest Canadian breweries, Molson and Labatt. Both offer remarkably similar beers – Molson Canadian, Molson Export, Labatt Ice, Labatt Blue – that inspire, for reasons that elude most foreigners, intense loyalty. There is also a niche market for foreign beers, although Heineken, the most popular, is made under licence in Canada; American beers such as Budweiser and Coors are common.

Drinking bottled beer will be more expensive than draught, which is usually served by the 170ml glass; even cheaper is to purchase it by the pitcher, which contains six or seven glasses.

Where Vancouver does score is in a handful of brewpubs and microbreweries, though these have a tendency to go out of business, change hands, merge or lose impetus when a brewmaster moves on: the long reach of restrictive laws and provincial bureaucracy, as ever in anything to do with alcohol in British Columbia, doesn't help. Long-standing exceptions include the *Yaletown Brewing Company* (see p.151), *Steamworks Brewing Company* (see p.152) and the *Granville Island Brewery* (see p.75), through this last has no proper bar outlet. A recent addition to the microbrew community is *Dockside Brewing Company* (see p.152).

Note that the legal **drinking age** is 19 and that alcohol can only be bought from government-run stores (Ⓦwww.bcliquorstores.com) and some branches of the private BC VQA (Vintners Quality Alliance) stores. At present, only a handful of places are open on Sundays (11am–9pm), notably the Marquis Wine Cellar at 1034 Davie St near Thurlow St (Ⓣ604/684-0445, Ⓦwww.marquis-wines.com).

However, while things are easing up bureaucratically, there has yet to be a real renaissance in the city's relatively restrained drinking culture. This said, many daytime cafés, bistros, tapas bars and restaurants – generated by the old "must-serve-food" legal clause – also operate happily in the evening, turning into bars with a more night-owlish clientele and a more mellow nocturnal buzz, as do many of the clubs and live-music venues "Nightlife" chapter (see p.154). The city also has a good selection of **gay and lesbian bars** (see p.168).

Vancouver has several **brewpubs** and **hotel bars** – two notable and recommended examples of the latter are the Downtown *900 West* bar (see below) of the *Hotel Vancouver*, a good place for an early- or late-evening drink even if the hotel itself is beyond your budget; and the *Bacchus*, also Downtown, in the *Wedgewood* hotel (see review, p.123), which evokes the decadent ambience of a gentleman's club (and has a open fire for cold or rainy days). The bars reviewed below are open daily, unless otherwise specified.

Downtown

Bayside Lounge 1755 Davie St at Denman St Ⓣ604/682-1831, Ⓦwww.bestwesternsandshotelvancouver.com. Position is all in this peaceful and little-known lounge on the second floor of a Best Western Hotel, its location offering wonderful views of English Bay from the circular bay and large picture windows. Ideal for a quiet drink, though later on (it's open daily 11am–2am) there are nightly DJs.

Bin 941 941 Davie St between Burrard and Hornby Ⓣ604/683-1246, Ⓦwww.bin941.com. This is a great place to eat (see review on p.142), but vast numbers of people come here primarily to drink, attracted by the place's high-energy and cramped good vibes. Be prepared to wait in line – there are no reservations.

900 West 900 West Georgia St at Burrard St Ⓣ604/684-3131, Ⓦwww.fairmont.com. Hotel bars and lounges can be bland and anonymous affairs – not the bar of the *Hotel Vancouver*. Despite its location off the main lobby of one of the city's biggest and grandest hotels, it's a cosy space of dark wood, comfortable chairs and low lighting. 900 West is at its best immediately after businesses close, when the bar fills with an animated crowd catching a drink before heading home or moving on to a restaurant or club. Later in the evening it tends to be used more by hotel guests, and the atmosphere becomes mellower.

C9 Live Lounge Empire Landmark Hotel, 1400 Robson St at Nicola Ⓣ604/687-0511, Ⓦwww.empirelandmarkhotel.com or www.cloud9restaurant.ca. Vancouver has several bars with a view – notably the lounge in the *Sylvia* (see p.118) – but none that can match the one from this super-sleek lounge bar on the 42nd floor of the *Empire Landmark Hotel*. The bar rotates, so your view changes by six degrees every sixty seconds.

Gerard Lounge Sutton Place Hotel, 845 Burrard St between Robson and Smithe sts Ⓣ604/682-5511, Ⓦwww.suttonplace.com. A smooth, wood-panelled 25-seat lounge and piano bar in the smart *Sutton Place Hotel* that aims – successfully – to recreate the look and atmosphere of an English gentleman's club, complete with leather chairs, tapestries, oil paintings and wall-mounted taxidermic animals. It all makes for elegant and rather distinctive Downtown drinking. This is also, at least until fashions change, one of the places to spot the stars currently filming in town – plus plenty of the wannabes.

Ginger 62 1219 Granville St at Davie St Ⓣ604/682-0409, Ⓦwww.ginger62.com. A dress code here requires that you are pretty well turned out, but it's worth making the effort (plenty of regulars do) to enjoy the louche and deliberately affected 1960s-style lounge decor – red and gold room, couches, ottomans and big bar. Food consists of sophisticated tapas and Asian titbits.

La Bodega 1277 Howe St near Davie St ⓣ604/684-8815, ⓦwww.labodegavancouver.com. This place towards the south of Downtown recreates a Spanish bar that could almost be in Spain. As a result, it's one of the city's best and most popular places to drink, with fine tapas (great chorizo) and excellent main courses to mop up the alcohol (including sangria and other Spanish drinks). It's packed later on, especially on Fri and Sat, so try to arrive before 8pm. Closed Sun.

Lennox 800 Granville St at Robson St ⓣ604/408-0881. One of the city's busiest junctions is not perhaps the ideal place for a bar, but if you want a drink and time-out from the Downtown bustle, this comfortable and straightforward pub is a good and convenient choice. The selection of beers and single malts is extremely broad, but prices, given the site, are a touch over the odds. There's a small outside seating area for summer drinking and people-watching. Food is of the basic pub-grub variety, but the quality's reasonable.

Morrissey Pub 1227 Granville St between Davie and Drake sts ⓣ604/682-0909, ⓦwww.morrisseypub.com. Situated at the cheaper and less salubrious southern end of Granville St, this only halfway authentic "Irish" pub is better than the environs: spacious, lots of leather, dark wood and a fireplace. It's a cheerful and popular spot, with inexpensive beer and food. If you want something a little more out-there, try the affiliated Ginger 62 (see above) a couple of doors down.

Shark Club Bar & Grill in the Sandman Hotel, 180 West Georgia St at Cambie St ⓣ604/687-4275, ⓦwww.sharkclubs.com. Currently the best and busiest of several sports bars in the city. This being Canada, ice hockey is popular, but you'll also catch basketball, baseball, soccer and American and Canadian football (especially the last, as it's close to BC Place, home to the local team). There are thirty screens, a 180-seat oak bar, more than twenty beers on tap, Italian food from the kitchen and lots of testosterone, though the place is by no means confined to rowdy jocks.

Yaletown

Afterglow 1079 Mainland St near Helmcken St ⓣ604/642-0577, ⓦwww.glowbalgrill.com. The very mellow bar attached to the *Glowbal Grill* (see p.146), with its candlelight, intimate seating and easy-listening grooves, is a good place for a pre- or post-dinner drink – or for a night's drinking without pause for food.

Atlantic Trap & Grill 118 Robson St on the corner of Beatty St ⓣ604/806-6393, ⓦwww.trapandgrill.com. A place of considerable Celtic revelry and drinking (Guinness and Keith's are the tipples of choice), with allusions to Ireland and the Canadian Maritime Provinces throughout, not least in the prevailing green colour scheme. Live music some nights, currently Thursday and Saturday. Emphatically not the place for a quiet drink.

Bar None 1222 Hamilton St at Davie St ⓣ604/689-7000, ⓦwww.dhmbars.ca. A busy and reasonably smart under-forty-something Yaletown bar and club, in business since 1992, with an elegant brick and wooden-beam interior where you can eat, drink, watch TV, smoke cigars (there's a walk-in humidor), play backgammon or shoot pool and listen to live music. A house band plays Mon and Tues, with a DJ the rest of the week, though patrons are generally a touch too cool to make fools of themselves on the small dance floor. Generally closed Wed & Sun for private functions.

George Ultra Lounge 1137 Hamilton St at Helmcken St ⓣ604/628-5555, ⓦwww.georgelounge.com. If you want a smart, urban lounge bar, this is a good bet, a place that appeals to a young, beautiful set, with easy-on-the-palate cocktails, well-priced wines by the glass, just-right subdued lighting and a choice between sitting at the long bar or on the sofas of the lounge.

Section (3) 1039 Mainland St between Nelson and Helmcken sts ⓣ604/684-2777, ⓦwww.sectionthree.com. With a name like this you know you're in for a place with certain pretensions, and the hyper-modern and self-consciously arty decor and knowing crowd don't disappoint. The bar is curved, the bar stools wrought-iron, the floor hardwood, the art bizarre and the booths silver. Music and food are similarly modern and eclectic.

Soho Billiards 1283 Hamilton St at Drake St ⓣ604/688-1180, ⓦwww.sohocafe.ca. Primarily a place to play billiards, but also a bar that is less in-your-face trendy than some Yaletown establishments. The *Soho* opened in 1991 – one of the first to do so in the area – and despite a recent change of location remains a cosy spot for tea, coffee, a stronger drink or a full meal, or drink in unfussy surroundings.

SuBeez Café 891 Homer St at Smithe St ⓣ604/687-6107, ⓦwww.subeez.com. The sort of place you will love or hate, the SuBeez is a typical Yaletown warehouse-type space, with high ceilings supported by brutalist concrete columns. The lighting is low, the music is alternative to a fault, and strange art on the walls competes with screens showing silent films. You can eat here, but most of the regulars are here to drink. There are DJs on Thursday, Friday and Saturday evenings and a sister establishment, the WaaZuBee Café, at 1622 Commercial Drive (ⓣ604/253-5299, ⓦwww.waazubee.com).

Yaletown Brewing Company 1111 Mainland St at Helmcken St ⓣ604/681-2739. There's no danger of missing this extremely large, modern bar and restaurant with its own on-site brewery. It's very popular, and one of the long-established leaders in the funky Yaletown revival. All six varieties of beer brewed here are excellent, as are the snacks and Italian and West Coast food in the restaurant, but this is a better place to drink than to eat seriously. The patio is good in summer, and if the weather's bad you can retreat to several cosy indoor rooms.

West End

Cardero's 1583 Coal Harbour Quay on Cardero St ⓣ604/669-7666, ⓦwww.vancouverdine.com. The location of this waterfront pub-restaurant is neither here nor there – it's at the northern end of Cardero St roughly midway between Stanley Park and Burrard St – but the patio (heated on cooler evenings) offers great views of the park, moored boats, Burrard Inlet and the North Shore. The clientele is mostly young and well dressed, with many patrons en route to the adjoining restaurant, and the decor is low-key maritime.

Jupiter Café 1216 Bute St near Davie St ⓣ604/609-6665. You need to be in the mood for this bar's unsparing industrial look – all exposed a/c pipes, black ceilings and superstructure – or concentrate on the softer edge provided by comfy chairs, rich fabrics and over-the-top chandeliers. There's a big outdoor drinking area, ideal for taking in the very mixed but never less than well-dressed punters. There is food – the usual pastas, burgers and a dozen ways with chicken – but it's something of an afterthought.

▲ Yaletown Brewing Company

Sylvia Hotel 1154 Gilford St at Beach Ave ⓣ604/688-8865. Though not very appealing at first glance, this nondescript and easygoing hotel bar is popular for quiet drinks and superlative waterfront views, and makes a very pleasant retreat after a stroll in Stanley Park and/or English Bay Beach.

Gastown and around

Alibi Room 157 Alexander St between Columbia and Main sts ⓣ604/623-3383, ⓦwww.alibi.ca. Various movie-makers and shakers put money into this unashamedly hip and happening bar-restaurant – and the result is a crowd that is trendy, but not to the extent that it spoils this as a good place for drinks and – perhaps – dinner. Excellent and eclectic food is served upstairs, with a short, modern menu and surprisingly reasonable prices; downstairs you can drink and venture onto the small dance floor.

The Bourbon 50 West Cordova St between Abbott and Carrall sts ⓣ604/684-4214, ⓦwww.thebourbon.ca. A fine recent addition to the Gastown drinking scene, and rapidly establishing a reputation for excellent live music (it has a 300-seat capacity). Occupies a cavernous old building, with beams and bare-brick Victorian-era walls. Over 200 brands of drinks behind the bar, including many bourbons, at student-friendly prices. Open until 2am daily (3am Fri & Sat).

Blarney Stone 216 Carrall St between Powell and East Cordova sts ⓣ604/687-4322, ⓦhttp://blarneystone.ca. This lively pub and restaurant in Gastown features nightly live Irish music from the house band and a dance floor. If it looks a bit rough and ready, or just too plain rowdy, try The *Irish Heather* almost opposite across the street (see below). Closed Sun.

The Cambie 300 Cambie St at West Cordova St ⓣ604/684-6466. An obvious place to drink if you're staying at the linked hostel (see p.126), but the roomy (and invariably crowded) outdoor area and cheap pitchers of beer bring in a fair number of locals and other passing trade. Inside, it's all smoke, pool tables and down-to-earth drinking.

The Irish Heather 217 Carrall St at between Powell and East Cordova sts ⓣ604/688-9779, ⓦwww.irishheather.com. This charming Gastown place is a definite cut above the usual mock-Irish pub, with an intimate bar, varied clientele – anyone from students to local gallery owners – lots of nooks and crannies, live Irish music some nights and good Guinness (apparently it sells the second largest number of pints of the stuff in Canada). The Irish-influenced food – hearty stews and soups and so forth – is also excellent, and there's an unexpectedly pretty outdoor eating and drinking area at the back.

Honey Lounge 455 Abbott St between Hastings and Pender sts ⓣ604/685-7777. Don't expect to make much conversational headway against the occasionally booming music, but do come to the Honey if you're en route for the hip little gay- and lesbian-friendly Lotus Sound Lounge club downstairs (see p.169). The bar area of the lounge is spacious and more laid-back than the dance area, with lots of comfortable chairs piled with velvet cushions. Closed Sun.

Steamworks Brewing Company 375 Water St at West Cordova St ⓣ604/689-2739, ⓦwww.steamworks.com. This Gastown microbrewery and pub sells about a dozen of its own rightly well-regarded brews and has plenty of different rooms. Upstairs, the drinkers are likely to include leery and besuited financial types; by the staircase, the old clublike setting – wood panelling, comfortable chairs and windows overlooking the harbour – appeals to a more congenial crowd, while the basement has the appearance and atmosphere of a German beer hall. Fri night until about 9pm is when the place is liveliest.

Granville Island and Kitsilano

The Arts Club 1585 Johnston St, Granville Island ⓣ604/687-1354, ⓦwww.backstagelounge.com. *The Arts Club's* popular *Backstage Lounge and Grill*, part of its theatre complex, has seating with a waterfront view on Granville Island beneath the bridge; an easygoing atmosphere; decent food; and blues, jazz and other live music Fri and Sat evenings. It's especially well known for its 50-plus varieties of whisky. Early in the week (notably Wed) it's a hangout for students from the nearby Emily Carr Institute of Art and Design.

Bimini's Tap House 2010 West 4th Ave between Arbutus and Maple sts ⓣ604/732-9232, ⓦwww.biminis.ca. Anglo-style pub at the heart of the West Fourth Ave strip. Pool and cheap drinks attract a youngish crowd, but at the time of writing the pub is closed for renovation after fire damage.

Bridges 1696 Duranleau St, Granville Island ⓣ604/687-4400, ⓦwww.bridgesrestaurant.com. When the sun's shining it's hard to choose which is the nicest place to have a waterside drink on Granville Island – the busy patio here (where you can also eat) or the lounge bar of the Dockside Brewing Company (see below). Bridges is more central and thus more convenient.

Darby's Pub 2001 Macdonald St and West 4th Ave ⓣ604/731-0617, ⓦhttp://www.darbyspub.ca. This pub – generally known simply as Darby's – is relatively handy for the youth hostel and Kits Beach. People often start the evening here with a beer or game of darts – meals are served 11.30am–7pm, snacks till 10pm – and then move on to the *Fairview* for live blues (see p.156). Live music (a mixture of jazz, blues and rock) is generally played only on Fri and Sat evenings with jam sessions on Sat afternoons.

Dockside Brewing Company in the Granville Island Hotel, 1253 Johnston St, Granville Island ⓣ604/685-7070, ⓦwww.docksidebrewing.com. Beer buffs should try the stylish Dockside Lounge in the *Granville Island Hotel* to sample some of the on-site microbrewery's ales. The atmosphere is relaxed and the clientele a generally well-heeled crowd of thirty-somethings. Things tend to be more lively early in the evening, and in summer there's a fine outdoor patio.

King's Head 1618 Yew St between York and West 4th Ave ⓣ604/738-6966. A Kits fixture that divides opinion: to some it's an atmospheric and character-filled dive that never changes (in a good way) and to others it's simply a dive.

Wolf & Hound Pub 3617 West Broadway between Alma and Dunbar sts ⓣ604/738-8909, ⓦwww.wolfandhound.ca. Welcoming neighbourhood pub at the western end of the Broadway (West 9th Ave) entertainment strip that offers live music (generally traditional Celtic sessions) Wednesday to Sunday nights (no cover).

The North Shore

The Raven 1052 Deep Cove Rd ⓣ604/929-3834, ⓦwww.theravenpub.com. It's way out east on Deep Cove near the mouth of Indian Arm, so probably only appropriate if you've been in Mount Seymour Provincial Park just to the west (see p.156) or are a real beer fan, for there are half a dozen foreign imports and around twenty microbrews. Whisky fans will also find a good selection of malts.

Rusty Gull 175 East 1st St between Lonsdale Ave and St George ⓣ604/988-5585, ⓦwww.rustygullpub.com. Just 1min or so from Lonsdale Quay, this jovial neighbourhood pub is the most convenient place for a drink if you're on a flying visit to the North Shore or have time to kill before catching the SeaBus back to Downtown. The choice of beer and food is good, and you'll often be able to catch some live music, but the main draw here is the great view from the small patio over the warehouses and docks towards the Downtown skyline.

Sailor Hägar's 86 Semisch Ave at West 1st St ⓣ604/984-7669, ⓦwww.bestbeerbc.com. A brewpub with six good locally brewed beers on tap, plus a wide selection of other microbrewery and imported beers, uphill and about 200m (650ft) west of Lonsdale Quay. The interior is unexceptional, save for a big oak fireplace, but this is part of the appeal of what is a no-nonsense neighbourhood pub. The outdoor patio has fine views of Vancouver, and there's good pub and Scandinavian-influenced food.

Nightlife

Vancouver offers plenty to do come sundown, laying on a varied and cosmopolitan blend of **live music**, clubs and discos. Clubs here are just as adventurous as in other Canadian cities such as Toronto, particularly the fly-by-night alternative dives in the backstreets of Gastown and around Commercial Drive in the east. There's also a choice of smarter places (where you need to dress up), notably on the city's big, brash entertainment "strip" on Granville Street Downtown between Robson and Davie streets, plus more conventional clubs, a handful of discos and a smattering of good **gay** and **lesbian** clubs and bars. The city's northerly latitude occasionally makes for unreliable weather, but summer nightlife often takes to the streets in West Coast fashion, with outdoor terraces and – to a certain extent – beaches becoming venues in their own right. And when the fine weather does arrive, it allows the city to host a range of **festivals**, from jazz to theatre (see Chapter 17 for details of the main events).

The most comprehensive listings guide for nightlife is *The Georgia Straight* (Ⓦ www.straight.com), a free weekly published on Thursdays and available in dump bins at stores and other points around the city. Many other free magazines devoted to different musical genres and activities are available at the same points, but they come and go quickly. Selected club listings can also be found by visiting Ⓦ www.clubvibes.com, though note that entries on this site can be out of date.

Tickets for many major events are sold through Ticketmaster, with forty outlets around the city (Ⓣ 604/280-3311 for general tickets or 604/280-4444 for rock concerts, Ⓦ www.ticketmaster.ca); they'll sometimes unload discounted tickets for midweek and matinee performances. Half-price and last-minute same-day tickets are available via Tickets Tonight (Ⓦ www.ticketstonight.ca) at participating venues or through the outlet at the Touristinfo Centre at 200 Burrard St (see p.36).

Live music

Vancouver's nighttime **venues** are generally ill-defined places, and few restrict themselves solely to live music. Many bars, pubs and clubs offer live music all or some nights of the week, often with DJs and dancing on the same evenings or on nights when live music isn't offered. Clubs may also offer many types of music, from rock one night to jazz or 1970s revival bands the next. You'll also find live music and/or dancing in some of the places we've listed in Chapter 10 ("Drinking").

Here we've concentrated on places where music is predominant. They are dotted across the city and showcase a variety of largely local bands, none of which is likely to make the big time. Mainstream **rock** groups are the most common bill of fare, though **jazz** is generally hot news in Vancouver, with several spots specializing in the genre. And, while Vancouver isn't as cowpoke as, say,

Calgary, it does have several clubs dedicated to **country music**, though most are in the outer suburbs. At the other end of the spectrum to these small clubs, the 60,000-seat Pacific Coliseum and other bigger venues such as the Orpheum Theatre are on the touring itinerary of most international acts.

Cover charges in most smaller clubs and venues are typically a few dollars (anything from $5 to $20) but creep up when bigger acts perform. Prices are also higher on Friday and Saturday: the most you would expect to pay would be in the region of $40 on a big night at one of the city's smartest clubs. Occasionally you may have to pay a "membership fee" at clubs of a few dollars, usually a means of circumventing club licensing laws.

Pick up tickets on the night, through Ticketmaster (see opposite) for bigger events, or through many of the CD and vinyl stores listed on p.179, especially Red Cat Records.

Rock, hip-hop, reggae, R&B and punk

The Bourbon 50 West Cordova St between Abbott and Carrall sts ⓣ604/684-4214, ⓦwww.thebourbon.ca. You can drink here, or enjoy the DJs in the small hours, but this Gastown spot is also an excellent place to catch live music in roomy, unpretentious surroundings. Open until 2am daily (3am Fri & Sat).

Cellar 1006 Granville St ⓣ604/605-4357, ⓦwww.cellarvan.com. Live "underground rock" plus DJs on non-music nights, with themes such as Singles Games Night and Radio One Thursday (live British rock).

Commodore Ballroom 868 Granville St and Smithe ⓣ604/739-4550 or 739-7469. The city's best midsize venue (there's room for around 1000 people) benefited from a $1 million face-lift after being empty for three years, a makeover that retained some of the original Art Deco decor (the venue's over 75 years old) but sacrificed a little of the previous down-and-dirty atmosphere. However, it remains an excellent place to catch major international and other touring bands (the Clash, Nirvana and the Talking Heads all played here). There is an adventurous music policy that embraces many different types of band (rock, pop, jazz and blues), and they feature a new DJ every two to three weeks.

Fabric 66 Water St and Abbott St ⓣ604/683-6695, ⓦwww.fabricvancouver.com. The name changes from year to year, but this remains one of central Vancouver's best and most heavily patronized music venues, largely by virtue of its cool, funky vibe and convenient mid-Gastown location. The live music nightly often seems something of a distraction – the place is also a good dance club and known as something of a pick-up spot. The clientele is mainly a casual bunch of 19- to 24-year-olds, and the music anything from jazz, reggae, trance and soul to rock, hip-hop, techno and progressive house. Bar food and piano lounge until 9pm, when the band strikes up and the more serious dancing and partying begin.

Lamplighter 92 Water St at Abbott St ⓣ604/687-4424 or 681-6666, ⓦwww.thelamplighter.ca. This Gastown institution had little to recommend it, other than its claim to be the city's oldest inn, until two recent refurbs turned what was formerly a rather downbeat, old-style pub into a sleek, contemporary bar. Not all regulars approve of the changes, but the plum Gastown location (on the corner one block from the Steam Clock), plus live (usually local and cover) bands and DJs some nights (currently Thurs–Sat), means it looks destined to remain one of the area's key bars and small music venues.

Media Club 695 Cambie St at West Georgia St ⓣ604/608-2871, ⓦwww.themediaclub.ca. A pleasing, noisy, intimate and good-time 150-person-capacity place that books key touring bands most nights, plus up-and-coming local outfits that run the musical gamut.

Pub 340 340 Cambie St at West Hastings St ⓣ604/602-0644. A 110-person-capacity venue that never pretends to be other than what it is: a no-nonsense pub, with cheap beer and food, and live music nightly from loud and enthusiastic rock, punk, electronic and hardcore metal bands. There's also the inevitable karaoke, currently on Wed nights.

Railway Club 579 Dunsmuir St and Seymour St ⓣ604/681-1625, ⓦwww.therailwayclub.com. This is one of the city's best small pub-music-type venues – the place is tiny – a longtime favourite with excellent bookings, casual atmosphere and a wide range of live music (folk, blues, jazz and rock), with a preference for indie bands. It's also a good place just for a drink and a game of darts – the upstairs pub is quieter and more relaxed than the stage bar downstairs. There's a separate "conversation" lounge where it's more peaceful, so it's ideal if you don't want to come here just for the music.

Red Room 398 Richards St at West Cordova St ⓣ604/687-5007, ⓦwww.redroomonrichards .com. You'll hear eclectic musical fodder at this 400-person capacity Downtown venue, including Latin, Top 40, hip-hop (currently on Fridays), plus touring and local bands on some nights.

Roxy 932 Granville St and Nelson St ⓣ604/331-7999, ⓦwww.roxyvan.com. The *Roxy* – "where life is like a beer commercial" – has been around for a while, providing a successful, casual and fun place for the city's UBC college crowd and people in from the 'burbs. Four bars feature slick bartenders showing off their moves and there are live bands most nights – often the two very competent house bands – with an emphasis on 1950s to 1970s music. It also has theme dance nights and karaoke sessions.

The Venue 881 Granville St at Smithe St ⓣ604/646-0064, ⓦwww.venuelive.ca. Opened in the summer of 2009, to great fanfare, The Venue is a 500-person capacity space with excellent sightlines and a glam-rock-inspired interior, with velvet booths and LED lights across the walls. There's a miscellany of live music Monday to Thursday and DJs on Friday and Saturdays.

Jazz, blues and country

Arts Club Theatre Backstage Lounge 1585 Johnston St, Granville Island ⓣ604/687-1354, ⓦwww.thebackstagelounge.com. Given Granville Island's popularity, at least by day, it has surprisingly few places to sip a late-night beer or catch some live music. This good lounge, tucked away behind one of the city's best-known small theatres (see p.161), makes up for the shortage elsewhere. It's a nice spot to hear R&B, jazz and blues, or watch the boats and the sun set on False Creek. It's also pretty lively most nights, which may have something to do with the fact that it has one of the best selections of whiskies in Vancouver. There's a cover charge at weekends and occasionally on weekdays as well, depending on the band.

Boone County Cabaret 801 Brunette Ave, Coquitlam ⓣ604/523-3144, ⓦwww .boonecountycountry.com. Suburbia's favourite country-music club is some 20km (12 miles) east of town just off the Trans-Canada (take bus #151) in residential Coquitlam. The cramped, 300-capacity place is invariably raucous and crowded. Closed Sun and Mon.

Calhoun's Bakery Café 3035 West Broadway at Balaclava St ⓣ604/737-7062, ⓦwww.calhouns .bc.ca. The fact that Calhoun's is open 24 hours a day, seven days a week, has always made it a popular student retreat at night (and a favourite of Kits mothers by day), but recently it has broadened its appeal by presenting live music three or so nights a week, with a mix of jazz and Latin, currently on Tuesday, Thursday and Sunday.

Capone's 1141 Hamilton St at Davie St ⓣ604/684-7900, ⓦwww.caponesrestaurant.net. *Capone's* is one of the better fixtures that has opened in burgeoning Yaletown. On the face of it, the place is primarily a restaurant – mostly pizza and pasta – but it also takes its jazz seriously, and there's a stage for nightly live performances (generally house and local bands during the week, bigger names Friday and Saturday). The restaurant's layout is oddly long and narrow, however, so arrive early or book a table near the stage if you want a decent view of what's going on.

Cellar Restaurant & Jazz Club 3611 West Broadway ⓣ604/738-1959, ⓦwww.cellarjazz .com. Kitsilano has only recently acquired this club, a tiny 70-seat red-walled basement with black booths and low tables that frequently offers the best live jazz in the city four or more nights a week (generally Wed–Sat). Join the enthusiastic crowd for top local outfits or big international names.

Fairview in the Ramada Inn, 898 West Broadway at Dunbar St ⓣ604/872-1262. Good local blues and 1950s rock 'n' roll in something resembling a pub atmosphere – fans seem unperturbed by the hotel setting – which means there's generally a lively buzz but precious little room to move on the small dance floor. Snacks are served during the day and good-value meals in the evening. Live music nightly from Mon to Sat, with a cover charge at weekends depending on the band.

O'Doul's 1300 Robson St at Jervis St ⓣ604/661-1400, ⓦwww.odoulsrestaurant.com. Upscale drinking and dining accompanied by live mainstream jazz most nights in a central Downtown location.

Rossini's Kits Beach 1525 Yew St at Cornwall Ave ⓣ604/737-8080, ⓦwww.rossinisjazz.com.

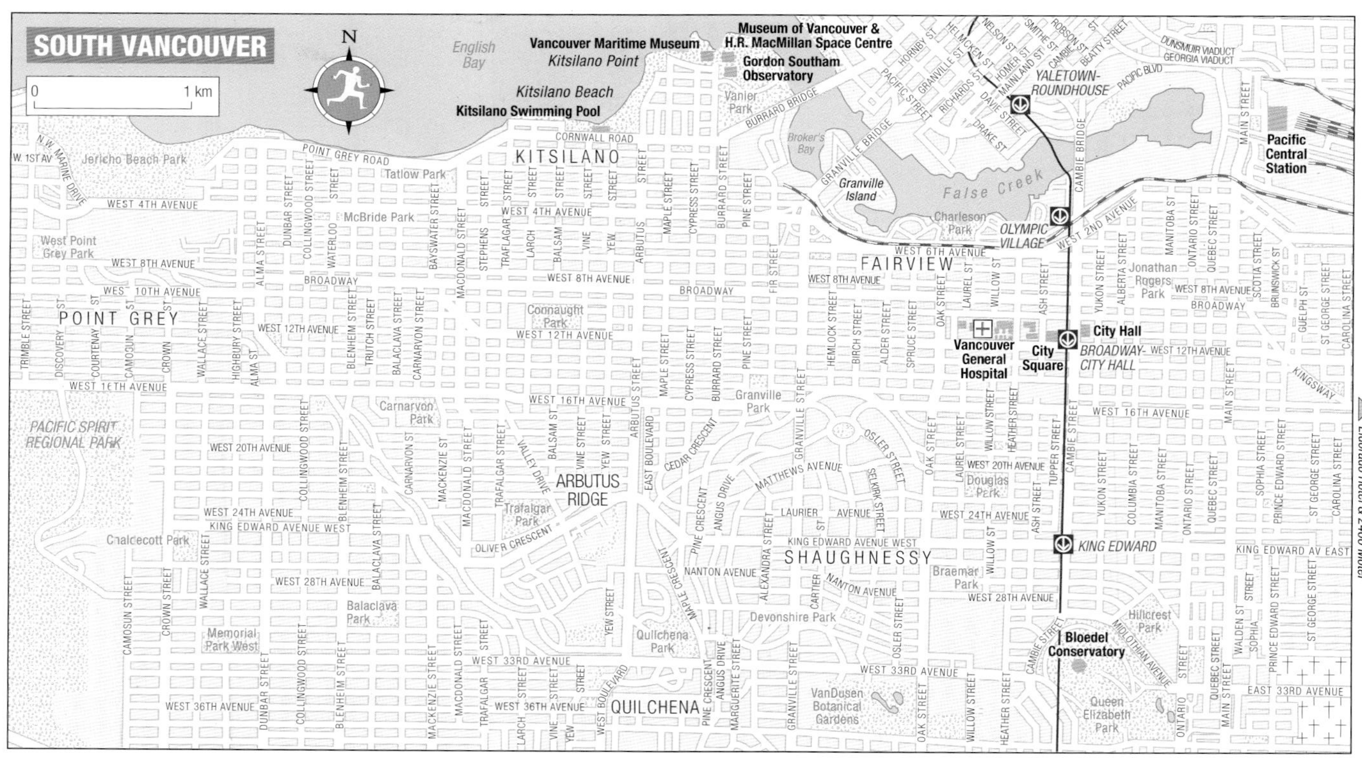

SOUTH VANCOUVER
0
1 km
N
English Bay
Vancouver Maritime Museum
Kitsilano Point
Kitsilano Beach
Kitsilano Swimming Pool
Museum of Vancouver & H.R. MacMillan Space Centre
Gordon Southam Observatory
Vanier Park
Broker's Bay
Granville Island
False Creek
Charleson Park
OLYMPIC VILLAGE
YALETOWN-ROUNDHOUSE
Pacific Central Station
City Hall
BROADWAY-CITY HALL
City Square
Vancouver General Hospital
KING EDWARD
Bloedel Conservatory
Queen Elizabeth Park
Hillcrest Park
VanDusen Botanical Gardens
Jonathan Rogers Park
Douglas Park
Braemar Park
Granville Park
Devonshire Park
Quilchena Park
Connaught Park
Trafalgar Park
Carnarvon Park
Balaclava Park
Memorial Park West
Tatlow Park
McBride Park
Jericho Beach Park
West Point Grey Park
PACIFIC SPIRIT REGIONAL PARK
KITSILANO
FAIRVIEW
SHAUGHNESSY
ARBUTUS RIDGE
QUILCHENA
POINT GREY
CAMBIE BRIDGE
GRANVILLE BRIDGE
BURRARD BRIDGE
DUNSMUIR VIADUCT
GEORGIA VIADUCT
PACIFIC BLVD
MAIN STREET
KINGSWAY
BROADWAY
CAMBIE STREET
OAK STREET
GRANVILLE STREET
BURRARD STREET
ARBUTUS STREET
MACDONALD STREET
DUNBAR STREET
POINT GREY ROAD
CORNWALL ROAD
N.W. MARINE DRIVE
WEST 4TH AVENUE
WEST 8TH AVENUE
WEST 12TH AVENUE
WEST 16TH AVENUE
KING EDWARD AVENUE WEST
WEST 33RD AVENUE
WEST 36TH AVENUE
Eldorado Hotel & 2400 Motel

Eating out in Vancouver

As food is one of Vancouver's great pleasures, dining out here can be an experience every bit as memorable as any number of gallery visits, views or mountain hikes. Not only does the rich bounty of ocean, field and forest provide a wealth of superb natural ingredients, but the city's multicultural population has produced a plethora of different ethnic cuisines, many of which provide the various strands for the city's favoured fusion cooking.

Blue Water Café specializes in Pacific Rim seafood ▲

Vancouver has a strong Asian culinary influence ▼

Culinary roots

Fine dining on seasonally available food is nothing new in Vancouver. For thousands of years, the **aboriginal population** that inhabited the present-day Downtown peninsula feasted on, among other things, wild salmon (fresh, or dried and smoked for the winter), camas bulbs (quamash), and nuts, roots berries and game from the nearby forests and mountains. Vancouver has no restaurant devoted entirely to the aboriginal tradition, but you'll find hints of the past in many of the city's menus.

How it began

If a year can be highlighted in which Vancouver's food and wine began its progress to its current elevated position – dining here, by common consent, is every bit as good as in London, Sydney or New York – then it was 1985. This was the year that a 42-year-old British-born chef, **John Bishop**, who had come to Vancouver in 1973 after a cosmopolitan grounding in cooking that took him from London to the Caribbean by way of Ireland, first opened his eponymous restaurant on what was then a relatively undistinguished stretch of 4th Avenue. The restaurant is still there, and regularly wins plaudits as the best in the city.

The West Coast way

What Bishop did seems commonplace today – indeed, his ideas caught on in virtually every major restaurant in the city and beyond. Before long, the Vancouver restaurateur found himself in the vanguard of a gastronomic movement that also had its champions in California, notably Alice Waters and her restaurant in Berkeley, *Chez Panisse*, and a cast of

West Coast–trained disciples, such as Sally Clarke in London, who spread a particular approach to cuisine far and wide. And what was this approach? Bishop's mantra is "**buy locally, eat seasonally**", an attitude now shared by most of Vancouver's leading chefs. The actual cooking goes by many names: fusion, Californian, West Coast, Pacific Rim. But at heart it's about taking ideas and influences from different ethnic cuisines and applying them to locally sourced ingredients of the highest quality.

▲ Seasonal scallops

▼ Futomaki sushi

The menu decoded

Bishop's dishes change seasonally, but an almost random look at two recent **dishes** – BC Spotted Shrimp Salad with kimchi, two-year-old miso, dashi custard and kelp crunch, and grilled Thomas Reid Farms organic chicken breast with herb gnocchi and wild mushroom ragout – illustrates what's going on. In the first, the kelp is an ingredient straight from the city's aboriginal culinary heritage; the miso and dashi (a Japanese

▼ Pacific salmon

Pacific salmon

For all the organic, obscure and exotic ingredients you'll find in Vancouver's markets and restaurants, perhaps the most ubiquitous and straightforward is wild **Pacific salmon**. For those accustomed to farmed salmon, with its lurid artificial colour and bland-tasting flesh, this is a different fish and a very different dining experience. It's no longer as common as it was – aboriginal peoples used to shovel salmon onto the land as fertilizer – and can be expensive, but a stroll through the fish stalls of Granville Island market and a simply grilled salmon steak remain two of the city's best gastronomic experiences.

soup) provide the hint of **Asian influence** (often Chinese and Japanese) that almost always pervades Vancouver's cooking; and the house-made kimchi (a Korean pickle), acknowledges Korean cooking, one of the latest ethnic cuisines to make its presence felt in the city.

In the second dish, the gnocchi are a nod to **Italy**, whose cuisine is also invariably present in the West Coast approach. The wild mushrooms hark back to the days when food was easily plundered from the natural environment, and the aioli (garlic sauce) and ragout bring the richer, more traditional influences of **France** to bear. The BC shrimp and chicken from a named British Columbia farm underline the penchant for locally sourced (and, these days, organic) natural ingredients.

Wine-tasting in British Columbia ▲

Grapes on the vine ▼

Canadian wine

Whereas no-one questions the quality of Canadian wild salmon, **Canadian wine** used to be something of a joke. Not anymore. British Columbia now has two premier wine-producing regions, one on southern Vancouver Island and the other, larger one in the Okanagan Valley in the province's dry southwest corner. Both produce wines as good as their Californian, New Zealand and Australian New World cousins – though outside Canada they are all but unknown.

To get a taste, head to any of the multitude of Vancouver restaurants that favour locally sourced ingredients – most now also have long lists of BC wines by the glass and bottle. Names to look out for include the superlative **Inniskillen** estate, along with **Sumac Ridge** and **Jackson-Triggs**, all three based in the Okanagan. Closer to Vancouver, **Wild Goose** and **Starling Lane** are small but highly rated Vancouver Island producers.

A restaurant with a polished thirty- and forty-something clientele that offers reliably high-quality and non-threatening jazz. Downtown there's the similar *Rossini's Gastown* at 162 Water St (Ⓣ604/408-1300).

Yale 1300 Granville St and Drake St Ⓣ604/681-9253, Ⓦwww.theyale.ca. An outstanding venue and *the* place in the city to hear hardcore blues and R&B – check out the hall-of-fame photographs in the entryway of the blues maestros who've played here. It has a relaxed air and big dance floor and occasionally presents outstanding international names alongside lesser homegrown talent.

Clubs and discos

Many of the live-music venues above double as **clubs** and **discos** – the boundaries between the three are generally pretty blurred – and as in any city with a healthy alternative, student and music scene there are also plenty of fun, one-off clubs that have an irritating habit of cropping up and disappearing quickly. Most clubs of note or long standing are dotted around Downtown, Gastown and – increasingly – at the southern end of Richards and Granville streets – while the fly-by-night places are more likely to spring up on and around Main Street and Commercial Drive. See *The Georgia Straight* listings weekly for the latest. Cover charges are usually nominal ($5–15), with women often free before 11pm, and tickets are often available (sometimes free) at record shops. Bring ID if appropriate, as you will be need to be at least 19 and, often over 25, for most clubs.

Au Bar 674 Seymour St between Dunsmuir and West Georgia sts Ⓣ604/648-2227, Ⓦwww.aubarnightclub.com. Downtown club for suits and miniskirts, with martinis the (expensive) drink of choice. Strict dress code and vetting on the door (you'll spot the Seymour St queues from afar), but the exclusive air is what attracts punters. If you get in, people-watching may prove the most entertaining part of your evening. Three bars and small dance floor with safe Top 40, hip-hop and R&B.

Boss 1320 Richards St at Pacific Blvd Ⓣ604/619-9416, Ⓦwww.bossnightclub.net. This large Yaletown club changes identity (and name) from year to year, but makes the most of its cutting-edge music, lights and dance floor, and has a sharp clientele to match. There's plenty of room at the rear bar (one of eight) for a drink and a break from the music, with hip-hop currently on Sat and a wide range of sounds on theme nights the rest of the week.

Caprice 967 Granville St between Smithe and Nelson sts. Club Ⓣ604/685-3288, lounge 685-3189, Ⓦwww.capricenightclub.com. This club is the relocated and reincarnated *Luv-a-Fair*, which for years was one of the city's best. Its airy, modern successor, a converted cinema, lives up to its predecessor's high standards, with an excellent dance floor and state-of-the-art sound, light and video systems. If you don't want to dance, then the *Caprice Lounge* alongside offers a quieter retreat where you can eat and chill out in front of a fire and large-screen TVs.

Lotus Sound Lounge 455 Abbott St at West Pender St Ⓣ604/685-7777. An underlit underground club with some great nights, notably drum 'n' bass and lots of house. Elsewhere in the same building is the equally amenable *Honey* lounge (see p.152).

Tonic 919 Granville St between Nelson and Smithe sts Ⓣ604/669-0469, Ⓦwww.thetonicclub.com. One of the big, popular, no-nonsense dance clubs that characterize the Granville Street Downtown entertainment "strip" with great sound and lighting in a setting that has been described as a "country and Western saloon crossed with a Nevada whorehouse". Very similar, and one block south, is the cavernous Stone Temple, 1082 Granville St (Ⓣ604/488-1333, Ⓦwww.stonetemplenightclub.com).

Richard's on Richards 1036 Richards St and Nelson St Ⓣ604/687-6794, Ⓦwww.richardsonrichards.com. This club and disco – probably the best-known in the city – has been around for years and invariably invites sneers from young and hip clubbers. This is because it's a smart, trendy and somewhat pretentious place – check out the valet parking – aimed at the older, richer and better-heeled set. It's also hugely popular, so be prepared for long waits. And put on something other than a T-shirt and sneakers – there's a dress code.

Music is generally safe covers from the occasional live bands and recorded Top 40 and other mainstream dance fodder. Usually closed Sun, but opening times can vary.

Shine 363 Water St at Richards st ⓣ604/408-4321, ⓦwww.shinenightclub.com. Conveniently located and happening Gastown club which attracts some of the city's top DJs. Understated decor, pleasant staff, fair drink prices, with comfortable retro 1960s couches and all-white colour scheme that provide a sophisticated setting for house, reggae, soul, R&B, hip-hop and other sounds, usually arranged around musically themed nights. Dress up a touch, or you'll feel out of place.

Comedy

It's not that the inhabitants of Vancouver have no sense of humour, just that it's proved difficult here over the years to make money out of clubs that offer comedy and nothing else. As a result there's currently only one comedy club of long standing, though occasional venues add comedy to their schedules: see *The Georgia Straight* (see p.154) for the latest details.

Balthazar's House of Comedy 1215 Bidwell St at Davie St ⓣ604/689-8822, ⓦwww.balthazarvancouver.com. Small venue that usually hosts just one night of professional stand-up a week, currently on Monday.

Darby's Pub 2001 Macdonald St and West 4th Ave ⓣ604/803-8429, ⓦwww.darbyspub.ca. Fun bar (see p.152) that hosts a Mon-night comedy show with a different host and headliner each week.

Jupiter Café 1216 Bute St between Davie and Burnaby sts ⓣ604/609-6665, ⓦwww.jupitercafe.com. A West End bar (see p.151) that showcases professional stand-ups once weekly, currently on Mon.

12

The performing arts

Vancouver serves up enough top-quality highbrow culture to suit the whole spectrum of its cosmopolitan population and its visitors, with plenty of unusual and avant-garde **performances** to spice up the mainstream entertainment you'd expect of a major North American city. It also boasts a wide range of festivals devoted to the performing arts, the best of which are included in the calendar of events in Chapter 17 (see p.201). This being a well-integrated multicultural city, Vancouver also offers a range of performances that fully acknowledges and involves all parts of its diverse population.

As the western capital of Canada's **film industry**, Hollywood studios favour Vancouver in their pursuit of cheaper locations and production deals. It's therefore no surprise that the spread of **cinemas** is good – though the films shot in the city, with the odd exception, are rarely more than B-movie action flicks or "straight-to-video" offerings. Home-produced and Hollywood first-run films play in the Downtown movie houses on the central "Theatre Row" – the two blocks of Granville between Robson and Nelson streets – and at other big complexes, and there's no shortage of cinemas for more esoteric productions.

Major performance spaces

Centre in Vancouver for the Performing Arts 777 Homer St ⓣ604/602-0616, ⓦwww.centreinvancouver.com. In 1996 the Queen Elizabeth Theatre (see below) was joined by this world-class 1824-seat complex, an impressive three-level modern space opposite the central library – it was designed by the library's architect, Moshe Safdie: check out the amazing mirrored staircase and dramatic glass cone in the lobby. It has had a chequered career, the original owners having gone bust, and until 2002 the building sat empty. Now owned by Hong Kong property developers, it is once again hosting large-scale productions of popular theatre and musicals as well as various musical acts.

Chan Centre for the Performing Arts 6265 Crescent Rd, University of British Columbia ⓣ604/822-9197, ⓦwww.chancentre.com. The 1400-seat Chan Shun Concert Hall, the main space of the three-hall UBC performance complex, has the best acoustics in the city, and hosts shows by university music, drama and other groups, as well as fashion shows, world music concerts and other events. The UBC also has a smaller recital hall at Gate 4, 6361 Memorial Rd.

Orpheum Theatre 884 Granville St at Smithe ⓣ604/665-3050 or 876-3434, ⓦwww.vancouver.ca/theatres/orpheum. The refurbished and beautifully ornate 3000-seat Orpheum is Vancouver's oldest theatre. Built in 1927 as a cinema – the original Wurlitzer organ survives – it is all rococo gilt, deep-red carpets, ornamental plaster and chandeliers topped off by a painted dome ceiling, and serves as the headquarters of the well-respected Vancouver Symphony Orchestra and several small choirs.

Queen Elizabeth Theatre 600 Hamilton St between Dunsmuir and Georgia. Information ⓣ604/299-9000, tickets ⓣ604/665-3050, ⓦwww.vancouver.ca/theatres/qet. This modern 2929-seat theatre is the chief focus of the city's performing arts scene, playing host to a steady procession of visiting theatre, opera and dance troupes, and even

Information and tickets

Check the **listings** pages of *The Georgia Straight* weekly (widely available in dump bins around the city and online at ⓦwww.straight.com) or the *Vancouver Sun* (ⓦwww.vancouversun.com), whose full listings appear in the Thursday edition. The **Dance Centre** (ⓣ604/606-6400, ⓦwww.thedancecentre.ca) offers details of current and forthcoming dance performances.

For classical-music recitals, check the above sources or fliers posted at the city's main music stores.

Tickets for most musical, theatrical and other events can be obtained from individual box offices or through Ticketmaster (ⓣ604/280-4444, ⓦwww.ticketmaster.ca), which has around forty outlets around the city. Cut-price **same-day tickets** for events can often be obtained from the "Tickets Tonight" desk (ⓦwww.ticketstonight.ca) at the main Burrard Street infocentre (see p.36).

the occasional big rock band. It also houses the 668-seat Vancouver Playhouse, used for smaller recitals, dance and chamber-music concerts and by the resident Vancouver Playhouse Theatre Company.

Classical music

Vancouver has many of the ingredients required for a thriving classical music scene, not least an excellent symphony orchestra and several outstanding performance spaces. It also has a wide range of societies and ensembles that cater to more specialized areas of the classical canon, such as baroque, choral and chamber music.

Early Music Vancouver 1254 West 7th Ave ⓣ604/732-1610, ⓦwww.earlymusic.bc.ca. This society, one of several musical associations in the city, promotes medieval, baroque and other early music, preferably played with the original instruments of the time. Concerts with leading international or local performers are held at venues across the city, including St Andrew's Wesley Church at 1012 Nelson St, the Chan Centre and UBC Recital Hall, 6361 Memorial Rd. Look out, too, for performances at the Early Music Festival in July and August (see p.204).

Friends of Chamber Music PO Box 38046 RPO King Edward Mall ⓣ604/437-5747, ⓦwww.friendsofchambermusic.ca. Highly regarded organization that offers around eight concerts a year, almost all of them performed in the Vancouver Playhouse.

Music-in-the-Morning Concert Society PO Box 95024, Kingsgate RPO, Vancouver ⓣ604/873-4612, ⓦwww.musicinthemorning.org. This society began modestly in musician-educator June Goldsmith's front room but now organizes innovative and respected morning concerts of old and new music with local and visiting musicians. Morning concerts are held at various locations at 10.30am (Sept–May Tues–Fri); one-hour "Rush Hour" concerts take place in the Vancouver Art Gallery, 750 Hornby St (see p.46). Other spinoffs include "Composers & Coffee", in which musicians discuss a composer's work and illustrate it through performance; and afternoon "Family Musik", aimed at families with children.

Pacific Baroque Orchestra ⓣ604/215-0406, ⓦwww.pacificbaroque.com. Dedicated to presenting performances using original (or authentic replica) seventeenth- and eighteenth-century baroque instruments. Often has month-long, themed programmes, such as 'Salzburg Serenade: Mozart, the early Years'. Venues vary.

University of British Columbia School of Music UBC Recital Hall, Gate 4, 6361 Memorial Rd ⓣ604/822-5574, ⓦwww.music.ubc.ca. The UBC presents around eight major and many smaller performances during January and February and between September and November. Many of the concerts are free.

Uzume Taiko ⓣ604/873-6378, ⓦwww.uzume.com. Vancouver has become a major centre for Japanese-influenced Taiko music, and in Uzume Taiko the city has North America's first professional drumming ensemble (three drummers, a flautist, a cellist and African and Latin percussionists). See website for latest concert locations.

Vancouver Bach Choir 805–235 Keith Rd, West Vancouver ⓣ604/921-8012, ⓦwww.vancouver bachchoir.com. The city's top non-professional 150-strong choir performs between three and five major

concerts yearly of Bach and other choral works at the Orpheum Theatre (see p.159). Its Christmas sing-along performance of Handel's *Messiah* is something of a city institution.

Vancouver Cantata Singers 125 West 7th Ave ⓣ604/730-8856, ⓦwww.vancouvercantatasingers.com. Various locations are used by this forty-strong, semi-professional choir for performances of traditional and contemporary choral music.

Vancouver Chamber Choir 1254 West 7th Ave ⓣ604/738-6822, ⓦwww.vancouverchamberchoir.com. This is Vancouver's best and most internationally renowned professional choir. Founded in 1971, the choir performs at a dozen locations, including the Orpheum, the Chan Centre and even the *Fairmont Waterfront Hotel* and *Hotel Vancouver* (see p.121).

Vancouver Chopin Society 400-601 West Broadway ⓣ604/871-4450, ⓦwww.chopinsociety.org. Presents about half-a-dozen recitals a year devoted to Chopin at different small venues.

Vancouver New Music Society 837 Davie St ⓣ604/633-0861, ⓦwww.newmusic.org. This association is responsible for promoting cutting-edge twentieth-century and contemporary classical music, including opera and mixed-media dance and film performances. It presents around seven major concerts annually between September and June, usually at the Vancouver East Cultural Centre (see p.162), and occasionally links with other orchestras and musical organizations to present festivals of new music.

Vancouver Opera 500–845 Cambie St ⓣ604/638-0222 for tickets, 682-2871 for information, ⓦwww.vancouveropera.ca. The Vancouver Opera produces four operas during its season (Oct–May) at the Queen Elizabeth Theatre: productions enjoy an excellent local and national reputation and consist of operas from the mainstream repertoire, often performed by international stars, and works by more obscure Canadian composers. The box office is open Mon–Fri 9am–4pm.

Vancouver Recital Society 304–873 Beatty St ⓣ604/736-0363, ⓦwww.vanrecital.com. Hosts two of the best and most popular cycles in the city – the summer Chamber Music Festival (various locations) and the recital cycle at the Vancouver Playhouse (Sept–April). Concerts are also held at other venues, including the Chan Centre. Presents a few major international names each year, as well as up-and-coming performers.

Vancouver Symphony Orchestra 601 Smithe St ⓣ604/876-3434, ⓦwww.vancouversymphony.ca. The highly regarded VSO presents most concerts at the Orpheum or the Chan Centre but also sometimes gives free recitals in the summer at beaches and parks, usually culminating in a concert on Whistler Mountain. Its repertoire includes so-called "Masterworks" (great classical works), "Kids' Koncerts" (aimed at school children) and "VSO Pops", a mixture of pop, Broadway and other show tunes. The box office (Mon–Fri 1–5pm) is at the Orpheum Theatre at Smithe and Granville (see p.159).

Theatre

Theatre in Vancouver is what you would expect from a vibrant, urbane and multicultural city. It has a healthy mainstream presence, but there are also a number of smaller and long-established performance spaces that feed productions – and actors and actresses – onto larger stages, both literally and metaphorically. Film and TV star Michael J. Fox, for example, graduated from the Arts Club Theatre on Granville Island. There is also a thriving community theatre scene and plenty of opportunities to catch a performance outdoors during some of the city's summer festivals (see p.203).

Arts Club Theatre 1585 Johnston St, Granville Island ⓣ604/687-1644, ⓦwww.artsclub.com. Established in 1964, this is one of the leading lights in the city's drama scene, and one of the most active. Performances are staged at several venues: the 425-seat main stage offers mainstream drama, comedies and musicals; the bar next door presents small-scale revues and cabaret; while the 650-seat refurbished Art Deco Stanley Theatre at 2750 Granville St south of Broadway – a former vaudeville theatre and movie house – offers a mixture of musicals, long-run shows and mainstream and avant-garde plays by Canadian and other dramatists.

Boca del Lupo Third Floor, 1405 Anderson St ⓣ604/684-2622, ⓦwww.bocadellupo.com. This is a superb and well-respected troupe that offers innovative and highly entertaining shows of all kinds, including free performances in Stanley Park in the summer.

Electric Company 1883 Venables St ⓣ604/253-4222, ⓦwww.electriccompanytheatre.com. A dynamic, small company that presents hugely exciting and dramatic original productions at different venues.

Firehall Arts Centre 280 East Cordova St and Gore ⓣ604/689-0926, ⓦwww.firehallartscentre.ca. The leader of Vancouver's community and avant-garde pack, presenting mime, music and visual arts. The 150-seat theatre is housed in a historic fire station and generally hosts three major (often ground-breaking) productions each season from the resident Firehall Theatre Company, as well as cutting-edge contemporary dance. There's also a nice lounge and gallery, plus an outdoor stage for summer shows.

Green Thumb Company Suite 320, 309 West Cordova St ⓣ604/254-4055, ⓦwww.greenthumb.bc.ca. A predominantly children's and family-oriented company that often produces plays that address serious social issues in an accessible and light-hearted way. Most productions take place at the Vancouver East Cultural Centre (see below).

Mortal Coil 164-555 Great Northern Way ⓣ604/874-6153, ⓦwww.mortalcoil.bc.ca. Like the Green Thumb Company (see above), this innovative troupe will appeal to children, thanks to their magical and extravagant productions, complete with elaborate costumes, stilts, masks and superb physical theatre. Locations vary.

▲ Yevgeny Sudbin at the Vancouver Playhouse

Presentation House Theatre 333 Chesterfield Ave, North Vancouver ⓣ604/990-3474, ⓦwww.phtheatre.org. The North Shore is short of venues, largely having to make do with this former 1902 schoolhouse, the setting for contemporary theatre productions and performance art.

Theatre Under the Stars Malkin Bowl, Stanley Park ⓣ604/687-0174 or 257-0366, ⓦwww.tuts.ca. July and August productions by "TUTS" at the Malkin Bowl – built in 1934 as a bandstand – are fun, popular and lightweight (and, note, not free), but can suffer from being staged in one of Canada's rainiest cities. Try for a dry night – productions will be cancelled on very bad days – and bring something to sit on and something warm to wear. For more outdoor drama, head to the Bard on the Beach Shakespeare Festival (p.203).

Touchstone Theatre Suite 200, 873 Beatty St ⓣ604/709-9973, ⓦwww.touchstonetheatre.com. Touchstone has been presenting the best plays by Canadian playwrights at various venues for over thirty years, during which time it has established a reputation for top-quality staging and performance.

Vancouver East Cultural Centre 1895 Venables St and Victoria Drive ⓣ604/251-1363, ⓦwww.vecc.bc.ca. This highly renowned 350-space in East Vancouver – known colloquially as the "Cultch" – is housed in a late nineteenth-century former church adapted for performance and is used by a highly eclectic mix of drama, dance, mime and musical groups. Performances are usually modern, sometimes controversial and almost always far better than the "neighbourhood" tag – suggesting small-scale local productions – the place modestly attaches to itself. To get here take bus #20 from Downtown to Commercial Drive at Venables and walk east two blocks uphill.

Vancouver Playhouse Theatre Company Hamilton St at Dunsmuir ⓣ604/665-3050, ⓦwww.vancouverplayhouse.com. One of western Canada's biggest theatre companies. It usually presents six top-quality shows from the mainstream theatrical canon, employing some of the region's premier performers, directors and set designers.

Waterfront Theatre 1411 Cartwright St, Granville Island ⓣ604/685-6217, ⓦwww.giculturalsociety.org. This popular and intimate 224-seat theatre is used by three resident and several occasional local companies. You

Dance

Vancouver serves dance enthusiasts well, especially those whose bent is for **contemporary dance**, an area where the work over many years of talented individuals such as Karen Jamieson has provided the impetus for a flourishing and nurturing environment for modern choreography. Many leading lights of the city's dance world, as well as those from farther afield, come together for the annual Dancing on the Edge festival (see below and p.203).

can expect a wide range of shows – anything from musicals to improvisation – plus drama workshops and readings.

Anna Wyman Dance Theatre 707–207 West Hastings St ⓣ604/685-5699, ⓦwww.annawyman.com. Although its repertoire is wide, this troupe specializes in contemporary dance. As well as staging shows in a variety of conventional spaces, it occasionally puts on free outdoor performances on Granville Island and at Robson Square near the Vancouver Art Gallery.

Ballet British Columbia 677 Davie St, sixth floor ⓣ604/732-5003, ⓦwww.balletbc.com. The province's top company performs – along with major visiting dance companies – at the Queen Elizabeth Theatre (see p.159). The corps is highly respected and known for its bold and powerful performances and its sophisticated approach and interpretations. It presents both modern and more traditional dance.

EDAM Western Front Lodge, 303 East 8th Ave ⓣ604/876-9559, ⓦwww.edamdance.org. Experimental Dance and Music was founded in 1982 by six dancers and a musician and has long favoured developing dance through improvisation. It presents multimedia productions mixing dance, film, music and art at a variety of venues.

Karen Jamieson Dance Company 4036 West 19th Ave ⓣ604/893-8807, ⓦwww.kjdance.ca. Jamieson is an award-winning choreographer whose company, founded in 1983, often uses solely Canadian composers and artists and incorporates aboriginal themes into its work.

Kokoro Dance Company 339 West Hastings St ⓣ604/662-7441, ⓦwww.kokoro.ca. An innovative company whose name means "heart" in Japanese and whose works combine elements of modern dance and traditional Japanese dance. Most performances are held at the Vancouver East Cultural Centre.

Scotiabank Dance Centre 677 Davie St ⓣ604/689-0926, ⓦwww.thedancecentre.ca. This dance centre sits in a former bank building converted in 2001 by Arthur Erickson, architect of the Museum of Anthropology and other Vancouver buildings (see p.89). It provides studio and rehearsal space for around 30 companies and is open to the public for workshops, classes, exhibitions and other events. It also houses the Vancouver Dance Centre (ⓣ604/606-6400, ⓦwww.thedancecentre.ca), a major source of information on dance in Vancouver and beyond. Contact it for details of the major Dancing on the Edge Festival in July (for more on the festival, see p.203).

Film

Vancouver may feature prominently in the world of film production, but this is a city that still appears to be no more or less obsessed with watching films than any other place its size. This said, it has plenty of multiplex screens for first-runs and several repertory movie houses dotted around the city's fringes that cater to more dedicated film buffs. Cinema enthusiasts should time a visit to the city to coincide with the Vancouver International Film Festival (North America's third largest) in late September and October (see p.204).

Cinemark Tinseltown 88 Pender St at Abbott ⓣ604/806-0799, ⓦwww.cinemark.com. Just two blocks south of Water St and the heart of Gastown, this multi-screen in the International Village complex has the most modern and high-tech of the city centre's first-run cinemas, with big screens, underground parking and good seating.

Fifth Avenue Cinemas 2110 Burrard St at West 5th Ave ⓣ604/734-0300, ⓦwww.festivalcinemas.ca. Fiveplex cinema in South Vancouver run by the founder of the Vancouver Film Festival. It is one of the better in the city for art-house or more arty first-run films.

Films and filming in Vancouver

Vancouver's burgeoning **film and TV industry** – as a production centre it now rates third in terms of size behind Los Angeles and New York – has seen it rather hyperbolically dubbed "Hollywood North". Others, more unkindly, have christened it "Brollywood" – Hollywood with rain – not least *The X-Files* lead David Duchovny, who lamented that it rained "400 inches a day". The star's unhappiness with the climate was apparently one of the reasons the show fled Vancouver after five seasons had been shot in the city.

That said, *The X-Files* was a major catalyst for a business that sprang from a venture worth just US$12 million in 1978 to an industry that now generates at least $650 million plus $1 billion in indirect revenues.

The reason is simple – money. It costs less to produce films and TV in Vancouver, though there are those who claim, Duchovny's complaints aside, that it was the weather that first lured *The X Files'* makers to the city – the rainy, overcast days were perfect for the sombre pall that infused many of the show's early episodes.

True or not, the US producers of this and other shows loved the favourable exchange rates, the cheap (and union-lite) labour, the easy flight from LA and, above all, the wide range of locations that easily double for US locations. Tenements, skyscrapers, alleys – especially the alleys – docks, waterfront and more need little or no disguise to stand in for New York, Philadelphia, Chicago or other stateside cities.

Thus remakes of *Perry Mason* and *Ironside*, for example, feature the Vancouver Art Gallery, while chunks of the city also appeared in Schwarzenegger's *The Sixth Day*. Vancouver can also do London, Hong Kong and Russia, appearing as the last in *The Russia House* with Sean Connery. Inland, British Columbia offers forests, lakes, mountains and, around Kamloops, areas of near desert – much of *First Blood*, for example, Sylvester Stallone's first Rambo movie, was shot in and around Hope in the Fraser Valley east of Vancouver, the town being wasted by Stallone in spectacular fashion near the film's end.

The merits, or otherwise, of *First Blood* aside, the majority of films and TV shows made in Vancouver are usually forgettable at best, and B-movie straight-to-video or unmitigated rubbish at worst. Over the years, better-known outings include *The Accused* (with Jodie Foster), *Little Women*, *We're No Angels* (with Sean Penn), *This Boy's Life* (Robert de Niro) and *Bird on a Wire* (Mel Gibson and Goldie Hawn). More recently, Oscar-winning *Juno* (2007) was shot in and around Vancouver, the city standing in for Minnesota, as were superhero movie *Fantastic Four* (2005) and *Eclipse* (2010), third in the 'Twilight' series based on the books of Stephenie Meyer.

In the same way that Vancouver- and Canadian-produced films may be little known, so there is a long roster of "American" stars who actually hail from the land of the maple leaf: Dan Ackroyd, Jim Carrey, Christopher Plummer, Keanu Reeves, Donald Sutherland and William Shatner, with Pamela Anderson, Raymond Burr (of *Ironside* and *Perry Mason* fame), Michael J. Fox and James Doohan (the immortal Scotty in *Star Trek*) hailing from Vancouver itself. One Bill Pratt also worked in the city as a 22-year-old, and might have remained a longshoreman-cum-stagehand had he not moved to Hollywood and changed his name – to Boris Karloff.

Among local filmmakers, the best-known name is Atom Egoyan, who grew up in Victoria; his films include *Speaking Parts* (1989), *The Adjuster* (1991), *The Sweet Hereafter* (1997), *Diaspora* (2001) and *Adoration* (2008).

To find out more about the city's film and TV business, pick up *Reel West* magazine from newsstands (Ⓦwww.reelwest.com) or contact the BC Film Commission (Ⓣ604/660-2732, Ⓦwww.bcfilmcommission.com), which provides updates on movies and TV series currently being shot in the city.

Granville Cineplex 855 Granville St between Robson and Smithe ⓣ604/684-4000, ⓦwww.cineplex.com. What's happened to Granville Street? Once there were a dozen or so cinemas on the strip: now this is the last one, a multiplex that's also known locally as the Granville 7, and an obvious Downtown choice (with the Paramount – see below) to catch a big-budget first-run movie.

Hollywood 3123 West Broadway at Balaclava ⓣ604/738-3211, ⓦwww.hollywoodtheatre.ca. A Kitsilano repertory cinema that can also always be relied on for good (and good-value) double bills and second-run (or just over first-run) movies. It celebrated its 70th birthday in 2005, during which time it's been run by several generations of the same family, the Farleighs.

Pacific Cinémathèque 1131 Howe St near Helmcken ⓣ604/688-8202, ⓦwww.cinematheque.bc.ca. The nonprofit film society that runs this screen is devoted to furthering the understanding of cinema and contemporary visual arts. As part of its brief, it shows a good range of art-house, overseas and experimental films, all of which makes it the best non-mainstream cinema in the city. The programmes can be hit or miss, but film buffs will usually find something tempting.

Paramount 900 Burrard St at Smithe ⓣ604/630-1407, ⓦwww.cineplex.com. A state-of-the-art nine-screen multiplex that opened in 2005 with sound system and screens guaranteed to show first-run blockbusters to best effect.

Ridge Theatre 3131 Arbutus St at West 15th Ave ⓣ604/732-3352, ⓦwww.festivalcinemas.ca. A little too far south to catch its target Kits audience, but still a great neighbourhood place for second-run, classic and other films. Look out for its provocatively paired double bills and late-lunch (1.30pm) "Movies for Mommies" screenings. Built in 1950, it's virtually unchanged – there's even an enclosed "crying room" for parents with boisterous children or howling infants.

Vancity Theatre Vancouver International Film Centre, 1181 Seymour St at Davie ⓣ604/685-0260, ⓦwww.vifc.org. Opened in 2006, this modern and extremely comfortable cinema comes from the people who produce the city's international film festival and presents a dynamic repertory programme.

13

Gay Vancouver

While it may lack the profile or élan of San Francisco, Vancouver enjoys the same laid-back West Coast attitudes and *joie de vivre*. The city boasts a large, vibrant and unabashed gay, lesbian and transgender community, much of which is culturally and politically active. There's also a lively and diverse scene when it comes to entertainment and nightlife, with plenty of clubs – theme nights are a popular phenomenon – drag shows and up-to-the-minute bars and discos.

Gays and lesbians live and socialise across the city but especially on and around Davie and Denman streets and, to a lesser extent, the edgier environs of Commercial Drive. Those in these communities, plus an increasing number of visitors, now have the benefit of British Columbia's enlightened rulings and subsequent legalization of same-sex marriage.

It hasn't always been this way, homosexuality having only been decriminalized in Canada in 1969. This followed a slow process of protest and liberalization which started five years earlier with the creation in Vancouver of the Association for Social Knowledge, Canada's first openly gay and lesbian discussion forum. Today, the easygoing self-confidence of the city's gays and lesbians is traced by many to 1990, when Vancouver hosted Celebration 90: Gay Games III and Cultural Festival, a week-long event that attracted 8500 participants and spectators to around thirty sports and associated cultural events.

Same-sex marriage in British Columbia

The moment was 6.09pm on July 20, 2005 – but it was a long time coming. Up until this point, moves to secure the legitimacy in law of **same-sex marriage** in Canada had met with plenty of conflict and confusion on the part of federal and provincial legislators. Twenty couples, including ten from BC, had begun the concerted legal campaign, taking the federal government to court to fight for equality rights in marriage some five years earlier. Rulings in lower and provincial courts were largely favourable, and in 2003 the ruling was handed down that the law must be changed from July 12, 2004. Then the Ontario appeal court ruled that there was no reason for implementation to be delayed – the change should take place with immediate effect from June 10, 2003 (and weddings from 2001 should be registered). The problem? Despite the ruling having federal force, only in Ontario did it seem to have any teeth. Couples applying for marriage licences in BC were turned down. This was a federal law that, paradoxically, seemed to apply in only one province. Then on July 8, 2003, the BC appeal court lifted the suspension in granting licences – same-sex couples were free to marry. However, almost two years of wrangling, not helped by elections and political point-scoring, would ensue before a pan-Canadian law finally hit the statute books.

For information and links on same-sex marriages, visit Ⓦwww.gayvan.com/gaymarriage.

Gay and lesbian events

The main draw in Vancouver's gay calendar is **Pride**, which celebrated its thirtieth anniversary in 2008. It usually takes place over three days or more during the first long weekend in August. Special events are held in clubs across the city, while the traditional parade along Denman and Beach has, by general consent, become bigger and better each year, with ever more exuberant floats. Over the years, the parade has spawned stalls and stages at Sunset Beach up to Davie Street, with lots of beer gardens and live performances.

For further information contact the Vancouver Pride Society (Ⓣ604/687-0955, Ⓦwww.vancouverpride.ca or www.vancouverpride.com); special club events can be found in the listings sections of the free publications *The Georgia Straight* and *Xtra! West* – and on their websites – in the week or so preceding the event (see below and p.154). The success of Pride's procession, in particular, has spawned the Vancouver Dyke March (Ⓦwww.vancouverdykemarch.com), founded in 2004. It currently takes place in Pride week around McSpadden Park, at Victoria Drive and Fourth Avenue, and is followed by a free festival at Grandview Park.

The Queer Film and Video Festival (Ⓦwww.outonscreen.com) takes over the city's movie theatres shortly after Pride in August. It marked its twentieth anniversary in 2008.

Change has continued apace, and today the city's progressive attitude is making it a prime destination for gay couples wanting to wed, same-sex marriages having been made legal in 2003. At the same time, a slightly ageing population and a general shift in lifestyles have led the city's gay and lesbian culture to diversify beyond clubs and pubs in recent years. Now there's a plethora of courses and group activities available in the city – anything from gay quilting to gay Ping-Pong and gay square-dancing.

That's not to say the city's gay nightlife is second-rate. Davie Village, which runs from Burrard along Davie to Denman, is where you will find the highest concentration of long-established gay clubs, pubs and stores, though there are plenty of other venues throughout the city; lesbians, for their part, have traditionally gathered on or around Commercial Drive (The Drive). Most clubs are open late, usually until 4am, a relatively new freedom following the relaxation of licensing laws.

There are also plenty of **events** and **festivals** that have become, or are becoming, permanent fixtures. These include the city's Pride celebration in August (see box above) and the Stonewall Festival in June, the latter a mixed bag of cultural and other events, usually held in Grandview Park on Commercial Drive between Charles and Williams streets.

Contacts, media and information

The best source of information pertaining to gays and lesbians is **Xtra! West** (Ⓦwww.xtra.ca), produced by the not-for-profit Pink Triangle Press. It's available from kerbside boxes and from music, video and other stores around the city, and has articles on news, events and people, as well as a classified section and full gay and lesbian nightlife and entertainment listings.

Other general contacts include the **Gay & Lesbian Centre Help Line** (Ⓣ604/684-6869 or 1-800/566-1179) and the **Gay & Lesbian Business Association** (Ⓣ604/253-4307 or 739-4522, Ⓦwww.glba.org), the latter being a source for gay- and lesbian-friendly businesses in the city. The **Gay Lesbian Transgendered Bisexual Community Centre** – The Centre for short – has a good library at 1170 Bute St between Davie and Pendrell sts (Ⓣ604/684-5307, Ⓦwww.qmunity.ca).

Little Sister's Book and Art Emporium at 1238 Davie St (Ⓣ604/669-1753, Ⓦwww. littlesistersbookstore.com) sells everything from dildos to greetings cards, and also has a comprehensive noticeboard. It also sells tickets for various events, as does GayMart at 1148 Davie (Ⓣ604/681-3262).

Fetish fans should also look at theme nights at Club 23 West (see opposite) and the PumpJack Pub (see opposite): there is a strict fetish dress code. Visit Ⓦwww .vancouverdungeon.com for details of monthly play parties, dungeon nights and workshops.

Nightlife

Gay and lesbian **clubs** tend to open and close with alarming speed, so it is always worth checking listings magazines (see p.154), websites and flyers and posters for latest details. Gay and lesbian pubs tend to be rather better established, and to help you find a place operating, or still with a gay and/or lesbian emphasis, we have indicated which bars and clubs below have been open for some time. Cover charges, varying according to the act or night, are charged at most venues other than pubs on theme nights. A word of warning: while Vancouver is a welcoming city for the gay traveller, it is still important to keep your wits about you. There has been the occasional case of queer-bashing, as in most cities, and a man was murdered in the cruising area of Stanley Park in 2001.

Pubs and restaurants

Café Luxy 1235 Davie St Ⓣ604/669-5899, Ⓦwww.cafeluxy.com. Davie Village and the West End have no shortage of gay-friendly places to eat and drink, but this stands out by virtue of its fresh, home-made pastas and jazz-groove DJ nights, currently every Tues.

Davie Village Cafe 1141 Davie St Ⓣ604/228-1819. A fine, gay-owned and gay-operated place that opened in 2005 and has quickly become popular for breakfast, lunch and dinner. Has a pleasant patio for outdoor dining and people-watching.

816 Granville 816 Granville St Ⓦwww.club816 .com. A Downtown dance club with a high percentage gay clientele, especially on Sat, when it's open until 6am the following morning. No alcohol. $20 cover.

Fountainhead Pub 1025 Davie St between Burrard and Thurlow Ⓣ604/687-2222, Ⓦwww.thefountainheadpub.com. A popular and pleasantly buzzing place at the heart of Davie Village for good food, drink (including microbrewed beers) and a large, heated patio from which to spy on all the street action. Also has a pool table, darts and multiple TV screens. Tends to attract a slightly older, more mellow crowd. Gay-owned and operated. Open daily from 11am until late. No cover.

Oasis 1240 Thurlow St between Davie and Burnaby Ⓣ604/685-1724, Ⓦwww .oasisvancouver.com. Boasts, among other things, a piano bar and Vancouver's longest cocktail and martini menu (over 200 types). Comfortable upstairs place for people who want to be heard above the music. Also has a tapas menu with daily specials, and a rooftop patio. The staff is especially friendly. Open daily 9pm until late.

1181 1138 Davie St near Bute St Ⓣ604/687-3991, Ⓦwww.tightlounge.com. At the heart of Davie Village, this is a stylish and popular "straight-friendly" gay-owned and gay-run bar with a polished, contemporary interior.

Event organizers

The HerShe Bars (Ⓦwww.flygirlproductions.com) are popular lesbian nights held in different venues mainly on the Sunday of any holiday or long weekend. Other useful websites to visit if you are looking for one-off events and information include Ⓦwww .lesbigay.com and www.girlgigs.com.

PumpJack Pub 1167 Davie St between Thurlow and Bute ☎604/685-3417, ⓦwww.pumpjackpub.com. A spacious spot and Vancouver's leather bar of choice. Arrive early to guarantee a window-side bar stool to watch the men go by. There are pool tables and uniform nights. Expect queues at the weekends.

Speakeasy Bar & Grill 1239 Davie St at Bute St ☎604/685-5761, ⓦwww.thespeakeasy.ca. One of the more recent additions to the Davie Village scene, this airy bar opened in autumn 2008, and features big screens for sports events, cosy booths, a sit-down bar, good-value meal specials, is open for breakfast, lunch and dinner, and has a lovely second-floor patio.

Sugar Daddy's 1262 Davie St ☎604/632-1646. This welcoming neighbourhood pub and sports bar is another West End gay rendezvous of some standing, thanks to video sports, big-screen TVs, and good burgers, beer and margaritas. It has the area's largest outdoor patio. Open for lunch and dinner daily.

Clubs

Celebrities 1022 Davie St near Burrard ☎604/681-6180, ⓦwww.celebritiesnightclub.com. Vancouver's current high-profile and showcase gay and lesbian club, completely renovated and overhauled in 2005, with Davie Street's largest dance floor, the latest lighting and sound systems and a roster of the city's top DJs. Also numerous theme and one-off nights, plus excellent entertainers. Cover charge most nights.

Club 23 West 23 West Cordova ☎604/662-3277, ⓦwww.club23.ca. A cool, dark, split-level club, perfect for the various theme nights held here, such as the naked parties organized by the Pacific Canadian Association of Nudists (☎604/684-9872, ext 2026, ⓦwww.p-can.org), Lesbians on the Loose and Sin City fetish nights.

Lotus Sound Lounge 455 Abbott St ☎604/685-7777. The bars here host a number of gay and lesbian nights, with men-only, women-only and various theme nights: call for latest details. There are some mixed nights and occasional fetish and other theme parties. Call before you go for latest permutations and times.

Numbers 1042 Davie St between Burrard and Thurlow ☎604/685-4077, ⓦwww.numbers.ca. The city's longest-established gay bar, this is a cruisey, multilevel venue (gay-owned and -run) that has been in business since 1980, with a gay disco, kitschy dance floor, movies and pool tables upstairs, men and women downstairs – but with very few women. It was given a glitzy overhaul in 2005 that included opening the front of the building on to Davie St and adding new video screens and a powerful new sound system. It tends to attract a slightly more mature crowd and is very busy at weekends. As with virtually all the clubs listed here, there is a wide variety of theme nights, when a cover charge may apply.

Odyssey 1251 Howe St near Davie ☎604/689-5256. A young gay and bisexual club with house and techno disco and theme shows on most nights. Expect to queue on Fridays and Saturdays as it is one of the hippest and wildest places in town. Novelty nights include Gay Bingo, Shower Power and Feather Boa. Cover charge most nights.

Pulse 1138 Davie St near Thurlow St ☎604/669-2013, ⓦwww.pulsenightclubvancouver.com. New gay nightclubs are a rarity in Vancouver, and though this is a revamped former club (the Majestic), the overhaul has produced a new dance floor and state-of-the-art sound system, giving the more established Davie Village clubs a run for their money.

Male saunas

F212 Steam 1048 Davie St ☎604/689-9719, ⓦwww.f212.com. This bathhouse is found at the heart of Davie's gay "village" in the West End. It has three rooms, lockers, a twelve-man Jacuzzi, steam rooms, an adult-video room and a weight area. Open 24hr. There is a second co-owned outlet, New West, at 430 Columbia St in New Westminster (☎604/540-2117), 40min on the SkyTrain from Downtown.

M2M 1210 Granville St (downstairs) near Davie ☎604/684-6011, ⓦwww.m2mplayspace.com. A Downtown spot that caters to the leather, steam, jocks and Levi fraternity. Open 24hr.

14

Shopping

Vancouver affords excellent **shopping** possibilities. Unlike many colder Canadian cities, it has largely eschewed the indoor mall, offering instead a wide variety of smaller specialist stores and a good selection of markets. It also has the range of designer and upmarket boutiques you would expect in a city of this size and wealth, as well as the predictable rash of souvenir and other tourist shops.

In **Downtown**, the key shopping thoroughfare is **Robson Street**, and in particular the stretch near the corner of Burrard Street, an intersection that supposedly has the highest pedestrian count of any city block in Canada. Robson's character has changed in the last few years, its former array of small European restaurants and specialist stores having given way to smart designer-clothing stores – with the emphasis on youth fashion – slick cafés and upscale restaurants. In the five blocks or so west of Granville you'll also find flagship stores for national and international chains, such as Banana Republic, Gap, Nike, Roots, French Connection, Zara and Chapters.

These days, the funkier (and more expensive) specialist shops are to be found in **Yaletown**, which has plenty of fashion, furniture and home-design stores. As rents rise, however, some of the businesses that made the area interesting in the first place are being forced out, and top international designer names are increasingly colonizing the streets. For food and fun browsing in small offbeat shops, **Granville Island** and its superb market have no rivals – though the island can be very busy, especially at weekends. In **Gastown**, specialist stores – the antiques, cigar and other stores on Water and Abbott streets in particular – leaven the weight of souvenir shops. Furniture and homeware stores are also beginning to make their presence felt in Gastown, and the area also has some of the finest galleries of Inuit and other aboriginal art in the city.

Away from Downtown, **Chinatown** boasts a good night market and plenty of food shops and stores selling Chinese kitchenware and goods. Further afield still, young local designers have begun to open stores on the southern reaches of **Main Street** (so-called SoMa) around 21st Avenue. The same area, from around 19th Avenue to 27th Avenue, is also thick with antiques stores, most dealing in a particular specialist area such as Art Deco or Second Empire. Another small corner of Main Street at 4th Avenue is rapidly being colonized by artists' and designers' studios, small cafés and specialist stores and galleries. Main Street's only problem, however, is its distance from the city centre, but if you want a taste of the emerging and funky new world of edgy East Vancouver, this is the street to visit.

To the south of Downtown, **Kitsilano**'s best specialist stores and secondhand bookshops cluster on **West 4th Avenue** between Burrard and Alma streets. There are also retail hotspots on Broadway, and though this is an emerging shopping street it doesn't yet have West 4th's eclectic mix of stores carrying anything from clothing, home furnishings and candles to books, sportswear and crystals.

Further south still, the **South Granville** enclave – the ten-block stretch of Granville Street from about West 7th to 17th Avenue – is a key shopping area. Once a place where older, wealthy denizens of old-money Shaughnessy came to shop, the area now has a trendier edge, with clothing stores and delicatessens complementing upscale galleries and stores selling antiques, Oriental carpets, furniture and designer clothes. When film companies want a double for New York's Fifth Avenue, this is where they come.

Much further afield, there are a handful of ethnic enclaves with food markets and stores aimed at the local community – though in all cases the areas' original ethnic identities are quickly being blurred by the arrival of Downtown hipsters and other new inhabitants. This is especially true of **Commercial Drive** east of Chinatown and the railway and bus station – more commonly known as "the Drive" – and in particular the stretch from 1st Avenue to Venables Street in East Vancouver, which for years was the city's **Little Italy**. The delis, coffee bars and Italian mammas are still in evidence, but the ethnic mix (Vietnamese, Korean, Chinese and others) is now more varied, as is the range of trendy clothing stores, bookshops and interesting speciality outlets.

Much the same can be said of **Little Greece**, to the west in Kitsilano, where the traditionally Greek-dominated area of Broadway from Trafalgar to Waterloo streets now has a far more diverse ethnic mix – though several good Greek restaurants and cafés survive. Farther south, a district where the ethnic flavour is still marked is the **Punjabi Market** – on Main Street between 49th and 51st avenues – where in the Guru Bazaar and other stores you'll find a wide range of Indo-Pakistani goods such as saris, fabrics and Indian spices and food. The area is also crammed with lots of tiny jewellery stores – bartering is acceptable in most.

The **opening hours** of most Vancouver stores are Monday to Saturday from 9 or 10am to 5.30 or 6pm (7pm for malls), with some staying open late (until 9pm) on Thursdays and Fridays. Many stores on Robson Street stay open until 9pm every night, at least in summer. Most malls and stores on Robson and other Downtown malls also open on Sunday, though hours are generally a little shorter – typically 10am or noon to 5pm. Opening times that are markedly different are given in individual entries below.

Note that visitors can no longer **claim back GST** (the goods and services tax) on purchases.

Aboriginal arts and crafts

Coastal Peoples Fine Arts Gallery 1024 Mainland St ⓣ604/685-9298, ⓦwww.coastalpeoples.com. This airy modern gallery was one of the first in Yaletown to deal in aboriginal art and artefacts. It sells small totems, paintings, prints and Inuit sculpture at top-dollar prices, but specializes in fine gold and silver jewellery. This is the place where you're likely to find the work of both established and up-and-coming artists.

Hill's Native Art 165 Water St ⓣ604/685-4249, ⓦwww.hillsnativeart.com. If you find the art of Water Street's museum-like galleries too precious or expensive, you might like Hill's. Established in 1946, it has a selection of items and artefacts aimed more squarely at ordinary visitors – T-shirts, prints, books, CDs of aboriginal music and so forth – as well as paintings, sculptures, masks and – if you have $35,000 to drop – full-sized totems.

Images for a Canadian Heritage 164 Water St ⓣ604/685-7046, ⓦwww.imagesforcanada.com. This government-licensed gallery sells some of Canada's finest (and most expensive) pieces of Inuit and other Pacific Northwest aboriginal art. The quality of its pieces makes it more of a museum than a store or gallery, a feeling reinforced by its tasteful brick and wood-beamed setting. Check out the fine soapstone sculptures and reindeer-antler carvings by Kevin Peters.

Inuit Gallery of Vancouver 206 Cambie St ⓣ604/688-7323, ⓦwww.inuit.com. Like the similar and nearby Images for a Canadian Heritage, this gallery showcases some of the finest and most expensive Inuit art available

on the open market – masks, works on paper, ceremonial bowls, stone and bone sculptures, painted chests, wood and argillite carvings and much more. Prices are high, but it's worth admiring the exquisite pieces even if you have no intention to buy. Often there's work here by some of the top names in aboriginal art, notably Bill Reid, Richard Davidson and David Neel.

Khot-La-Cha Salish Handicrafts 270 Whonoak St, North Vancouver ⓣ604/987-3339, ⓦwww.khot-la-cha.com. Crafts, sweaters, jewellery and inexpensive accessories are part of the large selection of goods at this Salish-run store a block off Capilano Rd.

Leona Lattimer Gallery 1590 West 2nd Ave at Fir St ⓣ604/732-4556, ⓦwww. lattimergallery.com. A great-looking gallery just west of Granville Island with a wide range of Pacific Northwest peoples' prints, paintings, sculpture, masks, jewellery and totems: not everything is expensive – prices for most pieces range from a few to a few hundred dollars.

Marion Scott Gallery 308 Water St ⓣ604/685-1934, ⓦwww.marionscottgallery.com. This gallery is now in its fourth decade and remains noted for its contemporary aboriginal art, in particular its well-chosen and individual Inuit prints, drawings and sculpture. It is also increasingly showing the work of young non-aboriginal artists.

Spirit Wrestler Gallery 47 Water St ⓣ604/669-8813 or 1-888/669-8813, ⓦwww.spiritwrestler.com. The Gastown location precludes low prices, but then the work here was never going to be inexpensive, for the smallish gallery specializes in high-quality sculpture and graphics by leading Inuit, Maori, Haida and other aboriginal artists inspired by shamanism.

Antique shops

Mihrab 4578 Main St at 29th Granville St ⓣ778/737-5959. Owner Lou Johnson makes repeated trips to India and the rest of the subcontinent to replenish the stock of this slick gallery-shop. It sells one-off tribal, modern and antique pieces – everything from tiny door handles to teak bed frames.

Salmagundi 321 West Cordova St ⓣ604/681-4648. A Gastown hoard of covetable items, some hidden in the 100-odd drawers of an old Japanese medicine chest.

Shaughnessy Antique Gallery 3025 Granville St at West 14th Ave ⓣ604/739-8413. Where some stores specialize, this gallery has a wide range of classy antiques (notably Victoriana) and more modern 1950s, 60s and 70s pieces.

Uno Langmann 2117 Granville St near West 6th Ave ⓣ604/736-8825, ⓦwww.langmann.com. It's unlikely you'll be buying anything here unless you've recently come into an inheritance, but if you're nearby it's worth looking in on a treasure trove that is more museum than shop. Particularly good for eighteenth- and nineteenth-century Canadian paintings.

Vancouver Antique Centre 422 Richards St ⓣ604/669-7444. A heritage building with around 15 antique stores on two floors. New stores are opening in neighbouring buildings.

Books and magazines

Antiquarius 609–207 West Hastings St at Cambie ⓣ604/669-7288. A treasury of secondhand books across a wide range of subjects, plus old magazines, posters, photographs, sheet music and a small assortment of bric-a-bric and antiques.

Banyen Books and Sound 3608 West 4th Ave between Stevens and Trafalgar ⓣ604/732-7912, ⓦwww.banyen.com. Tremendous bookshop devoted to all things New Age, organic gardening, alternative medicine and healing, yoga, Buddhism and other mind, body and spirit titles. Also sells CDs, incenses, yoga mats and other associated articles.

Antique hunting

Though a long way to come from Downtown, **Antique Alley** at New Westminster, near Westminister Quay, contains a dozen or more antique shops and hosts a flea market on Saturdays in summer.

A better-known and more accessible alternative is **Antique Row**, a run of antique shops between 16th and 25th avenues on Main Street south of King Edward Avenue. Sunday afternoon is the busiest time for browsers. Standout stores include Legends, 4366 Main St (ⓣ604/875-0621), which is great for retro and vintage clothes and jewellery.

Barbara-Jo's Books to Cooks 1740 West 2nd Ave ☎604/688-6755, Ⓦwww.bookstocooks.com. A specialist store that was inspired by a similar shop in London's Notting Hill and is typical of the imaginative shops that formed Yaletown's first wave but have now moved on. It stocks over 2500 cookery, food and wine books, plus literary works and fiction titles with a food theme. The store also hosts occasional talks and lectures and has a demonstration kitchen where you can watch dishes from various books being prepared. There is also an outlet in Granville Island's Net Loft building.

Blackberry Books 1663 Duranleau St, Granville Island ☎604/685-4113, Ⓦwww.bbooks.ca. This Granville Island store isn't large, but it makes up for what it lacks in size in its eclectic good taste and range of titles. It is also the sort of small, specialist bookstore with a knowledgeable staff that appeals to the variety of bookish baby boomers who frequent Granville Island on Saturday and Sunday mornings.

Biz Books 302 West Cordova St at Cambie St ☎604/669-06431, Ⓦwww.bizbooks.net. Biz Books serves Vancouver's movie fans, would-be screenwriters and others with a wide range of books connected with all aspects of the film business.

Book Warehouse 1015 Denman St at Nelson St ☎604/685-5711, Ⓦwww.bookwarehouse.ca. A recent arrival in Vancouver, but this small independent chain already has five central outlets, including an outpost in Yaletown (1065 Homer St at Helmcken St), thanks to its excellent staff, welcoming stores and discounting policy.

Chapters 788 Robson St at Howe ☎604/682-4066 or 1-888/648-0889, Ⓦwww.chapters.ca. Many of Vancouver's more highbrow inhabitants were less than pleased when Chapters, a vast bookshop chain, opened this megastore in the city. Smaller and much-loved Downtown stores such as the more traditional Duthie's felt the heat and closed. However, the sheer range of titles – it has over 110,000 in stock – comfortable chairs and the pleasant, airy feel of the store have won people round, and it's hard to fault either the service or the presentation. The travel section on the street-level floor is particularly good for outdoor activity or natural history guides to British Columbia and the Canadian Rockies. There are also vast sections devoted to international newspapers and magazines and a music store with the chance to listen to a wide range of CDs before you buy. There is another reasonably central outlet at 2505 Granville St (☎604/731-7822).

Duthie Books 2239 West 4th Ave between Vine and Yew ☎604/732-5344, Ⓦwww.duthiebooks.com. Duthie had been Vancouver's main bookstore chain since 1957 until financial Armageddon forced the closure of all but this large and browser-friendly Kits store.

Kidsbooks 3083 West Broadway at Barclay ☎604/738-5335, Ⓦwww.kidsbooks.ca. The city's biggest children's bookshop, though it doesn't confine itself to books: there are also puppets, games, toys and occasional readings. There is another branch in North Vancouver at 3040 Edgemount Blvd (☎604/986-6190).

MacLeod's Books 455 West Pender St at Richards ☎604/681-7654. A great place to browse for well-priced secondhand books, with a particularly good stock of fiction and nonfiction titles relating to western Canada. It also has a smaller selection of antiquarian titles.

Magpie Magazine Gallery 1319 Commercial Drive between Charles and Kitchener ☎604/253-6666. If you don't find the magazine you want among the 5000 or more titles on sale here (the city's biggest selection), then you probably won't find it anywhere.

Mayfair News 1535 West Broadway at Granville St ☎604/738-8951. If you're homesick for home-written newspapers or magazines, this is the place, for it has hundreds of local, US, UK and other periodicals. It's open until 10.30pm daily.

Wanderlust 1929 West 4th Ave between Cypress and Maple ☎604/739-2182, Ⓦwww.wanderlustore.com. A Kitsilano store (five blocks back from the beach) with everything you could want from a travel bookshop, including many hundreds of books, maps, guides and travel accessories.

Crafts and jewellery

Circle Craft in the Net Loft Building, Granville Island ☎604/699-8021, Ⓦwww.circlecraft.net. Main draws in this shop, one of several in the Net Loft ensemble opposite the Public Market, are ceramics, jewellery and sculpture made from "retrieved" items.

Forge & Form 1334 Cartwright St ☎604/684-6298. The studio just beyond the False Creek Community Centre doesn't look like

much, but it's the working base of two master gold- and silversmiths, Dietje Hagedoorn and Jürgen Schönheit. Their work has been bought by the likes of X-Files star Gillian Anderson, among others, in particular their "tension-set" stones – stone held in place without a setting.

Gallery of BC Ceramics 1359 Cartwright St, Granville Island ⓣ604/669-5645, ⓦwww.bcpotters.com. This gallery opposite the False Creek Community Centre is owned and run by the Potters Guild of British Columbia. At any one time you can buy or admire the work of around 100 guild members. Pieces range from the functional – domestic tableware and the like – to sculpture and other display pieces. Prices cover a correspondingly wide spectrum. A large selection of books on ceramics and pottery is also available.

Henry Birks & Sons 698 West Hastings St ⓣ604/669-3333, ⓦwww.birks.com. An institution since 1879, which makes this traditional jeweller almost as old as the city itself.

Jade 4–375 Water St, Gastown ⓣ604/687-5233, ⓦwww.jademine.com. This sort of shop can easily become little more than a glorified souvenir store, but Jade is a serious sort of place, with the stone in all shapes and sizes and pieces costing from a few cents to several thousand dollars. Much of its jade is sourced from the Polar Mine near Dease Lake in northern British Columbia, home of what is generally considered the world's best jade. Even if you don't want to buy, this is a fascinating place to browse.

Kites on Clouds 201–131 Water St, Gastown ⓣ604/669-5677. An unusual and eye-catching shop devoted to quality kites, wind socks and "airtoys". The stock is fun and colourful – if only you could say the same for the service.

Malaspina Printmakers Society 1555 Duranleau St, Granville Island ⓣ604/688-1827, ⓦwww.malaspinaprintmakers.com. An excellent gallery and workshop that showcases the work of numerous local printmakers. Ideal for a reasonably priced gift to take home.

Martha Sturdy Originals 16 West 5th Ave ⓣ604/872-5205, ⓦwww.marthasturdy.com. Sturdy is celebrated across North America for her jewellery and designs in glass, furniture and cast-resin homeware. Her pieces are expensive, as you'd expect of work that has been exhibited in museums and galleries across the country.

The Crafthouse 1386 Cartwright St, Granville Island ⓣ604/687-7270, ⓦwww.craftcouncilbc.ca. A glorious showcase for the work of decorative and functional pottery, textiles and other crafts by Canadian (and mostly BC) artists. The gallery is run by the nonprofit Crafts Association of British Columbia.

Chinese goods

Buddha Supplies Centre 4158 Main St at 26th Ave ⓣ604/873-8169. This extraordinary store sells over five hundred deliberately combustible items, all designed as joss – paper replicas of earthly belongings that are burned at Chinese funerals to help make the deceased's life in the underworld more pleasant. Buy $1 million denomination notes from the Bank of Hell or more ambitious and equally materialistic items such as a paper

Galleries

Vancouver has a plethora of small **private art galleries**, with a particular preponderance of established and somewhat staid outlets on a southern stretch of Granville Street between West 3rd Avenue and West 7th Avenue and beyond. For listings, check The Georgia Straight (see p.175) or Vancouver Magazine or visit ⓦwww.art-bc.com and ⓦwww.preview-art.com, the latter the site for the free quarterly gallery magazine Preview. Many galleries have free openings on the first Thursday of every month from 5 to 8pm.

If you want to browse among the best, **Buschlen Mowatt**, 111–1445 West Georgia St (ⓣ604/682-1234, ⓦwww.buschlenmowatt.com), is generally considered the city's foremost mainstream gallery. Other well-regarded and long-established spaces include the Bau-Xi Gallery, 3045 Granville St at West 14th Ave (ⓣ604/733-7011, ⓦwww.bau-xi.com), devoted largely to leading local artists, and the Equinox Gallery, 2321 Granville St at West 7th Ave (ⓣ604/736-2405, ⓦwww.equinoxgallery.com) for major local and international names in painting, sculpture and installations.

cellular phone, CD player or fax machine – or a paper penthouse complete with carport and Mercedes.

Keefer Chinese Bakery 251 East Georgia St near Main ⓣ604/685-2117. You have plenty of bakeries to choose from in and around Chinatown, but a wide range of high-quality cakes, buns and tarts makes this one of the best. Coconut buns and barbecued pork buns are tasty buys. As with most food stores in Chinatown, the customers are mostly local Chinese-Canadians.

Ming Wo 23 East Pender at Carrall ⓣ604/683-7268, ⓦwww.mingwo.com. Ming Wo has some ten outlets around the city selling an amazing selection of Chinese and other kitchenware. If you ever wanted a gigantic cleaver, this is the place to come, but you'll also find more innocuous items such as woks, pasta machines, plates, knives and serving bowls. Other outlets in Kitsilano at 2839 Broadway at Macdonald plus 2707 Granville St at 11th Ave and 2170 West 4th Ave.

South China Seas Trading Company Granville Island Public Market ⓣ604/681-5402, ⓦwww.southchinaseas.ca. An outlet that sells fresh Chinese and Asian produce, noodles, Asian cookbooks and a wide variety of specialist spices, sauces, and hard-to-find ingredients such as Thai basil, fresh Kaffir lime leaves, rambutans and mangosteens.

T & T Supermarket 179–181 Keefer St near Abbott ⓣ604/899-8836, ⓦwww.tnt-supermarket.com. The shelves here and at other T & T supermarkets around the city are a cornucopia of Chinese food and other Asian products, many of them likely to be of mind-boggling obscurity and unknown culinary purpose unless you have profound knowledge of Chinese cooking. If you're just browsing, be sure to look in the seafood bins – full of extraordinary-looking creatures of the deep – and to take in the many exotic fresh fruits and vegetables.

Ten Lee Hong 500 Main St at East Pender ⓣ604/689-7598. Wonderfully authentic Chinese tea and herb shop, with a vast range of red, green, white and black teas, and charming staff who will offer guidance and free tastings to help you choose and brew your tea.

Ten Ren Tea & Ginseng Company 550 Main St between Keefer and East Pender ⓣ604/684-1566, ⓦwww.tenren.com. Canada's best-stocked teashop is filled with jars of medicinal and drinking teas of all descriptions from China and around the world. A Chinatown institution, the store sells strong black China teas and others more familiar to Western palates, but you might also try delicately scented teas such as jasmine, ginger flower and chrysanthemum. American, Korean and Siberian ginseng is also available.

Tung Fong Hung Medicine Company 536 Main St ⓣ604/688-0883. Chinatown is full of herbalists, but if you have time for only one, then Tung Fong Hung is the first choice for product. A lot of what is on sale is frankly of dubious efficacy – dried seahorse and sliced deer antler, for example – though you can't help but be fascinated by the various potions, powders, lotions and other concoctions on display. Some of these "cures" can have side effects, so don't embark on a course of treatments without advice – there is an on-site herbalist for consultations.

Cigars

La Casa del Habano 980 Robson St at West Hastings ⓣ604/609-0511. Havana House is one of Cuba's largest suppliers of cigars, and this central store with a walk-in humidor avails itself of many hundreds of examples of its stock. Smokes here cost from a few dollars to more than a hundred.

Vancouver Cigar Company 1093 Hamilton St at Helmcken ⓣ604/685-0445 or 1-888/94-CIGAR, ⓦwww.vancouvercigar.com. It's said that the infamous cigar in the Bill Clinton and Monica Lewinsky affair was acquired during Clinton's visit to Vancouver for a world summit. This Yaletown store was perhaps too far from the Waterfront Hotel where he was staying to be the source, but it does have one of the city's better selections of Cuban and other cigars, with all leading brands such as Bolivar, Cohiba and Romeo y Julieta. There's also a full range of accessories. The store stays open until midnight Thurs–Sat. Also at 250-780 Beatty St at Robson.

Condoms

O! Zone Condoms 953 Denman St at Barclay and Haro ⓣ604/683-3423 or 1-888/423-7193, ⓦwww.ozonecondoms.com. A visit to this fun store lays to rest forever the notion that Canadians are strait-laced or in any way uptight. It stocks thousands of condoms from around the world in an eye-opening range of colours and designs.

The good-natured staff will answer just about any question you care to pose on the subject.

Department stores

Gay-Mart 1148 Davie St between Thurlow and Bute ⓣ604/681-3262, ⓦwww.gaymart.com. More bazaar than department store, but collects a wide range of clothes, accessories, toys, movies and more aimed at a gay clientele under one roof.

The Bay 674 Granville St at Georgia ⓣ604/681-6211, ⓦwww.hbc.com. There's no missing The Bay, a big old-fashioned department store outlet for the famous Hudson's Bay Company. The company began trading fur in the seventeenth century, its trading posts seeding the growth of many Canadian towns and cities. Today, it has stores such as The Bay from coast to coast, as well as other lucrative business interests. While you can no longer buy furs here, you can still buy the Hudson's Bay Company's celebrated original "point" blanket, whose colourful stripes once referred to the number of beaver pelts each blanket was worth as a trade. Otherwise this store has the reasonable prices and all the predictable clothes, shoes and household goods you would expect of a department store, including designer concessions such as Polo, Tommy Hilfiger and DKNY.

Sears 701 Granville St and Robson ⓣ604/685-3121, ⓦwww.sears.ca. Famous US mid-market name in the huge retail space vacated by a noted Canadian department-store name, Eaton's, after the latter company's financial meltdown.

Urban Fare 177 Davie St ⓣ604/975-7550, ⓦwww.urbanfare.com. Yaletown and the smart denizens of False Creek's condominiums got the impossibly hip supermarket they deserved in this supremely slick store. Supermarket basics are complemented by lots of organic and ethnic foods, an olive bar, a pasta bar and a wide variety of high-quality prepared foods. Some idea of the shop's ambition can be gained from the fact that while it bakes much of its own bread, many of the basic ingredients are flown in from Poilâne, one of France's best bakeries. Has expanded and now has five other central locations.

Computers and electrical

Future Shop 796 Granville St at Robson ⓣ604/683-2502, ⓦwww.futureshop.ca. Granville used to be the preserve of small electrical stores and repair workshops, among other things, and this gadget, games, DVD and all-things-electric store carries on the tradition, albeit in a much more stylish setting than the former mom-and-pop stores.

MAC Station 101-1014 Homer St at Helmcken ⓣ604/806-6227, ⓦwww.macstation.com. It was only a matter of time before Yaletown's Mac-toting designers, writers and condo-dwellers got a shop to feed their passion for Apples – and a place to fix them when things go wrong. Two other central locations.

Health and beauty

Beauty Bar 2142 West 4th Ave near Arbutus St ⓣ604/733-9000, ⓦwww.beautybarcosmetics.com. Fabulous range of make-up, cosmetics and other feel-good lotions and potions for women, but also more of the same for men.

Beauty Mark 1120 Hamilton St near Davie ⓣ604/642-2294, ⓦwww.beautymark.ca. Small-scale body maintenance (manicures, pedicures and so forth), plus cosmetics, jewellery and other must-have accessories.

Skoah 1011 Hamilton St ⓣ604/642-0200, ⓦwww.skoah.com. Drop by this Yaletown spa for superb facials for men and women (from about $90 for the signature 75min facial), plus locally made own-brand organic cosmetics.

Household and design

Birks 698 West Hastings St ⓣ604/669-3333, ⓦwww.birks.com. When many Canadian couples get married they send their wedding list to Birks, a chain with a reliable stock of fine china, glassware, silver and the like.

Chintz & Company 950 Homer St ⓣ604/689-2022. Large landmark store on the northern edge of Yaletown, an area that is home to more than its share of design and homeware stores. This one covers all bases from fabrics to furniture.

Drinkwater and Company 3036 West Broadway at Balaclava ⓣ604/224-2665. It may not look like much from the outside, but professionals and public alike storm this family-run kitchenware store for all manner of cooking and other hardware.

House of Villeroy & Boch 420 Howe St at West Hastings ⓣ604/681-5884. Offers the best in contemporary tableware, expensive gifts and stationery.

Inform 97 Water St between Abbott and Carrall ⓣ604/682-3868, ⓦwww.informinteriors.com. Large Gastown showroom for the best in modern furniture from B&B Italia, Philippe Starck, Mies van der Rohe and other leading names.

Liberty Design 1635 West Broadway between Pine and Firsts ⓣ604/682-7499, ⓦwww.libertyliving.ca. A store that has become a favourite among Vancouver's design-conscious shoppers looking for furniture, designer items and other beautiful things for the home from around the world.

Living Space Interiors 188 Kingsway at 10th Ave ⓣ604/683-1116, ⓦwww.livingspace.com. Cutting-edge Italian and French designs in furniture and other household must-have items.

Koolhaus 1 Water St at Carrall ⓣ604/684-9033, ⓦwww.koolhausdesign.com. A stylish store that sells the best in design, whether it's kitchenware or furniture for the home, garden or office. Also has a Yaletown outlet at 896 Cambie St at Smithe.

The Cross 1198 Homer St near Davie ⓣ604/689-2900 ⓦwww.thecrossdesign.com. More central than many of the city's design stores, with a wide range of accessories, artefacts and one-off items of homeware.

Glasses

Eyes on Burrard 775 Burrard St ⓣ604/688-9521, ⓦwww.eyesonline.com. Large and central eyewear store known for its witty window displays and the latest frame styles from Persol, Boucheron, Paul Smith, Oliver Peoples and others.

Granville Eyeland 1666 Johnston St, in the Net Loft Building ⓣ604/488-0909, ⓦwww.granville-eyeland.com. If you want a new pair of spectacles, join the long line of locals and celebrities (including Elton John, Ed Asner and Robin Williams) who have patronized designer Klaus Sebök's Granville Island studio. The attention to detail is minute – Sebök, who has been in the trade for over 35 years, takes a cast of the bridge of your nose to ensure a perfect fit – while the variety of materials used can border on the ludicrous: buffalo horn, leather and salmon-skin frames are all available. One client wanted – and was made – glasses in 18-carat gold. Cost? $17,000 the pair.

Malls

The Landing 375 Water St ⓣ604/454-5050, ⓦwww.the-landing.com. The Landing occupies a superbly restored 1905 warehouse in Gastown and includes a mostly upmarket selection of souvenir stores, restaurants and elegant designer outlets such as Polo Ralph Lauren.

Pacific Centre ⓣ604/688-7236, ⓦwww.pacificcentre.com. Vancouver's major central Downtown mall stretches north from Robson St for almost three blocks between Dunsmuir and Pender streets: to the east and west it is bordered by Howe and West Georgia streets. The emphasis among its more than two hundred stores is on clothes and shoe stores, but there are plenty of specialist shops such as Crabtree & Evelyn (toiletries and cosmetics), the Nike Shop and major general-clothing stores such as Holt Renfrew, a sort of Canadian version of Saks Fifth Ave. A three-storey waterfall is the main non-retail highlight. Another 115 top-end and mid-priced speciality stores are enclosed in the adjoining Vancouver Centre, which has its main entrance at 650 West Georgia St (ⓣ604/688-5658).

Park Royal Shopping Centre 2002 Park Royal South, West Vancouver ⓣ604/925-9576, ⓦwww.shopparkroyal.com. This is one of those rather dated megamalls (actually two facing malls, North and South) in which you could, if forced, probably spend your entire life without having to leave – 250 stores, cinemas, golf range, bowling, a food court and various special events are all on hand. The malls are astride Marine Drive just west of the Lions Gate Bridge. The Village at Park Royal opened in 2005, adding an outdoor component to the complex, with walkways and landscaping (there are even waterfalls) amidst top-end clothing, organic food, homeware and lifestyle stores.

Royal Court 1055 West Georgia St at Burrard ⓣ604/689-6711. This underground mall is something of a poor relation among the Downtown malls, but only because it's smaller than its rivals – it has around sixty stores and a food hall. The variety of shops and services is good, however, with everything from high-fashion boutiques to emergency dental clinics. One of the more fascinating stores is Geomania (ⓣ604/683-2818), which sells crystals, minerals and fossils, plus works in stone.

Sinclair Centre **757 West Hastings St ⓣ604/666-4484, ⓦwww.sinclaircentre.com.** The Sinclair Centre is a classy mall that occupies four historic converted buildings – the old Vancouver Post Office (1910), Winch Building (1911), Customs Examining Warehouse (1913) and Federal Building (1937). Most of the stores are upmarket outlets such as Armani or the ultra high-fashion Leone store.

Maps and guides

International Travel Maps **12300 Bridgeport St, Richmond ⓣ604/273-1400, ⓦwww.itmb.com.** Now departed from its former and far more convenient Downtown location, this store offers an extensive selection of world travel books, guides and maps, as well as an excellent selection of specialist guides to Vancouver and a bewildering range of outdoor and other activities in British Columbia. You can also buy detailed hiking maps of the province.

The Travel Bug **3065 West Broadway at Bayswater ⓣ604/737-1122, ⓦwww.travelbugbooks.ca.** A tiny store crammed with maps, guides and accessories on the funky strip of small shops, cafés and restaurants on the stretch of Broadway from Larch to Bayswater.

Wanderlust **1929 West 4th Ave at Cypress ⓣ604/739-2182, ⓦwww.wanderlustore.com.** Kitsilano point of pilgrimage for maps, guide-books, luggage and other travel accessories.

Markets

Chinatown Night Market **200 Keefer St and 200 Pender St ⓣ604/682-8998. May–Sept Fri–Sat 6.30pm–1.30am.** Two separate blocks in Chinatown are closed to traffic for three nights a week in the warmer months of the year to make way for booths, tables and stalls selling a wide variety of fruit and vegetables, imported clothes, cooked food and miscellaneous junk, fake luxury goods, art and trinkets. The area is crowded and the atmosphere buzzing.

Granville Island Public Market **1669 Johnston St ⓣ604/666-5784, ⓦwww.granvilleisland.bc.ca. Daily 9am–6pm. Closed Mon in winter unless a public holiday.** This covered food market is by far the best in the city, and contains a staggering array of fresh fruit and vegetables, fish, meat, pastas, chocolates, hams, cheese and a variety of gourmet foods and wines. Stalls that are particularly worth

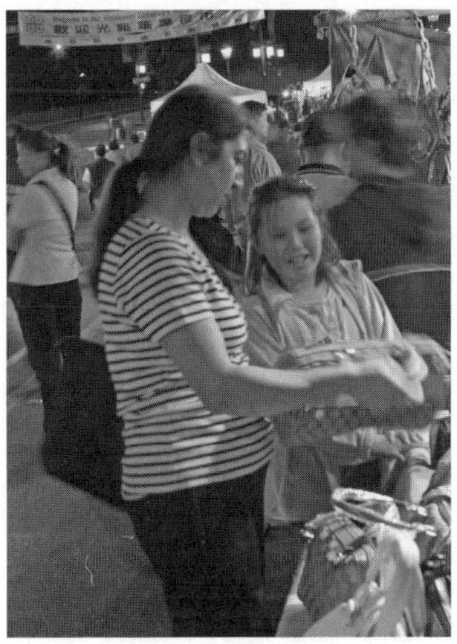

▲ Chinatown night market

hunting out include Dussa's (ⓣ604/688-8881), for ham and cheese, and the Stock Market (ⓣ604/687-2433). The latter has a wonderful concept, selling home-made soup stocks and sauces by the litre, plus three daily soups to take home or eat there. It also sells a wonderful seven-grain hot cereal for breakfast topped with apple sauce, maple syrup and cream. Currently there's also a Farmer's Truck Market on the island every Thursday from 9am to 6pm. See also p.75.

Lonsdale Quay Market **123 Carrie Cates Court, North Vancouver ⓣ604/985-6261, ⓦwww.lonsdalequay.com. Sat–Thurs 9.30am–6.30pm, Fri 9.30am–9pm.** A smaller and only slightly less exhilarating version of the Granville Island Public Market, this market is just seconds away from the North Vancouver SeaBus terminal (see p.98), with a ground floor devoted primarily to fruit and vegetable stalls and food counters and an upper floor given over to fashion stores, bookshops and gift stores. Perhaps the best thing here, however, is the view across the water to Downtown.

River Market at Westminster Quay **810 Quayside, New Westminster ⓣ604/520-3881, ⓦwww.rivermarket.ca. Mon–Thurs 10am–7pm, Fri 10am–8pm, Sat 9am–6pm, Sun 10am–6pm.** It's hard to see why you would want to pay a special visit to this market 25min by SkyTrain from Downtown, for it's a pale imitation of Granville Island and Lonsdale Quay markets, with a similar mixture of food

stalls, speciality stores and food court. But it's worth a look if you happen to be down here, especially if you combine a visit with a walk along the river.

Robson Public Market 1610 Robson St at Cardero ⓣ604/682-2733, ⓦwww.robsonpublicmarket.com. Daily 9am–9pm. This long-established neighbourhood food market is something of an aberration on a street that has an increasing number of high-rent designer shops and smart restaurants. It has plenty of fruit and vegetable stalls, a couple of good bakeries, a salmon stall and an outstanding butcher, R B Meats. The upper level has a food court with ethnic restaurants (French, Italian, Japanese, Greek and such) and takeaway concessions.

Vancouver Flea Market 703 Terminal Ave; admission 75¢; ⓣ604/685-0666, ⓦwww.vancouverfleamarket.com. Sat & Sun 9am–5pm, public holidays 10am–4pm. Vancouver's largest flea market lies close to the bus and rail terminal about 5min walk from the Main St SkyTrain station. There are more than 350 stalls, and while many sell little more than T-shirts, cheap trinkets or sheer tat, you'll also find plenty of junk, old books, used tools, secondhand clothes and other flea-market staples. As ever with this sort of place, you'll have to arrive early if you want to find the real bargains or treasures.

Music and video

Highlife Records and Music 1317 Commercial Drive between Charles and Kitchener ⓣ604/251-6964, ⓦwww.highlifeworld.com. Excellent world-music specialist which has been in business over 20 years. Also has a selection of vintage instruments.

HMV 788 Burrard St at Robson ⓣ604/669-2289. This is the only place in Vancouver you'll need to visit for CDs, videos, laser discs and books on music and other forms of entertainment. Housed in Vancouver's former public library, this is the largest music store in Canada, a vast retail area over three floors with over 150,000 titles. The store is extremely central and prices, at least if you're coming from Europe, are far better than anything you'll find at home. There are listening stations where you can listen to a choice of CDs, as well as a good selection of computer multimedia software for Mac and PC.

Red Cat Records 4307 Main St at East 27th Ave ⓣ604/708-9422, ⓦwww.redcat.ca. Owned by a local musician and the first choice in the city if you want a handle on what is happening in the Vancouver music or tow hunt through an electic collection of new and used vinyl and CDs, with an emphasis on indie, country and rock 'n' roll.

Scratch Records 726 Richards St at West Georgia St ⓣ604/687-6355, ⓦwww.scratchrecords.com. Tremendous independent record shop with knowledgeable staff and great collection of rare, obscure, unusual and covetable vinyl and other music.

Sikora's Classical Records 432 West Hastings St at Homer St ⓣ604/685-0625, ⓦwww.sikorasclassical.com. Sikora's has been in business over thirty years, and boasts more than 25,000 classical CD and DVD titles, plus a wide choice of music on vinyl.

Zulu 1972 West 4th Ave at Burrard St ⓣ604/738-3232, ⓦwww.zulurecords.com. Not only is this the most amiable record store in the city, it's also the best for secondhand records, tapes and CDs, as well as a big selection of imports, rare vinyl and non-mainstream music. A newer store, without the second-hand stock, can be found nearby at 1869 West 4th Ave (ⓣ604/738-0856).

New clothing

Aritzia 1110 Robson St at Thurlow ⓣ604/684-3251, ⓦwww.aritzia.com. Main outlet for a trendy and design-savvy chain that carries clothes for young women by Canadian and Vancouver-based designers that you probably won't find elsewhere. Also has an outlet in the Pacific Centre (see p. 000).

Atomic Model 1036 Mainland St at Nelson ⓣ604/688-9989, ⓦwww.atomicmodel.com. Yaletown store that imports leading women's high-fashion lines and diffusion lines such as Is (Voyage) and Urchin (Mark Eisen) and much-frequented by models, stylists and other industry people.

Bacci's 2788 Granville St at West 12th Ave ⓣ604/733-4933, ⓦwww.baccis.ca. The formula in this attractive store is a little bit of designer everything, from clothes and shoes to homeware and cosmetics.

Betsey Johnson 1033 Alberni St at Burrard ⓣ604/488-0314, ⓦwww.betseyjohnson.com. This New York designer doesn't open many international stores, so this is a treat for Vancouver women and visitors who like her soft and often unconventional clothes.

The Block 350 West Cordova St ⓣ604/685-8885, ⓦwww.theblock.ca. Carries a good assortment of women's clothes by a variety of mostly Canadian designers and is the main Vancouver outlet for clothes by UK company Ghost.

Club Monaco 1034 Robson St at Jervis ⓣ604/687-8618, ⓦwww.clubmonaco.com. Canadian-founded, now Ralph Lauren–owned, this chain borrows more than a little from Banana Republic in its approach and style. This is no bad thing, however, and you can be sure of classic styles, up-to-the-minute fabrics and cuts, and prices that don't cause too much of a double-take. There are several outlets around the city, including in the Pacific Centre.

Crocodile 2156 West 4th Ave at Yew ⓣ604/742-2762, ⓦwww.crocodilebaby.com. The beautiful people who want their babies to be equally beautiful flock to this store, not only for clothes, but also for stylish (and expensive) accessories such as the ubiquitous Mountain Buggy prams.

Diane's Lingerie 2950 Granville St at West 13th Ave ⓣ604/738-5121, ⓦwww.dianeslingerie.com. If it's fun, slinky, naughty, sensible or sexy, or from local or international designers, then it'll be here.

Dorothy Grant 138 West 6th Ave between Columbia and Manitoba sts ⓣ681-0201, ⓦwww.dorothygrant.com. A celebrated Canadian designer whose clothes, accessories and jewellery are inspired by traditional Haida and other aboriginal art and culture.

Dream 311 West Cordova St between Homer and Cambie ⓣ604/683-7326, ⓦwww.dreamvancouver.com. One of several small shops on Cambie (including some vintage stores – see p.183) where you can find distinctive clothes by local designers, Dream also has a fine selection of jewellery. Another outlet, Little Dream, has opened on Granville Island at 130-1666 Cartwright St (ⓣ604/683-6930).

Eugene Choo 3683 Main St at East 21st Ave ⓣ604/873-8874, ⓦwww.eugenechoo.com. Cock of the walk among the new fashion outlets opening on south Main, this store has metamorphosed from a vintage outlet to a must-stop fashion retreat for men and women.

Holt Renfrew 733 Dunsmuir St at Granville ⓣ604/681-3121, ⓦwww.holtrenfrew.com. A definite first choice for one-stop designer shopping. All the leading labels in a smart new store, plus cosmetics and an excellent selection of shoes.

Leone Sinclair Centre, 757 West Hastings St ⓣ604/683-1133, ⓦwww.leone.ca. Look out for the stars shopping at this elegant and top-end store, which is filled with Sui, Miu Miu by Prada, Dolce & Gabbana, Versace, Armani and other leading labels. A second store, L2, has opened just round the corner to the north at 350 Howe St at West Cordova (ⓣ604/685-9327).

Mark James 2941 West Broadway at Bayswater ⓣ604/734-2381, ⓦwww.markjamesclothing.com. Menswear central, with all the major Italian and other labels (Byblos, Boss, DKNY), plus a jeans/sportswear section in a different part of the store.

Narcissist Design 3659 Main St at East 21st Ave ⓣ604/879-8431, ⓦwww.narcissist.com. Another big player on the southern part of Main St, with men's and women's clothes, plus homeware.

Roots Canada 1001 Robson St at Burrard ⓣ604/683-4305, ⓦwww.roots.ca. Think The Gap with a Canadian twist and a slightly more varied range. This chain stocks lots of sports and casual wear, leather jackets and footwear.

TNA 2899 Granville St at West 13th Ave ⓣ604/714-5937, ⓦwww.tna.ca. Light, deceptively simple clothes in fine fabrics for teenagers and young women in a chic store that, like many a similar outlet, resembles a rather smart apartment, complete with classic pieces of modern furniture.

Sporting goods stores

Comor 1980 Burrard St at 4th Ave ⓣ604/736-7547, ⓦwww.comorsports.com. Comor is one of the city's major ski and winter-sports retailers, and it stocks a full range of skis, snowboards, clothing, skates, sunglasses and other items from leading manufacturers such as Oakley, North Face, Salomon, Patagonia, K2 and Rollerblade. The store also does repairs, features a wide range of rental equipment and will deliver free to major Downtown hotels.

Europe Bound Outfitters 195 West Broadway and Columbia ⓣ604/874-7456, ⓦwww.europebound.com. This store is part of a chain with outlets across Canada, and carries a full range of top outdoor brands.

Lululemon Athletica 1148 Robson St at Thurlow ⓣ604/681-3118, ⓦwww.lululemon.com. The man behind this store, Chip Wilson, was

Outdoors and sports equipment

Given its setting and the spectacular scenery on its doorstep, it's no surprise that Vancouver is one of the best cities in North America to find equipment for hiking, camping and numerous other outdoor activities. Mountain Equipment Co-op (see below) was one of the first major outdoor stores, and its existence has led to several other similar stores opening nearby on the three blocks of West Broadway around Cambie and Columbia streets.

Stores in this axis include Valhalla Pure Outfitters, 222 West Broadway (ⓣ604/872-8872, ⓦwww.vpo.ca), and A J Brooks, 147 West Broadway (ⓣ604/874-1117, ⓦwww.ajbrooks.com).

Farther west, a similar thing has happened at the junction of West 4th and Burrard streets, but this time you'll find a concentration of skate, surf, diving, ski and snowboard stores for sales and rentals. Key players here are Pacific Boarder, 1793 West 4th Ave (ⓣ604/734-7245, ⓦwww.pacificboarder.com); The Boardroom, 1717 and 1745 West 4th Ave (ⓣ604/734-7669, ⓦwww.boardroomshop.com) – there is also an outlet in North Vancouver at 2057 Lonsdale Ave at West 21st St (ⓣ604/985-9669); Thriller, 3467 Main St at 19th Ave (ⓣ604/736-5651, ⓦwww.thrillershop.com); and Westbeach (see below).

also the brains behind the celebrated Westbeach shop (see below). Pick up the absolute latest (and hottest) in sports gear and yoga wear (yoga is huge in Vancouver), either by Lululemon or leading brands such as Gaia. The shop and its concept have been so successful that you can now find the store as far afield as Asia.

Mountain Equipment Co-op 130 West Broadway at Columbia St ⓣ604/872-7858, ⓦwww.mec.ca. Canada's largest outdoor-equipment and supplies store is a block long and something of a Vancouver institution. Because it really is a cooperative, you need to pay $5 membership to make a purchase, but you'll soon recoup this if you buy something from the store's staggering range of tents, boots, winter sports gear, climbing gear and other outdoor activity equipment and clothing.

Sigge's 2077 West 4th Ave at Arbutus ⓣ604/731-8818 or 1-877/731-8818, ⓦwww.sigges.com. Specializes in cross-country ski apparel and accessories, with all leading brands, savvy staff and the backup for lessons and guided skiing. Open Sept–mid-April only.

Westbeach 1766 West 4th Ave between Pine and Burrard sts ⓣ604/731-6449, ⓦwww.westbeach.com. An internationally renowned sports, board and skateboarding store which is something of an institution, almost as well known in Germany and Japan as it is in Vancouver. It has its own line of street and technical gear, and often hosts skateboarding shows.

Shoes and leather ware

Bionic 1072 Mainland at Helmcken ⓣ604/685-9696, ⓦwww.bionicfootwear.com. Unashamedly aimed at the youth market, with an emphasis on trainers and sneakers, as well as of-the-moment styles that only the hip and young can get away with.

Boys' Co 1044 Robson St ⓣ604/684-5656. A good one-stop shop for shoes, thanks to its range, central location and reasonable prices.

David Gordon 840 Granville St between Robson and Smithe sts ⓣ604/685-3784. A long-established store specializing in all sorts of boots, from Western to Doc Martens, as well as accessories and other fashionable and alternative street footwear.

Dayton Boots 2250 East Hastings St at Nanaimo ⓣ604/253-6671, ⓦwww.daytonboots.com. These work boots, a staple piece of kit for loggers and farmers, have become highly fashionable thanks to the patronage of film crews, film stars and other trendsetters. This is the original factory outlet.

Gravity Pope 2205 West 4th Ave at Yew ⓣ604/731-7673, ⓦwww.gravitypope.com. One of the city's largest selections of shoes that are desirable by virtue of their brand or trendiness, though it's not all froth – there's everything from clogs and espadrilles to cowboy boots and stilettos.

Ingledew's 535 Granville St near the Pacific Centre ⓣ604/687-8606, ⓦwww.ingledews.com. Ingledew's has been a byword for

good shoes, bags, accessories and other leather ware since 1915. It also trades on its excellent service.

John Fluevog 837 Granville between Robson and Smithe ⓣ604/688-2828, ⓦwww.fluevog.com. Cult name Fluevog has made a splash in the international fashion world, noted for his inspired takes on traditional shoes and his funky urban footwear – and for some pretty outrageous platforms, fetish and other items that are more high art than high fashion.

Speciality food and drink

A Bosa & Company 562 Victoria Drive near Turner St ⓣ604/253-5578, ⓦwww.bosafoods.com. This sensational Italian delicatessen two blocks east of Commercial Drive has been run by the same family for three generations. It stocks more than 2500 items of food – the cheeses, olive oils and hams are exceptional – as well as a wide range of Italian kitchenware and gadgets.

Alberni Street BC Liquor Store 1120 Alberni St at Thurlow ⓣ604/660-4572, ⓦwww.bcliquorstores.com. A larger-than-average store with longer-than-average hours (until 11pm, 6pm Sun).

All India Food 6157 Main St near 49th Ave ⓣ604/324-1686. All the Indian spices and produce you can imagine under one (very large) roof in the Punjabi Market area. Many people come here just for the amazing sweet outlet – All India Surat Sweets – where you can sample a buffet of brightly coloured sweets and sugar-saturated Indian puddings. The store is also known for its fine samosas.

First Ravioli Store 1900 Commercial Drive ⓣ604/255-8844. Almost anything and everything Italian can be purchased at the most venerable and celebrated of Vancouver's Italian supermarkets.

Fujiya Japanese Food 912 Clark Drive at Venables St and branches ⓣ604/251-3711, ⓦwww.fujiya.ca. This store east of Chinatown (five blocks west of Commercial Drive) stocks a big range of Japanese food and kitchenware. It also prepares fresh fish for sushi and sells sushi to take away.

Kaplan's Delicatessen & Restaurant 5775 Oak St at 41st Ave ⓣ604/263-2625. Just southwest of Queen Elizabeth Park, Kaplan's is as authentic a 1940s Jewish delicatessen as you could wish for, selling a wide range of kosher food, a big spread of sandwiches and 265 other menu items.

Les Amis du Fromage 1752 West 2nd Ave ⓣ604/732-4218, ⓦwww.buycheese.com. This store's 400-plus cheeses would put many a French cheese shop to shame. Also has a branch at 845 East Hastings St between Hawkes and Campbell (ⓣ604/253-4218).

Longliner Sea Foods 1689 Johnston St ⓣ604/681-9016. Granville Island market has several fresh salmon and seafood stalls: this is generally considered the best, and is favoured by many of the city's chefs.

Marquis Wines 1034 Davie St at Burrard ⓣ604/684-0455, ⓦwww.marquis-wines.com. Many liquor stores are owned by the state: not this one, which has a central Downtown location and also sells glasses and other wine-related accessories. It's in a reasonable, convenient location, the staff know their stuff – and its opening hours are longer than most – daily 11am–9pm.

Meinhardt Fine Foods 3002 Granville St at West 14th Ave ⓣ604/732-4405, ⓦwww.meinhardt.com. A pretty delicatessen with on-site patisserie and café.

Murchie's Tea & Coffee 825 West Pender St at Howe ⓣ604/669-0783, ⓦwww.murchies.com. A western Canadian institution (there's another branch in Victoria – see p.226 – and several other outlets dotted around Vancouver), Murchie's sells more than forty different blends of coffee and around fifty types of tea.

Parthenon Wholesale and Retail Food 3080 West Broadway near Bayswater ⓣ604/733-4191. This Greek grocery and deli south of Jericho Beach (four blocks west of Alma St) sells, among other things, everything you need to make the consummate Greek meal. It also has a big selection of prepared foods to take away.

Patisserie Lebeau 1728 West 2nd Ave at Pine St ⓣ604/731-3528. Glorious bread made in imported French ovens, and you can also buy equally good coffee, cakes and waffles, and sandwiches.

Taylorwood Wines 1185 Mainland at the corner of Davie ⓣ604/684-0455, ⓦwww.taylorwoodwines.com. There are plenty of people in Yaletown with the cash to splash on decent wine, and

For more excellent food stores, also see Capers Whole Food Markets (p.131) and T&T Supermarket (p.175), as well as the Chinese goods section (p.174).

when the mood takes them, this is where they come. Look out for free tastings midweek and Sunday afternoons.

Vintage clothing

Deluxe Junk Co 310 West Cordova St at Cambie ⓣ604/685-4871, ⓦwww.deluxejunk.com. The "junk" in the name is no accident – this Gastown store is full of the stuff – but among the mountains of unwearable polyester there's always the possibility of uncovering a real find. The store is just moments from Virgin Mary's (see below).

Legends Retro-Fashion 4366 Main St at East 29th Ave ⓣ604/875-0621. It's a long way to come from Downtown, but this treasure trove is much loved by vintage connoisseurs both for the often immaculate condition of the old clothes, hats and accessories and for the fact that most are unique and often out-of-the ordinary gems.

Mintage 1946 West 4th Ave St ⓣ604/MIN-TAGE, ⓦwww.mintagevintage.com. Great range and display, with a sister store at 1714 Commercial Drive (ⓣ604/871-0022).

True Value Vintage 710 Robson St at Granville, basement level ⓣ604/685-5403. One of the city's best-known and most central vintage stores, with clothing from the 1920s through to the 1990s, including a big selection of used Levis, lots of fake fur, leather jackets, evening wear, period swimwear and accessories.

Value Village 1820 West Hastings at Victoria Drive ⓣ604/254-4282, ⓦwww.valuevillage.com. A large collecting house for clothes dug out from thrift stores and charity shops across BC and beyond, and as such as good a source of vintage clothing as you'll find – owners of vintage stores in more central parts of the city also use this as a source. There's a second store at 6415 Victoria Drive (ⓣ604/327-4434).

Virgin Mary's 430 Homer St between West Hastings and West Pender ⓣ604/844-7848. Another good little shop in the Gastown cluster of secondhand and vintage stores near Cambie.

15

Kids' Vancouver

Have no fears if you're travelling to Vancouver with children – the city is a child-friendly place, with plenty of sights that appeal to youngsters and adults alike. It also has attractions designed specifically with children in mind, numerous parks and gardens, boat and plane tours, and a wide miscellany of good cafés and restaurants – many with outdoor seating – where children won't be out of place. You'll also have few problems finding places to change or feed younger children in hotels or major malls. The city is also physically safe, save in parts of Chinatown and its environs (see p.57), though you should exercise caution in places and situations with obvious potential for problems – on or near water, on busy streets and junctions, and on upland trails in the parks of the North Shore and elsewhere.

The city has plenty of sources of information and ideas for travel with children (see box opposite), especially when it comes to **organized tours** (see p.27). Seaplane tours, while not cheap, offer great views and the thrill of taking off in a small plane, and should be sure-fire winners with most kids (see p.28). Less expensive but equally appealing tours include whale-watching expeditions – there is more choice of tours from Victoria (see p.221), but trips also run from Vancouver – and the many boat, horse-drawn and wildlife ventures possible in and around the city.

One of the best ways to indulge your children is to time your visit to Vancouver to coincide with the city's **International Children's Festival**, an annual event held for a week each May in colourful tents set up in Vanier Park. It draws over two hundred children's entertainers – jugglers, magicians and the like – and storytellers from around the world. Tickets for events go on sale through Ticketmaster (see p.154) in March but are also available at the festival. Many events sell out quickly, but even if you miss your show of choice, the small daily admittance fee to the festival allows you to enjoy the myriad free events and performances outside the show tents. There are also tents where children can participate in activities such as dancing or kite-making. For information, call Ⓣ604/708-5655 or visit Ⓦwww.youngarts.ca. Many of the city's other festivals will also appeal to children – see p.201 for further details.

Note that most sights that charge an **entrance fee** usually allow some children to enter free, typically those under five or six. Some sights are more generous than others, however – the Vancouver Art Gallery, for example, allows children under twelve in without charge, whereas at Science World and the Vancouver Aquarium the cutoff is a more miserly four years old. Some, but by no means all, sights offer better-value **family tickets**, allowing entrance to two adults and two (occasionally three) children.

The account below briefly highlights the various child-friendly sights, activities and attractions around the city. For fuller details, see the relevant sections of the guide.

Information and ideas

The main Vancouver Touristinfo Centre (see p.36) is a good place to start for **information and ideas** on activities for children, especially for organized tours. It is also the place to pick up the free, annually updated *Kids' Guide Vancouver*, which you'll also find at the infocentres at the Peace Arch Border Crossing on Hwy 99 in Surrey and on the domestic and international arrivals levels at Vancouver International Airport. It carries a map and suggests around 100 places and ideas for activities with children.

The **Granville Island Kids Market** (see p.186) usually has free information, news sheets and fact sheets such as *BC Parent* (Ⓣ604/221-0366, Ⓦwww.bcparent.com) and *West Coast Families* (Ⓣ604/689-1331, Ⓦwww.westcoastfamilies.com) whose pages contain listings and calendars of events. There are also several dedicated **websites**, the best being Ⓦwww.kidsvancouver.com, which has extensive listings and ideas under several headings such as Rainy Days, Playgrounds, Animals and Parks & Gardens. It also includes good practical information on parking, safety and access by public transport, as well as a tip-filled "Good to Know" section. Also good for listings – but with less in the way of practical help – is the informal Ⓦwww.findfamilyfun.com, a jolly, colloquial site compiled by local parents and their children.

Major sights

Downtown attractions that should keep children happy include **Canada Place** (see p.42), which has fun views of the active port, an IMAX cinema, and the spectacle of boats, seaplanes and helicopters taking off; if you're lucky, you'll be able to admire the vast cruise ships that often dock here and, if you're luckier still, watch one of the ships as it leaves or comes into port. Be sure to have a few quarters (25¢) to feed into the telescopes.

You'll also want clear weather to make the most of the views at the nearby **Harbour Centre** (see p.43), where the lifts and viewing deck offer captivating city panoramas. On **Robson Street**, children should like the waterfalls, pools and fountains of Robson Square, and the adjacent Vancouver Art Gallery (see p.46) holds regular monthly events aimed at children with lots of hands-on activities, shows and drop-in art-making sessions.

To the east, the buskers and steam-powered clock in **Gastown** (see p.54), with its toots and whistles, provide a few moments of light relief. Relatively close by there's also the **Dr Sun Yat-Sen Garden** (see p.60), where every day at noon children can feed the fish and turtles (older children will enjoy Chinatown's night market – see p.178). Down in **Yaletown**, the shops are all pretty grown-up, but the safe, quiet streets, and their laid-back vibe, are perfect for children. The main sight here is the old steam train at the **Roundhouse** (see p.50) community centre, the Canadian Pacific Railway's former yard and turntable, where children can clamber into the cab of Engine 374, the locomotive that pulled the first passenger train into Vancouver in 1887.

Across in North Vancouver, the **SeaBus** is a fun ride in its own right, with the lure of the Lonsdale Quay Market (see p.98) and its sights, sounds and dedicated kids' stalls as an additional treat for children. Another fun ride is the cable-car trip up **Grouse Mountain** (see p.99). Older children with a scientific bent might also enjoy learning about the life cycle of salmon at the **salmon hatchery** in Capilano River (see p.102); younger children here should be captivated by the sight of leaping salmon.

South of the Downtown core, **Science World** (see p.76) has countless hands-on displays and an OMNIMAX screen very much aimed at children; it's also one of the places on False Creek accessed by small **ferries** (see p.25) – of obvious appeal to children – that ply back and forth between Downtown, Granville Island and Vanier Park.

▲ Kids Market, Granville Island

Granville Island

Granville Island (see p.71) is a major attraction, great in the sun or rain, and one whose general buzz, street performers and market should captivate children of all ages. It also boasts a duck pond, several small museums (the model ship and model train museums have obvious appeal for children – see below), plenty of child-friendly cafés and restaurants, Sutcliff Park (lots of grassy areas, picnic tables and a long promenade) and a dedicated **Kids' Playground and Water Park** (see p.75).

Best of all is the **Kids Market** (daily 10am–6pm; ⓣ604/689-8447, ⓦwww.kidsmarket.ca), one of the city's key children's attractions. It boasts around thirty children's toy shops – selling kites, books, puppets, crafts, clothing and much more – plus play areas upstairs (small fee) for toddlers and older children, a food outlet, and an indoor playground known as the Adventure Zone and Circuit Circus. It's a busy, not to say chaotic, place at weekends. On Saturdays in summer free events happen around the island, including performances by clowns, magicians and musicians and face-painting.

Museums

Vancouver's finest museum, the **Museum of Anthropology** (see p.87), should interest children by virtue of the scale and spectacle of the totem poles and other carvings in its main hall. In Vanier Park, the Vancouver Museum is of more limited allure, unlike the more compelling **Maritime Museum** (see p.81) with its historic boats and displays (notably the *St Roch* and tugboat wheelhouse), the Pirates! display and Children's Maritime Discovery Centre, where children can play on the computers, use the telescopes trained on boats in English Bay and dress up in pirate clothes and naval uniforms. Close by are the more modern planetarium and multimedia displays of the **H.R. MacMillan Space Centre** (see p.80).

Children whose eyes don't glaze over in museums may also want to visit the **Vancouver Public Library**'s well-stocked children's library, play area, pre-school learning centre and more (see p.48). Also Downtown, the **Vancouver Art Gallery** (see p.46) holds special children's afternoons (usually the third Sunday of the month, noon–5pm), during which lots of hands-on and interactive creativity are on offer. Activities are partly designed to illuminate the temporary exhibitions in the gallery – and may include anything from working with clay and finger-painting to watching dance performances.

Farther afield, the **BC Museum of Mining**, off Hwy 99 about 45 minutes' drive from Downtown en route for Squamish (see p.238), has an underground train, guided tour of the mine, gold-panning area and live demonstrations of mining equipment.

Parks, gardens and animals

Most first-time visitors, or those with limited time, should make for **Stanley Park** (see below), the city's obvious open-space destination for those with children.

In southern Vancouver, the flowers of the **VanDusen Botanical Garden** at Oak Street and 37th Avenue probably won't appeal, but the Elizabethan Hedge Maze just might – adults can keep an eye on their charges from a grassy mound alongside (see p.85). In **Queen Elizabeth Park** (see p.83), children should respond enthusiastically to the fifty-odd varieties of exotic birds in the Bloedel Conservatory.

Across on the **North Shore**, Cypress Provincial Park, Lynn Canyon, Lighthouse and Mount Seymour parks are full of easy, fun trails and boulders and fallen trees to scramble over. Lynn Canyon also has a suspension bridge over rapids (see p.105), a free alternative to the touristy and expensive Capilano Suspension Bridge (see p.103), Lighthouse Park has tidal pools and Cypress Falls boasts two cracking waterfalls. Be careful, however, as many of these parks have areas of wilderness. Much gentler is **Ambleside Park** (see p.104), with a flat sand beach, playground and small summer water park. Farther afield, the spectacular **Shannon Falls** (see p.238) on the way to Squamish should capture children's imaginations.

Stanley Park

Stanley Park vies with Granville Island as Vancouver's most compelling destination for those travelling with children. There is a huge variety of things to do here, from the **Vancouver Aquarium** (see p.69), with its whale and dolphin shows and many exhibits specifically aimed at children to the more low-profile sights such as the Miniature Train and Children's Farmyard (see p.68), where children can look at peacocks, Shetland ponies, pigs, cows, chickens and other barnyard animals.

There are also several **beaches** and swimming areas such as the heated pool at Second Beach (see p.68) and plenty of open spaces – notably the Stanley Park Playground – for youngsters to run off excess energy. You can also rent children's bikes, rollerskates and in-line skates, as well as "jogging" buggies and hitch-on bike buggies for small children. Then there are the many peripheral or incidental temptations: Stanley Park horse-drawn tours (see p.28); the Nine O'Clock Gun (fired at nine daily); the totem poles at Brockton Point; and the host of ducks, geese and swans (don't feed them) on Lost Lagoon and Beaver Lake.

Zoos and animals

You might – if you are lucky – see birds and small creatures in the parks of the North Shore (though you may not want to encounter the black bears and cougar that roam the Coast Mountains) and there are plenty of opportunities for birdwatching on and around the Fraser Delta. In the city itself, however, Stanley Park's Vancouver Aquarium and Children's Farmyard (see above) are about the only places to take children to see animals.

A little farther afield is **Maplewood Farm** (daily April–Oct 10am–4pm; adults \$5.25, children 19 months–16 years \$3, special events \$5.75/\$4.75; Ⓣ604/929-5610, Ⓦwww.maplewoodfarm.bc.ca), located in the heart of North Vancouver at 405 Seymour River Place. The five-acre site was one of many farms that once operated in the area but were put out of business by the big agricultural holdings in the Fraser Valley. The BC parks department saved this one from oblivion, and it now has around 200 barnyard animals, including pigs, sheep, donkeys, ducks and chickens. Various special events take place throughout the year, among them pony rides, a summer Sheep Fair, Country Christmas Weekend, 101 Pumpkins Day (late Oct) and Farm Fair

(mid-Sept). Right next to the farm is the **Maplewood Mudflats Bird Sanctuary**, great if your children are birders.

About 45 minutes' drive and 48km east of the city is the **Greater Vancouver Zoo** (daily: April–Sept 9am–7pm; Oct–March 9am–4pm; adults $20, children 4–15 $15, two adults & two children family pass $60; ⓣ604/856-6825, ⓦwww.gvzoo.com), a large site at 5048 264th St, Aldergrove, with around 125 species of animals either roaming relatively freely or in spacious enclosures. Creatures here include elephants, lions and tigers (whose 1pm feeding time is popular), buffalo, elk, zebras, giraffes, hippos, a rhino and camels.

Games and amusement parks

For an old-fashioned experience, visit the **Playland Family Fun Park** (visit website for current hours; ⓣ604/252-3583, ⓦwww.pne.ca/playland; adults and children over 48in in height $29.95, children under 48in $19.95 for unlimited rides; discounted tickets are available online and at Save On Food stores). This amusement park is in Exhibition Park (or Hastings Park) at East Hastings St and Cassiar St and can be reached on buses #14 or #16. There are around 35 rides, including an old-fashioned roundabout and wooden rollercoaster, plus an arcade of electronic games and a Nintendo Pavilion.

Beaches, swimming pools and water parks

Vancouver has plenty of places to **swim**, including several good beaches, though as the best ocean temperature you can hope for is about 18–21°C (65–70°F) you may want to take younger children to some of the indoor pools: diehards can compromise by swimming in the fresh- and saltwater outdoor pools (see below). The city also has a small water park on Granville Island for younger children and a monster park out of the city with a range of watery attractions that should appeal to children of all ages.

Swimming pools and water parks

Granville Island Water Park Granville Island ⓣ604/257-8195. Open and supervised daily 10am–6pm in summer, weather allowing. This water park and adjoining adventure playground are near the False Creek Community Centre (which has changing facilities) off Cartwright St to the right as you enter the island (behind the island's infocentre). The park has a central wading pool with fire hose for the children; the playground has a waterslide and lots of rope- and log-built facilities.

Kitsilano Beach and Pool The seawater at Kits Beach (see p.83) may be a touch cool for adults, but it doesn't seem to worry children. Lifeguards are on duty all summer. Nearby, the area's grassy spaces have swings and monkey bars. Kits' heated outdoor pool lies right by the water and has a gently sloped section for youngsters: it's busy on summer weekend afternoons, so time a visit for the morning.

Splashdown Park 4799 Nu Lelum Way, Tsawwassen ⓣ604/943-2251, ⓦwww.splashdownpark.ca. If you have time to kill before catching a ferry, or your children clamour for the joys of a water park, head over to this big complex 3min drive from the Tsawwassen ferry terminal south of Vancouver – it offers thirteen vast slides, swimming pool, giant hot tub, picnic areas, inner tubes and basketball and volleyball courts. Call or check website for opening hours; adults and children over 48in in height $20.95, children under four and 48in $14.95; family tickets $72.95.

Stanley Park Children can swim in the supervised pool at Second Beach (it also has waterslides) or splash around at the water adventure playground across from Lumberman's Arch.

UBC Aquatic Centre ⓣ604/822-4522, ⓦwww.aquatics.ubc.ca. The university's aquatic centre, next door to the Student Union Building and bus loop, boasts two fifty-metre pools (one indoor, one outdoor), with lots of inflatable toys, inner tubes, basketball nets and floating mats in summer for children. Drop by the pools on a visit to the Museum of Anthropology (see p.87), but call

for pool hours first, as only certain times are designated for the general public.

Vancouver Aquatic Centre ⓣ**604/665-3424,** ⓦ**www.vancouver.ca/parks/rec.** This Downtown center offers drop-in swimming for the public ($5.15) daily from 7am (except Sunday, from 10pm) until 4.15pm and again from 7pm to 9.30pm (4.15pm on Saturday and Sunday). Lanes for lengths are also available. Other facilities include a sauna and whirlpool (tickets are $2.65 if you want to use these without the pool) plus fitness centre and weight room.

16

Sports and outdoor activities

Come up with an outdoor activity and chances are you'll be able to indulge in it somewhere in or around Vancouver. The city's close proximity to scenic mountains, forests and ocean make it a superb playground for outdoor enthusiasts of every stripe: snow-covered slopes for skiing, snowboarding and other winter activities; woodland and wilderness for hiking, climbing and mountain biking; and open water for sailing, kayaking, windsurfing, diving and other aquatic sports – with ample opportunities for running and in-line skating, golf, tennis and more.

Beyond Vancouver lies the vast interior of British Columbia, where immense areas of wilderness constitute an almost limitless natural playground. Whistler is the most obvious out-of-city destination (see p.240), thanks to its well-deserved reputation as one of North America's finest winter-sports resorts, but other centres, such as Squamish (for climbing and windsurfing) and Powell River (for diving), are also outstanding.

Vancouver's options for watching sports rather than doing them are more restricted, for this is not a city with any great teams in the top **spectator sports**. The one notable exception is ice hockey, where the Vancouver Canucks play in the National Hockey League. If you're not too worried about the quality of your sport, you can watch baseball and Canadian football, among others, at a variety of first-class venues. If you wish to see top-flight basketball, however, note that the NBA's Vancouver Grizzlies are no more – the team has relocated to Memphis.

The city is packed with companies aimed at helping you find and enjoy your chosen activity, and the initial **contact details** on the following pages are meant simply to set you on the right track. The Vancouver Touristinfo Centre (see p.36) has the lowdown on numerous activities and will book tickets for some of the bigger sporting events. You'll also find plenty of information at the city's larger outdoor shops, not to mention the chance to **rent** just about any piece of outdoor or other sporting equipment or clothing (see "Shopping" p.181). For more information, order or pick up a copy of *The Vancouver Book*, the infocentre's official visitor's guide, or visit Ⓦ www.tourismvancouver.com.

Outdoor activities

Certain activities in Vancouver have their obvious seasons – such as skiing and winter sports – though even here you should note that there can be surprising exceptions. In Whistler (see p.240), for example, you can ski year-round, not just

in winter, thanks to summer glacier skiing. You'll also find that the winter season in Whistler may be longer than at the slopes close to Vancouver itself. Hiking, too, can be a year-round activity, though be aware of the very real risks involved in cold-weather hiking at higher altitudes even in parks close to the city. Fair-weather activities such as golf are self-evident, but don't overlook things like birdwatching, which can be most rewarding during spring and autumn migrations, or fishing, which also has seasonal variations.

Bicycling

Bicycling is popular in Vancouver, whether it's mountain biking or cycling on city trails or in Stanley Park. Most rental outfits – see p.65 for details on those near Stanley Park – provide maps with recommended routes, as do most bicycle shops around the city.

Expect to pay from about $5 an hour, $15 a half-day and $30 to $40 for a full day, depending on the quality of the bike. You may also find that some hotels and hostels, particularly in the West End, hire or loan bikes to guests. Note that you can take bikes on SkyTrain and SeaBus free of charge, and that some buses have bike racks.

For **further information**, contact Cycling BC (Ⓣ 604/737-3034, Ⓦ www.cycling.bc.ca) or visit Ⓦ www.momentumplanet.com. Bear in mind that the law in BC requires you to wear a helmet when cycling.

There are a number of routes from which to choose, with a total of 16 designated cycleways totalling 129km in the city and about the same again in the city environs. The most obvious and popular is the flat 8.8-kilometre run around the **Stanley Park Seawall** (allow 1hr; see p.65), a combination of paved surface, trail and road. The Seawall circuit forms part of one of the city's most scenic and popular routes, which runs westward from Canada Place pier and finishes up in Pacific Spirit Regional Park via the Seawall, English Bay and Sunset beaches, Granville Island, Vanier Park and Kitsilano and Jericho beaches (or continue from English Bay along the north side of False Creek to Science World). Other designated routes are the run around **False Creek** (10km) and the **BC Parkway** (19km) that shadows the SkyTrain route from the Science World–Main Street station to New Westminster.

More ambitious rides take you to Spanish Banks from Granville Island (17km round-trip) and to **Horseshoe Bay** in North Vancouver by way of Stanley Park, the Lions Gate Bridge and Marine Drive (40km round-trip).

The best of the **mountain-biking** trails are found in North Van's **parks and mountains** (see Chapter 7). Winter cross-country ski trails are used by bikers, notably on Hollyburn Mountain in Cypress Provincial Park – Hollyburn Ridge alone has some 16km of trails. The steep Good Samaritan Trail on Mount Seymour (with links to Bridle Path and the Baden-Powell Trail) is a notorious route – recommended for very fit bikers only – though this park also has

▲ Biking in Stanley Park

many excellent and less demanding trails. Beginners and intermediates should also look at the trails in Pacific Spirit Park (see p.93).

Remember that you can take bikes on the SeaBus to get to North Van (see p.25), and on some of the small Aquabus ferries from Downtown to Granville Island (see p.25). Note, though, that Granville Island, while convenient to access by bike, is a touch too congested with people for cycling, though there are cycle paths close by around False Creek.

Birdwatching

The wide variety of habitats in and around Vancouver provides shelter for more than 360 species of **birds**. Even Downtown in Stanley Park you'll be able to see birds such as bald eagles, swans and great blue heron. The park also has a heronry just outside the Vancouver Aquarium.

The city's key birdwatching spot is the **George C. Reifel Migratory Bird Sanctuary** (daily 9am–4pm; $4; Ⓣ604/946-6980, Ⓦwww.reifelbirdsanctuary.com), 850 acres of natural marshes and managed wetland at 5191 Robertson Rd, Westham Island, 35km south of Vancouver on the southern shore at the entrance to the Fraser River Delta. It attracts some 1.5 million migratory birds annually, with more than 268 species spotted here year-round, most notably the vast wintering flocks of lesser snow geese from Wrangle Island above the Arctic Circle. The so-called Fraser-Skagit flock numbers anything between 30,000 and 60,000, depending on the success of the nesting season in the Arctic.

Some birds winter on the Fraser, others on the nearby Skagit Estuary in Washington State. In spring, the most common visitors are millions of Western sandpipers, but this is also a good time to see fish-eating birds of prey (including ospreys), which follow migrating salmon up the Fraser. Low dikes serve as walkways (3km in total) around the reserve and are wheelchair accessible, while in the west of the reserve there is a two-storey observation tower on the foreshore. Some walkways are edged with trees, offering habitats for forest birds and roost sites for birds of prey such as owls, eagles and various hawks. Note that the sanctuary holds a Snow Goose Festival in the first weekend of November to celebrate the arrival of the eponymous birds, which generally stay in the region until around mid-December.

Elsewhere, you stand a good chance of seeing herons in the heronries in Stanley and Pacific Spirit parks (there are generally nesting herons right by the Vancouver Aquarium). In winter you'll almost certainly see bald eagles at Brackendale near Squamish en route for Whistler (see p.239). In January 1994 some 3700 eagles were officially counted here, the largest number ever recorded in North America.

Canoeing and kayaking

There are several places to **canoe** or **kayak** – or learn to do either – in and around Vancouver: **False Creek** (nearest to Downtown, and a good place for beginners); **English Bay** (but *not* in the vicinity of the Lions Gate Bridge, where the currents are strong and dangerous); **Deer Lake** in East Vancouver; and **Indian Arm**, a striking finger-shaped inlet and fjord flanked by 1200-metre mountains on the North Shore. For the last, rent a canoe or kayak at Deep Cove in North Vancouver (see below) and head either to Cates Park to the south or to Jug Island, Combe Park or Belcarra Regional Park across the inlet. For **rentals, tours and lessons** contact the following outlets:

Bowen Island Sea Kayaking Bowen Island (Ⓣ604/947-9266 or 800-60-KAYAK, Ⓦwww.bowenislandkayaking.com). Located farther afield than its competitors at Bowen Island, a short distance west across the water from Horseshoe Bay and Cypress Provincial Park in West Vancouver.

Rental rates are $45 for 3 hours in a single boat, then $10 an hour and $65 all day. Add $15 or $20 to these rates for double kayaks. Guided tours include 3-hour trips near the island (4 daily in summer 1–4pm; $65); a sunset paddle (daily in summer 6–9pm, $50); full-moon trips (call for dates; $65); and 7-hour trips around Howe Sound (Fri–Sun 9.30am–4.30pm; $120). There are also occasional weekend tours (one monthly June–Aug; $375) around Bowen Island and daily high-summer trips to Pasley Island ($120). Bowen Island is easily reached by ferry.

Deep Cove Canoe & Kayak Indian Arm at 2156 Banbury Rd (Ⓣ604/929-2268, Ⓦwww.deepcovekayak.com; April–Oct). Over in North Vancouver, this company is located thirty minutes from Downtown in a pretty waterside community on the shores of Deep Cove. This is an excellent outfit, and offers hourly, daily and multi-day rentals; kayak and canoe schools with lessons for paddlers of all abilities (and special children's classes); guided tours (including women-only tours); and private trips. The eighteen-kilometre fjord that is Indian Arm offers tremendous scenery and sheltered waters, while Deep Cove has plenty of cafés, restaurants, hiking trails and so forth once you come off the water. Call or visit website for latest tours and prices.

Ecomarine Ocean Kayak 1668 Duranleau St (Ⓣ1-888-425-2925 or 689-7575, Ⓦwww.ecomarine.com). Located on Granville Island just across the water from Ocean West Expeditions (see below), and with similar rates, lessons and tours of False Creek and beyond. It also has offices at 1700 Beach Ave on English Bay (same phone number) and at the Jericho Sailing Centre at 1300 Discovery St (Ⓣ604/689-7575) on Jericho Beach.

Climbing

Close to the city, there's the chance to **climb** at Juniper Point in Lighthouse Park (see p.111), on the cliffs and crags overlooking Indian Arm in Deep Cove, and on some of the mountains above North Van. However, the best climbing in the Vancouver vicinity is at Squamish (see p.239). For much more on climbing locally and in the rest of BC, contact the Alpine Club of Canada–Vancouver Section, 130 West Broad way (Ⓣ604/878-5272, Ⓦwww.alpineclubofcanada.ca or www.accvancouver.ca), or visit Ⓦwww.out-there.com, which has an extraordinary number of climbing-related links. Also good is Ⓦwww.bivouac.com, which also carries hiking information. **Ice-climbing** locations on Vancouver Island and elsewhere can be found at Ⓦwww.summitpost.org, and the Alpine Club (see above) and Vancouver-based Mountain School (47 West Broadway at Manitoba St, one block east of the Mountain Equipment Co-op Ⓣ604/878-7007, Ⓦwww.themountainschool.com) offer ice-climbing courses, the latter from $375 for two days. Alternatively, you can climb indoors at the following centres:

Cliffhanger Indoor Rock Climbing Centre 670 Industrial Ave (Ⓣ604/874-2400, Ⓦwww.cliffhangerclimbing.com; Mon 10am–11pm, Tues–Fri noon–11pm, Sat 10am-10pm, Sun 10am–9.30pm, earlier opening times in summer). Crack climbing, lead climbing, training room, bouldering cave and large climbing wall. A day pass costs $18.

Edge Climbing Centre 1485 Welch St, Suite 2, North Vancouver, off Capilano Rd near Marine Drive (Ⓣ604/984-9080, Ⓦwww.edgeclimbing.com; Mon–Fri 1–11pm, Sat–Sun noon–9pm). A very well-equipped North Vancouver climbing gym, with wall and lessons. A day pass costs $17.

Fishing

Key places for **fishing** around the city are **Burrard Inlet** (open all year), **Howe Sound** and **Horseshoe Bay** – the last is the best place for salmon and one of the most popular **fishing** areas on the coast. There are also marinas at

Fishermen's Cove, Sunset Beach, Lions Bay and Whytecliff. North Vancouver has Seymour River, Lynn Creek and the Capilano River. Farther afield, there is the **Sunshine Coast** (see p.248), especially between Secret Cove and Egmont and near Pender Harbour. East of the city you can fish on the Fraser River, Buntzen Lake and Harrison Lake.

If you want to fish you'll need a nonresident saltwater or freshwater **licence**. A freshwater **licence** costs $20 a day ($36 for eight days, $50 for non-residents); tidal-waters licence $7.35 daily. They can be obtained online (Ⓦwww.fishing.gov.bc.ca) or from tackle shops around the city, most of which carry current regulations for fishing. For more on fishing around the city and in BC generally, visit Ⓦwww.pac.dfo-mpo.gc.ca. The *Vancouver Sun* also carries a daily fishing report detailing the fish in season and where they can be fished.

Good **tackle shops** include Bonnie Lee Fishing Charters, at 1676 Duranleau St on the dock at the entrance to Granville Island (Ⓣ604/290-7447 or 866/933-7447, Ⓦwww.bonnielee.com); many of the charter companies below will also be able to help with bait and tackle.

The **months to visit** if you're planning a fishing trip are April and May, when the chinook (or king) salmon run at the mouth of the Fraser River and Howe Sound, or August, when millions of sockeye salmon run up the coast. Charters generally rent by the half-day, day or week, and are available through numerous operators (see below). There are also plenty of companies that offer seaplane and helicopter trips to remote lakes and rivers for fly-in fishing trips. Full details are available from the Vancouver Touristinfo Centre (see p.36).

Charter companies to contact include Bites-On Salmon, 450 Denman St (Ⓣ877/688-2483 or 604/688-2483, Ⓦwww.bites-on.com); Bonnie Lee Fishing Charters (see above); and Sewell's Landing, 6409 Bay St, West Vancouver(Ⓣ604/921-3474, Ⓦwww.sewellsmarina.com).

Golf

There are more than a dozen **golf courses** within an hour's drive of Downtown Vancouver, and more than seventy between Whistler to the north and Hope to the east. Reckon on **green fees** of about $55 ($40 if you take a "twilight" slot) to play most courses. For details of other public courses, contact the Vancouver Board of Parks and Recreation (Ⓣ604/257-8400, Ⓦwww.city.vancouver.bc.ca/parks/golf). You can book tee times at three major public courses (Langara, McCleery and Fraserview). An excellent source of general information is Ⓦwww.golfbc.com.

Fraserview 7800 Vivian Drive (Ⓣ604/257-6923 or 280-1818, Ⓦwww.vancouver.ca/parks). Around 5km east of the University Golf Club (see below), and almost equally popular, this course has a park setting with rolling hills and mature trees.

Furry Creek 150 Country Club Rd, Furry Creek (Ⓣ604/896-2224 or 1-888/922-9462, Ⓦwww.golfbc.com/courses). This par-72 course lies among the mountain forests and woods of Howe Sound on the North Shore and has won the accolade of BC's "Most Scenic Golf Course".

Gleneagles 6190 Marine Drive at Orchill Rd (Ⓣ604/921-7353). Like Furry Creek, the chief attraction of this nine-hole West Vancouver course is the stunning backdrop of ocean and mountains.

Langara 6706 Alberta St at 49th Ave and Cambie (Ⓣ604/713-1816 or 257-8400, Ⓦwww.vancouver.ca/parks). A much-loved par-71 course from 1926 whose popularity has only increased following recent renovation and redesign. Book at least five days in advance to be sure of a round.

Northview Golf & Country Club 6857 168th St, Surrey (Ⓣ604/574-0324 or 1-888/574-2211, Ⓦwww.northviewgolf.com). The two prestigious

courses here were designed by Arnold Palmer and host the Vancouver Open, part of the US PGA tour, held over the Labour Day weekend.

University Golf Club 5185 University Blvd at UBC (T 604/224-1818, W www.universitygolf.com). The closest public course to Downtown is this par-72, situated near the eastern entrance to the UBC campus where West 10th Ave meets Blanca Street.

Hiking

Hiking opportunities beyond Vancouver's boundaries to the north and east in the Coast and Interior mountains of BC are almost unlimited. Closer to Downtown, most of the best trails are in the parks above North Vancouver – see Chapter 7 for details of recommended hikes. Bear in mind that they are often in wilderness or near-wilderness areas, and you should therefore have suitable **equipment and clothing** and be prepared for sudden changes of weather. There are trails to suit all levels of fitness – and if you don't fancy doing it alone you can contact the Vancouver Touristinfo Centre for details about hiring a **guide**. See p.173 for shops where you can find detailed hiking maps.

The best **urban trails** include Burnaby Mountain, with its good views of Burrard Inlet and Indian Arm; Pacific Spirit Regional Park, which has quiet walks and forest trails; Richmond Dyke and its windswept trails on the Fraser River and Strait of Georgia; and the most obvious and convenient, Stanley Park and its Seawall.

For **creek and shoreline walks** consider the Lighthouse Park, a great spot for sunsets, sea cliffs and old-growth forest (see p.111), and the Lynn and Capilano canyons (see p.105 and p.101). For something longer, plump for the **Baden-Powell Trail**, a forty-kilometre hike from Horseshoe Bay on Howe Sound to Deep Cove on Indian Arm and Cates Park on the Dollarton Hwy. It links several of the area's best trails and can be joined – among other places – at Grouse Mountain, where you can follow a popular leg of the trail to Mount Seymour (start early and allow a full day). If you have a car, then head out to **Pitt Lake**, about an hour east of the city: it's North America's largest tidal freshwater lake and is surrounded by lots of pretty trails.

Ice-skating

If you can't – or don't – **skate** in Vancouver in winter you're in a pretty small minority. Rinks are open from about November to mid-March or early April at the West End Community Centre, 870 Denman St (T 604/257-8333, W www.westendcc.ca), where you can rent skates for a few dollars, and in winter you can skate at the top of Grouse Mountain (see p.99). The celebrated rink at Robson Square under Robson St between Howe and Hornby has been closed, to considerable public outrage, but may reopen – contact the city's infocentre for latest details. If you want to skate where the pros do, trek out to the eight-rink Ice Sports Centre at 6501 Sprott in Burnaby (T 604/291-0626, W www.icesports.com), the practice facility for the Vancouver Canucks hockey team. It's open year-round, but you'll need to call to check on opening hours for the public. Lessons and rentals are available.

In-line skating

The Seawall promenade in Stanley Park is the obvious choice for **in-line skaters**: watch out, though, for cyclists, who share the path. There are plenty of places to rent skates near the park: outfits that rent bikes invariably have skates, too (see p.65).

Stanley Park aside, the route most favoured by skaters is the shared cycleway on and around Granville Island and False Creek: start at the bottom of Denman Street and Beach Avenue and head east. If you're a confident skater, there's a designated – but occasionally steep and difficult – eleven-kilometre

route known as the Mainline in North Vancouver in the Seymour Demonstration Forest.

While **in-line skating is banned on pavements** across the city, the police appear to turn a blind eye to transgressors most of the time. Visit Ⓦwww.rollerbladevancouver.com for more background.

Rafting

You won't find much **whitewater rafting** in Vancouver's immediate vicinity, but in the mountains nearby are some of the finest stretches of white water on the continent. Relatively gentle rafting experiences are available in and around Squamish and Whistler (see p.250); for more variety and more exciting trips you need to head to the Interior Mountains. Bear in mind that longish drives (an hour at least) are usually required before you reach the river. Several Vancouver-based and regional companies organize trips (see below), and most offer a variety of grades (1–6), with class 3 and 4+ trips on the Squamish, Elaho and Chilliwack rivers, for example, and gentler class 1 and 2 rides on the Cheakamus and Lower Squamish rivers.

Canadian Outback Adventure 100–657 Marine Drive, West Vancouver (Ⓣ604/921-7250 or 1-800/565-8735 in Vancouver area, international 604/921-7250, Ⓦwww.canadianoutback.com). Organizes a wide variety of trips of differing severity. The gentlest (suitable for children as young as five), the Cheakamus Splash, has 90min on the river, costs $110 and departs from May–Sept at weekends at noon.

Chilliwack River Rafting Adventures 49704 Chilliwack Lake Rd, Chilliwack (Ⓣ604/824-0334 or 1-800/410-7238, Ⓦwww.chilliwack-rafting.com). A 90min drive out of town (take Hwy 1 and Sardis exit 119 south on Vedder Rd and then Chilliwack Lake Rd); offers half- and one-day trips on the Chilliwack River from around $89 and $110 for overnight tours.

Hyak Wilderness Adventures 203-3823 Henning Drive, Burnaby (Ⓣ1-800/663-7238, Ⓦwww.hyak.com). Organises trips on the Thompson and Chilliwack rivers, with afternoon river trips on the Chilliwack ($105, departs 3.30pm, returns 6.30pm mid-June to mid-July) or day-long tours on both (May to mid-July Sat at 10am for $129, Sun–Fri 10.30am for $119).

REO Rafting 845 Spence Way, Anmore (Ⓣ604/461-7238 or 1-800/736-7238, Ⓦwww.reorafting.com). Present $145 between June and August ($115 April, May & Sept) to this excellent company and you'll get a transfer out to the Nahatlatch river, about two and a half hours' drive from the city, and then four or five hours on the river, with breakfast, lunch and all specialist gear and clothing included. REO also offers multi-day trips, including a one-night getaway ($205).

Sailing

Great possibilities for sailing trips can be found in the Gulf Islands between Vancouver and Vancouver Island. If you're not so sure of your abilities, you can hire a skipper for half- or full-day sailing (around $160 for a half-day, $250 a day) around English Bay or farther afield on longer trips: for details, enquire at the following charter companies. Experienced sailors can choose from a large range of dinghies and other sailing boats from numerous operators in and around the city.

The best first port-of-call in both cases is the **Jericho Sailing Centre** in Jericho Beach Park western Kitsilano at 1300 Discovery St, home to many sailing companies and a laid-back **café**, the *Galley Patio & Grill*, with a patio that offers lovely views of the bay. **Boat charter companies** include:

Cooper Boating 1620 Duranleau St (Ⓣ604/687-4110 or 1-888/999-6419, Ⓦwww.cooperboating.com). A good first choice, if only because it is conveniently located on Granville Island. It

offers cruises, boat rentals, sailing lessons on boats up to 13m. Rentals start at about $165 a day off season, but up to the $500 in full season, depending on the boat. A skipper will cost from $325 a day.

Vancouver Yacht Charters 1551 Johnson St (Ⓣ604/779-9193, Ⓦwww.boatcharters.net). A wide range of yachts for the serious enthusiast.

Scuba diving

Around Vancouver most people **dive** in Howe Sound and Indian Arm: the water is cold (6°C) – you'll need a six-millimetre neoprene wetsuit – and it's worth going out with an experienced local diver for your first dives. Hiring an instructor will cost from $80 a dive, while a place on a weekend dive boat will cost from $90. Tremendous diving is available, however, at three locations outside the city – around the Gulf Islands; near the town of Powell River (see p.252); and around the artificial reefs on specially scuttled boats such as the *Cape Breton* and *Saskatchewan* near Nanaimo (visit Ⓦwww.artificialreef.bc.ca for more information).

More specific places to dive include West Van's **Whytecliff Park** off Marine Drive, which has a special Marine Protected Area (the best diving here is between Oct and April, and the most celebrated dive is the "Cut", a wall hundreds of metres deep and with some 200 marine species); **Lighthouse Park**, a great spot but accessible only to better intermediate and advanced divers; and **Porteau Cove** on Hwy 99 (24km north of Horseshoe Bay), a popular place with a protected provincial marine park, campsite, boat launch, showers, old minesweeper and an artificial reef made from sunken hulls.

Most **dive stores** will rent out all gear by the day, as well as organizing occasional weekend and night dives. You'll need proof of diving certification for all gear and air. Good places to start are:

Diving Locker at 2745 West 4th Ave at Macdonald St (Ⓣ604/736-2681 or 1-800/348-3398, Ⓦwww.divinglocker.ca). This long-established Kitsilano outfit is one of Canada's largest dive centres and retailers. It rents full equipment to certified divers from about $100 and organizes dives (with rental) and monthly night dives.

Great Pacific Diving 10020-152 Street, Surrey (Ⓣ604/986-0302, Ⓦwww.greatpacific.net). Out-of-city company that rents out equipment, but is aimed more at local divers, organizing Wednesday-night dives and weekend trips (typically around $350, depending on destination) on and around Vancouver Island.

Rowands Reef Scuba Shop 1512 Duranleau St (Ⓣ604/669-3483, Ⓦwww.rowandsreef.com). Rental of the full kit from this convenient Granville Island-based shop costs around $135, plus $65 for a divemaster. Boat dives (minimum of four people) are $89.

Skiing and snowboarding

If you want a few hours' boarding, downhill or cross-country skiing close to the city, you can find it here – Vancouver has three hills less than thirty minutes' drive from Downtown. Serious skiers, snowboarders and other winter-sports enthusiasts, however, head for the big-name resorts outside Vancouver such as Whistler (see p.240) or the less exalted runs of Mount Baker 120km away in the United States. For more on the parks below, see Chapter 7.

Cypress Bowl, 1610 Mount Seymour St, North Vancouver (Ⓣ604/926-5612,Ⓦwww.cypressmountain.com), is 16km from Downtown and offers decent downhill skiing and snowboarding, and the closest cross-country skiing to Vancouver. Lift passes for a day's skiing cost $47.62 ($44.76 off season), $16.98 for cross-country skiing. Multi-day and reduced-cost evening passes are also available at this and the ski areas below. The area has the longest vertical drop of the resorts near the city – 533m – and a base elevation of 980m.

Grouse Mountain lies about 12km from the city centre in North Vancouver, a 20-minute drive from Downtown. The Grouse Mountain Ski Resort, 6400 Nancy Greene Way, North Vancouver (Ⓣ604/980-9311 or 984-0661, snow reports Ⓣ604/986-6262, Ⓦwww.grousemountain.com), has lift tickets for adults good for a day's skiing that cost $50.

Mount Seymour is located in Mount Seymour Provincial Park about 16km north of Vancouver. The Mount Seymour Ski Resort, 1700 Mount Seymour Rd, North Vancouver (Ⓣ604/986-2261, Ⓦwww.mountseymour.com), has all-day lift passes that cost $42. The area has a vertical drop of 365m and a base elevation of 1010m, making this the highest of Vancouver's resorts.

Swimming

Water temperatures at Vancouver's sandy beaches rarely achieve a summer peak much above 21°C (70°F). Seven of these beaches are patrolled by lifeguards from mid-May to mid-September (Second Beach, Third Beach, English Bay Beach, Kitsilano Beach, Jericho Beach, Locarno Beach and Spanish Banks Beach). See box, p.79, for more on the city's beaches. The city's major pools are:

Kitsilano Pool Cornwall Avenue and Yew Street on Kitsilano Beach (late May to mid-June Mon–Fri noon–8.45pm, Sat–Sun 10am–8.45pm; mid-June to early Sept Mon–Fri 7am–8.45pm, Sat–Sun 10am–8.45pm; rest of Sept Mon–Fri 7am–7.15pm, Sat–Sun 10am–7.15pm; $5.15; Ⓣ604/731-0011). Like its rival at Second Beach, this major outdoor pool is another gargantuan affair, though this one is saltwater and heated to around 25°C (77°F) in high summer. It has both a play area (excellent for families with children) and a zone for laps.

Second Beach Pool, Second Beach, Stanley Park (mid-May to mid-June Mon–Fri noon–8.45pm, Sat–Sun 10am–8.45pm; mid-June to July daily 10am–8.45pm, then closes 15min earlier each week from Aug 4 to mid-Sept; $5.15; Ⓣ604/257-8371 or 257-8370). The closest of the city's two major outdoor pools to Downtown is an enormous freshwater pool beside the Seawall that has lifeguards, a handful of small waterslides and a playground.

UBC Aquatic Centre 6121 University Blvd (call or visit website for the latest hours; $4.95; Ⓣ604/822-4522, Ⓦwww.aquatics.ubc.ca). The UBC Aquatic Centre has one of Vancouver's best indoor pools – it sits alongside the Student Union Building – as well as an outdoor pool, but students take priority, and hours for the general public can be restricted. It is also a long way from Downtown, though you could try to combine a swim here with a visit to the Museum of Anthropology (see p. 000).

Vancouver Aquatic Centre 1050 Beach Ave at the foot of Thurlow (Mon–Fri 7am–9.30pm, lanes only from 4.30pm, Sat 8am–9.30pm, with some restrictions, Sun 10am–9.30pm, with some restrictions; Ⓣ604/665-3424; $5.15). The centre is conveniently located on the southern edge of Downtown (and handy for ferries to and from Granville Island) and has an Olympic-size fifty metre pool heated to 28°C.

YWCA Fitness Centre 535 Hornby St near Dunsmuir (Mon–Fri 6am–10pm, Sat & Sun 8am–5.30pm; the day pass, $16, includes all the centre's facilities; Ⓣ604/895-5777, Ⓦwww.ywcavan.org or www.ywcahealthandfitness.com) has another excellent and very central pool, but it's only 25m long and six lanes wide. On the plus side, it's ozonated rather than chlorinated.

Tennis

Vancouver's very popular 180 public tennis courts can be used on a first-come, first-served basis for a maximum of an hour per session between 8am and dusk. All the courts are free and can be booked up to a week in advance; reservations are taken between mid-May and Labour Day weekend

(early Sept) and courts cost $11.70 per hour Mon–Fri 3pm to dusk, weekends 9am to dusk (Ⓣ604/605-8224).

Other central courts are in Stanley Park by Lost Lagoon at the foot of Robson; in Kitsilano Beach Park (ten courts); in Jericho Beach Park behind the Jericho Sailing Centre; in Queen Elizabeth Park (eighteen courts) at 33rd Avenue and Cambie Street; at the False Creek Community Centre on Granville Island; and at the UBC Coast Tennis Club at the UBC campus (6184 Thunderbird Blvd at East Mall; indoor courts can be booked in advance on Ⓣ604/822-2505, Ⓦwww.tennis-ubc.ca).

If you don't have a racquet handy, rent one at Bayshore Bicycle and Rollerblade Rental, 745 Denman St (Ⓣ604/688-2453), for around $10 a day.

Windsurfing

If you want to windsurf, kitesurf or skimboard for a morning or so, then you can have lessons and rent (or buy) boards, wetsuits, lifejackets and other equipment at Jericho Beach at Windsure Windsurfing School, 1300 Discovery St (daily April–Oct 9am–8pm; Ⓣ604/224-0615, Ⓦwww.windsure.com). Rentals start at around $20 a day, wetsuit and lifejacket included. Note that you can windsurf off Jericho, Locarno, Kits and English Bay beaches (see p.79) between the yellow buoys only, but not at the mouth of False Creek between the Granville Street and Burrard Street bridges near Granville Island.

Serious windsurfers should head for Squamish on the way to Whistler (see p.239).

Spectator sports

None of the Vancouver teams that take part in North America's leading sports – baseball, ice hockey and football – can really be said to make the grade in the big-time leagues. This is true even in the sports where the city fields teams in the cross-border leagues with the United States, such as the National Hockey League (NHL); the **Vancouver Canucks** rarely do more than put on a respectable showing in the NHL. This said, all the city's teams have a passionate following, something that is especially true of the Canucks, but also of the **Vancouver Canadians** baseball team and the **BC Lions** football team.

This means **tickets** for many events sell quickly, especially those that involve major visiting teams or one-off events. Even so, you can usually find a seat somewhere right up to the start of the game. Tickets for many events can be obtained from the Vancouver Touristinfo Centre (see p.36), from the box offices listed below, or from one of the forty or so branches of Ticketmaster dotted around the Greater Vancouver area. You can buy tickets with a credit card over the phone from Ticketmaster by calling Ⓣ604/280-4444 or visiting Ⓦwww.ticketmaster.ca.

Baseball

The **Vancouver Canadians** (Ⓣ604/872-5232, Ⓦwww.canadiansbaseball.com) play in the Single-A Northwest League against seven other groups at the charming, 7500-seat Nat Bailey Stadium, at 4601 Ontario St and West 29th Ave on the east side of Queen Elizabeth Park (see p.83). To reach the stadium, take bus #3 south on Main St to West 30th Ave and walk one block west. The season runs from June to September and there are afternoon and evening games. **Tickets** can usually be bought at the door, however, and cost from $11 for general admission, from $14 for a box and $20 for reserved Diamond Club admission.

Football

Canadian football is slightly different from its American cousin. In the

Canadian version there are three downs instead of four, the field is longer and wider, there are twelve players instead of eleven, and a point (known as a rouge) is gained for a missed field goal. The game is exciting but comes in a poor second to American football in commercial terms and in the calibre of players it can attract – the money and real talent head to the United States.

Canadian teams play in the Canadian Football League (CFL). Vancouver's representatives are the **BC Lions** (Ⓣ604/589-ROAR, Ⓦwww.bclions.com), who play at the 60,000-seat BC Place Stadium at 777 Pacific Blvd at the foot of Robson and Beatty streets. The season runs from June to late October and tickets cost from $30 to $80. The best approach to the stadium is to take the SkyTrain (see p.25) to Stadium station.

Horse racing

For a day out or a flutter, head to the delightful **Hastings Park Racecourse** in East Vancouver at Exhibition Park, Renfrew St at East Hastings and Cassiar (Ⓣ604/254-1631 or 1-877/977-7702, Ⓦwww.hastingspark.com). Races are usually run weekend afternoons from April to November (plus Friday evening June–Sept). Admission is free. Free bus shuttles usually run from Renfrew SkyTrain station and the junction of East Hastings and Renfrew streets.

Ice hockey

If you want just one taste of live sport during your stay, you'll probably find an ice hockey game the most exciting choice. In ice hockey (or plain "hockey") Canada ranks among the world's best, though in the **Canucks** (Ⓣ604/899-4625 or 899-4600, Ⓦwww.canucks.com) Vancouver has a team that doesn't always reach the heights of rivals such as the Edmonton Oilers and Calgary Flames. The Canucks play at General Motors Place Stadium – known colloquially as "The Garage" – at 800 Griffiths Way close to Beatty St and Pacific Blvd (Ⓣ604/899-7469, event hotline Ⓣ604/899-7444). They draw big crowds in a season that runs from October to mid-April. Ticket prices range from $55 to $131.

Soccer

Vancouver's men's and women's football (soccer) teams are the Whitecaps, formerly the 86ers (Ⓣ604/899-9283, Ⓦwww.whitecapsfc.com), and play in the USL's Division 1 in a season that runs from the end of April to mid-September (men) and May to the end of July (women). Matches take place at the Swanguard Stadium at Kingsway and Boundary Rd (take the SkyTrain to Patterson), and admission costs between about $18 and $35.

Festivals and events

Whatever time of year you visit Vancouver, a festival or annual event of some description is probably being held somewhere in the city. While we've listed the major ones below; you can learn more about these as well as various one-off events and shows by contacting Tourism Vancouver (Ⓣ604/683-2000, Ⓦwww.tourismvancouver.com) or picking up *The Vancouver Book,* an annually updated listing of festivals and general information available free from the city's infocentre (see p.36). Other listings can be found by visiting Ⓦwww.foundlocally.com/vancouver.

January

Polar Bear Swim Every New Year's Day since 1819 hardy locals jump into the icy waters at English Bay Beach in a mass swim. In 1920 the event was formalized as the New Year's Day Polar Bear Swim. In a good year, some two thousand people take the plunge, though not all manage the "required" 90m swim to a special buoy. In 2003, there were 1200 participants, including 91-year-old Ivy Granstrom. Most sensible people – and crowds can number over 10,000 – come simply to stand and watch, but if you take the plunge, bear in mind that temperatures range from 3 to 8°C. Ⓣ604/665-3424 or 257-8400. Ⓦwww.vancouver.ca/parks/events.

Annual Bald Eagle Count First Sunday of the month At 9am at the Brackendale Art Gallery, people come to watch the annual count of the huge numbers of bald eagles that gather to gorge on the salmon near Brackendale en route for Whistler (see p.239). In 1994, the record year, volunteers counted 3700 eagles. Ⓣ604/898-3333, Ⓦwww.brackendaleartgallery.com/festival.

Dine Out Vancouver For limited periods in January, many of Vancouver's better restaurants offer three-course meals at discounted prices. Contact the infocentre for further details. Ⓦwww.tourismvancouver.com/visitors/diningout.

PuSh Festival Around 25,000 people attended the 2008 version of this increasingly popular and dynamic festival of groundbreaking music, opera, dance and performing arts. It takes place in various venues over 20 days towards the end of the month and the beginning of February. Ⓣ604/605-8284 or 1-866/608-8284, Ⓦwww.pushfestival.ca.

International Chinese New Year Festival The precise dates of the Chinese New Year depend on the lunar calendar – it's held

▲ Dragon Dance, Chinese New Year

sometime between late January and early February – but whenever it occurs you can rely on some fifteen days of festivities in Chinatown and around the city. There's a Dragon Parade (Sun afternoon), music, dancing, storytelling, art exhibitions and lots of fireworks. There are similar events in the Chinese communities of Victoria and Burnaby. Ⓦwww.cbavancouver.ca.com.

February

Vancouver International Boat Show over five days near the start of the month. This is western Canada's largest and oldest boat show. It features the latest in power and sail vessels, accessories, electronics, fishing gear and sports, fishing and sailing lodges. The show takes place in the BC Place Stadium. Ⓦwww.vancouverboatshow.ca.

Vancouver International Storytelling Festival A charming event over three or four days that champions and celebrates the storyteller's art, with lots of readings and events, usually around a different annual theme. Ⓣ604/876-2272, Ⓦwww.vancouverstorytelling.org.

Vancouver International Dance Festival Dance is big news in Vancouver, and this month-long festival embraces numerous events, workshops and live performances from local, Canadian and international troupes. Ⓣ604/662-7441 for information, Ⓣ604/662-4966 for tickets, Ⓦwww.vidf.ca.

CelticFest Five days of Celtic music, culture and entertainment centered on St Patrick's Day in the middle of the month. Takes place most years. Ⓣ604/683-8331, Ⓦwww.celticfestvancouver.com.

Spring Break Theatre Festival The invariably excellent Arts Club is behind this week-long festival of theatre aimed primarily at children at venues mostly on and around Granville Island. Ⓣ604/687-1644, Ⓦwww.artsclub.com.

April

Vancouver Playhouse International Wine Festival near the start of the month or mid- or late March One of North America's largest annual wine festivals allows you to sample over six hundred wines from 125 wineries around the world at the Vancouver Convention and Exhibition Centre and leading hotels and restaurants throughout Greater Vancouver. The event has been running since 1979, when it was launched to help provide funds for the Vancouver Playhouse Theatre Company, and has grown in stature each year – 1600 wines from 183 wineries were presented in 2009. Ⓣ604/873-3311, Ⓦwww.playhousewinefest.com.

Baisakhi Day Parade mid-month This vibrant parade, which celebrates the Sikh Indian New Year, takes place on and around Ross St off Marine Drive in North Vancouver. Ⓣ604/324-2010.

Vancouver Sun Run third weekend of the month The Sun Run is one of the world's largest 10k runs – in past years it has attracted over 17,000 runners. You can run (or walk) the scenic route through Downtown, starting and finishing at BC Place Stadium, where there are refreshments and entertainment. Ⓣ604/689-9441, Ⓦwww.sunrun.com.

May

Vancouver International Marathon first Sunday of the month Canada's largest marathon attracts over six thousand runners and takes you from BC Place Stadium and along False Creek to Stanley Park and then Kitsilano. Ⓣ604/872-2928, Ⓦwww. bmovanmarathon.ca.

The New Play Festival on Granville Island first week of the month This weeklong celebration of the best of new Canadian theatre involves many workshop sessions and some of the city's best actors, actresses and directors. Ⓦwww.playwrightstheatre.com.

New Music West Festival second weekend of the month An international festival of new pop and rock music, with lots of events, seminars and special music and band nights at a variety of the city's clubs. Ⓣ604/684-9338, Ⓦwww.newmusicwest.com.

Cloverdale Rodeo and Exhibition third weekend of the month Some of the top male and female stars of the North American professional rodeo circuit compete in bull-riding and other rodeo events at the Cloverdale Rodeo and Exhibition Fairgrounds in Surrey. Ⓣ604/576-9461, Ⓦwww.cloverdalerodeo.com.

Hyack Festival third weekend of the month New Westminster is the setting for this popular festival, usually held on the long weekend. It includes a family day, May Day celebrations, fireworks, a parade and an antiques fair. Ⓦwww.hyack.bc.ca.

Vancouver International Children's Festival towards the end of the month or early June Music, theatre, dance and puppetry from around the world. Staged in Vanier Park over about a week, the event is attended

by upwards of 70,000 people. For more, see p.184. ⓣ604/708-5655, ⓦwww.childrensfestival.ca.

June

VanDusen Flower and Garden Show first week of the month The city's premier garden festival, held in the botanic garden (see p.85), will appeal to anyone with green fingers. The show features some two hundred stands devoted to everything from flowers and shrubs to gargoyles and garden gnomes. ⓣ604/878-9274, ⓦwww.Vancouver.ca/parks.

Bard on the Beach Shakespeare Festival from the second Tuesday of the month until last week of September This is a popular and long-established theatre festival in which Shakespeare plays are performed in a five-hundred-seat tent on the beach in Vanier Park overlooking English Bay. Two plays are usually performed each year. Box office ⓣ604/739-0559, information ⓣ604/737-0625 or 1-877/739-0559, ⓦwww.bardonthebeach.org.

Commercial Drive Festival Visit ⓦwww.thedrive.ca for details of numerous events during the year designed to promote Commercial Drive, an ever-more dynamic street in East Vancouver, including two days in mid-June and mid-July when the street is closed to traffic in favour of street performers, stalls and cultural and other events.

Dragon Boat Festival third weekend of the month A weekend of boat races on False Creek involving some 150 teams and two thousand international competitors. Other events include a wide range of family-oriented cabaret and other stage shows. ⓣ604/688-2382, ⓦwww.dragonboat.ca.

Festival d'Eté Francophone de Vancouver four days in mid-June Vancouver may be a long way from Canada's francophone heartlands to the east, but it still puts on a French-themed street festival and performances in venues around the city by leading Québecois artists. ⓦwww.lecentreculturel.com.

International Jazz Festival from the third Friday of the month, for ten days One of Vancouver's major festivals, this jazz-and-blues event brings together some of the world's biggest names in jazz, who perform at some 25 venues around the city – from nightclubs to outdoor stages on Grouse Mountain and in the Dr Sun Yat-Sen Garden. The event, which draws around eight hundred musicians, includes a two-day Mardi Gras-style street festival in Gastown. ⓣ604/872-5200, ⓦwww.coastaljazz.ca.

National Aboriginal Day Community Celebrations the 21st Part of a nationwide celebration of First Nation, or aboriginal, culture. Many of Vancouver's events take place at the Vancouver Aboriginal Friendship Centre, 1607 East Hastings St at Commercial Drive. ⓣ604/251-4844.

July

Canada Day the 1st Canada celebrates its confederation, a national holiday, with festivities, including big fireworks displays, that are held around the city. The special focus is on Canada Place (fireworks start at 10pm), Granville Island and Grouse Mountain. Canada Place ⓣ604/666-8477, ⓦwww.canadaplace.com; Granville Island ⓣ604/666-5784, ⓦwww.granvilleisland.bc.ca.

Dancing on the Edge early to mid-month The city's major dance festival brings together leading dance companies from across North America for around ten days. Most performances are staged at the Firehall Arts Centre, 280 East Cordova St. ⓣ604/689-0926, ⓦwww.dancingontheedge.org.

Pacific National Exhibition (PNE) from mid-August to early September A traditional, family-oriented exhibition that offers a wide range of events, including rodeo, logging shows, demolition derbies, fashion shows, livestock displays, dog shows and much more. Especially good for younger children. It is linked to the Playland amusement park close by (see p.188). East Hastings St and Renfrew. ⓣ604/253-2311, ⓦwww.pne.ca.

Theatre Under the Stars from the middle of the month to the middle of August Two amateur city theatre groups perform two major productions outdoors in the Stanley Park Malkin Bowl. ⓣ604/687-0174, ⓦwww.tuts.ca.

Vancouver Folk Festival third weekend of the month One of Vancouver's biggest and most respected festivals, this event attracts around 30,000 to Jericho Beach Park. Some 100 performances are given by local and international singers, songwriters and storytellers on seven different stages, with shows throughout the day and evening. There's also a special Little Folks Festival for children. Tickets start at about $48 (on the gate) for a Friday ticket ($76 on Sat or Sun) and $140 (bought in advance) for the weekend. ⓣ604/602-9798, ⓦwww.thefestival.bc.ca.

Vancouver Global ComedyFest towards the end of the month Local and international comedians perform at Granville Island and other venues for ten days. ⓣ604/685-0881, ⓦwww.comedyfest.com.

MusicFest Vancouver second half of the month or first half of August One of the city's newest music festivals, this is an ambitious fourteen-day event held across several venues. Canadian and international musicians perform orchestral, choral, world music, jazz and opera in around eighty concerts. The festival is often themed to a single composer, or to the music of one country. ⓣ604/688-1152, ⓦwww.musicfestvancouver.ca.

HSBC Celebration of Light towards the end of the month or early August Three different countries every year compete in a spectacular fireworks competition – the world's largest – on English Bay, usually over four nights. Each night features a show by a single country; the three come together on the fourth night to lay on a majestic joint spectacle that attracts upwards of 500,000 people to the city's West End. ⓣ604/642-6835, ⓦwww.celebration-of-light.com.

Caribbean Days Festival towards the end of the month A two-day celebration of Caribbean art, music and culture organized by the Trinidad and Tobago Cultural Society of British Columbia held in Waterfront Park, North Vancouver. It's the largest cultural event of its kind in the province. ⓦwww.caribbeandays.ca.

Vancouver Early Music Festival from the end of the month to early August The University of British Columbia (UBC) School of Music organizes this celebration of medieval, baroque and other early music. Performances are held over about three weeks at the UBC Recital Hall, 6361 Memorial Rd. ⓣ604/732-1610, ⓦwww.earlymusic.bc.ca.

Vancouver Chamber Music Festival end of the month The Vancouver Recital Society has been running this two-week festival since 1986. Events are broadcast on national radio and held in the park-like campus of Crofton House School in Vanier Park. This may sound low-key, but it's considered one of the finest events of its kind in Canada, bringing together many of the most talented classical musicians from Canada and abroad. ⓣ604/602-0363, ⓦwww.vanrecital.com.

August

Powell Street Festival first weekend of the month A celebration of Japanese and Japanese-Canadian culture, this festival provides an eclectic mixture of parades, food, workshops, music and other entertainment, often drawing leading exponents of Japanese culture from around the world. ⓣ604/739-9388, ⓦwww.powellstreetfestival.com.

Harmony Arts Festival beginning of the month North Shore artists are showcased in this two-week event, with numerous exhibitions, free events, demonstrations, concerts, markets and workshops. ⓣ604/925-7268, ⓦwww.harmonyarts.ca.

Abbotsford Air Show second weekend of the month Plane enthusiasts reckon this is one of the world's best air shows. The event is held at Abbotsford airport, 56km southeast of Vancouver. ⓣ604/852-8511, ⓦwww.abbotsfordairshow.com.

Vancouver Pride Parade towards the beginning of the month One of Vancouver's pivotal summer events, with 600,000 attending the main parade and 110,000 at the festival site on Sunset Beach. Events vary from year to year, but there's usually plenty happening on and around Denman St and lots of celebrations in the city's gay and lesbian clubs and pubs. ⓣ604/737-7433, ⓦwww.vancouverpride.ca.

Wooden Boat Festival last weekend of the month Boat owners and enthusiasts gather on the west dock at Granville Island to show off and admire wooden boats of all kinds. ⓣ604/688-9622, ⓦwww.vcn.bc.ca/vwbs.

September

Vancouver Fringe Theatre Festival mid-month A highly popular event dating from 1985 in which over one hundred theatre, dance and comedy groups from around the world put on five hundred shows at various indoor and outdoor venues around the city. The event usually lasts for between ten and fourteen days. Further information ⓣ604/257-0350, ⓦwww.vancouverfringe.com.

Vancouver International Film Festival from the end of the month to mid-October North America's third-largest film festival presents up to five hundred screenings of three hundred new films, revivals and retrospectives from some fifty countries. It runs for around seventeen days, and events take place in cinemas around the

city. The festival is popular – upwards of 114,000 people attend. ⓣ604/685-0260, ⓦwww.viff.org.

Moon Festival late September or early October This outdoor Chinese mid-autumn festival takes place on the fifteenth day of the eighth month of the Chinese calendar, which means it varies from year to year depending on the lunar cycle. The festival is staged at the Dr Sun Yat-Sen Garden (see p.60) and involves music, moon cakes, storytelling and a lantern parade. ⓣ604/662-3207.

October

International Writers & Readers Festival third week of the month Around sixty national and international literary stars and new writers give readings and workshops on Granville Island and other locations around Vancouver and BC. The festival attracts some big-hitters – Martin Amis, Margaret Atwood, Peter Carey, John Irving, P. D. James, Alice Munro, Frank McCourt and J. K. Rowling are some of the past speakers. ⓣ604/681-6330, ⓦwww.writersfest.bc.ca.

Vancouver Snow Show end of the month The Canada Place Conventions Centre hosts Canada's winter-sports show. This is a place to pick up cheap clothes and equipment as companies unload old stock. ⓣ800/626-1538, ⓦwww.canwestshows.com/snowshow.

November

Remembrance Day Nov 11 Armistice Day – marking the moment hostilities ceased in World War I – is the day when all Canada, in common with many countries, remembers soldiers who died in the war. In Vancouver a 21-gun salute is fired from Deadman's Island in Stanley Park at noon, and vintage aircraft fly over the park and Canada Place.

VanDusen Market and Festival of Light late November and early December This popular and high-quality craft and gift market is held in the VanDusen Botanical Garden (see p.85). Throughout December the Festival of Light sees the gardens illuminated by over 20,000 lights. ⓦwww.vancouver.ca/parks.

December

Christmas Carol Ship Parade three weeks leading up to Christmas This is one of Vancouver's more magical events, in which a flotilla of decorated and illuminated boats of all descriptions cruises around the harbour on different nights. People onboard sing carols or broadcast taped Christmas music. ⓣ604/878-8999, ⓦwww.carolships.org.

18 Directory

Airlines Air Canada, Air Canada Jazz & Air Canada Tango (Ⓣ604/688-5515, 1-888/247-2262 or 888/661-247-2262, Ⓦwww.aircanada.ca, www.flyjazz.com, www.flytango.com); American Airlines (Ⓣ604/222-2532 or 1-800/433-7300, Ⓦwww.aa.com); Baxter: float-plane services to Victoria's Inner Harbour (Ⓣ604/683-6525 or 1-800/661-5599, Ⓦwww.baxterair.com); British Airways (Ⓣ604/270-8131 or 1-800/247-9297, Ⓦwww.ba.com); Harbour Air Seaplanes: services to Victoria Inner Harbour (Ⓣ604/274-1277 or 1-800/665-0212, Ⓦwww.harbour-air.com); Helijet Airways: helicopter service to Victoria (Ⓣ604/273-1414 or 1-800/665-4354, Ⓦwww.helijet.com); KLM (Ⓣ604/303-3666); United (Ⓣ1-800/241-6522, Ⓦwww.ual.com); Northwest (Ⓣ1-800/225-2525, Ⓦwww.nwa.com); West Coast Air: seaplane services to Victoria and Gulf Islands (Ⓣ604/688-9115, 606-6888 or 1-800/347-2222, Ⓦwww.westcoastair.com); WestJet (Ⓣ1-800/538-5696, Ⓦwww.westjet.com); Whistler Air: direct flights to Whistler from Vancouver Harbour Air Terminal by *Pan Pacific Hotel* (Ⓣ604/932-6615 or 1-888/806-2299, Ⓦwww.whistlerair.ca).

Airport tax All passengers departing from Vancouver have to pay departure tax, but it is currently included in the cost of all tickets.

American Express Park Place Building, 666 Burrard St, enter at Hornby and Dunsmuir (Ⓣ604/669-2813 or 1-800/772-4473); open Mon–Fri 8.30am–5.30pm, Sat 10am–4pm.

Area code The area code for the greater Vancouver area is Ⓣ604.

BC Parks Ⓣ604/924-2200, Ⓦwww.gov.bc.ca/bcparks.

Bike rental Bayshore Bicycles & Rollerblade Rentals, 745 Denman St (Ⓣ604/688-2453, Ⓦwww.bayshorebikerentals.ca) and 1610 West Georgia St at Cardero in the *Westin Bayshore Hotel* (Ⓣ604/689-5071); Harbour Air, Harbour Air Terminal at the waterfront west of Canada Place (Ⓣ604/688-1277), which also rents blades and motorcycles; Spokes, 1798 West Georgia St at Denman (Ⓣ604/688-5141, Ⓦwww.vancouverbikerental.com).

Buses Airporter (Ⓣ604/946-8866 or 1-800/668-3141, Ⓦwww.yvrairporter.com) for shuttle from Vancouver Airport to bus depot and Downtown; BC Transit for city buses, SeaBus and SkyTrain (Ⓣ604/953-3333, Ⓦwww.translink.bc.ca); Greyhound (Ⓣ604/662-3222, 482-8747 or 1-800/661-8747, Ⓦwww.greyhound.ca) for BC, Alberta, Yukon and long-haul destinations including Seattle and other points in the US; Malaspina Coach Lines (Ⓣ1-877/227-8287, Ⓦwww.malaspinacoach.com) for the Sunshine Coast, Powell River, Whistler, Pemberton and Nanaimo on Vancouver Island; Pacific Coach Lines (Ⓣ604/662-8074 or 1-800/661-1725, Ⓦwww.pacificcoach.com) for Victoria, Vancouver Island; Perimeter (Ⓣ604/266-5386 or 604/717-6600, Ⓦwww.perimeterbus.com) for services between Whistler and Vancouver Airport; Quick Shuttle (Ⓣ604/940-4428 or 800/665-2122, Ⓦwww.quickcoach.com) for Bellingham Airport, downtown Seattle and SeaTac Airport.

Car rental Alamo, 1132 West Georgia St at Thurlow (Ⓣ604/684-2869, Ⓦwww.alamo.ca); Avis, 757 Hornby St at West Georgia (Ⓣ604/606-2869, Ⓦwww.avis.ca); Budget, 416 West Georgia at Richards, and 1705 Burrard St (Ⓣ604/668-7000 or 1-800/268-8900 in Canada, 1-800/527-0700 in US, Ⓦwww.bc.budget.com); Hertz, 1128 Seymour St at Helmcken (Ⓣ604/606-4711 or 1-800/263-0600, Ⓦwww.hertz.com); Lo-Cost, 1835 Marine Drive (Ⓣ604/986-1266 or 800/986-1260, Ⓦwww.locost.com); National 1130 West Georgia St at Thurlow (Ⓣ604/609-7150, 1-800/227-7368,

ⓦwww.nationalcar.com); Rent-a-Wreck, 1349 Hornby St (ⓣ604/688-0001 or 1-888/665-3777, ⓦwww.rentawreckvancouver.com).

Consulates Australia, 1225 Dunsmuir St, Suite 888, at Hornby (ⓣ604/684-1177); Ireland, 1400-100 West Pender St at Abbott (ⓣ604/683-8440 or 683-9233); New Zealand, 1200-Suite 888 Dunsmuir St at Hornby (ⓣ604/684-7388); UK, 800–1111 Melville St at Thurlow (ⓣ604/683-4421); US, 1075 West Pender (ⓣ604/685-4311, ⓦwww.usconsulatevancouver.ca).

Currency Exchange Custom House Currency, Unit 60–200 Granville St (ⓣ604/608-1763, ⓦwww.customhouse.com); International Securities Exchange, 1169 Robson St near Thurlow (ⓣ604/683-9666); Travelex–Thomas Cook, 999 Canada Place, Suite 130 (ⓣ604/641-1229); Vancouver Bullion & Currency Exchange, 402 Hornby St (ⓣ604/685-1008, ⓦwww.vbc.ca).

Dentists Many major hotels have a dentist on call. Otherwise, for your nearest dentist, call the College of Dental Surgeons for a referral (ⓣ604/736-3621) or the British Columbia Dental Association (ⓣ604/736-7202, ⓦwww.bcdental.org). Drop-in dentist Dentacare (Mon–Fri 8am–5pm only; ⓣ604/669-6700) is in the lower level of the Bentall Centre at 1055 Dunsmuir St and Burrard.

Directory enquiries ⓣ411.

Doctors The College of Physicians can provide names of three doctors near you (ⓣ604/733-7758). Drop-in service (no appointments necessary) at Vancouver Medical Clinics, Bentall Centre, 1055 Dunsmuir St (Mon–Fri 8am–4.45pm; ⓣ604/683-8138); Carepoint, 1175 Denman St (daily 9am–9pm; ⓣ604/681-5338); Stein Medical Clinic, Bentall 5 Lobby, 188–550 Burrard St at West Pender (Mon–Fri 8.30am–5.30pm; ⓣ604/688-5924, ⓦwww.steinmedicalclinic.com); or Ultima Vancouver Airport Medical Clinic, Vancouver International Airport, Domestic Terminal (ⓣ604/207-6900, ⓦwww.ultimamedical.ca).

Electricity Canada uses 110-volt, 60-cycle electricity, which means that travellers from the US should find that their appliances work without a hitch, but Europeans and others will need an adaptor.

Emergency services (police, fire and ambulance) ⓣ911.

Hospitals St Paul's Hospital, 1081 Burrard St (ⓣ604/682-2344); Vancouver General Hospital, 855 West 12th Ave (ⓣ604/874-4111); or British Columbia's Children's Hospital, 4480 Oak St (ⓣ604/875-2345). In North Van there is the Lions Gate Hospital, 231 East 15th St (ⓣ604/988-3131).

Internet access Free access at the Vancouver Central Library, 350 West Georgia St (ⓣ604/331-3600, ⓦwww.vpl.ca; access not available on Sun); or from about $4 an hour at the *Internet Café*, 1104 Davie St at Thurlow (ⓣ604/682-6668), which opens daily until 11pm.

Laundries Davie Laundromat, 1061 Davie St (ⓣ604/682-2717); Scotty's One Hour Cleaners, 834 Thurlow St near Robson (ⓣ604/685-7732).

Left luggage At Pacific Central Station ($2 per 24hr) and at CDS Baggage at the city airport (national and international arrivals) from $2 per item for 24hr.

Liquor laws The legal drinking age in British Columbia is 19.

Lost property BC Transit, Stadium SkyTrain station, 590 Beatty St (ⓣ604/682-7887); West Vancouver Transit (ⓣ604/985-7777); police (ⓣ604/717-2726); airport, customer service counter, Level 3, International Departures (ⓣ604/276-6104). If you leave items in a taxi, call the appropriate cab company.

Maps Geological Survey of Canada, 101–605 Robson near Richards (Mon–Fri 8.30am–4.30pm; ⓣ604/666-0529). Superb source of official survey maps, including *all* 1:50,000 maps of BC and Yukon.

Optician Opticana Eyewear, 455 Granville St (ⓣ604/685-1031, ⓦwww.opticana.ca).

Parking Main Downtown garages are at The Bay (entrance on Richards St near Dunsmuir), Robson Square (on Smithe St and Howe) and the Pacific Centre (on Howe St and Dunsmuir) – all are expensive and fill up quickly. A better idea might be to leave your car at the free Park'n'Ride in New Westminster (off Hwy 1).

Pharmacies Shopper's Drug Mart, 1125 Davie St and Thurlow (ⓣ604/669-2424), is open 24hr and has five other outlets open Mon–Sat 9am–midnight, Sun 9am–9pm. London Drugs, 1650 Davie St (ⓣ604/669-2884), is open daily until 11pm. Carson Midnite Drug Store, 6517 Main St at 49th Ave, is open daily until midnight. Safeway supermarket pharmacies are also often open late: the store at Robson St at Denman is open until midnight.

Police Non-emergency 24hr (Ⓣ604/717-3321). Royal Canadian Mounted Police (RCMP) (Ⓣ604/264-3111); Vancouver City Police, 2120 Cambie St (Ⓣ604/665-3535 or 717-3535, Ⓦwww.vancouver.ca/police).
Post office Main office at 349 West Georgia St and Homer (Mon–Fri 8am–5.30pm; Ⓣ604/662-5722 or 1-800/267-1177). Post office information (Ⓣ1-800/267-1177, Ⓦwww.canadapost.ca). Post office outlets with longer hours can be found in many 7-Eleven and Shopper's Drug Mart stores.
Student cards Most places will accept a school ID for student discounts; an International Student Identity Card (Ⓦwww.isiccard.com), however, is the most widely recognized and accepted card of all.
Smoking All indoor public transport and other public spaces, including bars and restaurants, are nonsmoking. Smoking is generally allowed on restaurant and bar terraces and patios. You need to be 19 to purchase tobacco.
Tax Provincial sales tax (PST) is 7.5 percent on most goods and services, rising to 8 percent on hotel bills and 10 percent in restaurants and bars; this is supplemented by the nationwide goods and services tax (GST), a 7 percent levy equivalent to VAT in Europe.
Taxis Black Top (Ⓣ604/731-1111 or 681-2181); Vancouver Taxi (Ⓣ604/871-1111); Yellow Cab (Ⓣ604/681-3311 or 681-1111).
Temperature Vancouver averages 55–70°F (13–21°C) in the summer months, 33–42°F (1–6°C) in the winter.
Time zones Vancouver runs on Pacific Time, or eight hours behind GMT, the same as Seattle, Portland and San Francisco. Daylight saving time applies between April and October.
Tipping 15 percent is generally expected.
Tourist information Vancouver Touristinfo Centre, 200 Burrard St (Ⓣ604/683-2000, Ⓦwww.tourismvancouver.com); BC Tourism /Hello BC (Ⓣ800/435-5622, Ⓦwww.hellobc.com); Granville Island, 1398 Cartwright St, Granville Island (Ⓣ604/666-5784, Ⓦwww.granvilleisland.com).
Train enquiries Amtrak (Ⓣ1-800/872-7245, Ⓦwww.amtrak.com); Rocky Mountain Railtours (Ⓣ604/606-7200 or 1-800/665-7245, Ⓦwww.rockymountaineer.com) for expensive rail tours through the Rockies; VIA Rail (Ⓣ604/669-3050 or toll-free in Canada only Ⓣ1-888/842-7245, 1-800/561-3949 in the US, Ⓦwww.viarail.ca).
Weather information Ⓣ604/664-9010.

The great outdoors

Only the luckiest cities can lay claim to ravishing landscapes. London, Paris, New York and Tokyo may be great cities, with iconic landmarks and distinctive skylines, but they don't combine the splendour of their urban landscapes with the majesty of a glorious natural setting in the manner of Venice, Sydney and Rio de Janeiro. Here, nature often comes to define the city as much as any social, cultural or historical context. Vancouver is one of this lucky group, framed by mountains, embraced by the ocean and edged with rivers and forests that contain a glorious profusion of flora and fauna and innumerable opportunities for outdoor activities.

Snowboarding at Whistler ▲

Hiking in Mount Seymour's forests ▼

The mountains

The most obvious and defining of Vancouver's landscapes are the **mountains** above the North Shore, sudden glimpses of which are one of the great, unexpected pleasures of wandering the city. These are part of the Coast Mountains, the colossal range that runs for hundreds of miles parallel to the Pacific coast to the Alaska border and beyond. They were formed between 60 and 75 million years ago by ructions of the Pacific and North American tectonic plates, part of the same mountain-building episode that gave birth to the Rockies in the BC interior. Much of the **North Shore mountain area** is easily accessible, whether you simply take the cable-car up Grouse Mountain (see p.98) or opt for hiking in Cypress, Mount Seymour and other North Shore parks (see pp. 107–112).

The rainforest

If there's one feature of Vancouver's great outdoors you'll probably remember more than any other, it's **trees**: lots of them. The west coast's torrential rainfall, mild maritime climate, deep soils and long growing season produce Canada's most impressive forests and its biggest trees. In the mountains above Vancouver, and

Whistler

One of the world's great winter and summer resorts. Whistler's credentials as a winter-sports destination need little underlining, especially after the resort's role in the **2010 Olympics**, but what is less well known is its superb range of summer activities, notably high-level hiking and biking, but also golf, climbing and rafting (see p.250).

Flora and fauna

Shrubs and **bushes** such as salal, huckleberry, bunchberry, salmonberry and twinberry thrive alongside mosses, ferns, lichens, liverwort, orchids and skunk cabbage. All sorts of animals can be found here, not close to the city, perhaps, but if you're lucky, you'll come across some fauna only a trail's length into the wilderness. The most notable large animals are **cougar** and their main prey, **Columbian blacktail deer**, as well as **black bears**; smaller creatures include red squirrels. Birds are legion, with a wealth of woodland species, including rarities such as the **Rufous hummingbird**, which migrates from its wintering grounds in Mexico to feed on the forest's numerous nectar-bearing flowers.

▲ Black bear

▼ Humpback whale

in wondrous Stanley Park, this means luxuriant swathes of temperate **rainforest**, dominated by Sitka spruce, western red cedar, Pacific silver fir, western hemlock, western yew and, biggest of all, Douglas fir, some of which tower 90m high and are over 1200 years old.

The Fraser River

Gazing north from Vancouver's Downtown foreshore to the Coastal Mountains, you might easily forget that in the other direction, beyond the suburbs of South Vancouver, is an entirely different environment, one that in its own way is just as grand and naturally fecund. It centres on the **Fraser**, one of the great rivers of North America, which empties into the sea in a mighty delta of shifting sands, mudflats, swirling waters and windswept marsh.

Among the 360 species of **birds** found here are blue heron, osprey, bald eagles

and other birds of prey, lured by the prospect of rich pickings amid the millions of spawning salmon that run the river year after year. The salmon run, plus the fact that this is the first landfall reached by many migratory species, also brings over 1.5 million transitory birds through the region annually.

Some of the most magical sights here occur with the arrival of around 60,000 wintering **lesser snow geese**, seduced from the chilly climes of Wrangle Island above the Arctic Circle.

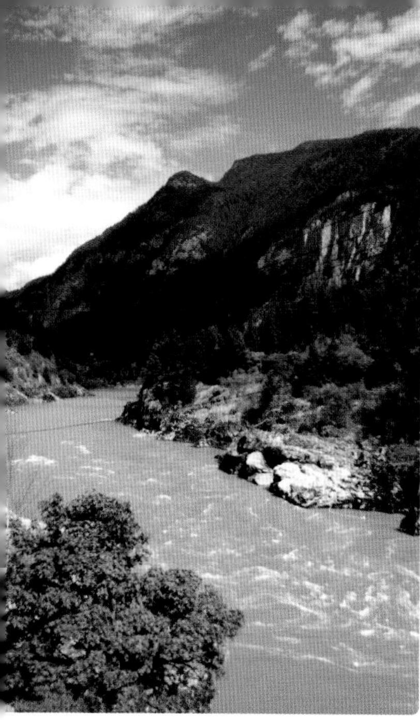

The Fraser River ▲

Orca ▼

The ocean

Beyond the Fraser's broad estuary lies the open ocean, yet another outdoor playground – sailing, diving and kayaking are all possible. But the Pacific coast off Vancouver, warmed by the Japanese current, also has the greatest number of **marine species** of any temperate coast in the world. For all its natural diversity, though, the ocean here holds only one maritime attraction for most visitors – the chance to see whales.

Grey whales are the most common, and are often easily spotted from headlands or boats (see p.221) between February and May and from September to October as they migrate between the Arctic and their breeding grounds off Mexico. **Humpback whales** are another favourite, largely because of their surface acrobatics and long, haunting "songs". Vancouver's waters also support one of the world's most concentrated populations of **orcas**, or killer whales. These are often seen in family groups, or pods, close to shore, usually on the trail of shoals of salmon. The orca, however, is the only whale whose diet runs to warm-blooded animals – hence the "killer" tag – and it will gorge on walrus, seal and even minke, grey and beluga whales.

Out of the City

Out of the City

19

Victoria

Victoria is British Columbia's provincial capital and the region's second city after Vancouver. It's a popular excursion from Vancouver, 69km to the northeast across the Georgia Strait, and though it's possible to come here for the day – especially if you take a seaplane from Vancouver's harbour – you'd be better advised to stay overnight and give the city the two or so days it deserves.

This said, Victoria has a lot to live up to. Leading US travel magazine *Condé Nast Traveler* has voted it one of the world's top ten cities to visit, and world number one for ambience and environment. It's not named after a queen and an era for nothing. Much of the waterfront area has an undeniably quaint and likeable English feel – "Brighton Pavilion with the Himalayas for a backdrop," said the writer Rudyard Kipling – and Victoria has more British-born residents than anywhere in Canada. However, its tourist potential is exploited chiefly for American visitors, served up with lashings of fake Victoriana and chintzy commercialism, and ersatz echoes of empire at every turn. Despite the seasonal influx, and the sometimes atrociously tacky attractions designed to part tourists from their money, it's a small, relaxed and pleasantly sophisticated place, worth lingering in if only for its inspirational museum. It also provides plenty of pubs, restaurants (and the odd club) and serves as a base for a range of outdoor activities and slightly more far-flung attractions. Chief of these is **whale-watching**, with a plethora of companies on hand to take you out to the teeming waters around the city. And as a final lure the weather here – though often damp – is extremely mild; Victoria's meteorological station has the distinction of being the only one in Canada to record a winter in which the temperature never fell below freezing.

A brief history of Victoria

Salish peoples originally inhabited Victoria's site, and in particular the Lekwammen, who had a string of some ten villages in the area. Here they cultivated camas bulbs – vital to their diet and trade – and applied advanced salmon-fishing methods to the shoals of migrating salmon in net-strung reefs offshore. At the time the region must have been a virtual paradise. Captain George Vancouver, who was mapping the North American coast apparently ignorant of the aboriginal presence, described his feelings on first glimpsing this part of Vancouver Island: "The serenity of the climate, the innumerable pleasing landscapes, and the abundant fertility that nature puts forth, require only to be enriched by the industry of man with villages, mansions, cottages and other buildings, to render it the most lovely country that can be imagined."

Getting to Victoria

There are three ways to reach **Victoria** – by bus and ferry, by car and ferry, or by air. Most people travelling under their own steam from Vancouver use the first, which is a simple matter of buying an all-inclusive through-ticket from Vancouver's bus terminal (see p.23) to Victoria's bus depot. By far the quickest approach, however, is to take a seaplane from Vancouver's **port**: this takes just 25 minutes – as opposed to 3 hour 30 minutes by bus and ferry – and drops you right in Victoria's Inner Harbour; however, it works out around three times as expensive.

By bus and ferry from Vancouver

If you're without your own transport, the most painless way to Victoria from Vancouver is to buy a ticket on **Pacific Coach Lines** (Ⓣ604/662-8074, 250/385-4411 or 1-800/661-1725, Ⓦwww.pacificcoach.com) at the Vancouver bus terminal at 1150 Station St, which takes you, inclusive of the ferry crossing and journeys to and from ferry terminals at both ends, to Victoria's central bus station at 700 Douglas St. Buses leave hourly in the summer, every two hours in the winter; total journey time is about 3 hour 30 minutes and a single ticket costs $43 ($84 return). No bookings are necessary: overflow passengers are simply put on another coach. Be sure to keep your ticket stub for reboarding the bus after the crossing. You can save yourself about $15 by using public transport at each end and buying a ferry ticket separately, but for the extra hassle and time involved it hardly seems worth it.

A similar all-inclusive bus/ferry arrangement also operates from Vancouver to Nanaimo on Vancouver Island (113km north of Victoria) via the Horseshoe Bay Terminal, located about fifteen minutes north of West Vancouver on Hwy 1. You can reach the Horseshoe Bay Terminal by taking bus #250 or #257 from Georgia Street. The ferry charges are the same for foot passengers.

You can also reach Victoria directly from Vancouver Airport by inclusive coach and ferry arrangements: ask for details at the bus desk in international arrivals of Pacific Coach Lines bus services (7 daily; $48 single). Journey time is about 3 hour 30 minutes. However, if you intend to visit Victoria before Vancouver, and are flying, then it usually only costs a little more to fly direct to the city from farther afield: it's not usually worth flying to Vancouver and then taking the bus-ferry option to save money.

By car from Tsawwassen, Horseshoe Bay and Powell River

BC Ferries operates four routes to Vancouver Island across the Georgia Strait from mainland British Columbia (information on Ⓣ1-888/223-3779 in BC, otherwise Ⓣ250/386-3431, Ⓦwww.bcferries.com). Reservations (on Ⓣ1-888/724-5223 in BC, otherwise Ⓣ604/444-2890) are essential in summer to avoid long waits. The route used by most Vancouver–Victoria drivers is the Tsawwassen–Swartz Bay connection, also the route used by Pacific Coach Lines' buses. Ferries ply the route almost continuously from 7am to 10pm (sixteen sailings daily in summer, minimum of eight daily in winter). Car tickets in high season (from late June to early Sept) cost $45. Bicycles cost $2 year-round. You need to add on per-person fares, which are $13.50.

The Mid-Island Express Tsawwassen–Nanaimo (Duke Point terminal), midway up the island, has eight or so departures daily on the two-hour crossing. More boats cover the Horseshoe Bay–Nanaimo (Departure Bay terminal) route, a 95-minute journey from a terminal about fifteen minutes' drive from West Vancouver. Fares for both these routes are the same as for Tsawwassen to Swartz Bay. The fourth

The first step in this process began in 1842 when Victoria received some of its earliest **white visitors**, notably Hudson's Bay Company representative James Douglas, who disembarked at present-day Clover Point during a search for a new local headquarters for the company. One look at the natural harbour and its surroundings was enough: this, he declared, was a "perfect Eden", a feeling only reinforced by the friendliness of the indigenous population, who helped him build

route is Powell River–Comox, Powell River being some 160km northwest of Vancouver on the Sunshine Coast.

By air from Vancouver

Flying into Victoria from Vancouver Airport is an expensive option. Open return fares typically run to around $150, excursion fares (with restrictions) around $100. It's more fun and more direct to fly from Vancouver harbour to Victoria harbour by helicopter or float plane: Harbour Air (Ⓣ250/384-2215 in Victoria, Ⓦwww.harbour-air.com) and West Coast Air (Ⓣ250/388-4521 or 1-800/347-2222, Ⓦw.westcoastair.com) fly in 35 minutes from just west of Canada Place in Vancouver (see p.206 for details) for a one-way price of $134 ($268 return). Helijet Airways (Ⓣ1-800/665-4354, Ⓦwww.helijet.com) flies either from the helipad east of Canada Place or from Vancouver Airport for $245 one-way, standby from $75. You can also fly direct float plane from Seattle (Lake Union or North Lake Washington) with Kenmore Air (Ⓣ250/384-2499 or 1-866/435-9524, Ⓦwww.kenmoreair.com), with up to five departures daily MayAug, 2–3 daily the rest of the year. Journey time is 45 minutes.

By ferry from the US

Washington State Ferries, at 2499 Ocean Ave, Sidney (in Victoria Ⓣ250/381-1551; in Sidney Ⓣ250/656-1531; in Seattle Ⓣ206/464-6400; in Washington State Ⓣ1-888/808-7977; Ⓦww.wsdot.wa.gov/ferries) runs **ferries** from Anacortes, ninety minutes north of Seattle, to Sidney, thirty minutes (and 30km) north of Victoria (summer 2 daily in each direction, winter 1 daily; 3hr–3hr 30min). One of the two summer departures goes via Orcas Island and Friday Harbor on the San Juan Islands. Passenger fares for the full trip are around US$15.60, a car and driver US$41.90. Car reservations are required from Orcas and Friday Harbor and can be made by calling at least a day in advance (Ⓣ360/378-4777 in Friday Harbor).

Black Ball Transport, 430 Belleville St, Victoria (in BC Ⓣ250/386-2202 or 800-972-6509; in WA Ⓣ360/457-4491 or 1-800/833-6388; Ⓦwww.cohoferry.com) operates a ferry across the Juan de Fuca Strait from Port Angeles right to Victoria's Inner Harbour (1–4 daily; 95min). Passenger fares are US$11, plus US$42.50 for a car and US$5 for a bicycle. Reservations are not accepted. Car drivers should call ahead in summer to have some idea of how long they'll have to wait. For foot passengers, and day-trippers in particular, a speedier option is Victoria Express's seasonal service from Port Angeles to Victoria's Inner Harbour (late June to Aug 3 daily; late May to late June & Sept to mid-Oct 2 daily; 55min; in Canada Ⓣ250/361-9144; in the US Ⓣ360/452-8088 or Ⓣ1-800/633-1589; Ⓦwww.victoriaexpress.com). The fare is US$12.50 one-way, US$25 return; bicycles or canoes cost $5 one-way or return. There is also a service between Victoria and Friday Harbor (US$35 one-way).

The 300-passenger-only Victoria Clipper catamaran travels between Pier 69 in downtown Seattle and Victoria's Inner Harbour (mid-May to mid-Sept 4 daily; early May and late Sept 2 daily; rest of year 1 daily) in around 3 hours, sometimes less (250 Bellevue St, Victoria; in Victoria Ⓣ250/382-8100; in Seattle Ⓣ206/448-5000; elsewhere in North America Ⓣ1-800/888-2535; Ⓦwww.victoriaclipper.com). Ticket prices in summer are US$84 single and US$139 return in peak season (June–Aug & various other holiday weekends) and from US$69/116 off season.

Fort Camouson, named after an important aboriginal landmark (the name was later changed to **Fort Victoria** to honour the British queen). The aboriginal peoples from up and down the island settled near the fort, attracted by the new trading opportunities it offered. Soon they were joined by British pioneers, brought in to settle the land by a Bay subsidiary, the Puget Sound Agricultural Company, which quickly built several large company farms to accommodate

Reserving provincial campsites

Tent and RV sites at many public campsites in British Columbia's provincial parks can be reserved through Discover Camping (March to mid-Sept Mon–Fri 7am–7pm, Sat & Sun 9am–5pm Pacific time; ⓣ1-800/689-9025 or ⓣ604/689-9025). Reservations can be made up to three months in advance but no later than 48 hours before the first day of arrival. A nonrefundable booking fee of $6.30 per night, up to a maximum of three nights ($18.90), is charged. Reservations can also be made at ⓦwww.discovercamping.ca. General information on the parks is on ⓣ250/387-4550 or 1-800/663-7867, ⓦwww.elp.gov.bc.ca/bcparks.

settlers. In time, the harbour became the busiest West Coast port north of San Francisco and a major base for the British navy's Pacific fleet, a role it now fulfills for the bulk of Canada's modern **navy**.

Boom time came in the 1850s following the mainland gold strikes, when Victoria's port became an essential stop off and supplies depot for prospectors heading across the water and into the interior. Military and bureaucratic personnel moved in to ensure order, bringing morals and manners of Victorian England with them. Alongside there grew a rumbustious shantytown of shops, bars and brothels, with one bar run by "Gassy" Jack Deighton, unwittingly soon to become one of Vancouver's founders.

Though the gold-rush bubble soon burst, Victoria carried on as a military, economic and political centre, becoming the capital of the newly created British Columbia in 1866 – years before the founding of Vancouver. British values were cemented in stone by the **Canadian Pacific Railway**, which built the *Empress Hotel* in 1908 in place of a proposed railway link that never came into being. Victoria's planned role as Canada's western rail terminus was surrendered to Vancouver, and with it any chance of realistic growth or industrial development. These days the town survives quite well almost entirely on the backs of tourists (four million a year), the civil-service bureaucracy and – shades of the home country – retirees in search of a mild-weathered retreat. Its population today is around 350,000, almost exactly double what it was just thirty years ago.

Arrival, information and transport

Victoria International Airport (ⓣ250/953-7500, ⓦwww.victoria airport .com) is 26km north of downtown on Hwy 17 near the Sidney ferry terminal. Hwy 17 runs south and takes you to the city outskirts where it becomes Douglas Street, which runs to the heart of downtown. The Airporter shuttle bus heads downtown (where it stops at major hotels) every half-hour between about 4.30am and 1am; a single fare for the 45-minute journey is $18 (ⓣ250/386-2525 or 1-877/386-2525, ⓦwww.victoriaairportshuttle.com). They can also arrange pick-ups to the airport.

The **bus terminal** is downtown at 700 Douglas St and Belleville St, close to the Royal British Columbia Museum. Pacific Coach Lines' buses (ⓣ250/385-4411, ⓦwww.pacificcoach.com) from Vancouver or Vancouver airport drop you here, and it is the base for Greyhound (ⓣ250/388-5248 or 1-800/663-8390, ⓦwww.greyhound.com) as well as onward connections on Vancouver Island provided by Greyhound (ⓣ250/385-4411 or 1-800/318-0818, ⓦwww .greyhound.ca). Victoria's **train station**, at the northern end of Wharf Street, is

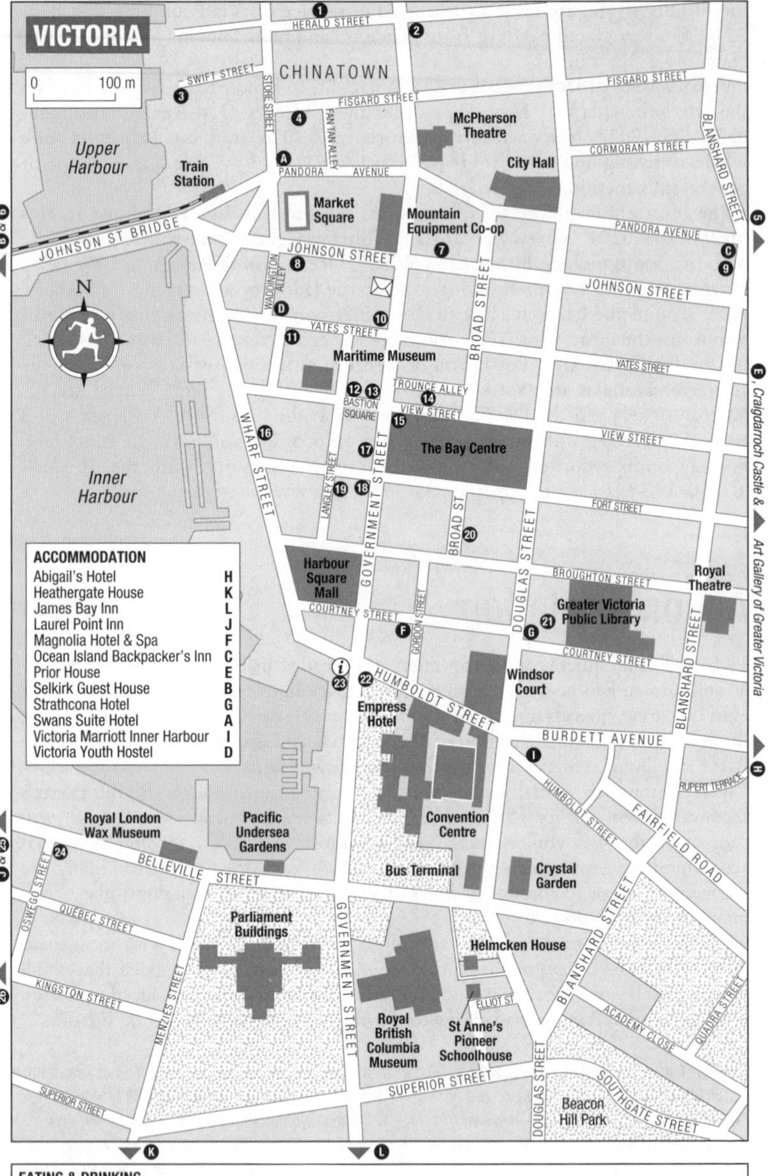

EATING & DRINKING

Barb's Place	25	Canoe	3	Lady Marmalade	7	Swans Brewpub	A
The Bard & Banker	18	Coffee House	4	The Mark	24	Tapa Bar	14
Bartholomew's Bar & Rockefeller Grill	22	Darcy's Wharfside Pub	16	Milestone's	23	The Temple	19
Big Bad John's	21	Demitasse Coffee Bar	9	Murchie's	17	Willie's Bakery & Café	8
Blethering Place	5	Earl's	15	Pagliacci's	20		
Blue Crab Bar & Grill	26	Herald Street Café	1	Rebar	12		
Brasserie L'Ecole	2	The Irish Times	13	The Reef	10		
		Il Terrazzo	11	Spinnakers BrewPub	6		

useful only if you are taking the one daily service on Via Rail (Ⓣ1-888/842-7245, Ⓦwww.viarail.ca) to or from Nanaimo and points north (journey time to Nanaimo is 2hr 25min).

Victoria's busy **infocentre** is at 812 Wharf St, in front of the *Empress Hotel* on the harbour (daily: May–Sept 8.30am–6.30pm; Oct–April 9am–5pm; Ⓣ250/953-2033, Ⓦwww.tourismvictoria.com). The staff can help you book whale-watching and other tours (see box, p.221), and provide a huge range of general information.

The most enjoyable means of transport are the tiny Inner Harbour **ferries** (Ⓣ250/708-0201, Ⓦwww.victoriaharbourferry.com) that run around the harbour. Stops include Fisherman's Wharf, Ocean Pointe Resort and West Bay Marina, but they're worth taking just for the ride: try an evening mini-cruise ($20) around the harbour: buy tickets ($2.25) on ferries in the Inner Harbour or book at the infocentre. You're unlikely to need to take a local **bus** if you stick to the downtown area, but if you do venture out, most services run from the corner of Douglas and Yates streets. The fare within the large central zone is $2.25 – tickets and the DayPass ($7) are sold at the infocentre, 7-Eleven stores and other marked outlets, or you can pay on board if you have the exact fare. For 24-hour recorded information on city transport, call the BusLine (Ⓣ250/382-6161, lost property 995-5637, Ⓦwwww.bctransit.com).

Accommodation

Victoria fills up quickly in the summer, and most of its budget **accommodation** is well known and heavily patronized. Top-price hotels cluster around the Inner Harbour area; **hostels** and more downmarket alternatives are scattered all over, though the largest concentration of cheap **hotels** and **motels** is around the Gorge Road and Douglas Street areas northwest of downtown.

Reservations are virtually obligatory in all categories, though the infocentre's accommodation service (Ⓣ1-800/663-3883, Ⓦwww.tourismvictoria.com) will root out a room if you're stuck. They are more than likely to offer you B&B accommodation, of which the town has a vast selection; prices for many are surprisingly elevated, though owners of many of the more far-flung places will pick you up from downtown.

Victoria's commercial campsites are full to bursting in summer, with most space given over to RVs. Few of these are convenient for downtown – given that you'll have to travel, you might as well head for one of the more scenic provincial park sites. Most are on the Trans-Canada Hwy to the north, or on Hwy 14 east of Victoria.

Hotels, motels and B&Bs

Abigail's Hotel 960 McClure St Ⓣ250/388-5363 or 1-800/561-6565, Ⓦwww.abigailshotel.com. A very classy, small hotel in a fine building with log fires, voluminous duvets, Jacuzzis and a good breakfast. If you want to treat yourself, this is the place. All rooms are non-smoking. Situated on the corner of Quadra St, a block east of Blanshard St and within easy walking distance of the city centre. $189–420

James Bay Inn 270 Government St at Toronto St Ⓣ250/384-7151 or 1-800/836-2649, Ⓦwww.jamesbayinn.com. This 45-room hotel vies with the *Cherry Bank* as Victoria's best reasonably priced option, though rates have climbed in the last couple of years. The Edwardian building was the home of painter Emily Carr. Simple rooms at varying prices, with a restaurant and pub in the basement. $131–175

Laurel Point Inn 680 Montréal St Ⓣ250/386-8721 or 1-800/663-7667, Ⓕ250386-9547,

Ⓦ www.laurelpoint.com. Don't be put off by the size of this 200-room resort-style hotel. All rooms have a balcony and good harbour view, thanks to a position on a well-landscaped promontory (with a Japanese garden) on the Inner Harbour. The contemporary aesthetic is simple and clean, and a far cry from the chintzy look of many of Victoria's hotels. There are two wings, north and south – you want to be in the southern one, designed by Arthur Erickson (see p.89) in 1989. Here, the rooms are all pale wood and dark marble, with Japanese-style sliding doors, Asian works of art and airy, stylish bathrooms. $189–420

Strathcona Hotel 919 Douglas St Ⓣ250/383-7137 or 1-800/663-7476, Ⓦwww.strathconahotel.com. Large, modern hotel where rooms include baths and TVs. There's a British-style pub and restaurant downstairs with booming live and DJ music which may not be to all tastes. $109–149

Swans Suite Hotel & Brewpub 506 Pandora Ave Ⓣ250/361-3310 or 1-800/668-7926, Ⓦwww.swanshotel.com. Brewpub aside, the appeal of the 30 rooms here is the setting, a converted 1880s grain store that means many of the suites and larger rooms are quirky, loft-style spaces, often on a split level and with exposed beams and bold, original artwork. The one- and two-bedroom suites take up to six people, making them perfect for families, and there are fully equipped kitchens and dining and living rooms. $199–359

The Magnolia Hotel & Spa 623 Courtney St Ⓣ250/381-0999 or 1-877/624-6654, Ⓦwww.magnoliahotel.com. One of the new wave of Victorian lodgings, this 63-room boutique hotel lays on the character thick, the small lobby setting the period Edwardian tone, though the effect, especially in the high-quality rooms (the best have harbour views and fireplaces) and superb bathrooms, is never stuffy. The Aveda Spa is one of the best in the city. $289–359

Bed and breakfasts

Heathergate House 122 Simcoe St Ⓣ250/383-0068 or 1-888/683-0068, Ⓦwww.heathergatebb.com. This small B&B offers three rooms plus a separate two-bed cottage within walking distance of the Inner Harbour and the sights. All rooms are en suite. There's a private floor for guests with a lounge and TV room. $115-149

Prior House 620 St Charles St Ⓣ250/592-8847 or 1-877/924-3300, Ⓦwww.priorhouse.com. A very smart six-room B&B; once the home of Victoria's lieutenant governor – ask for his suite, where the bathroom features a chandelier. About 2.5km east of downtown in the smart Rockland area, so it's better if you have transport. $249–299

Selkirk Guest House 934 Selkirk Ave Ⓣ250/389-1213 or 1-800/974-6638, Ⓦwww.selkirkguesthouse.com. Fine historic waterfront home dating from 1909 northwest of the Inner Harbour: take bus #14 from Douglas St (to within two blocks) or cross the Johnston Bridge and follow the water past Bay St and Banfield Park: then take Arcadia, a right turn from Craigflower Rd to Selkirk Ave. It's well placed for bike and walking trails (it's on the Galloping Goose Trail) and you can rent boats and canoes. Dorm places cost $20; doubles $145–155.

University residences and hostels

Ocean Island Backpacker's Inn 791 Pandora Ave at Blanshard St Ⓣ250/385-1788 or 1-888/888-4180, Ⓦwww.oceanisland.com. A good, reasonably central location in the northeast corner of downtown. Facilities include private and shared rooms, Internet access, a music room with instruments, no curfew, free morning coffee, laundry room, free bike storage, linen and towels provided and limited parking at $4 a day. The restored 1893 heritage building has a wide variety of dorms and rooms (singles and doubles with and without bathroom) on a sliding scale depending on the time of year, the day of the week (more on Fri and Sat) and whether you have a HI card. Dorm beds cost $19; private doubles cost from $28, family rooms from $36. Weekly and monthly rates are available on dorms and rooms.

University of Victoria Corner of Sinclair and Finnerty Rd Ⓣ250/721-8395, Ⓦwww.hfcs.uvic.ca. Good, if plain rooms (single or double) on the university campus are available May–Sept when not required for students or conferences. Shared bathroom, laundry and kitchen facilities. Good-value four-room suites with bathroom, kitchen and living room are also available. For a small extra fee guests have access to the university pool and other sports facilities.

It is a half-hour car or bus (#4 or 14) ride to downtown. Singles $45 (with breakfast), doubles $55.
Victoria Youth Hostel (HI) **516 Yates and Wharf sts ⓣ250/385-4511 or 1-888/883-0099, ⓦwww.hihostels.ca.** Large, modern, welcoming and extremely well-run place just a few blocks north of the Inner Harbour. The bunk rooms, though, can be noisy: the reception, rather ominously, sells earplugs. The notice boards are packed with useful information on the city. Members $24 (June–Sept), $22 (April, May & Oct), rest of the year $20; nonmembers $28/26/24. Private rooms cost $62 ($50 Nov–March) for members, $70/58 for nonmembers.

Campsites

Fort Victoria RV and Park Campground **340 Island Hwy 1A ⓣ250/479-8112, ⓦwww.fortvictoria.ca.** Closest site to downtown, located 6km north of Victoria off the Trans-Canada Hwy. Take bus #14 (for Craigflower) from the city centre; it stops right by the gate. Large 300-pitch site mainly for RVs but with a few tent sites; free hot showers. $37 for two people.
Goldstream Provincial Park **2930 Trans-Canada Hwy ⓣ604/689-9025 or 1-800/689-9025, ⓦwww.discovercamping.ca.** Bus #50 from Douglas St downtown. Although 20km north of the city off Hwy 1, this site is set in old-growth forests of cedar and Douglas fir and is Victoria's best camping option. Flush toilets and free hot showers, with plenty of hiking, swimming and fishing opportunities. $24 per site.
Thetis Lake **Trans-Canada Hwy at 1938 West Park Lane ⓣ250/478-3845, ⓔthetislake@shaw.ca.** Runs a close second to Goldstream Provincial Park's campsites for the pleasantness of its setting, and is only 10km north of downtown. Family-oriented, with 147 sites, as well as laundry and coin-operated showers. $20 per two people.

The City

The Victoria that's worth bothering with is very small: almost everything worth seeing, as well as the best shops and restaurants, is within walking distance of the **Inner Harbour** area and the Old Town district behind it. On summer evenings this area is alive with strollers and buskers, and a pleasure to wander as the sun drops over the water. Foremost among the daytime diversions are the **Royal British Columbia Museum** and the **Empress Hotel**. Most of the other trumpeted attractions are dreadful, and many charge entry fees out of proportion to what's on show. If you're tempted by the Royal London Wax Museum, the Pacific Undersea Gardens, Miniature World, English Village, Anne Hathaway's Thatched Cottage or any of Victoria's other dubious commercial propositions, details are available from the infocentre. Otherwise you might drop by the modest **Maritime Museum** and think about a trip to the celebrated **Butchart Gardens**, some way out of town, but easily accessed by public transport or regular all-inclusive tours from the bus terminal. If you're around for a couple of days you should also find time to walk around **Beacon Hill Park**, a few minutes' walk from downtown to the south.

The best of the area's beaches are well out of town, around three or four miles on Hwy 14 and Hwy 1, but for idling by the sea drop down to the pebble shore along the southern edge of Beacon Hill Park. For some local swimming, the best option by far is **Willows Beach** on the Esplanade in Oak Bay, 2km east of Victoria; take bus #1 to Beach and Dalhousie Road. Other good stretches of sand can be found on Dallas Road and at Island View Beach.

The Royal British Columbia Museum

The Royal British Columbia Museum (daily 9am–5pm, National Geographic IMAX Theatre daily 10am–8pm; museum $15, IMAX Theatre $11, combined

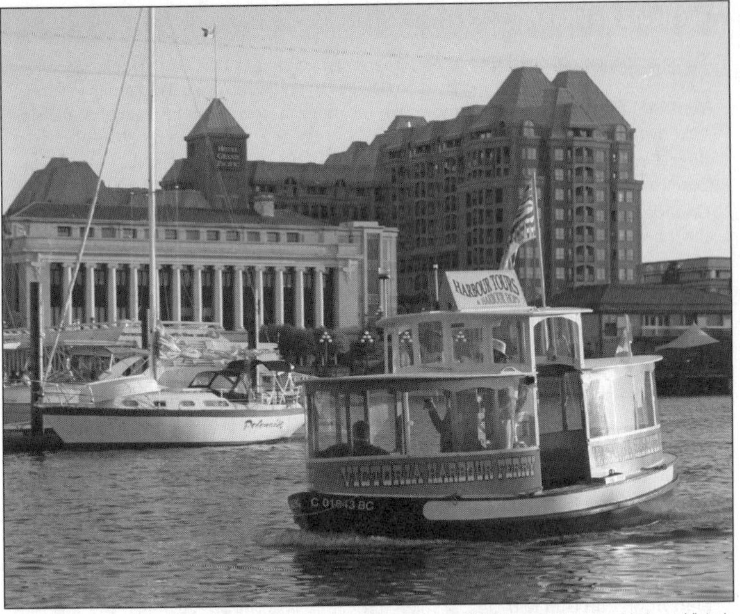

▲ Waterfront on the Inner Harbour, Victoria

ticket $35, IMAX double feature $16.75; Ⓦwww.royalbcmuseum.bc.ca) is a short stroll along the waterfront from the infocentre at 675 Belleville St. Founded in 1886, it is arguably the **best museum in Canada**, and regularly rated, by visitors and travel-magazine polls, as one of North America's top ten. All conceivable aspects of the province are examined, but the aboriginal peoples section is probably the definitive collection of a much-covered genre, while the natural-history sections – huge re-creations of natural habitats, complete with sights, sounds and smells – are mind-boggling in scope and imagination. Allow at least two trips to take it all in.

The **second floor** contains dioramas, full-scale reconstructions of some of the many natural habitats found in British Columbia. The idea of re-creating shorelines, coastal rainforests and Fraser Delta landscapes may sound far-fetched, yet all are incredibly realistic, down to dripping water and cool, dank atmospheres. Audiovisual displays and a tumult of information accompany the exhibits (the beaver film is worth hunting down), most of which focus attention on the province's 25,600km of coastline, a side of British Columbia usually overlooked in favour of its interior forests and mountains.

Upstairs on the **third floor** is the mother of all the tiny museums of bric-a-brac and pioneer memorabilia in BC. Arranged eccentrically from the present day backwards, it explores every aspect of the province's social history over two centuries in nitpicking detail. Prominently featured are part of an early twentieth-century town, complete with cinema and silent films, plus comprehensive displays on logging, mining, the gold rush, farming, fishing and lesser domestic details; all the artefacts and accompanying information are presented with impeccable finesse.

Up on the mezzanine **floor** is a superb collection of **aboriginal peoples' art, culture and history**. It's presented in gloomy light against muted wood walls and brown carpet, which creates a solemn atmosphere in keeping with the tragic

Festivals in Victoria

Summer brings out the buskers and free entertainment in Victoria's people-places – James Bay, Market Square and Beacon Hill Park in particular. Annual highlights include:

TerrifVic Jazz Party April. A showcase for about a dozen top international bands held over four days.

Jazz Fest June. More than 100 assorted lesser-known bands perform in Market Square.

Canada Day July 1. Celebration of Canada's national day concentrated in and around the Inner Harbour and including fireworks, food, music and other cultural events.

Victoria International Festival July & Aug. Victoria's largest general arts jamboree.

Folk Fest Last week of July. Multicultural arts extravaganza.

First People's Festival Early Aug. Celebration of the cultures of Canada's aboriginal peoples.

Canadian International Dragon Boat Festival Mid-Aug. Over 100 international teams take part in dragon-boat races on the Inner Harbour.

Classic Boat Festival Aug 30–Sept 1. Dozens of wooden antique boats on display.

Royal Victoria Marathon Early Oct. Marathon and half-marathon around the city streets and surroundings held on the Canadian Thanksgiving weekend.

Fringe Festival Sept. Avant-garde performances of all kinds.

Great Canadian Beer Festival Second week of Nov. Selections of beer from some of the province's best microbreweries can be tasted at the Victoria Conference Centre, 720 Douglas St.

Merrython Fun Run Mid-Dec. A 10km run through downtown Victoria.

nature of many of the displays. The collection divides into two epochs – before and after the coming of Europeans – tellingly linked by a single aboriginal carving of a white man, starkly and brilliantly capturing the initial wonder and weirdness of the new arrivals. The whole collection takes a thoughtful and oblique approach, taking you to the point where smallpox virtually wiped out in one year a culture that was eight millennia in the making. A section on land and reservations is left for last – the issues are contentious even today – and even if you're succumbing to museum fatigue, the arrogance and duplicity of the documents on display will shock you. The highlights in this section are many, but try to make a point of seeing the short film *In the Land of the War Canoes* (1914), the **Bighouse** (a facsimile of a meeting hall) and its chants, and the audiovisual display on aboriginal myths and superstition.

The **National Geographic Theatre** in the museum plays host to a huge IMAX screen and a changing programme of special-format films. Outside the museum, there's also **Thunderbird Park**, a strip of grass with a handful of totem poles.

Helmcken House and around

Helmcken House (irregular hours – check the Royal British Columbia Museum website for the latest details; $5) stands off Belleville Street, directly adjacent to the museum. The oldest house in BC still on its original site, built in 1852, it is a predictable heritage offering that showcases the home, furnishings and embroidery talents of the Helmcken family. Dr John Helmcken was Fort Victoria's doctor and local political bigwig, and his house is a typical monument to stolid Victoria values. Upstairs it contains various attic treasures and some fearsome-looking medical tools. It's probably only of interest, however, if you've so far managed to avoid any of Canada's many thousands of similar houses.

Just behind the house there's another old white-wood building, the **St Ann's Pioneer Schoolhouse**, originally purchased by a Bishop Demers for four sisters of the Order of St Ann, who in 1858 took it upon themselves to leave their Québec home to come and teach in Victoria. Built between 1843 and 1858, it's believed to be the oldest building in Victoria still in use.

The Parliament Buildings

The huge Victorian pile of the **Parliament Buildings** (daily mid-May to early Sept Mon–Thurs 9am–5pm, Fri–Sun 9am–7pm; guided tours, but times may vary according to parliament business; ⓣ250/387-3046 or 1-800/663-7867 in BC), one block west of the museum at 501 Belleville St, is old and imposing in the manner of a large and particularly grand British town hall. Beautifully lit at night by some three hundred tiny bulbs (though locals grumble about the cost), the domed building is fronted by the sea and well-kept gardens – a pleasant enough ensemble, though it doesn't really warrant the manic enthusiasm visited on it by hordes of summer tourists. You're more likely to find yourself taking time out on the front lawns, distinguished by a perky statue of Queen Victoria and a giant sequoia, a gift from the state of California.

Designed by 25-year-old Francis Rattenbury, who was also responsible for the nearby Empress Hotel, the building was completed in 1897 at a cost of

Whale-watching from Victoria

The waters around Victoria are not as whale-rich as those around Tofino on the west coast of Vancouver Island, but there's still a very good chance of spotting the creatures. Three pods of orcas (killer whales) live in the seas around southern Vancouver Island, around a hundred animals in all, so you may see these, though minke are the most common whale spotted, with occasional greys and humpbacks also present. Few outfits offer guaranteed sightings, and many cover themselves by preparing you for the fact that if you don't see whales you stand a good chance of seeing Dall's porpoises, harbour or elephant seals and California and Steller sea lions.

While there are many outfits to choose from, they offer almost identical trips at the same prices, typically around $80 to $100 for a three-hour outing. There's usually a naturalist, or at least a knowledgeable crew member, to fill you in on what you're seeing (or not). The only real variables are the boats used, so you need to decide whether you want a rigid-hull cruiser (covered or uncovered), which is comfortable and sedate (and usually the most expensive at around $100), a catamaran ($75–90), or a high-speed aluminium-hull inflatable known as a "Zodiac" ($80–1000), which is infinitely more exhilarating, but can offer a sometimes bumpy ride and lacks toilets on board.

The two companies below have been around longer than most; the infocentre (p.216) has details on others.

Seacoast Expeditions Located at the Coast Victoria Harbourside, 45 146 Kingston St (ⓣ250/383-2254 or 1-800/386-1525, ⓦwww.seacoastexpeditions.com) – a ten-minute walk across the Johnson Street bridge or a three-minute harbour ferry crossing (it also has a shuttle-bus pick-up from downtown hotels). Victoria's founding whale-watching company, Seacoast has been in the business over a decade and offers between four and six three-hour trips daily between April and October ($89).

Five Star Charters 706 Douglas St (ⓣ250/388-7223 or 1-800/634-9617, ⓦwww.5starwhales.com). Has been in business since 1985 and in the past claimed the highest percentage of whale sightings out of all the tour operators (thanks to spotter boats and a good network of contacts). It runs two daily three-hour trips from mid-April through Sept ($99). Trips are in 12-passenger open cruiser or 40-person "Supercat" boats.

$923,000, in time for Queen Victoria's jubilee. Figures from Victoria's grey bureaucratic past are duly celebrated, the main door guarded by statues of Sir James Douglas, who chose the site of the city, and Sir Matthew Baillie Begbie (aka the "Hanging Judge"), responsible for law and order during the heady days of gold fever. Sir George Vancouver keeps an eye on proceedings from the top of the dome. Free tours start to the right of the main steps and are led by guides who are chirpy and full of anecdotes. Look out for the dagger that killed Captain Cook, and the gold-plated dome, painted with scenes from Canadian history.

Beacon Hill Park

The best park within walking distance of the town centre is **Beacon Hill Park**, south of the Inner Harbour and a few minutes' walk up the road behind the museum. Victoria is sometimes known as the "City of Gardens", and at the right times of the year this park shows why. Victoria's biggest green space, it has lots of paths, ponds, big trees and quiet corners, and plenty of views over the **Juan de Fuca Strait** to the distant Olympic Mountains of Washington State (especially on the park's southern side). These pretty straits, incidentally, are the focus of some rather bad feeling between Victoria and the US for the city has a dark secret: it dumps raw sewage into the strait, excusing itself by claiming it's quickly broken up by the sea's strong currents. Washington State isn't so sure, and there have been plenty of arguments over the matter and, more to the point for city elders, economically damaging convention boycotts by American companies. Either way, it's pretty bad PR for Victoria and totally at odds with the city's image.

The gardens in the park are by turns well tended and wonderfully wild and unkempt, a far cry from its earliest days, when it was known by the local Salish as Meeacan, their word for a belly, as the hill was thought to resemble the stomach of large man lying on his back. The park was a favoured retreat of celebrated Victorian artist Emily Carr. They also claim the **world's tallest totem pole**, as well as the "Mile Zero" marker of the Trans-Canada Hwy and – that ultimate emblem of Englishness – a cricket pitch. Some of the trees are massive old-growth timbers that you'd normally only see on the island's unlogged west coast. Come here in spring and you'll catch swaths of daffodils and blue camas flowers. Some 30,000 other flowers are planted in the gardens annually.

The Empress Hotel

A town is usually desperate when one of its key attractions is a hotel, but in the case of Victoria the **Empress Hotel** is so physically overbearing and plays such a part in the town's tourist appeal that it demands some sort of attention. You may be unlikely to stay here – rooms are expensive – but it's worth wandering through the huge lobbies and palatial dining areas for a glimpse of well-restored colonial splendour. In a couple of lounges there's a fairly limp "Smart Casual" dress code – no dirty jeans, running shoes, short shorts or backpacks – but elsewhere you can wander freely. If you want to **take tea** in the Tea Lounge, you can enjoy scones, biscuits, cakes and, of course, tea over six courses but you have to abide by the dress code and be prepared for an enormous outlay. In other lounges like the *Bengal* (see below) you can ask for just tea and scones.

The hotel's **Crystal Ballroom** and its lovely Tiffany-glass dome form the most opulent area on view, but the marginally less ornate entrance lounge is the top place for the charade of afternoon tea, and indulging can be a bit of a laugh. There's also a reasonably priced bar and restaurant downstairs, **Kipling's**, and the

The Butchart Gardens

If you're into things horticultural you'll want to make a trek out to the celebrated and much-hyped Butchart Gardens, 22km north of Victoria at 800 Benvenuto Ave, Brentwood Bay on Hwy 17 towards the Swartz Bay ferry terminal (daily: mid-June–Aug 9am–10pm, first two weeks of Sept & Dec 9am–9pm; rest of the year 9am–sunset; rates $16.25 in early Jan, then on a sliding scale through the year to $28 between mid-June and Sept; ⓣ250/652-4422 or 652-5256 for recorded information, ⓦwww.butchartgardens.com). The gardens are renowned among visitors and locals alike for the stunning firework displays that usually take place each Sat evening in July and Aug. There is also a restaurant and various other commercial enterprises, with musical entertainment well to the fore. The gardens are illuminated during the late-evening opening hours between mid-June and the end of Sept.

The gardens were started in 1904 by Jenny Butchart, wife of a mine-owner and pioneer of Portland Cement in Canada and the US, her initial aim being to landscape one of her husband's quarries. The garden now covers fifty breathtaking acres, comprising rose, Japanese and Italian gardens and lots of decorative details. About half a million visitors a year tramp through the foliage, which includes over a million plants and seven hundred different species. At the same time, the amount of space actually given over to gardens may strike you as slightly disproportionate to the space allotted to the car park, gift shop and restaurant.

To get here by public transport take bus #75 for "Central Saanich" from downtown. Otherwise, there are regular summer shuttles (May–Oct daily, hourly in the morning, half-hourly in the afternoon; ⓣ250/388-6539) from the main bus terminal, where tickets ($9) are obtainable not from the main ticket office but a separate Gray Lines desk.

attractive **Bengal Lounge**, complete with tiger-skin over the fireplace, where you can have a curry and all the trimmings for about $15. For a bigger treat, take dinner amidst the Edwardian splendour of *The Empress Dining Room*.

The old town

The oldest part of Victoria focuses on **Bastion Square**, original site of Fort Victoria, from which it's a short walk to Market Square, a nice piece of old-town rejuvenation (the vast and bizarre tulip sculpture excepted), and the main downtown shopping streets. Bastion Square's former saloons, brothels and warehouses have been spruced up and turned into offices, cafés and galleries.

The modest **Maritime Museum** at 28 Bastion Square (daily 9.30am–4.30pm; $10; ⓦwww.mmbc.bc.ca) is of interest mainly for the lovely chocolate and vanilla-coloured building in which it's housed, the former provincial courthouse. Displays embrace old charts, uniforms, ships' bells, old photographs, lots of models and a BC Ferries section on the second floor. On the top floor is the restored vice-admiralty courtroom, once the main seat of justice for the entire province. Note the old open elevator built to reach it, commissioned by Chief Justice Davie in 1901, supposedly because he was too fat to manage the stairs.

Two blocks away to the north of the square lies the attractive **Market Square** (ⓣ250/386-2441, ⓦwww.marketsquare.ca), the old heart of Victoria but now a collection of some 35 speciality shops and cafés around a central courtyard (bounded by Store, Pandora and Johnson streets). This area boomed in 1858 following the gold rush, providing houses, saloons, opium dens, stores and various salacious entertainments for thousands of chancers and would-be immigrants. On the Pandora Avenue side of the area was a ravine, marked by the current sunken courtyard, beyond which lay **Chinatown** (now centred slightly further north on Fisgard Street), the oldest on

North America's west coast. Here, among other things, 23 factories processed 90,000 pounds of opium a year for what was then a legitimate trade and – until the twentieth century – one of BC's biggest industries.

As for the **shopping streets**, it's worth looking out for E.A. Morris, a wonderful old cigar and tobacco shop next to Murchie's coffee shop at 1110 Government St, and Roger's Chocolates, 913 Government St, whose whopping Victoria creams (among other things), are regularly dispatched to Buckingham Palace for royal consumption.

Other attractions

Outside the Inner Harbour, Victoria has a scattering of **minor attractions** that don't fit into any logical tour of the city – and at any rate are only quick-stop diversions – the most compelling of which is Craigdarroch Castle.

Craigdarroch Castle and the Art Gallery of Greater Victoria

Craigdarroch Castle (daily: mid-June to early Sept 9am–7pm, rest of year 10am–4.30pm; $12; Ⓦwww.craigdarrochcastle.com) is perched on a hilltop at 1050 Joan Crescent in Rockland, one of Victoria's more prestigious neighbourhoods. It was built by Robert Dunsmuir, a caricature of a Victorian politician, strike-breaker, robber baron and coal tycoon, who was forced to put up this gaunt Gothic pastiche to lure his wife away from Scotland. Only the best was good enough, from the marble, granite and sandstone of the superstructure to the intricately handworked panels of the ceilings over the main hall and staircase. The dastardly Dunsmuir never enjoyed his creation: he died in 1889, two years after the castle was begun and a year before it was finished. Among the 39 rooms there's the usual clutter of Victoriana and period detail, in particular some impressive woodwork and stained and leaded glass. To get here by **bus** take the #11-University or #14-University from downtown to the foot of Joan Crescent, two minutes' walk from the castle. If you decide to walk the whole way, allow 45 minutes from the Inner Harbour.

The **Art Gallery of Greater Victoria** (Mon–Sat 10am–5pm, Thurs till 9pm, Sun noon–5pm, closed Mon Sept–April; $12, but may be higher for some exhibitions; Ⓦwww.aggv.bc.ca) is near Craigdarroch Castle at 1040 Moss St, just off Fort St. It's of little interest unless you're partial to contemporary Canadian paintings and the country's best collection of Japanese art; the building, housed in the 1890 Spencer Mansion, boasts the only complete Shinto shrine outside Japan. It does, however, have a small permanent collection of Emily Carr's work (see p.48) as well as a temporary exhibition. To get here by **bus**, take the #10-Haultain, #11-Uplands/Beacon Hill or #14-University from downtown.

The Emily Carr House, Point Ellice and Craigflower Manor

Ten rooms are open to the public at **Emily Carr House** (Tues–Sat 11am–4pm; $6; Ⓦwww.emilycarr .com), two blocks from the Inner Harbour at 207 Government St. This was the early home of British Columbia's best-known artist, born here during a blizzard in 1871 in the old wooden bed still visible in what would become

her bedroom. The building was constructed in 1864, and has been painstakingly restored to its former state. Fans of the artist may want to pay homage, but the works on the walls are copies.

The 1861 Victorian-Italianate **Point Ellice House and Gardens** (guided tours May–Sept daily 11am–5pm; $6; ⓣ250/380-6506, ⓦwww.pointellicehouse.ca) at 2616 Pleasant St is magnificently re-created but less enticing than Craigdarroch Castle because of its slightly shabby surroundings. These can be overlooked, however, if you make a point of arriving by sea, taking one of the little Harbour Ferry services to the house (10min) from the Inner Harbour. The restored Victorian-style gardens here are a delight on a summer afternoon. The interior – one of the best of its kind in western Canada – retains its largely Victorian appearance thanks partly to the reduced circumstances of the O'Reilly family, whose genteel slide into relative poverty over several generations (they lived here from 1861 to 1974) meant that many furnishings were simply not replaced. Tea is served on the lawns in the summer; it's a good idea to book ahead. Bus #14-University will get you here from downtown if you don't fancy the approach by water.

In its day, **Craigflower Manor and Farmhouse** (currently closed for restoration after fire damage; ⓣ250/387-4697) on Admiral's Rd about 9km and fifteen minutes' drive from downtown, was among the earliest of Victoria's farming homesteads, marking the town's transition from trading post to permanent community. It was built in a mock-Georgian style in 1856, apparently from timbers salvaged from the first four farmhouses built in the region. Its owner was Kenneth McKenzie, a Hudson's Bay Company bailiff, who recruited fellow Scottish settlers to form a farming community on Portage Inlet. The house was to remind him of Scotland, and soon became the foremost social centre in the fledgling village – mainly visited by officers because McKenzie's daughters were virtually the only white women on the island. As with Point Ellice House, reservations for tea are recommended. Take **bus** #14-Craigflower from downtown.

Eating, drinking and nightlife

Although clearly in Vancouver's culinary shadow, Victoria still has a plethora of **restaurants**, some extremely good, offering greater variety – and higher prices – than you'll find in most other BC towns. **Pubs** tend to be plastic imitations of their British equivalents, with one or two worthy exceptions, as are the numerous **cafés** that pander to Victoria's self-conscious afternoon-tea ritual. Good snacks and pastry shops abound, while at the other extreme there are budget-busting establishments if you want a one-off treat or a change from the standard Canadian menus that await you on much of the rest of the island.

Nocturnal diversions in Victoria are for the most part tame: highbrow tastes, though, are surprisingly well catered for, and there's a smattering of **bars**, as well as **live music** venues and **clubs** to keep you happy for the limited time you're likely to spend in the city. **Jazz** is particularly popular – for information on the city's jazz underground, contact the Victoria Jazz Society, 250–727 Johnson St (ⓣ250/388-4423, ⓦwww.vicjazz.bc.ca).

Listings appear in the main daily newspaper, the *Times-Colonist*, and in a variety of free magazines (titles change from year to year) you can pick up in shops, cafés and hotels: the most current is the excellent *Monday Magazine* (ⓦwww.mondaymag.com) published every Thursday. Vast amounts of information on events and performances are also available from the infocentre (see p.216). **Tickets** for most

offerings are available from the city's main performance space, the McPherson Playhouse, 3 Centennial Square, Pandora and Government streets (Ⓣ250/386-6121 or 1-888/717-6121, Ⓦwww.rmts.bc.ca).

Cafés, tea and snacks

Bakery Café 537 Johnson St Ⓣ250/381-8414. A pretty, rambling heritage building, with lots of flowers and a pleasant conservatory and outdoor patio. Handily placed for a coffee after exploring Market Square to the north.

Barb's Place 310 St Lawrence St, Fisherman's Wharf, off Kingston St Ⓣ250/384-6515, Ⓦwww.barbsplace.ca. A much-loved floating shack that offers classic home-cut chips, fish straight off the boat and oyster burgers and chowder to boot: the bathtub-size ferries from the Inner Harbour drop you close by.

Blethering Place 2250 Oak Bay Ave Ⓣ250/598-1413 or 1-888/598-1413. Along with the *Empress Hotel*, this rather overrated spot is known as a place to indulge in the tea-taking custom. Scones, cakes and dainty sandwiches are served up against the background of hundreds of toby jugs and royal-family memorabilia.

Coffee House 533 Fisgard St Ⓣ250/386-7115. Very popular and laid-back café, with attractive bare-brick walls, narrow frontage and a cosy interior, with excellent coffee, snacks and light meals.

Empress Hotel 721 Government St Ⓣ250/348-8111. Try tea in the lobby, with tourists and locals alike on their best behaviour amidst the chintz and potted plants. A strict dress code allows no dirty jeans, anoraks or sportswear.

Lady Marmalade 608 Johnson St Ⓣ250/381-2872, Ⓦwww.ladymarmalade.ca. A little off the visitor trail, and much-patronised by locals, especially young mothers with small children. There's an old sofa by the door, but beyond that the feel is fresh, modern and funky, with vivid green-painted walls. Snacks or fuller meals, including a good-value all-day breakfast from $7.50.

Murchie's 1110 Government St Ⓣ250/381-5451. This long-established place, with high-quality produce, is the best retreat for basic tea, coffee and cakes in the centre of Victoria's shopping streets.

Rebar 50 Bastion Square at Langley St Ⓣ250/360-2401, Ⓦwww.rebarmodernfood.com. A great place that serves teas, coffees (charcoal-filtered water) and health food at lunch (usually organic), but most remarkable for its extraordinary range of fresh-squeezed juices in strange combinations, smoothies, "power tonics" and frighteningly healthy wheatgrass drinks (Astro Turf: a blend of carrot, beetroot, garlic and wheatgrass).

Restaurants

The Bard & Banker 1022 Government St at Fort St Ⓣ250/953-9993, Ⓦwww.bardandbanker.com. Sure, it's 'themed pub' (Scottish, in this case), and is right on Victoria's main street, but the wonderful heritage building and the beautifully fitted period interior are likely to win you over, along with 30 beers on tap, live music nightly and an emphasis on food that is well above the average for a so-called pub (pizzas with chanterelles and truffle oil, for example, for $13.99, or slow-braised veal cheek with maple syrup at $19).

Blue Crab Bar and Grill 146 Kingston St Ⓣ250/480-1999, Ⓦwww.bluecrab.ca. The dining room of the Coast Hotel has wonderful views over the water to the mountains beyond, a lovely backdrop for some of Victoria's best fish and seafood – though main meat dishes, such as Fraser Valley duck, are also available for between about $25 and $35. The wine list is outstanding. Daily 6.30am–10.30pm; dinner served from 6pm.

Canoe 450 Swift St Ⓣ250/361-1940, Ⓦwww.canoebrewpub.com. In a short time, this restaurant and brewpub has become one of Victoria's most popular places to eat and drink. Its setting is impressive – this was once Victoria's power station, and the interior retains an old industrial feel, with sturdy walls and vast beams. Outside, the patio is superb, with views towards the harbour and the Johnson Street bridge, and the atmosphere lively and convivial. Best of all, the food is excellent, whether you take the more ambitious and refined restaurant offerings such as wild salmon or Moroccan-style tagine stews upstairs (mains from $12) or the simple bar snacks and pub food (oysters, pizzas, burgers) downstairs (from $5). And the beer, of course, is excellent. Sun–Fri 11am–midnight, Sat 11am–1am.

L'Ecole 1715 Government St Ⓣ250/475-6260, Ⓦwww.lecole.ca. Don't be fooled by the location close to Victoria's Chinatown, for this multi-award-winning

restaurant serves the best French country cooking in town, with classic moules, frites, steaks, local fish and other staples, all made with immaculate and well-sourced local ingredients. Menus change daily. The dining room is pleasantly small and intimate, much like the wine list, which eschews big names in favour of decent, unpretentious wines to match the cooking. And prices won't hurt, either, with main courses from about $18. Tues–Sat 5.30–11pm.

Earl's Bay Centre, 1199 Government St at Yates St ⓣ250/381-1886, ⓦwww.earls.ca. You'll find an *Earl's* in many Canadian towns, but the restaurants are none the worse for being part of a chain: good – not fast – food with mains (pizzas, sandwiches) starting at around $12, with a lively, pleasant interior and friendly service. Daily 11am–midnight.

The Irish Times 1200 Government St at View St ⓣ250/383-7775, ⓦwww.irishtimespub.ca. Just a block from the *Bard & Banker* (see above) and similar in most respects: themed, set in a lovely old building, and with a good, welcoming atmosphere and attractive period-style interior: a good place for simple, fairly priced meals with a pint and the chance to hear live music.

Il Terrazzo 555 Johnson St, Waddington Alley ⓣ250/361-0028, ⓦwww.ilterrazzo.com. Smooth, laid-back ambience with lots of red brick and plants and a summer patio that provides the setting for good North American versions of Italian food. With Pagliacci's (see below), this is the best place in town for moderately priced Italian food, with mains from $14 to $37 and brunch from $10. Mon–Sat 11.30am–3pm (closed for lunch Sat from October to April), daily for dinner 5–10pm.

The Mark Hotel Grand Pacific, 463 Belleville St ⓣ250/386-0450, ⓦwww.themark.ca. At between $25 and $50 for a main course, prices here are at the top end for Victoria, but this is the fine dining room of a good hotel, and the locally sourced ingredients are conjured into intricate and ambitious dishes. If you want a cap on spending, go for the set six-course seafood tasting menu at $70, and if you want to spend less (mains from $16), have simpler food and enjoy a fine terrace view of the harbour, head for the hotel's less formal *Pacific* restaurant. Daily 5–10pm (*Pacific* daily 6.30am–10pm).

Milestone's 812 Wharf St ⓣ250/381-2244, ⓦwww.milestonesrestaurants.com. Popular mid-priced place for burgers, pastas, steaks and the like (from about $8 to $25 for main courses), slap-bang on the Inner Harbour beneath the infocentre, so expect lots of bustle, passing trade and good views. Mon–Thurs 11am–10pm, Fri 11am–11pm, Sat 10am–11pm, Sun 9am–10pm.

Pagliacci's 1011 Broad St between Fort and Broughton ⓣ250/386-1662, ⓦwww.pagliaccis.ca. The best restaurant in Victoria if you want a fast, furious atmosphere, live music, good Italian food at fair prices (mains from $13) and excellent desserts. A rowdy throng usually begins to queue (there are no reservations) almost from the moment the doors are open. Mon–Thurs 11.30am–10pm, Fri–Sat 11.30am–11pm, Sun 10am–10pm.

Tapa Bar 620 Trounce Alley ⓣ250/383-0013, ⓦwww.tapabar.ca. A good little find, this buzzy place has inexpensive tapas (plates from $8) – try the excellent *gambas al ajillo* (prawns in a pungent garlic sauce) – wines by the glass and a long list of Martinis. Mon–Thurs 11.30am–11pm, Fri & Sat 11am–midnight, Sun 11am–10pm.

The Temple 525 Fort St ⓣ250/383-2313, ⓦwww.thetemple.ca. Unashamedly chic and contemporary in look, feel and food. The sleek main room has a wraparound bar (in glowing glass), a double chaise longue-bed for reclining couples and an imposing fireplace, while the more intimate Velvet Room has a couple of cosier tables. There's a DJ later in the evening, but the emphasis remains on good Pacific Northwest cooking and a seasonal menu, with small dishes from around $8, more substantial ones up to $20 or more. Mon–Fri 11.30am–2.30pm, daily for dinner from 5pm.

The Reef 533 Yates St ⓣ250/388-5375, ⓦwww.thereefrestaurant.com. It's a long way from home, but the Caribbean cooking here is authentic, especially the classic jerk sauce, a spicy Caribbean staple, added to meats, and chicken in particular. There are several jerk dishes, plus prawn and fish dishes (good grilled blue marlin) and some innovative salads. Reckon on between $11 and $20 for main courses, and settle down later in the evening to listen to DJ-spun sounds and a mellow lounge atmosphere. Mon–Thurs 11am–midnight, Fri–Sun 11am–1am.

Bars and pubs

Bartholomew's Bar and Rockefeller Grill Executive House Hotel, 777 Douglas St ⓣ250/388-5111. This is an upbeat pub with a steady diet of local bands. For the same sort of place, also try *Steamers*, at 570 Yates St, where you'll catch enthusiastic local bands most nights, and most types of music from reggae to Celtic.

Big Bad John's 919 Douglas St ⓣ250/383-7137. Next to the *Strathcona Hotel*, this is Victoria's most atmospheric bar by far, with bare boards and authentic old banknotes, messages and IOUs pasted to the walls. It also hosts occasional live bands and singers, usually of a country-music persuasion.

D'Arcy's Wharfside Pub 1127 Wharf St ⓣ250/380-1322. Victoria's original "Irish pub" has been going strong for years, thanks to a prime site on the edge of Bastion Square, reliable food and beer, and excellent occasional live Irish music plus bands and other performances above the bar in the Upstairs Cabaret.

Spinnakers BrewPub 308 Catherine St near Esquimalt Rd ⓣ250/384-6613, ⓦwww.spinnakers.com. Bus #23 to Esquimalt Rd. Thirty-eight beers, including several home-brewed options, a restaurant, live music, occasional tours of the brewery and good harbour views draw a mixed and relaxed clientele.

Swans Brewpub 506 Pandora Ave at Store St ⓣ250/361-3310, ⓦwww.swanshotel.com. This pretty and highly popular hotel-café-brewery, housed in a 1913 warehouse, is the place to watch Victoria's young professionals at play. Many foreign and home-brewed beers on tap, with live music nightly (no cover charge).

Clubs and live music

The Cambie 856 Esquimalt Rd ⓣ250/382-7161. A long-established venue with country bands most nights and occasional jam and open-mic sessions. Take bus #6.

Evolution 502 Discovery St ⓣ250/388-3000, ⓦwww.evotheclub.com. One of Victoria's more interesting clubs, thanks to plenty of techno, rave and alternative sounds.

Hermann's Jazz Club 753 View St ⓣ250/388-9166, ⓦwww.hermannsjazz.com. Dimly lit club thick with 1950s atmosphere that specializes in Dixieland but has occasional excursions into fusion and blues.

Hush 1325 Government St ⓣ250/385-0566, ⓦwww.hushnightclub.ca. A central, low-lit, low-ceilinged dance club that attracts a young, informal crowd, and takes its music and its DJs very seriously. Has a roster of resident DJs and special guests behind the decks two or three times a week.

Element 919 Douglas St ⓣ250/383-7137, ⓦwww.elementnightclub.ca. The biggest, best and noisiest of the live-music venues, this club occupies the garish, neon-lit basement of the *Strathcona Hotel*. Varied live bands, including the occasional big name, and dancing nightly. Upstairs, in the same hotel complex, The Roof, part of *The Sticky Wicket Pub*, offers DJs most nights

The Lucky Bar 17 Yates St at Wharf St ⓣ250/382-LUCK, ⓦwww.luckybar.ca. Good, old-fashioned type of music and dance club that offers a wide variety of live music most evenings plus DJ-based nights. Cover from $5.

Listings

American Express 1213 Douglas St (Mon–Fri 8.30am–4.30pm, Sat 10am–4pm; ⓣ250/385-8731).

Bike rental Cycle BC Rentals at 950 Wharf St and 707 Douglas St (ⓣ250/885-2453 or 1-866/380-2453, ⓦwww.cyclebc.ca) rents a big range of bikes (from $7 an hour, $24 daily) plus scooters, kayaks, rowing boats, motor boats and motorbikes.

Bus information Akal Airporter shuttle bus from Victoria Airport (ⓣ250/386-2525 or 1-877/386-2525, ⓦwww.victoriaairportshuttle.com). For services to Vancouver, there's Pacific Coast Lines (ⓣ604/662-8074 in Vancouver or 250/385-4411 at the Victoria bus terminal, ⓦwww.pacificcoach.com); for services on the island, Greyhound (ⓣ250/388-5248 or 1-800/663-8390, ⓦwww.greyhound.ca). Both operate from the bus terminal at 700 Douglas St and Belleville St.

Car rental Avis, 62B-1001 Douglas St (ⓣ250/386-8468 or 1-800/879-2847) and Victoria Airport (ⓣ250/656-6033, ⓦwww.avis.com); Budget, 757 Douglas St (ⓣ250/268-8900 or 1-800/668-9833,

Ⓦwww.budgetvictoria,com); National, 767 Douglas St (Ⓣ250/386-1213 or 1-800/227-7368).

Doctor and dentist Most hotels have a doctor or dentist on call. Otherwise contact Cresta Dental Centre in the Tillicum Street Mall at 3170 Tillicum Rd, Burnside St (Ⓣ250/384-7711). The Tillicum Mall Medical Clinic at the same address (Ⓣ250/381-8112) accepts walk-in patients.

Equipment rental Sports Rent, 1950 Government St at Discovery (Ⓣ250/385-7368, Ⓦwww.sportsrentbc.com). Rents a colossal range of equipment, including bikes, rollerblades, all camping, hiking, climbing and diving gear.

Ferries BC Ferries (Ⓣ250/386-3431 or 1-888/223-3779, Ⓦwww.bcferries.com); Black Ball Transport (Ⓣ250/386-2202 or 360/457-4491 in Port Angeles, Ⓦwww.cohoferry .com); Victoria Clipper (Ⓣ250/382-8100, 206/448-5000 or 1-800/888-2535, Ⓦwww.clippervacations.com); Washington State Ferries (Ⓣ206/464-6400 or 1-888/808-7977, Ⓦwww.wasdot.wa.gov/ferries).

Hospital Victoria General Hospital, 35 Helmcken Rd (Ⓣ250/727-4212).

Outdoor equipment Mountain Equipment Co-op, 1450 Government St. This large and excellent store offers a vast range of equipment for all outdoor activities, and occupies virtually an entire city block between Johnson St and Pandora Ave. Open Mon–Fri 10am–9pm, Sat 9am–6pm, Sun 11am–5pm.

Post office Main office, 714 Yates St at Douglas (Ⓣ250/953-1352, 1-800/267-1177 in Canada). Mon–Fri 8.30am–5pm.

Taxis Blue Bird Cabs (Ⓣ250/382-4235); Empress Cabs (Ⓣ250/381-2222); Victoria Taxi (Ⓣ250/383-7111).

Train information VIA Rail, 450 Pandora Ave (Ⓣ250/383-4324 or 1-800/561-8630 in Canada and 1-800/561-3949 in the US, Ⓦwww.viarail.ca).

20

The Gulf Islands

Scattered between Vancouver Island and the mainland lie several hundred tiny islands, most no more than lumps of rock, a few large enough to hold permanent populations and warrant a regular ferry service. Two main clusters are accessible from Victoria: the Gulf Islands and the San Juan Islands, both part of the same archipelago, except that the latter group belongs to the United States.

You get a good look at the Gulf Islands on the seaplanes from Vancouver (see p.213) and on the ferry from Tsawwassen – twisting and threading through their coves and channels, the ride sometimes seems even a little too close for comfort. The coastline makes for superb **sailing**, and an armada of small boats crisscrosses between the islands whenever the weather allows.

Hikers and campers are well served, and **fishing** is also good – some of the world's biggest salmon having met their doom in the surrounding waters. Indeed, there's an abundance of marine wildlife here including sea lions, orcas, seals, bald eagles, herons and cormorants, all of which you stand a good chance of seeing both on the islands and from the inter-island ferries.

And while the climate is hardly "Mediterranean", as claimed in the tourist blurbs, it is mild and the vegetation is particularly lush, making the Gulf Islands the dream idyll of many people from Washington State and British Columbia, whether they're artists, writers, pensioners or dropouts from the mainstream. For full details of what they're all up to, grab a copy of the local listings – you can find various free sheets in most cafés, organic food shops and the like.

Planning a visit

BC Ferries (Ⓣ250/386-3431 or 1-888/223-3779, Ⓦwww.bcferries.com) sails to five of the Southern Gulf Islands – **Saltspring**, **Pender**, **Saturna**, **Mayne** and **Galiano** – from Swartz Bay, 33km north of Victoria on Hwy 17. (A few other North Gulf Islands, notably Gabriola, can be reached from Chemainus and Nanaimo farther up Vancouver Island's East Coast). Reckon on at least two crossings to each daily, but be prepared for all boats to be jammed solid during the summer. Visit the website or pick up the company's *Southern Gulf Islands* timetable, widely available on boats and in the mainland infocentres, which is invaluable if you aim to exploit the many inter-island connections. All the ferries take cars, bikes and motorbikes, though with a car you'll need to make a **reservation**. Bear in mind that there's next to no public transport on the islands, so what few taxis there are can charge more or less what they wish. It costs only around $2 to take bikes on board, and **cycling** can be a great way to see the islands: most are small (if hilly), with few roads.

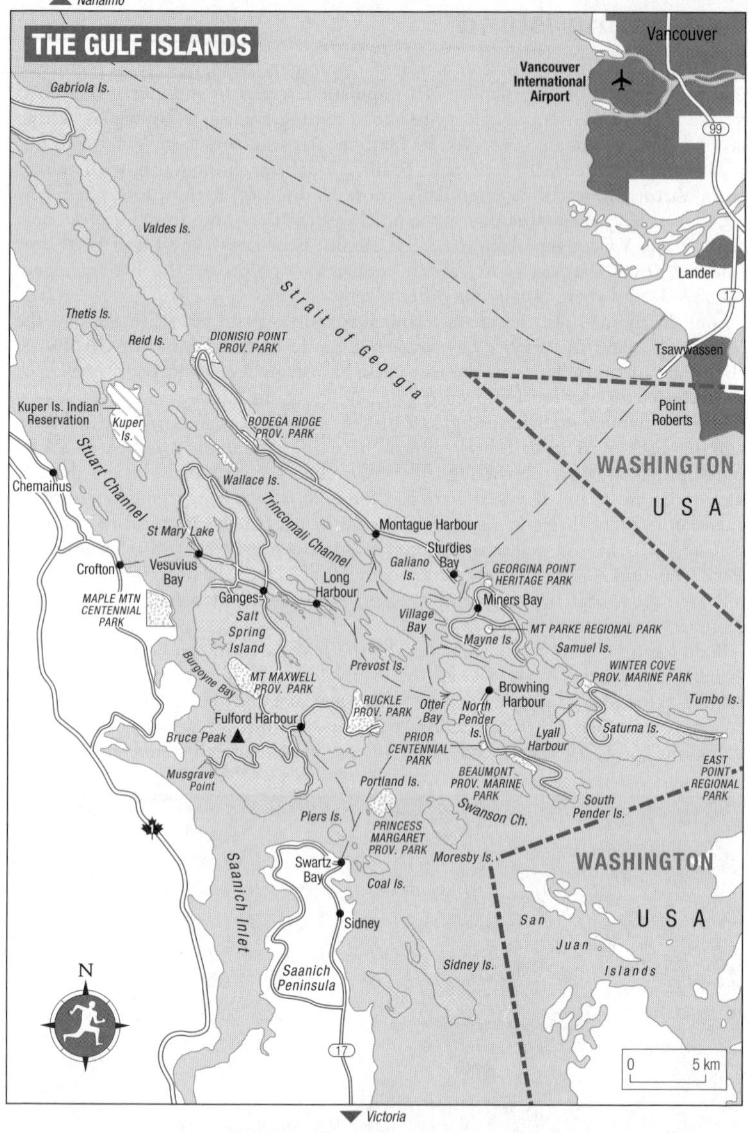

Have your **accommodation** worked out well in advance in summer. **Campers** should have few problems finding sites, most of which are located in the islands' provincial parks, though at peak times you'll want to arrive before noon to ensure a pitch – there are reservations in some parks. For help with B&Bs, use the *BC Accommodations* guide and the BC tourism bureau's phone and website (Ⓣ604/435-5622 or 1-800/435-5622, Ⓦwww.HelloBC.com), or contact the Victoria infocentre or **specialist agencies** such as the Gulf Islands Reservation Service (Ⓣ1-888/539-9984, Ⓦwww.gulfislandsreservations.com).

Salt Spring Island

SALT SPRING (pop. 9500), sometimes Saltspring, is the biggest, most populated and most visited of the islands – its population triples in summer – though if you're without transport think twice about coming here on a day-trip as getting around is pretty tough. It's served by Harbour Air seaplanes from Vancouver (see p.213) and has three ferry terminals: **Fulford Harbour** in the south, with sailings from Victoria's Swartz Bay (ten daily, more in summer; 35min; foot passengers $9.45, cars $28); **Vesuvius Bay** in the northwest, with sailings from Crofton, near Duncan, on Vancouver Island (13 daily; 20min; same fares); and **Long Harbour**, midway down the east coast, which connects to points on the BC mainland, notably Tsawwassen, usually via other islands.

Long Harbour is also the main terminal for inter-island travel. In the past the Saltspring Island Bus service has connected the ferry terminals with **GANGES**, the island's main village, on the east coast 5km from Long Harbour, but check with the Victoria or local infocentre (see below) for the latest.

Most enjoyment on Salt Spring, as with the other Gulf Islands, is to be had from sinking back into its laid-back approach to life: grabbing a coffee at a café overlooking the water, browsing galleries, cycling the backroads, hiking the odd easy trail, and so on. If you're here to slum it on a **beach**, the best strips are on the island's more sheltered east side – Beddis Beach in particular, off the Fulford to Ganges Road – as well as at Vesuvius Bay in the northwest and at Drummond Park near Fulford in the south. Like many Gulf Island beaches, several (but not all) are sandy, and in summer the water, while hardly tropical, is also warm enough for swimming.

Beddis can be seen en route to one of the best parks in the Gulf Islands, the **Ruckle Provincial Park**, a swath of lovely forest, field and maritime scenery tucked in the island's southeast corner 10km east of Fulford Harbour. It has 15km of trails, most leaving from trailheads at Beaver Point, the rocky headland that marks the end of the access road – the best path marches north from here along the

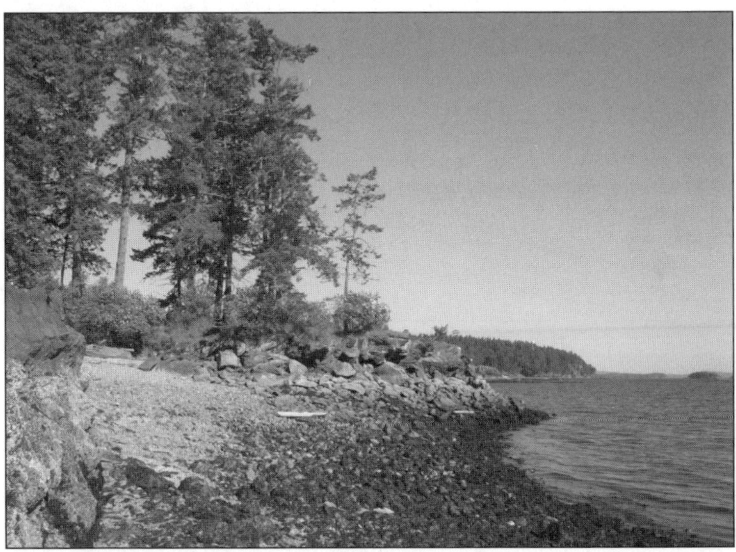

▲ Salt Spring Island

Gulf Islands Water Taxi

The **Gulf Islands Water Taxi** (Ⓣ250/537-2510, Ⓦwww.members.unet.ca/~watertaxi/) has been a feature of island life since 1978, complementing the BC Ferries service and carrying visitors, schoolchildren, fishermen and others on two scheduled routes from the Visitors' Dock below the Oystercatcher Bar & Grill in Ganges. The **first route** runs Salt Spring (Ganges Harbour) to Galiano (Sturdies Bay) and on to Mayne Island (Miners Bay); currently Sept–June 2 daily 6.45am & 4.30pm from Salt Spring; $25 round trip between any two points, $15 one-way, no extra charge for bicycles. Prices and departure details are the same on the **second route**: from Salt Spring (Ganges Harbour) to Saturna (Lyall Harbour) to Horton Bay and on to Pender (Port Washington). An "Island Hopping" third route operates in summer (Sat 9am & 3pm from Ganges) calling at Galiano and Mayne. Reservations are recommended for all services, which are timetabled so that you can realistically make short day or sight-seeing trips to other islands from Salt Spring.

coast of tiny coves and rocky headlands to Yeo Point. The park also has an outstanding campsite ($15) at the end of the access road (see below). **Mount Maxwell Provincial Park** lies midway up the west coast; the eponymous mountain provides a tremendous 588-metre viewpoint. The park is accessed on Cranberry Road, which strikes west midway down the island off the main Ganges to Fulford Road.

Between April and October, head for the **Saturday Market** (Sat 8am–4pm; Ⓦwww.saltspringmarket.com), in Ganges' Centennial Park, for food and crafts. Community spirit reaches a climax during the annual **Artcraft** crafts fair (late June to mid-Sept), held in Ganges' Mahon Hall, that displays the talents of the island's many dab-handed creatives. The other main focus for cultural events is the **ArtSpring** centre, 100 Jackson Ave in Ganges (Ⓦwww.artspring.ca), which hosts a summer performing arts festival (July & Aug).

Practicalities

Ganges, close to Long Harbour on the east coast, is armed with a small **infocentre** at 121 Lower Ganges Rd (daily: July & Aug 9am–5pm; April–June & Sept–Oct 10am–4pm; Nov–March 11am–3pm; Ⓣ250/537-5252, Ⓦwww.saltspringtourism.com) and a rapidly proliferating assortment of galleries, tourist shops and holiday homes.

Ganges' infocentre is the place to check out the island's relatively plentiful **accommodation**. You can choose from the hundred or more, often rather expensive, **B&B** options (whose owners can arrange to pick you up from the ferry), or one of the so-called "resorts" – usually a handful of houses with camping, a few rooms to rent and little else. Each of the ferry terminals also has a range of mid-price **motels**, notably *Harbour House*, 121 Upper Ganges Rd, Ganges (Ⓣ250/537-5571 or 1-888/799-5571, Ⓦwww.saltspringharbourhouse.com; $119–295); and the 28-unit *Seabreeze Inn* in a park-like setting above Ganges Harbour at 101 Bittancourt Rd (Ⓣ250/537-4145 or 1-800/434-4112, Ⓦwww.seabreezeinns.com; $105–195).

The island's best **campsite** is in Ruckle Provincial Park – a magnificent, waterfront, 78-pitch site ($15 in summer, $10 in winter) at Beaver Point, reached by following Beaver Point Road from the Fulford Harbour ferry terminal (10km).

In Ganges, there are numerous **cafés** and coffee shops for high-quality sandwiches: for something more ambitious, try the appealing *Tree House Café-Restaurant*, 106 Purvis Lane (Ⓣ250/537-5379, Ⓦwww.treehousecafe.ca), which serves breakfast,

lunch and dinner and has places to sit outside and low-key live (often acoustic) music most nights. For a treat, the place to go is *House Piccolo*, 108 Hereford Ave, Ganges (Ⓣ250/537-1844, Ⓦwww.housepiccolo.com, dinner only), which serves high-quality European and Scandinavian food and has won *Wine Spectator* magazine awards.

Galiano Island

Long and finger-shaped, **Galiano** (pop. 1040) is just 27km from north to south and barely five kilometres wide, but it remains one of the more promising islands to visit if you want variety and a realistic chance of finding somewhere to stay. There are two ferry terminals: **Sturdies Bay** in the southeast, which takes boats from the mainland (foot passengers $14.85, cars $47.60), and **Montague Harbour** on the west coast, which handles the Vancouver Island crossings from Swartz Bay (foot passengers $9.80, cars $31). You can also get here with the Gulf Islands Water Taxi and there are inter-island BC Ferries connections (1–4 daily) from Salt Spring via Pender and Mayne.

If you're **canoeing**, stick to the calmer waters, cliffs and coves off the west coast. **Hikers** can walk almost the entire length of the east coast, or climb Mount Sutil (323m) or Mount Galiano (342m) for views of the mainland mountains. To reach the trailhead for the latter, take Burrill south from the ferry at Sturdies Bay and along Bluff Road through the forest of Bluffs Park. A left fork, Active Pass Drive, takes you to the trailhead (total 5km from the ferry).

The locals' favourite **beach** is at Coon Bay at the island's northern tip, but there are excellent marine landscapes and beaches elsewhere, notably at **Montague Harbour Provincial Marine Park**, 10km from the Sturdies Bay ferry terminal on the west side of the island. The park has stretches of shell and pebble foreshore, a café, shop, three-kilometre waterfront trail to Gray Peninsula (though you can easily do your own foreshore walks) and, more to the point, a glorious provincial **campsite** ($19). Booking is essential in summer; see p.214 for details.

Practicalities

You can **stay** at Studies Bay at the very pleasant ten-room *Galiano Oceanfront Inn & Spa*, 134 Madrona Drive (Ⓣ250/539-3388, Ⓦwww.galianoinn.com; from $249); rates include a gourmet breakfast.

For **food and drink** the island's main pub, the *Hummingbird Inn* (Ⓣ250/539-5472), is about 2km from Sturdies Bay at 47 Sturdies Bay Rd. Food is reasonable at the *Hummingbird*, likewise at *La Bérengerie* (Ⓣ250/539-5392), a genteel restaurant, with meals at around $25, about the same distance from Montague Harbour on the corner of Montague and Clanton roads that usually rents three B&B rooms upstairs.

North and South Pender

The somnolent bridge-linked islands of **North** and **South Pender** muster about two thousand people between them, many of whom will try to entice you into their studios to buy local arts and crafts. Otherwise you can swim, snooze or walk on one of the many tiny **beaches** – there's public ocean access at some twenty points around the island. Two of the best are Hamilton Beach near Browning Beach on the east coast of North Pender and Mortimer Spit just south of the bridge that links the two islands. The latter is also the place to pick up trails to Mount Norman and Beaumont Provincial Marine Park.

Ferries come to North Pender from Swartz Bay (up to 7 daily; 40min direct or 2hr via Galiano and/or Mayne; foot passengers $9.80, cars $31) and Tsawwassen (foot-passengers $14.85 one-way; cars $47.60).

There's a handful of **B&Bs**, and a small wooded **campsite** at Prior Centennial Provincial Park, 6km south of the Otter Bay ferry terminal (March–Sept; $15). For the only **hotel**-type rooms, try the twelve-room *Inn on Pender Island*, prettily situated in 7.5 acres of wooded country near Prior Park at 4709 Canal Rd, North Pender (Ⓣ250/629-3353 or 1-800/550-0172, Ⓦwww.innonpender.com; $159), or the *Poets Cove Resort & Spa*, a plush resort at 9801 Spalding Rd, South Pender (Ⓣ250/629-3212 or 1-888/512-7638, Ⓦwww.poetscove.com; $279), which has a pool, marina, bistro-pub, restaurant, store, tennis, harbour views, canoe, boat and bike rentals, and a choice of rooms or cabins. Alternatively, try the three fully equipped self-catering cottages 500m sharp left from the ferry at *Arcadia by the Sea*, 1325 MacKinnon Rd, North Pender (Ⓣ250/629-3221 or 1-877/470-8439, Ⓦwww.arcadiabythesea.com; $107; May–Sept), with tennis court, outdoor pool and private decks.

Mayne Island

Mayne is the first island to your left (Galiano is on your right) if you're crossing from Tsawwassen to Swartz Bay – which is perhaps as close as you'll get, since it's the quietest and most difficult to reach of the islands served by ferries. One-way tickets from Tsawwassen (via Galiano/Montague Harbour) in high season cost $14.85 for foot passengers, $47.60 for cars. It also has few places to stay, which may be as good a reason as any for heading out here – particularly if you have a bike to explore the quiet country roads that snake over the island.

Best of several **beaches** is Bennett Bay, a sheltered strip with warm water and good sand. It's reached by heading east from the island's principal community at Miner's Bay (5min from the ferry terminal at Village Bay on the west coast) to the end of Fernhill Road and then turning left onto Wilks Road. If you want a **walk**, try the 45-minute climb up Mount Parke in the eponymous regional park; it starts near the Fernhill Centre on Montrose Road.

Village Bay – don't be fooled by the name: there's no village – has a summer-only **infocentre** booth (daily 9am–6pm; no phone, Ⓦwww.mayneislandchamber.ca) that should be able to fill you in on the limited **hotel** and **B&B** possibilities. Try the *Blue Vista Cottage Resort*, eight fully equipped cabins overlooking Bennett Bay at 563 Arbutus Drive, 6km from the ferry (Ⓣ250/539-2463 or 1-877/535-2424, Ⓦwww.bluevistaresort.com; $99–145), with ferry pick-up, sandy beach, park-like setting and bike, canoe and kayak rental. The *Tinkerer's B&B* on Miner's Bay at 417 Sunset Place off Georgina Point Rd (Ⓣ250/539-2280, Ⓔmayne_tinkerers@yahoo.com; $110–145; May–Oct), 2.4km from the ferry, is nicely offbeat: it rents bikes, provides hammocks and offers "demonstrations of medicinal herb and flower gardens". Also good is waterfront *Oceanwood Country Inn*, 2km south of the ferry at 630 Dinner Bay Rd (Ⓣ250/539-5074, Ⓦwww.oceanwood.com; from $185; March–Nov), which has twelve smart rooms, sauna, oceanfront hot tub and a superb, quiet garden setting.

Saturna Island

Saturna, to the south, has daily **ferries** from Swartz Bay on Vancouver Island (2–3 daily; foot passengers $9.80 return, vehicles $31) and from Tsawwassen but only via Mayne. The island boasts some good **beaches**, the best being at Russell Reef and Winter Cove Marine Park (no campsite) on its northwest tip. There's walking, wildlife and good views to the mainland from Mount Warburton Pike (497m) and on Brown Bridge in the southwest of the island.

For general information on Saturna, visit Ⓦwww.saturnatourism.com. The island is another **B&B** hideaway: try the three-room waterfront *Lyall Harbour B&B* (Ⓣ250/539-5577 or 1-877/473-9343, Ⓦwww.lyallharbour.com; $110–140), 500m from the ferry at 121 East Point Rd in Saturna Point. There are no campgrounds and only a handful of **places to eat**, notably the pub-restaurant at the modern, waterfront *Saturna Lodge,* 130 Payne Rd (Ⓣ250/539-2254, Ⓦwww.saturna.ca; $126–175; May–Oct), which also has six rooms to rent; rates include breakfast.

21

Whistler and the Sunshine Coast

Apart from Victoria and the southern Gulf Islands, two other major excursions from Vancouver are possible, each of which can easily be extended to embrace longer itineraries out of the city. The first, and far more tempting, is the inland route on the **Sea to Sky Highway** to **Garibaldi Provincial Park**, which contains by far the best scenery and hiking country within striking distance of Vancouver, and the famous world-class ski resort of **Whistler**. The last is well worth visiting at any time of the year, with winter an obviously busy time and summer almost equally popular, thanks to the area's many outdoor activities. En route to Whistler you'll pass through **Squamish**, nothing to rave over scenically, but rapidly emerging as one of North America's premier destinations for windsurfing, climbing and – in season – eagle-watching.

The second, and less enticing trip, is along the 150-kilometre Sunshine Coast, the only stretch of accessible coastline on mainland British Columbia, and a possible springboard to Vancouver Island: ferries depart from Powell River, the coast's largest town, to Comox on Vancouver Island. Most people on short trips, however, make the run to Powell River and then turn tail for Vancouver – there is no alternative route back to the city and no onward road route after the village of Lund and the end of Hwy 101 beyond Powell River.

The Sea to Sky Highway

A fancy name for Hwy 99 between North Vancouver and Whistler, the **Sea to Sky Highway** has a slightly better reputation than it deserves. It undoubtedly scores in its early coastal stretch, where the road clings perilously to an almost sheer cliff and mountains come dramatically into view on both sides of Howe Sound. Views here are better than along the Sunshine Coast, though plenty of campsites, motels and minor roadside distractions fill the route until the mountains of the Coast Range rear up beyond **Squamish** for the rest of the way to Whistler. This part of the highway is a stunner, with wonderful views of lakes and glaciers. Regular buses (see "Perimeter bus" details on p.241) connect Vancouver and Whistler (some continue to Pemberton), which you can easily manage as a day-trip (it's around 2hr one-way to Whistler from Vancouver by bus).

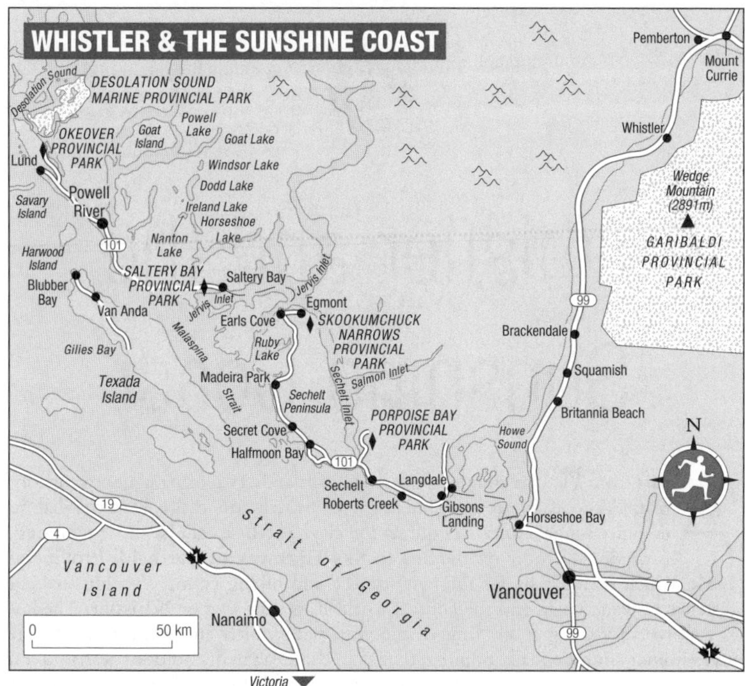

Britannia Beach

Road and rail lines meet with some squalor at tiny **Britannia Beach**, 53km from Vancouver, whose **BC Museum of Mining** is the first reason to take time out from admiring the views (Feb–Nov daily 9am–4.30pm, Dec–Jan Mon–Fri 9am–4.40; $18.50; ⓣ1-800/896-4044, ⓦwww.bcmuseumofmining.org). Centring on what was, in the 1930s, the largest producer of copper in the British Empire – 56 million tons of ore were extracted here before the mine closed in 1974 – the museum is housed in a huge building, derelict with age, on the hillside and is chock-full of hands-on displays, original working machinery, a 235-ton monster mine truck and archive photographs. You can also take guided underground tours (every 30min) around about 350m of the mine's galleries on small electric trains. And if parts of the complex look familiar it's because the mine has been used as a location in *The X-Files* and numerous other films and TV programmes.

Continuing north you pass several small coastal reserves, the most striking of which is **Shannon Falls Provincial Park**, 7km from Britannia Beach, signed right off the road and worth a stop for its spectacular 335-metre **waterfall**. It's six times the height of Niagara, and can be seen from the road but it's only five minutes' walk to the viewing area at the base, where the proximity of the road, plus a campsite and diner, detract a touch.

Squamish

The sea views and coastal drama end 11km beyond Britannia Beach at **SQUAMISH**, whose houses spread out over a flat plain amidst warehouses, logging waste and old machinery. However, if you want to climb, windsurf or mountain bike, there's

nowhere better in the region to do so. At a glance, all the town has by way of fame is the vast granite rock overshadowing it, "The Stawamus Chief", which looms into view to the east just beyond Shannon Falls and is claimed to be the world's "second-biggest free-standing rock" (after Gibraltar, apparently). The town rates as one of Canada's top – if not *the* top – spots for **rock climbing**. Around 200,000 climbers from around the world come here annually, swarming to more than four hundred routes covering the 625-metre monolith: the University Wall and its culmination, the Dance Platform, is rated Canada's toughest climb.

The rock is sacred to the local Squamish, whose ancient tribal name – which means "place where the wind blows" – gives a clue as to the town's second big activity: **windsurfing**. There are strong, consistent winds to suit all abilities, but the water is cold, so a wetsuit's a good idea (there are rental outlets around town). Most people head for the artificial **Squamish Spit**, a dyke separating the waters of the Howe Sound from the Squamish River. The area is run by the Squamish Windsports Society (Ⓦwww.squamishwindsports.com) and is 3km from town.

Rounding out Squamish's outdoor activities is the tremendous **mountain biking** terrain – there are 63 trails in the area ranging from gnarly single-track trails to readily accessible deactivated forestry roads. The best areas are the Valley Cliff Trails (stream-bed, single-track and woodland trails); Mamquam Forest Service roads (active logging roads with fine views of the Mamquam Glacier); the Cat Lake and Brohm Lake trails; and the Alice Lake trails, which include an abandoned railway for an easy ride.

The town has one more unexpected treat, for the Squamish River, and the tiny hamlet of Brackendale in particular (10km to the north on Hwy 99), which is the world's best place to see **bald-eagles**. In winter around 2000 eagles congregate here, attracted by the migrating salmon. The best places to see them are the so-called **Eagle Run** stretch of the river just south of the centre of Brackendale, and on the river in the Brackendale Eagles Provincial Park.

If you want to base yourself locally while seeing the eagles, contact the Sunwolf Outdoor Centre (Ⓣ604/898-1537 or 1-877/806-8046, Ⓦwww.sunwolf.net), signposted off Hwy 1 – take a left onto Squamish Valley Road at the Alice Lake junction 2km past Brackendale, continue for 4km and the centre is on the right. It has ten great three-person cabins on the shore of the Cheakamus River for $90; some have kitchens for an extra $10. To see the eagles from a raft costs $99 per person, including light lunch; a raft trip plus cabin accommodation costs $134 per person, if two share a cabin.

Practicalities

Most of the relevant parts of the town are concentrated on or near Cleveland Avenue, off Hwy 99, including the **infocentre** (May–Sept daily 9am–5pm, Oct–April Mon–Fri 9am–5pm, Sat & Sun 10am–2pm; Ⓣ604/892-9244 or 1-866/333-2010, Ⓦwww.tourismsquamish.com), a big supermarket and the most central **accommodation** if you're not at the hostel (see below), the *August Jack Motor Inn* (Ⓣ604/892-3504 or 1-888/892-3502, Ⓦwww.augustjack.com). Alternatively, the *Garibaldi Budget Inn*, 38012-3rd Ave (Ⓣ604/892-5204 or 1-888/313-9299), is excellent value. If you can afford more, then definitely plump for the *Howe Sound Inn & Brewing Company*, 37801 Cleveland Ave (Ⓣ604/892-2603 or 1-800/919-2537, Ⓦwww.howesound.com), which has 20 simple but modern rooms, great food and plenty of beer from its own microbrewery. The superlative *Squamish Hostel* at Mamquam Blind Channel on Hwy 99 (Ⓣ 604/892-9240 or 1-800/449-8614, Ⓦwww.hostels.com/squamish) is clean and friendly, with a kitchen, common room and 18 beds including two private rooms. Beds are $28.50 a night and private rooms are $70.

If you're looking into **renting equipment**, Vertical Reality Sports Centre at 37835 2nd Ave (ⓣ604/892-8248, ⓦwww.verticalrealitysports.com) rents climbing shoes and mountain bikes. For other **mountain bike hire**, contact Tantalus (ⓣ604/898-2588), by the Greyhound depot at 40446 Government Road, or Corsa Cycles (ⓣ604/892-3331, ⓦwww.corsacycles.com) at 800-1200 Hunter Place: rates for both start at about $45 for a day's hire. If you are here to climb, there are several **guides**, available from bookstores in Vancouver as well as the climbing shops in Squamish: Kevin McLane is the author of several books, including *The Climbers' Guide to Squamish* (Elaho, $34.95).

Garibaldi Provincial Park

After about 5km, the road north of Squamish enters the classic river, mountain and forest country of the BC interior. The journey thereafter up to Whistler is a joy, with only the march of electricity pylons to take the edge off an idyllic drive.

Unless you're skiing, **Garibaldi Provincial Park** is the main incentive for heading this way. It's a huge and unspoilt area that combines all the usual breath-taking ingredients of lakes, rivers, forests, glaciers and the peaks of the Coast Mountains (Wedge Mountain, at 2891m, is the park's highest point). Four rough roads access the park from points along the highway between Squamish and Whistler, but you'll need transport to reach the trailheads at the end of them. Other than camping, the only accommodation close to the park is at Whistler.

There are five main areas with trails, of which the **Black Tusk/Garibaldi Lake** region is the most popular and probably most beautiful, thanks to its high-mountain views. As so often in Canada, there are trails to suit most abilities, from easy day and half-day hikes which will require no specialist equipment, to multi-day treks and trails that involve a degree of scrambling. Further trails fan out from Garibaldi Lake, including one to the huge basalt outcrop of **Black Tusk** (2316m), a rare opportunity to reach an alpine summit without any rock climbing. The other hiking areas from south to north are **Diamond Head**, **Cheakamus Lake**, **Singing Pass** and **Wedgemount Lake**. Outside these small, defined areas, however, the park is untrammelled wilderness. For more **information**, including good advice on trails, visit ⓦwww.garibaldipark.com or pick the dedicated BC Parks pamphlet from infocentres in Vancouver and elsewhere, whose information can also be accessed at ⓦwww.gov.bc.ca/bcparks.

Whistler

Whistler, 56km beyond Squamish and 125km from Vancouver, is Canada's finest four-season resort, and frequently ranks among most people's world top-five winter ski resorts. Skiing and snowboarding are clearly the main activities, but all manner of other winter sports are possible and in summer the lifts keep running to provide supreme highline hiking and other outdoor activities (not to mention North America's finest summer skiing). It is a busy place, be warned – over two million lift tickets are sold here every winter, more than at any other North American resort. Fortunately it also has one of the continent's largest ski areas, so the crowds are spread thinly over the resort's 200-plus trails and twelve alpine bowls.

The resort consists of two adjacent but separate mountains – **Whistler** (2182m) and **Blackcomb** (2284m) – each with their own extensive lift and chair systems (but a joint ticket scheme) and linked by the PEAK 2 PEAK gondola (see box, p.244). The

mountains can be accessed from a total of five bases, including lift systems to both mountains from the resort's heart, the purpose-built and largely pedestrianized **Whistler Village**, the tight-clustered focus of many hotels, shops, restaurants and après-ski activity. The gondola (cable-car) for Whistler Mountain also leaves from the Village. Around this core are two other "village" complexes, **Upper Village** (for the gondola to Blackcomb Mountain), about a kilometre to the northeast and the newer Village North about 700m to the north. Around 6km to the south of Whistler Village is **Whistler Creekside** (also with a gondola and lift base), which has typically been a cheaper alternative but has undergone a fifty-million dollar redevelopment that has seen its accommodation and local services duplicating those of its famous neighbour. Further development took place in the build-up to the 2010 Winter Olympics, largely based in and around Whistler.

Arrival and getting around

There are several ways of **getting to** Whistler. If you're driving from Vancouver, allow about two and a bit hours for the 125-kilometre run on the highway – the road was only completed as recently as 1965: before that the area was little visited.

Perimeter (ⓣ604/266-5386 or 1-888/717-6066, ⓦwww.perimeterbus.com) runs a shuttle **bus** from Vancouver airport and various Vancouver hotels to Whistler Bus Loop and a selection of Whistler hotels. Reservations are required year-round for the service (April to mid-Dec 7 daily, 3 of which are express services and do not stop at Vancouver hotels – there are 8 southbound departures, including 3 express runs; mid-Dec to April 11 daily, including 8 express services; 2hr 30min–3hr; $49 plus tax one-way). Note that winter schedules can be affected by bad weather on the Sea to Sky Hwy.

Greyhound (ⓣ604/482-8747 in Vancouver, ⓣ604/932-5031 in Whistler, 1-800/661-8747 from anywhere in North America, 604/904-7060 from outside North America and 0800 731 5983 from the UK; ⓦwww.greyhound.ca or www.whistlerbus.com) runs 7–8 daily bus services from Vancouver's bus depot (see p.23) to the Village (2hr 20min; $27.90 one-way) via Britannia Beach, Whistler Creek and other stops.

After years as a freight-only operation, part of the old BC Rail line from North Vancouver to Prince George has been reopened to passenger traffic. The Whistler Mountaineer departs daily from May to mid-October from North Vancouver station at 8am, arriving in Whistler at 11.30am. The return trip leaves at 3pm. It's designed as an excursion trip rather than a passenger service, however, and it costs a steep $119 one way, $199 return. Bookings must be made in advance by phone only (ⓣ1-888/403-4727).

If you're staying in or near the Village, then you won't really need **local transport**, but WAVE (ⓣ604/932-4020) runs a shuttle bus service around Whistler Village, Village North and Upper Village as well as buses to Whistler Creek and other destinations ($2 flat fare, day pass $5, weekly pass $20). Buses have racks for skis and bikes. If you need taxis call ⓣ604/938-1515, ⓦwww.resortcabs.com.

Information

For **information** on Whistler-Blackcomb call ⓣ604/904-8134 or 1-866/218-9690 toll-free in North America or 0800/587-1743 toll-free in the UK, ⓦwww.whistlerblackcomb.com). Tourism Whistler (ⓣ604/932-3928) is another source of information, and runs the Whistler Activity and Information Centre, in the green-roofed Conference Centre near the Village Square (daily 9am–5pm; ⓣ604/932-2394 or 1-800/WHISTLER, ⓦwww.whistler.com). The **Chamber of Commerce** is in

▲ Hiking Whistler's High Note Trail

Whistler Village at 4230 Gateway Drive, off Village Gate Blvd (Mon–Thu 8.30am–6.30pm, Fri–Sat 8.30am–7.30pm; ⓣ604/932-5592, ⓦwww.whistlerchamberofcommerce.com). This office can assist with general information, tickets for events and last-minute accommodation. **Information kiosks** open daily 9am to 5pm between May and early September at several points, including the main bus stop and the Village Gate Boulevard at the entrance to Whistler Village.

For information on, and bookings for **activities** visit the **Tourism Whistler Activity Centre** at the Conference Centre near the Whistler Mountain gondola (ⓣ604/932-0606 or 1-800/WHISTLER toll-free in Northe America or 0808/180-0606 in the UK).

Accommodation

If you're here in summer and not on a package tour, all local **accommodation** can be booked through the excellent Whistler Central Reservations (ⓣ604/664-5625, 1-800/944-7853 toll-free in North America and toll-free in the UK ⓣ0800/731 5983, ⓦwww.whistler.com or www.mywhistler.com). In winter, reservations for those not on a package tour should be made well in advance (Sept at least), as many hotels have a thirty-day cancellation window and may insist on a minimum of three days' stay; prices are highest at this time, too. In winter there's no such thing as budget accommodation, unless you stay at the hostel, and with ever greater numbers of visitors in the summer, prices – and availability – of beds are increasingly a problem outside the ski season. But bear in mind that you don't have to stay in a "conventional" hotel, as there is a wide range of chalets, condos, apartments and houses to rent. These, as well as many hotels, often have kitchen facilities, enabling you save money on dining out. Virtually all types of accommodation, from B&B to condo, list nightly and weekly rates, and in season there's likely to be a minimum stay.

Hotels

Chalet Luise B&B Inn 7461 Ambassador Crescent ⓣ604/932-4187 or 1-800/665-1998, ⓦwww.chaletluise.com. Open May–Nov. Eight rooms in a peaceful garden setting that is convenient for the Village, lifts and various summer hiking trails. The European owners pride themselves on

providing big, home-made breakfasts. $119–175

Edgewater Lodge 8841 Hwy 99, 3km north of the Village ⓣ604/932-0688 or 1-888/870-9065, ⓦwww.edgewater-lodge.com. Set on a lovely forested waterfront promontory that pushes into Green Lake. As a result the 12 luxurious and recently renovated rooms enjoy sublime views, and you can canoe and hike virtually from the front door. $131–320

Executive Inn at Whistler Village 4250 Village Stroll ⓣ604/932-3200 or 1-800/663-6416, ⓦwww.executivehotels.net. Located at the heart of the Village, this "European-style" hotel has 37 rooms, each with big picture windows, kitchenettes, fireplaces and two-person Jacuzzis. $89–370

Fairmont Château Whistler 4599 Château Blvd, Upper Village ⓣ604/938-8000 or 1-800/257-7544; ⓦwww.fairmont.com. This was the resort's obvious first choice until the arrival of the *Four Seasons* (see below), which has left the vast English-manor-house-meets-French-château affair looking a little dated and its vast lobby and overall stylistic effect a little bombastic (the colossal lobby and its redoubtable wooden beams are a sight-seeing attraction in themselves for some visitors). You won't be disappointed here, certainly not in the fine spa, but if you have the money, the Four Seasons is the preferred choice. From $199

Four Seasons Resort Whistler 4591 Blackcomb Way, Upper Village ⓣ604/935-3400 or 1-888/935-2460, ⓦwww.fourseasons.com. Opened in June 2004, the *Four Seasons* stole the *Château Whistler's* upmarket thunder, quickly emerging as Whistler's luxury resort hotel of choice. Service reaches the *Four Seasons*' group's usual elevated standards, and the fabulous panoramic rooms, black-slate bathrooms, suites and town-house-style accommodation are the largest and most polished of their sort in town. Gas-burning fireplaces in the cosy wood-interior rooms are typical nice touches. All manner of facilities are available, along with every aid and guidance imaginable when it comes to skiing or indulging in other outdoor (or indoor) activities. From $445

Haus Heidi Pension B&B Inn 7115 Nesters Rd ⓣ604/932-3113 or 1-800/909-7115, ⓦwww.hausheidi.com. An eight-room inn that has been run by the same family for over 25 years, close to the Village, lifts and valley trails. A generous breakfast is included in the price. $125–225

Pan Pacific Mountainside 4320 Sundial Crescent ⓣ604/905-2999 or 1-888/905-9995, ⓦwww.panpacific.com. There's nowhere closer to the lifts than the older of Whistler's two Pan Pacifics– you can ski from the front door to the Whistler Mountain gondola station a few steps away. The contemporary lodge style is pleasant, and the 121 units include compact studios and one- and two-bedroom suites with kitchens. There's an outdoor pool, and the "Irish" pub and lounge are popular après-ski locations. From $219

Summit Lodge & Spa 4359 Main St ⓣ604/932-2778 or 1-888/913-8811, ⓦwww.summitlodge.com. A peaceful boutique-style hotel, with 81 rooms, all with kitchenettes, balconies and fireplaces. Granite worktops and cherry-wood décor add more than a dash of style, along with details such as free hot chocolate nightly, a ski shuttle, heated outdoor pool and above-average spa. $119–379

Westin Resort & Spa 4090 Whistler Way ⓣ604/905-5000 or 1-888/634-5577, ⓦwww.westinwhistler.com. The Westin chain came relatively late to Whistler (in 2000), but still managed to snaffle a prime location on the mountainside below the main run into the Village. With almost 1,000 beds, this is not an intimate place, but the rooms are spacious and well finished, with granite and cedar trim providing luxurious touches. Facilities include a spa and indoor and outdoor pools. From $339

Hostel

Hostelling International Whistler 5678 Alta Lake Rd ⓣ604/932-5492, ⓦwww.hihostels.ca; beds for members $28, nonmembers $32, private doubles $71/79. A 25-bed hostel with four- and eight-bed dorms 7km from the Village right on the shores of Alta Lake. One of the nicest hostels in BC, it's a signposted 50min walk from Whistler Creek or 10min drive to the Village centre; local buses leave the gondola base in the Village four times a day for the hostel 15min; ($2). As it's popular year-round, reserve many weeks, if not months ahead. Check-in is between 4 and 10pm.

Campsite

Riverside RV Resort and Campground ⓣ604/905-5533 or 1-877/905-5533,

www.whistlerlogcamping.com. Whistler's only central campsite is 1.4km north of Whistler Village at 8018 Mons Rd, and also has 14 five-person log cabins for $119–229 and 107 RV/tent sites for $35 for tents ($20 mid-Sept to mid-Dec), $37.50 for RVs.

Whistler Village

Whistler Village is the key to the resort, a rather characterless conglomeration of hotels, restaurants, mountain-gear shops and more loud people in fluorescent clothes than are healthy in one place at the same time. It's all a far cry from February 1966 when what was then known as London Mountain (local population 25) first started skiing operations. Apparently the International Olympics Committee (IOC) had let drop in the early 1960s that the region satisfied all the criteria for a successful Winter Olympic bid, and development began soon after. Someone on the IOC was obviously making mischief, however, for over the years, Whistler would make no fewer than three failed bids, losing out to Sapporo in 1972, Innsbruck in 1976 and Lake Placid in 1980. But the fourth time was lucky, and Whistler secured the lion's share of the 2010 winter games.

Skiing and snowboarding practicalities

The **skiing and snowboarding season** for Whistler and Blackcomb is one of the longest in North America, often running for almost 200 days from Nov to early June, weather permitting. The yearly average snowfall is an impressive ten metres, while the average winter alpine temperature rarely falls below –5C (compare this with a chillier –12C in Banff). Whistler sits in an area of temperate rainforest, and rain can certainly be a problem at lower altitudes. This said, what falls as rain in the Village is often falling as snow higher up.

Blackcomb closes at the end of April, while Whistler stays open until early June. Then the mountains switch places, as Whistler closes and Blackcomb reopens in early June for glacier skiing and snowboarding. Lifts open at 8.30am (9am from mid-April) and close at 3pm until late Jan, 3.30pm until late Feb, and at 4pm from late Feb. The Tube Park on Blackcomb is open Mon–Fri noon–8pm and 11am–8pm at weekends and holidays. **Summer hours** (June 5–July 30), for glacier skiing or high-level hiking are noon–3pm daily.

Lift tickets give you full use of both Whistler and Blackcomb mountains, and it will take days for even the most advanced skier or snowboarder to cover all the terrain. The best advice is to pick one mountain and stick to it for the day, or use the PEAK 2 PEAK, a $50-million, 4.4-kilometre gondola 415m above the valley floor that links the mountains. See the main text for the relative merits of each mountain. Tickets are available from the lift base in Whistler Village, but the queues can be horrendous. Instead, plan ahead and purchase your tickets and check all lift and other information online at www.whistlerblackcomb .com. Or book by phone on 604/904-8134 or 1-866/218-9690. Discounts are available for online booking, but you must book another element as well as a pass, such as rentals, lessons or accommodation. Your hotel can often set you up with tickets if you pre-book far enough in advance.

Prices increase slightly in peak season – over Christmas and New Year and from mid-Feb to mid-March – and lift tickets are subject to a seven-percent tax.

You can rent equipment from outlets at the Whistler and Blackcomb lifts, but it is first-come, first-served, and you need to be there first thing (8am) to beat the queues. Alternatively, Summit Ski (604/932-6255 or 1-888/608-6225, www.summitsport .com) has several outlets around the Village, including the Delta Whistler Resort and Market Pavilion.

Intermediate and expert skiers can join the **free tours** of the mountains: contact the infocentre for latest departure times.

The brouhaha that accompanied the awarding the games led to a fury of investment, building and upgrading, especially in Whistler Village, which took shape in the late 1970s (until then its site had been the community's rubbish tip). Whistler's name is said to derive either from the distinctive shriek of the marmot (a small, chubby mammal), or the sound of the wind whistling through Singing Pass up in the mountains. Whatever its origins, almost 40 years' worth of investments, plus the money associated with the Olympics, have paid off; the resort's services, lifts and general overall polish are almost faultless, and those of its nearby satellites are not far behind.

Whistler Mountain

Winter-sports enthusiasts can argue long and late over the relative merits of **WHISTLER MOUNTAIN** and its rival, Blackcomb Mountain (see below), both accessed from lifts at Whistler Village's lifts (the Blackcomb base is a little closer to the Upper Village). Both are great mountains, and both offer top-notch skiing and boarding, as evidenced by world-class events like the annual Snowboard FIS World Cup in December and the World Ski and Snowboard Festival in April – both held on Whistler. If this makes the slopes sound big-scale and intimidating, they're not, and if you become lost, confused or just want advice, there are 80 or so red-jacketed "Mountain Hosts" to answer questions.

Each mountain has its own distinctive character, and traditionally Whistler has been seen as the more homely of the two mountains, somewhere you can ski or board for days on end and never have to retrace your steps. One of Whistler's great advantages over Blackcomb is the sun, which the mountain catches much earlier: Seventh Heaven run aside, much of Blackcomb doesn't see the sun until after 11.30am.

The former's ski area is 4757 acres and there are over a hundred marked **trails** and seven major bowls. The breakdown of terrain is twenty percent beginner, fifty-five percent intermediate and twenty-five percent expert. Common consent has Whistler as the better mountain for beginners and intermediates – if you're attending ski school it's a mid-station. Blackcomb is steeper and has more narrow roads, which can test beginners' stopping abilities to the limit. The exception for beginners is for **children**, where the under-sixes should learn at the small hill at the base of Blackcomb, avoiding the bustle of the lift to mid-station on Whistler. Under-sixes ski free on the mountains. Day-care is available for toddlers aged three months to 48 months, for around $100, but should be booked well in advance. Contact the infocentre or visit Ⓦ www.whistlerblackcomb.com.

Whistler's **lifts** include two high-speed gondolas, six high-speed quads, two triple and one double chairlift, and five surface lifts. Helicopter drops make another 100 runs and glacier runs available. If you want the fast track to the best skiing on a quality powder day, take the Harmony and Peak chairlifts. Snowboarders are blessed with a half-pipe and park, though most boarders prefer Blackcomb, if only because it has fewer dull traverses where you have to unbuckle your board. Total vertical drop is 1530m and the longest run is 11km.

Blackcomb Mountain

BLACKCOMB MOUNTAIN, the "Mile-High Mountain", is a ski area laden with superlatives: the most modern resort in Canada, North America's finest summer skiing (on Horstman Glacier), the continent's longest unbroken fall-line skiing and the longest *and* second longest lift-serviced vertical falls in North America (1609m and 1530m).

Blackcomb is slightly smaller than Whistler, at 3414 acres, and has a similar breakdown of **terrain** (fifteen percent beginner, fifty-five percent intermediate and thirty percent expert). **Lifts** are one high-speed gondola, six express quads,

Mountain biking

Figures show that over the last few years the number of people visiting Whistler in summer has actually exceeded those coming in winter. One of the main reasons for this upsurge of warm-weather interest has been the phenomenal rise in the popularity of **mountain biking** in and around the resort, with an estimated 100,000 visitors annually coming to the resort specifically to take to two wheels. Free riding was all but invented in the mountains above Vancouver, so its proliferation in Whistler, an hour or so to the north is no surprise. The oft-made observation is what Hawaii is to the worldwide surfing community, Whistler is to the mountain-biking fraternity. Many believe that biking could soon be bigger in Whistler than skiing.

The resort's popularity is not all down to terrain and happy accident. It always did have hundreds of free trails, with a total of 100km of single-track and 80km of double-track trails, plus around 200km of lift-serviced trails, the last factor vital, for there's nothing better than having a ski lift do all the hard work of carrying your bike up the mountain and letting gravity do the work – and provide the pleasure – coming down.

What has made a big difference, however, is the opening of the deservedly celebrated **Whistler Mountain Bike Park** (ⓣ604/938-7275, ⓦwww.whistlerbike.com; open daily mid-May to early mid-Oct, 10am–5pm, plus 5–8pm on some lifts mid-June to early Sept, depending on the light). This includes those 200km of lift-serviced trails, two jump park areas, three or four access lifts (Whistler Gondola, Fitzsimmons, Magic and Garbanzo), three skills centres for all abilities (green circle, blue square and black diamond), expert staff on site, banked cruisers and dirt trails through canopied forest, a BikerCross park (fun to watch even if you don't take part), and self-guided rides over 1200-metre vertical trails.

Prices for the park aren't cheap: it'll cost you $55 for a day pass in high season (from mid-June), $44 the rest of the time, and $45/39 for seniors and youth 13–18. Children 10–12 are charged $28/23 – note that children under 12 must be accompanied by adults. Two- and three-day passes are also available. These prices cover riding, entry to the Magic Bike Park and access to the lifts from 10am–8pm. You can also rent a high-quality "Park" bike from $65 for half a day (or from $10/hr) from the park's eight various outlets (including the Westin, Four Seasons and Pan pacific hotels, and Glacier Lodge, Crystal Lodge, Whistler Mountainside and Blackcomb Base), or $99.99 for the whole day. Lesser "Youth Park" models cost $50/65. You can also rent individual bits of protective gear, or a full armour package (arm, leg, glove, chest and helmet) for $44.99 ($39.99 with a bike rental).

Of course, you don't have to sign up to the Bike Park to ride locally, or rent equipment from designated outlets. You can buy lift-only passes and do your own thing, and visit other rental outfits such as Cross Country Connection (ⓣ604/905-0071, ⓦwww.crosscountryconnection.com), which has bikes from $12 an hour, and also offers tours and lessons. If you want to research routes and further information, then ⓦwww.whistlermountainbike.com is an excellent resource.

If you're a beginner, then you can stick with the Valley Trail, the 30km paved pedestrian and cycle route in the valley around Whistler Village. You can rent bikes from outlets around the resort, including so-called "cruiser" bikes designed for beginners or those who want a more sedate and comfortable ride.

three triple chairlifts, and seven surface lifts. There are over a hundred marked trails, two glaciers and five bowls along with two half-pipes and a park for snowboarders. Runs such as Ruby, Sapphire, Garnet and Diamond are some of the world's best steep and avalanche-controlled powder, but note that it takes two chairlifts to reach them. Even if you're not skiing, come up here (summer or winter) on the ski lifts to walk, enjoy the **view** from the top of the mountain, or to eat in the restaurants (see below).

Eating

When it comes to **food**, Whistler Village and its satellites are loaded with cafés and around a hundred restaurants, though none really has an "address" as such. These can come and go at an alarming rate, and none – given the resort's purpose-built nature – can be said to have much in the way of original interiors or atmosphere. Most hotels have one or more restaurants, always open to non-residents. In smarter places such as the Four Seasons, where the *'Fifty Two 80 Bistro* (ⓣ604/966-5280) – named after Whistler and Blackcomb Mountain's "vertical mile" – has been winning plaudits, these can be of very high quality, if expensive. But if you're not prepared to pay the $60 and up a head for Whistler's more expensive places, then there are plenty of cafés and bars for snacks and light meals.

Don't forget the 17 mountain restaurants and cafés: on Blackcomb these include Rendezvous (at the top of the Solar Coaster Express), Glacier Creek Lodge (at the bottom of Jersey Cream Express and Glacier Express) and the Crystal Hut, a cabin at the top of the Crystal Chair Express: the last is one of the best options, and deservedly popular at lunch. On Whistler Mountain, the Chic Pea (top of Garbanzo Express) is a nice cabin for snacks and light meals, and has a sunny terrace; the Raven's Nest café-deli (top of the Creekside Gondola) also has a fantastic panoramic patio.

Araxi's Restaurant 4222 Village Square ⓣ604/932-4540, ⓦwww.araxi.com. A top-rated restaurant of long standing that serves up expensive Italian and West Coast-style food, with inventive pasta and very high-quality seafood bar and dishes – try the amazing mussels in chilli, vermouth and lemongrass followed by a perfect crème brûlée for dessert. The wine list runs to 27 pages and 12,000 bottles, but there's a good choice of wines by the glass. A meal for two here will cost $80-plus, with mains from about $30 – expensive, but you're paying for probably the best food in town.

Bearfoot Bistro 4121 Village Green ⓣ604/932-3433, ⓦww.bearfootbistro.com. A few years ago this was a simple French bistro: today it has a reputation of one of Canada's best restaurants, with superlative French food served in a variety of tasting menus (from $90–200-plus) that change from day to day. Reservations are essential.

Black's Restaurant and Pub 4270 Mountain Square ⓣ604/932-6408. Pizza, pasta and other slightly over-priced Mediterranean food (mains $10 and up) are the staples here, but it's the snug bar, *Black's Pub*, upstairs that provides the lure for most people here.

Caramba! Restaurante 12-4314 Main St ⓣ604/938-1879, ⓦwww.caramba-restaurante.com. On the face of it, the Mediterranean food in this casual but buzzy Lower Village spot – pastas, pizzas, roast meats – might seem unremarkable, but the regular queues out of the door bear witness to the quality of the food and dining experience. Main courses start at about $12, but run as high as $32.

Cittas Bistro Village Square ⓣ604/932-4177, ⓦwww.cittabistro.com. *Citta's* – pronounced "Cheetas" – is an American-style bistro offering a predictable but well-prepared variety of pizzas, gourmet burgers and the like at fair prices – main courses range from about $12–17, pizzas from $12.50. It opens at 11am and closes at 1am, which means it is also a busy and appealing late-night spot. During the day, the terrace, with its umbrella tables, is a great place for people-watching. At the time of publication, there was a chance *Cittas* would lose its lease and have to close, so check for the latest.

Ingrid's Village Café 4305 Skiers Approach-Village Square ⓣ604/932-7000, ⓦwww.ingridswhistler.com. *Ingrid's* is a favourite among locals and resort workers for breakfast (it opens 7am–6pm, later if busy), coffee and snacks. Prices are fair – the daily soup special will cost around $6.50,a veggie burger a dollar or so more – and the quality good.

Rim Rock Café & Oyster Bar 2117 Whistler Rd. ⓣ604/932-5565, ⓦwww.rimrockwhistler.com. This place is excellent for seafood, and for the traditional log-cabin-style atmosphere created by the long, narrow room and redoubtable fireplace at one end. Oysters are predictably good – try them in the house style: broiled with béchamel sauce and smoked salmon. Expect to pay between $20–40 for main courses.

Nightlife

Winter or summer, Whistler enjoys a lot of **nightlife** and après-ski activity, with visitors being bolstered by the large seasonal workforce. Like restaurants, clubs can come and go, but certain places have established well-defined niches on the nightlife circuit. These include Moe Joe's, Buffalo Bill's, Savage Beagle and Tommy Africa's for dancing (and more) and the Boot Pub, Crabshack and Dubh Linn Gate for live music. For peace and quiet, hit any of the bars and lounges in the luxury hotels such as the *Four Seasons* and *Fairmont Château Whistler* hotel. Note that some clubs may charge a cover on busy night, or for live music – anything from $10 to $30.

Boot Pub 7124 Nancy Greene Drive ⓣ604/932-3338. There's beer, live music some nights (generally Sun & Mon) and various other stage "shows" or dubious import on other nights. You might not like it, but it's a local institution.

Buffalo Bills Bar & Grill ⓣ604/932-6613 Across from the Whistler gondola, is a thirty-something bar/club with comedy nights, hypnosis shows, video screens, a moderate dance floor and live music.

Dubh Linn Gate Pan Pacific Mountainside, 4320 Sundial Crescent ⓣ604/905-4047, ⓦwww.dubhlinngate.com. An "Irish" pub with Whistler's largest selection of whiskies and draught beers, plus live modern and traditional Irish music every night (no cover charge).

Garfinkels Club 1-4308 Main St, Village North ⓣ604/932-2323, ⓦwww.garfswhistler.com. If you fancy yourself hip, are over 20 but under 25, and don't mind sports bars, then "Garf's" is for you. It's a good dance place week round, but Thurs is the big night, with indie, funk and classic dance tracks.

Longhorn Saloon and Grill 4280 Mountain Square ⓣ604/932-5999, ⓦwww.longhornsaloon.ca. Its position near the lifts make the Longhorn an obvious après-ski favourite, but don't expect too much beyond that, sports TV aside. Particularly lively on Sun.

Merlin's ⓣ604/938-7700. A lively and beer-heavy place in the Blackcomb Daylodge near the Wizard skilift and Blackcomb Mountain base. It has a good patio, with plenty of après-ski eating and cheap drinking options. Later, things liven up with a staff that "encourages bar-top dancing", live music some nights, theme parties, karaoke and pay-per-view sports on a giant screen. Popular with resort workers.

Moe Joe's 4115 Golfer's Approach ⓣ604/935-1152, ⓦwww.moejoes.com. Fri nights are popular at *Moe Joe's*, one of the best places in Whistler for dancing. It's smaller and more intimate than *Garf's* (see opposite) but attracts a similar clientele and espouses a similar musical policy.

Savage Beagle 4222 Village Stroll ⓣ604/938-3337, ⓦwww.savagebeagle.com. Like *Buffalo Bills*, the long-established and split-level *Savage Beagle* appeals to a slightly older, 30-something crowd, with a good little pub upstairs (with a great selection of drinks) and a dance floor downstairs. Tues is the key night.

Tommy Africa's 4216 Gateway Drive ⓣ604/932-6090, ⓦwww.tommyafricas.com. "Tommy's" is the best-known dance club in the Village and usually the most musically adventurous. The big night here is Mon.

The Sunshine Coast

A mild-weathered stretch of sandy beaches, rugged headlands and quiet lagoons running northwest of Vancouver, the **Sunshine Coast** receives heavy promotion – and heavy tourist traffic as a result – though in truth its reputation is considerably overstated and the scenic rewards are slim compared to the grandeur of the BC interior. Even as a taste of the province's mountain scenery it leaves much to be desired, and the best that can be said of the region is that in summer it offers some of western Canada's best diving, boating and fishing. If you are just coming out for the day, the best parts of the trip are the various **ferry crossings** en route: the first is from Horseshoe Bay at the western extreme of West Vancouver to Langdale and Gibsons Landing, where you pick up Hwy 101 for

the 79-kilometre run along the coast to Earl's Cove, and the beautiful (and slightly longer) crossing to Saltery Bay, where the boat provides views of some fine maritime landscapes. The road then continues 35km to Powell River before coming to an abrupt conclusion 23km later at the village of Lund.

Highway 101

Highway 101 runs almost the length of the coast from Gibsons Landing, often known simply as Gibsons, which is just 5km from the ferry terminal at Langdale for boats coming from **Horseshoe Bay** at the end of Marine Drive and the western edge of West Vancouver. You can reach the ferry terminal here from the city by taking bus #250 or the #257 express westbound from points on West Georgia Street downtown. Given that the coast is hardly worth full-scale exploration by car, and that the two ferry crossings provide two of the trip's highlights, you might consider saving the price of a rental and going by **bus**; it's perfectly feasible to get to **Powell River** in a day. Malaspina Coachlines (Ⓣ1-888/227-8287, Ⓦwww.malaspinacoach.com) runs two buses to Powell River at 8.30am (daily) and at 4.15pm daily except Saturday (5hr 45min; $58 one way). Returns leave at 6.45am daily and 2.45pm Friday to Sunday. Bus tickets include the price of the ferry crossings en route. Buses also run from the airport daily except Saturday at 4pm (6hr 45min; $73).

Gibsons to Powell River

Soon reached and well signposted from North and West Vancouver, **Horseshoe Bay** is the departure point for the first of the Hwy 101 **ferry** crossings, a 30–40-minute passage through the islands of fjord-like Howe Sound. There are regular sailings year-round, and tickets cost $11.85 for adults and $39 for cars: bikes cost $2; all tickets cost a little less outside the late-June to early September peak period. Note that each ticket is valid for one Horseshoe Bay-Langdale (return), Earl's Cove-Saltery Bay (return) or single journeys on both the Horseshoe Bay-Langdale and Earl's Cove-Saltery Bay crossings. Ferries also ply from here to Nanaimo on Vancouver Island, with hourly sailings in summer and every other hour off-season. Tickets cost $13.50 per adult and $45 for cars (less off-season and less for cars year-round outside weekends). For information on either of these services, contact BC Ferries in Vancouver (Ⓣ604/669-1211, 250/386-3431 or 1-888/223-3779, Ⓦwww.bcferries.com), or pick up a timetable from the Vancouver infocentre.

Gibsons, the terminal on the other side of Howe Sound, is spread widely over a wooded hillside – the nicest area is around the busy marina and public wharf, a better bet if you're pausing than Upper Gibsons a little further down the highway, which is little more than a busy strip. If you have time to kill, check out the town's two modest museums: the **Sunshine Coast Maritime Museum & Archives** on Molly's Lane (June–Aug Tues–Sat 10.30am–4.30pm; free; Ⓦwww.sunshinecoastmuseum.ca), which contains predictable displays of maritime and frontier memorabilia. For more on the town and details of local trails, beaches and swimming areas, visit the **infocentre** at 417 Marine Drive (daily 9am–6pm; Ⓣ604/886-2374 or 1-866/222-3806, Ⓦwww.gibsonschamber.com).

Farther west on Hwy 101 is Pender Harbour, a string of small coastal communities of which **Madeira Park** is the most substantial; whales occasionally pass this section of coast – which, sadly, is the source of many global aquariums' whales – but the main draws are fishing and boating. **Earl's Cove** is nothing but the departure ramp of the second ferry hop – a longer crossing (45min) that again offers fantastic views, including an immense waterfall that drops off a "Lost World"-type plateau into the sea.

Outdoor activities

In addition to skiing (see p.244) and mountain biking (see p.246), Whistler offers a wealth of **outdoor activities** year-round. For further information on the activities below, contact the various visitor centres (see p.241) or visit ⓦwww.whistler.com, which can book and advise on most activities. Numerous **rental outlets** around the resort provide bikes, blades and other equipment.

Hiking

You can ride the ski lifts up both mountains for tremendous views and easy access to high-altitude **walking** trails (June to early Sept daily 10am–8pm, early Sept to late Sept daily 10am–5pm, late Sept to mid-Oct Sat & Sun only 10am–5pm; lift passes $41.95 or $39.95 bought online).

Pick up the sheet of hiking trails from the infocentres (see p.241), or better yet buy the 1:50,000 *Whistler and Garibaldi Region* **map**. The two most popular high-level day walks are the **Rainbow Falls** and **Singing Pass** trails (both five to six hours). Other good choices are the easy and mostly level 4km trail to Cheakamus Lake or any of the high-alpine hikes accessed from the Upper Gondola station (1837m) on Whistler Mountain or the Seventh Heaven lift on Blackcomb. Among the eight walks from Whistler Mountain gondola station, consider the **Glacier Trail** (2.5km round trip; 85m ascent; 1hr) for views of the snow and ice in Glacier Bowl. The slightly more challenging **Little Whistler Trail** (3.8km round trip; 265m ascent; 1hr 30min–2hr) takes you to the summit of Little Whistler Peak (2115m) and gives grand views of Black Tusk in Garibaldi Provincial Park. Remember to time your hike to get back to the gondola station for the last ride down (times vary according to season).

If the high-level hiking seems too daunting (it shouldn't be – the trails are all very good and most are less than 5km – then there are plenty of trails (some surfaced) for bikers, walkers and in-line skaters around the Village. The **Valley Trail** system starts on the west side of Hwy 99 by the Whistler Park Golf Course and takes you through parks, golf courses and peaceful residential areas: the 30km of trails on and around **Lost Lake**, entered by the northern end of the Day Skier car park at Blackcomb Mountain, wend through cedar forest and past lakes and creeks; the eponymous lake is just over a kilometre from the main trailhead. There are also numerous operators offering guided walks to suit all abilities.

Other summer activities

Between May and September, Whistler River Adventures (ⓣ604/932-3532 or 1-888/932-3532, ⓦwww.whistlerriver.com; from $109 for a three-hour trip, one hour on the water) has **jet boating** on the Green River to below the Nairn Falls, with a good chance of spotting wildlife such as moose and bears. It also has a range of **rafting** trips from gentle to extreme priced from $89 for four-hour trips (one hour on the river): beginners are taken to the Green River, while experts can plump for the Class-IV thrills of the Elaho or Squamish River rapids. Bear in mind, though, that it can take two hours round-trip just to reach the water: only three hours of the six-hour ride, for example, are spent on the river. The same company offers half- and full-day catch-and-release **fishing** trips in surrounding rivers from about $150 per person.

If you want to **rock climb**, visit Whistler Core at the Whistler Conference Centre (ⓣ604/905-7625, ⓦwww.whistlercore.com; daily 10am–10pm, except autumn noon-9pm) which offers indoor facilities for climbing year-round and an outdoor summer climbing wall. A day's drop-in indoor climbing costs $17.50. A variety of guides and guided tours are available from $175 for a half-day climb.

From Jervis Bay, the opposite landing stage, it's a couple of kilometres up the road to the best of all the provincial parks in this region, **Saltery Bay Provincial Park**. Everything here is discreetly hidden in the trees between the road and the coast, and the campsite ($15) – beautifully situated – is connected by short trails to a couple of

You can **play tennis** at several public courts, or ask at the visitor centre for details of hotels such as the *Delta Whistler Resort*, *Fairmont Château Whistler* and *Château Whistler Resort* that allow players to use their courts and provide racket rental (from $10 an hour). Free public courts (ⓣ604/938-7529), include Meadow Park Sports Centre Myrtle Public School, Brio, Blackcomb Benchlands, White Gold, Emerald Park, Miller's Pond and Alpha Lake Park. The *Whistler Racquet & Golf Resort*, 4500 Northland Blvd (ⓣ604/932-1991, ⓦwww.whistlertennis.com) has three indoor and seven outdoor courts open to drop-in players from $16 an hour outdoor, $32 indoor. It also offers summer three-day camps for adults and children in summer, but they fill quickly, so book early.

The area has four great **golf** courses, including one designed by Jack Nicklaus. For further information on all, visit ⓦwww.golfbc.com. Despite a recent upgrade, the Whistler Golf Club course remains the cheapest to play, ranging from $75 in spring to $119 (ⓣ1-800/376-1777 or 604/932-4544), while the others, including Nicklaus North (ⓣ604/938-9898), cost from about $115 to $175. After any of these activities there are umpteen **spas** for massage, mud baths and treatments that soothe all aches and pains – for utter luxury – the top-of-the-range spa at the *Fairmont Château Whistler* (ⓣ604/938-2086, ⓦwww.fairmont.com).

Winter activities

Snowshoe rental and tours are available to get you across some of the safer snowfields in summer. For **snowshoe tours** for novices contact Outdoor Adventures@Whistler (ⓣ604/932-0647, ⓦwww.adventureswhistler.com; from $79 for 90 minutes' snowshoeing or $109 for an evening tour by Green Lake followed by dinner).

For gentle **sleigh rides**, contact Blackcomb Horsedrawn Sleigh Rides (ⓣ604/932-7631, ⓦwww.blackcombsleighrides.com). It offers a range of tours with or without lunch or dinner, with four tours (hourly from 5pm) every evening in winter ($55 for 40–50 min) and follow the ski trails to the woods for great views and a stop in a cabin for a mug of hot chocolate. For $105 you get a sleigh ride and dinner.

You can ride **snowmobiles** with Outdoor Adventures (see above) or Blackcomb Snowmobile (ⓣ604/932-8484, ⓦwww.blackcombsnowmobile.com). The trips are a 15-minute road transfer south of Whistler and you can choose between two- and three-hour rides in Family, Scenic, Wilderness, Extreme and Fondue (dinner included) categories. Two-hour Scenic rides (five daily) cost $129 for a single driver, $99 per person for two sharing (driver and passenger); three daily 3-hour trips cost $169/129. Children under 12 go free on Family tours. Similar tours and prices, including Family tours, are offered by Canadian Snowmobile Adventures (ⓣ604/938-1616, ⓦwww.canadiansnowmobile.com), weather allowing. Two-hour rides in the Fitzsimmons Creek area start from $125 and $99 for a passenger; three-hour "Mountain Safari" trips on Blackcomb Mountain cost from $159 and $125 respectively.

Blackcomb Snowmobile also offers a range of **dog-sled rides**: the "Mountain Mushing" tour (4 daily, 2hr 30min) costs $145.

If you want some **cross-country skiing**, the best spots are the 32km of groomed trails around Lost Lake and the *Château Whistler* golf course, all very easily accessible from Whistler Village, beginning just a block from the Blackcomb Mountain car park. The routes are suitable for beginners to experts and are groomed and patrolled. The visitor centre and resort websites have lots more background information. Visit ⓦwww.crosscountryconnection.com for more details and rental information.

swimming beaches. Farther along on the main road, the standout accommodation is the big *Oceanside Resort Motel* site which also has 11 cabins, 7km short of Powell River, which sits on a superb piece of shoreline (ⓣ604/485-2435 or 1-888/889-2435, ⓦwww.oceansidepark.com; ❸).

Powell River and beyond

Given its seafront location, **Powell River** has its scenic side, but like many a BC town its unfocused sprawl and nearby sawmill slightly dampen the overall appeal. If you're catching the **ferry** to Courtenay on Vancouver Island (4 daily; 75min), you might not see the town site, as the terminal is 2km to the east at Westview, and some of the **buses** from Vancouver are timed to coincide with the boats; if your bus doesn't connect, you can either walk from the town centre or bus terminal or call a taxi (Ⓣ604/483-3666). The local **infocentre** (summer daily 9am–5pm, winter Mon–Fri 9am–5pm; Ⓣ604/485-4701 or 1-877/817-8669, Ⓦwww.discoverpowellriver.com), which is at 111-4871 Joyce Ave, can supply a visitors' map showing the many trails leading inland from the coast hereabouts; they can also advise on boat trips on Powell Lake, immediately inland, and tours to Desolation Sound farther up the coast. The most central of several **campsites** is the 81-site *Willingdon Beach Municipal Campground* on the seafront off Marine Avenue at 6910 Duncan St (Ⓣ604/485-2242, Ⓦwww.willingdonbeach.ca; tent $17.50, RV $24).

The northern end-point of Hwy 101 – which, incidentally, starts in Mexico City, making it one of North America's longest continuous routes – is the hamlet of **Lund**, 28km up the coast from Powell River. **Desolation Sound Marine Provincial Park**, about 10km north of Lund, offers some of Canada's best boating and scuba diving, plus fishing, canoeing and kayaking. There's no road access to the park, but a number of outfitters in Powell River run tours to it and can hire all the equipment you could possibly need – try Westview Live Bait Ltd, 4527 Marine Ave, for **canoes**; Coulter's Diving, 4557 Willingdon Ave, for **scuba gear**; and Spokes, 4710 Marine Drive for **bicycles**. The more modest **Okeover Provincial Park**, immediately north of Lund, has an unserviced campsite ($15).

Contexts

Contexts

History

The following account provides a brief overview of Vancouver's history, from centuries of slow – or no – development to its relatively rapid rise in the last 130-plus years. For further reading on the city's background, check out the books listed on p.263.

Beginnings and early inhabitants

The area's **first inhabitants** probably arrived some 10,000 years ago, Asiatic peoples who crossed a land bridge which then existed across the present-day Bering Strait. From here they drifted southwards, evolving eventually into a variety of geographically distinct and culturally advanced peoples.

On the banks of the Fraser, the river which flows into the Pacific south of modern-day Vancouver, the ancient indigenous population was known as the **Stó:lo**, or "People of the River", a grouping of the Tsawwassen, Musqueam and another twenty or so peoples who probably consolidated their presence on Vancouver's Burrard Inlet around 3000 BC.

A highly developed people, the Stó:lo were skilled carpenters, canoe-makers and artists, although little in modern Vancouver – outside the city's museums – pays anything but lip service to their existence. They lived off the bounty of the sea and river – rich in salmon, shellfish, sturgeon and the like – and led more sedentary lives than the mostly nomadic peoples of the North American interior. They also hunted for deer, elk, bears and other animals, and gathered berries, fruit, roots and the *wapato*, a tuber that grew along the banks of the Fraser.

By about the eighteenth century, the area's indigenous groups lived in parts of what would become Greater Vancouver. Richmond and the Fraser delta were home to the Tsawwassen – the name now given to the city's principal ferry terminal. New Westminster was the preserve of the Kwantlen, while much of North Vancouver belonged to the Tsleil'waututh. The Squamish lived in villages on Howe Sound, Stanley Park, Jericho Beach, Kitsilano and North and West Vancouver. Other key areas in the modern city, like Locarno Beach and the North Shore east of the Capilano River, were largely occupied by the Coast Salish, who in turn divided into smaller tribes such as the Cowichan, Nanaimo and Saanich.

The first Europeans

Probably the first European to see the British Columbian coast was the British explorer **Sir Francis Drake** during a round-the-world voyage in 1579. The first recorded landing – at Nootka Sound on Vancouver Island – was made in 1778 by another Briton, **Sir James Cook**, during a voyage that took him up the Pacific coast from Oregon to Alaska. Ignorant of the area's true geography, Cook mistook Vancouver Island for the North American mainland. Mistaken or not, the mariner succeeded in sparking immediate British interest in the region.

The next fifteen years saw a variety of British, Spanish and French contacts with the area, all of which were prompted by the search for gold, new territory and improved trade routes, in particular the elusive Northwest Passage, the sea route across the roof of the American continent (see p.82). The Spanish dispatched three

expeditions to the region between 1774 and 1779, and it may be that **Juan Perez Hernandez**, captain on one of these missions, dropped anchor off Vancouver Island in 1774. In 1790, another Spaniard, the explorer Manuel Quimper, encountered the Songhees, a Coast Salish people, and apparently attempted to claim their land for Spain. In 1791, yet another Spaniard, **José María Narváez**, a Spanish pilot and surveyor, glimpsed the mouth of the Fraser from his ship, the *Santa Saturnia*. He also sailed into Burrard Inlet, but stopped short of what is today the inner harbour, mistaking Point Grey for a group of islands, which he christened the Islas de Langara.

Britain's interests at the time were represented by **George Vancouver**, a midshipman who had served under Cook in 1774, but who, by 1792, was a captain in command of his own ships, the *Chatham* and *Discovery*. Both vessels were engaged in mapping parts of the North American Pacific coast, a task that saw them shadowed by two Spanish ships under Dionisio Alcalá Galiano, with whom Vancouver pooled information. Vancouver eventually stumbled across the mouth of the Fraser, which he officially claimed for Britain in 1792. After studying the delta from a small boat, however, he deemed it too shallow to be of practical use.

Instead, he rounded a headland to the north, sailing into a deep natural port – the future site of Vancouver – which he named Burrard after one of his crew. He then traded briefly with the Squamish at X'ay'xi, a village on the inlet's forested headland – the future Stanley Park. The Squamish named the spot Whul-whul-Lay-ton, or "place of the white man". Vancouver then met Galiano and sailed on, having spent just a day in the region – scant homage to an area that would be named after him a century later.

Fur traders

What might have become long-running disputes between Britain and Spain over the region were settled in Britain's favour when Spain became domestically embroiled in the aftermath of the French Revolution. Exploration of the coast gave way to the exploration of the Canadian interior, prompted by the search for an easier route to export furs westwards to the Pacific instead of the arduous haul eastwards across the continent. **Alexander Mackenzie** of the North West Company, one of the great fur-trading companies of the day, made the first crossing of North America north of Mexico in 1793. He was followed by two further adventurers, Scottish-born explorers **Simon Fraser** (1776–1862) and **David Thompson** (1770–1857), whose names resonate as sobriquets for rivers, shops, motels and streets in Vancouver and elsewhere in British Columbia.

Fraser uncovered George Vancouver's error with regard to the Fraser River in 1808, when he made an epic 368-kilometre journey down the river from the Rockies to the sea. With the benefit of hindsight, this was one of the greatest feats in the annals of North American exploration, though Fraser – who had thought he was following the Columbia River – deemed the venture a failure. Nor did he travel the short distance north from the river's mouth to Burrard Inlet – not least because on emerging at the mouth of the river he was chased back upstream by the Musqueam.

In 1827, another fur-trading company, the **Hudson's Bay Company**, established a trading post at Fort Langley on the Fraser 48km from the sea – the area's first permanent European settlement. The post traded as far afield as Hawaii, but by 1839 had been abandoned for a more favourable site 35km upriver, where a reconstructed trading post survives to this day. Neither post, however, attempted to attract permanent homesteaders, the Hudson's Bay Company deciding that the presence of settlers would be detrimental to fur and other trades.

Victoria

The area that would become Vancouver remained a mixture of forest and aboriginal villages for the next twenty years, during which time the historical focus shifted to **Victoria** on Vancouver Island. Victoria received some of its earliest **white visitors** after 1842 when James Douglas, the Hudson's Bay Company's chief factor, founded Fort Camouson on the city's present site. The name was later changed to Fort Victoria to honour the British queen (see p.211 for more on Victoria's history).

The fort blossomed, attracting European immigrants, though the new settlement – like much of western Canada – remained a virtual fiefdom of the Hudson's Bay Company. The company's monopoly, among other things, antagonized the Americans and led to a flurry of diplomatic activity that persuaded the British to formalize its claims to the region in order to forestall American expansion. In 1846 the **Oregon Treaty** set the 49th parallel as the national boundary between the two areas. Vancouver Island, however, which lies partly south of the line, remained wholly British and was designated a crown colony in 1849.

Despite the treaty and the involvement of the Crown, the "Bay" still reigned in all but name and took no interest in promoting immigration; as late as 1855 the island's white population numbered only 774. As for the mainland – and what would become Vancouver – it remained almost unknown except to trappers and the odd prospector.

The gold rush

The event that transformed Victoria and led directly to the creation of Vancouver was the **discovery of gold**, first on the Fraser River in 1858 and then in the Cariboo region of British Columbia three years later. Some 30,000 prospectors, many of them old-timers from the California gold rush of 1849, surged to the area, heading first to Victoria to pick up supplies and then to the mainland for the trip up the Fraser. James Douglas, still Victoria's effective ruler, enlisted the support of the British government to control the influx, half-afraid that the Americans would use it as an excuse to expand territorially to the north. As a precautionary measure Britain declared the mainland north of the 49th parallel a crown colony, lending it the same status as Vancouver Island.

At the same time, the British government made available a detachment of the Royal Engineers under Colonel Richard Moody to build roads and a military garrison to keep watch on the flood of prospectors. Moody took one look at Fort Langley and decided its position was ill-suited to the task. Instead, he built a fort on the Fraser at **New Westminster** (now a southern suburb of Vancouver), which was then declared capital of British Columbia. The future downtown area of Vancouver remained no more than a tract of forest on the Burrard Inlet to the north.

All that began to change in 1859, when a trail – today's North Road – was blazed between New Westminster and the Burrard Inlet to provide guaranteed access to an ice-free harbour. In the same year, a British survey ship discovered coal on Burrard Inlet (at a spot still known as Coal Harbour). Another trail – which followed roughly the route of present-day Kingsway – was then cut in 1860 to link New Westminster and False Creek. Most development, however, continued on and around the Fraser, where the first saw mills were established in 1860.

Development of sorts began on the southern shore of **Burrard Inlet** in 1862, when three failed British prospectors – the so-called "Three Greenhorns" – bought

500 acres of land at $1.01 an acre with a view to founding a brickworks. This was a doomed idea, given the amount of timber around, and the project duly failed, as did the trio's attempts to develop the land for housing. Today the land is occupied by the West End and includes some of the most expensive real estate in North America.

By 1865 the gold rush was all but dead. A year later, the crown colonies of British Columbia and Vancouver Island were merged under the name **British Columbia**. New Westminster remained its capital. In 1867 the Dominion of Canada was created, a union of many of the British colonies and territories in eastern and central Canada. British Columbia, fearful it might eventually be absorbed by the United States, was brought into the new **Confederation of Canada** in 1871 with the promise of a transcontinental railway. **Port Moody**, a thriving settlement based around a sawmill at the eastern end of the Burrard Inlet, was earmarked as its eastern terminus. The railway, however, would take fifteen years to materialize.

Meanwhile, in 1867, the British entrepreneur Edward Stamp established **Hasting Mill** on the south shore of Burrard Inlet, one of the two seeds from which Vancouver would spring. The other was a tavern established close to the mill by one **"Gassy" Jack Deighton** (see p.53), around which a shantytown quickly developed, the site of which is now occupied by **Gastown**. In 1869, the settlement was incorporated as the town of **Granville**, the sum total of which amounted to six saloons, three hotels and a hardware store. The "town" prospered quietly for the next fifteen years on the back of its timber and modest coal deposits. Port Moody also continued to grow – in 1882 it gained the first electric lights north of San Francisco.

The railway and the Great Fire

By 1884 the long-promised transcontinental **Canadian Pacific Railway** (CPR) was within striking distance of Canada's west coast. Port Moody, however, would not be its terminus. Railway executives discovered the port was too small to handle the large ships that could be expected to dock once the railway was completed. Instead they chose an area 25km closer to the open sea – Granville – a decision that proved to be the turning point in Vancouver's history. The fact that the government granted the company 6000 acres of what everyone knew would become prime real estate was not entirely unconnected with the decision. Nor was the fact that various CPR executives already owned land near Granville.

The extent to which the CPR was influential in local affairs – much as the Hudson's Bay Company had been years earlier – was further illustrated when the company came up with a new name for Granville. The story goes that William Cornelius Van Horne, the CPR's larger-than-life vice-president, was being rowed around along the shore of the future Stanley Park when he decided the railway's terminus needed a more marketable name if visitors, businesses and immigrants were to be attracted to the new city. On April 6, 1886, the town of Granville – population 400 – was duly incorporated as the **City of Vancouver**.

Just three months later, on July 13, the entire "city" burned to the ground, the so-called **Great Fire** consuming Vancouver's 1000 or so wooden buildings in less than forty-five minutes. Twenty-eight people were killed and many left homeless. Rebuilding began almost immediately, this time using stone and brick, and by the end of the year, 800 buildings had risen from the ashes, many of which can still be seen in Gastown. In the same month, the first CPR train pulled into Port Moody – the track to Vancouver not being complete – and the Port of Vancouver received its first shipment: a consignment of tea from China. The next year saw the first CPR train complete the transcontinental journey to Vancouver.

The new city

The arrival of the railway changed everything. Within four years the city's population had soared from 400 to 13,000, and between 1891 and 1901 it grew to 29,000: in 1895 it surpassed that of Victoria for the first time. The CPR continued to shape the new city, developing the port and building swaths of residential housing in what would become the West End, Kitsilano and Shaughnessy Heights. The last was nicknamed "CPR Heaven" and was aimed at the city's new upper class, with the exception of Jews and Asians – the deeds of sale in CPR houses forbade the resale of property to either group. The company also built **Granville Street**, still one of the city's main thoroughfares, and paved Pender and Hastings streets. The port boomed, growing rich on shipments of local timber and vast supplies of wheat from the Canadian interior. So, too, did the population, bolstered by the arrival of **immigrants** from both Asia and Europe, immigration being a feature of the city that has continued, though not without problems, to the present day (see p.58).

Change continued apace. In 1901 the first proper **ferry services** began between Tsawwassen and Sidney on Vancouver Island. In 1908 the University of British Columbia was founded. Six years later, the opening of the Panama Canal – a major boost for the city – provided a quicker route to Europe for ships carrying Canadian wheat. By 1929 Vancouver's population was 80,000, making it Canada's third-largest city.

More far-flung areas on the north shore of Burrard Inlet were brought within the city's orbit following the opening of the original Second Narrows Bridge in 1925 (see p.96 for more on the history of the North Shore). The **Lions Gate Bridge** – more convenient for the centre of Downtown – was built in 1938 by the Guinness company, mainly to link its large residential developments in North Vancouver to the burgeoning Downtown peninsula. The first transcontinental air service to Montréal began a year later.

Contemporary Vancouver

Subsequent highlights in the city's twentieth-century history included the 1954 **British Empire Games**, a sporting forerunner of the Commonwealth Games. It was notable for being the first time two runners (Britain's Roger Bannister and the Australian John Landy) ran a mile in under four minutes; it was also the first sporting event broadcast live across North America. Also significant were the founding in 1969 of the organization that would become **Greenpeace** and the 1986 world-trade fair known as **Expo '86**, held to commemorate Vancouver's centenary. The latter event attracted 21 million visitors and considerably heightened Vancouver's profile on the world stage. A similarly high profile was achieved in 1993 and 1997, when the city hosted peace summits between presidents Clinton and Yeltsin.

Tourism to the city has benefited from such exposure, and is worth an estimated $4 billion a year and rising. Not that Vancouver, a city with a good economy and one of the five largest ports in the western hemisphere, needs tourism to survive. While factories and sawmills may occasionally close, the city now has a thriving **TV and movie industry** – launched partly on the back of *The X-Files*, the early seasons of which were filmed here – and a host of multimedia, software and service industries (see p.164 for more on film and TV production in the city).

Visitors to the city cannot help but notice the knock-on effects of its healthy economy, especially on the southern fringes of Downtown at False Creek, where dozens of high-rise condominiums are rising from formerly derelict railway yards. Nor, however, can they fail to notice the poverty and run-down neighbourhoods east of Downtown on and around Hastings Street, the most obvious blight on contemporary Vancouver. After years of talking but no action, it was the feeling that something needed to be done about this area – among other things – that helped **Larry Campbell** become mayor of Vancouver in November 2002.

Campbell had been involved with the BC Coroners' Office for twenty years, and had witnessed first-hand the deadly effects of the area's drug culture and other social problems. During 2003 concerted efforts were made by the police, welfare officers and other agencies to start tackling the issues. Campbell is no longer mayor, but results have been achieved, though at what cost remains to be seen, because representatives of the mostly affluent West End district of Downtown have since begun to complain that the drug dealers and others forced out of the city's eastern margins are now appearing on their own streets, and Davie and Denman in particular.

Vancouver's recent history has been dominated by one event, the **XXI Olympic Winter Games**, held in the city in February 2010. A long saga of defeated or stalled bids culminated in the city's successful $34 million bid in 2003, defeating Pyeongchang in South Korea and Salzburg. Behind the bid, among other things, was the memory of Expo '86, which greatly raised Vancouver's international profile, but also resulted in a property and commercial boom that bought considerable economic benefits to some in the city.

Crucially, however, not everyone was behind the bid – a citywide plebiscite in 2003 voted only 64 percent in favour. Notwithstanding the cost (estimated at $5–6 billion, with $1 billion on security alone), proponents of the Games claim considerable economic and infrastructure benefits. These include the new SkyTrain link between Richmond, the international airport and Downtown, and the upgraded Sea to Sky Highway that links Vancouver to Whistler. Numerous sports facilities were built or improved, including a $16.6 million upgrade for the Cypress Mountain resort (see p.59).

Behind these apparent triumphs, though, lurked murkier events. Chief among these were the driving of the Sea to Sky Highway through Eagleridge Bluffs in West Vancouver (despite much local resistance), an area of considerable environmental importance; the heavy-handed work of the organizing committee in dealing with local businesses to protect its "brand"; the opposition of some aboriginal groups to the Games; and – above all – the fact that at the time of publication, the amount of social housing promised as a legacy of the main Olympic Village, on the south shore of False Creek, seems unlikely to materialize.

Whatever the Games' legacy, or the controversy that inevitably surrounded it, Vancouver's continued good health seems assured. Figures from the census of 2011 will doubtless show the continued growth of both Greater Vancouver (with a population of 1,986,965 in the census of 2001) and the City of Vancouver (514,008). These and other figures suggest Vancouver is the fastest-growing metropolitan area in Canada, faster even than Toronto. Not only fastest growing, but also one of the most prestigious: year after year, social and other indices, and plaudits from international social commentators, suggest Vancouver is one of the best cities in the world in which to live. Not bad for a place that around 135 years ago was little more than a clearing in the wilderness.

Aboriginal cultures

Though few visible traces remain in modern Vancouver, aboriginal cultures have played an undeniable role in shaping the progress and development of the area. In particular, of all Canada's aboriginal peoples, the numerous linguistic groups that once inhabited – and in some cases still inhabit – Vancouver, Vancouver Island and parts of the northwest coast of British Columbia have the most sophisticated artistic tradition and the most lavish of ceremonials, a legacy well worth searching out.

Organization and ritual

Traditionally these groups' social organization stemmed from a belief in a mythical time when humans and animals were essentially the same: each tribe was divided into **kin groups** who were linked by a common supernatural animal ancestor and shared the same names, ritual dances, songs and regalia. Seniority within each kin group was held by a rank of chiefs and nobles, who controlled the resources of private property such as house sites; stands of cedar; and fishing, gathering and hunting territories.

Such privileges, almost unique among Canadian aboriginal groups, led to the accumulation of private wealth, and thus great emphasis was placed on their inheritance. Central to the power structure was the ceremonial **potlatch**, which was held in the winter village, a seasonal resting place for these otherwise nomadic people, located where the supernatural forces were believed to be most accessible. The potlatch marked every significant occasion from the birth of an heir to the raising of a carved pole, and underscored an individual's right to his or her inherited status. Taking its name from the Chinook word for "gift", the potlatch also had the function of **redistributing wealth**. All the guests at the potlatch acted as witnesses to whatever event or object was being validated, and were repaid for their services with gifts from the host chief. Though these gifts often temporarily bankrupted the host, they heightened his prestige and ensured that he would be repaid in kind at a subsequent potlatch.

The most important element of potlatches was the **masked dance**, which re-enacted ancestral encounters with supernatural beings and was the principal means of perpetuating the history and heritage of each kin group. Created by artists whose innovative ideas were eagerly sought by chiefs in order to impress their guests, the dramatic masks were often elaborate mechanisms that could burst open to reveal the wearer or – as was the case with the well-known Cannibal Bird – produce loud and disconcerting noises.

The **Kwakiutl** produced the most developed potlatches, featuring highly ranked dances like the *hamatsa*, or "**cannibal dance**", whose performers had served long apprenticeships as participants in less exalted dances. Before the *hamatsa*, the initiate was sent to the "Cannibal at the North End of the World", a long period of seclusion and instruction in the snowbound woods. On returning to the village he would seem to be in a complete cannibalistic frenzy and would rush around biting members of the audience. These apparent victims were all paid for their role, which usually involved cutting themselves with knives to draw a flow of blood – and the protagonist of the *hamatsa* would burst blood-filled bladders in his mouth to add to the carnage, while relatives shook rattles and sang to tame him. A fantastic finale came with the arrival of the loudly clacking "Cannibal Birds",

dancers dressed in long strips of cedar bark and huge masks, of which the most fearsome was the "Cannibal Raven", whose long straight beak could crush a human skull. The *hamatsa* would then return in ceremonial finery completely restored to his human state.

Foreign contact and consequences

As elsewhere in Canada, **European contact** was disastrous for the coastal peoples. The establishment of fur-trading posts in the early nineteenth century led to the abandonment of traditional economic cycles, the loss of natives' creative skills through reliance on readily available European goods, the debilitation from alcohol and internecine wars. Though most of BC remains non-treaty, lands on Vancouver Island were surrendered to become the "Entire property of the White people forever" in return for small payments – the whole Victoria area was obtained for 371 blankets. Infectious disease, the greatest of all threats, reached its peak with the 1862 smallpox epidemic, which spread from Victoria along the entire coast and far into the interior, killing probably a third of BC's aboriginal population.

In this period of decline, potlatches assumed an increased significance as virtually the only medium of cultural continuity, with rival chiefs asserting their status through ever more extravagant displays – even going as far as to burn slaves who had been captured in battle. Excesses such as these and the newly adopted "whiskey feasts" were seen by the **missionaries** as a confirmation that these peoples were enveloped in the "dark mantle of degrading superstition". With BC's entry into confederation the responsibility for the natives fell to the federal government in faraway Ottawa, much of whose knowledge of the indigenous peoples came from the missionaries – the subsequent **Indian Act**, passed in 1884, prohibited the potlatch ceremony.

For a while the defiant aboriginal groups managed to evade detection by holding potlatches at fishing camps rather than the winter villages, and there were few successful prosecutions until the 1920s. Things came to a head in 1922 with the conviction of 34 Kwakiutl from Alert Bay – all were sentenced to jail terms but a deal was struck whereby all those who surrendered their potlatch regalia were freed. Thirty years later, when potlatching was again legalized, aboriginal pressure began to mount for return of these treasures from the collections into which they had been dispersed, but it took a further twenty years for the federal government to agree to return the goods on condition that they be put on public display. Though the masks totally lose their dramatic emphasis in static exhibitions, many of the more local museums have a dual function as community centres, and as such are vital to the preservation of a dynamic aboriginal culture.

Books

Most of the following books should be readily available in the UK, US or Canada. We have given publishers for each title, with the UK publisher before the slash and the US publisher after it, unless the book is published in one country only; o/p means out of print. Note that virtually all the listed books published in the US will be stocked by major Canadian bookshops; we've indicated which books are published only in Canada. Books we especially recommend are flagged with the symbol.

Travel, culture and society

Douglas Coupland *City of Glass: Douglas Coupland's Vancouver* (Douglas & McIntyre, Canada). A Vancouver native – and better known for his pop culture treatises like *Generation X* and *Microserfs* – Coupland has put together a slender but rather fey volume that tries hard to be smart about the city's modern society, art and architecture. At least there are plenty of appealing visuals throughout.

Rhodri Windsor Liscombe *The New Spirit: Modern Architecture in Vancouver, 1938–1963* (MIT Press). The architecture examined in this large tome hardly looks modern when set against some of the buildings now going up in the city, but it's a good buy if you want the full story on the period which gave Vancouver many of its extant buildings.

Alan D. McMillan *Native Peoples and Cultures of Canada* (Orca, US). Comprehensive account of Canada's native groups from prehistory to current issues of self-government and land claims. Well-written, though more an academic textbook than a leisure-time read.

Jan Morris *O Canada: Travels in an Unknown Country* (Robert Hale, o/p/ HarperCollins, o/p). Musings from this well-known travel writer after a coast-to-coast Canadian trip.

Dennis Reid *A Concise History of Canadian Painting* (Oxford University Press). Not especially concise, but a thorough trawl through Canada's leading artists, including many you will see in Vancouver's art gallery (see p.46), with bags of biographical detail and lots of black-and-white (and a few colour) illustrations of major works.

Rex Weyler *Greenpeace* (Raincoast Books). Weyler was a founder member and director of the environmental organization Greenpeace, which had its origins in Vancouver and around. This is the definitive account of its birth from someone who was there.

History, art and biography

Pierre Berton Berton is one of Canada's finest writers, and many of his books touch on subjects with a powerful bearing on the history of Vancouver and Victoria: these include *The Last Spike* (Penguin US), an account of the history and building of the transcontinental railway, and *Flames across the Frontier* (Penguin US), episodes from the often uneasy relationship between Canada and the US.

Emily Carr *Growing Pains: The Autobiography of Emily Carr* (Douglas & McIntyre). Painter Emily Carr had an interesting life, to say the least (see p.48 for an abridged version),

travelling to Europe and struggling against the odds to become an artist of international repute. Here, in a book republished in 2005 to take account of the revived interest in a woman whose reputation has fluctuated, is the story through her own eyes. For the last word on the artist, there's *The Complete Writings of Emily Carr* (ed. Doris Shadbolt, University of Washington Press), but at 893 pages it's one for Carr obsessives only.

Paul Kane *Wanderings of an Artist among the Indians of North America* (Dover). Kane, one of Canada's better-known landscape artists, spent two and a half years travelling from Toronto to the Pacific Coast and back in the 1840s. His witty, racy account of his wanderings makes a delightful read.

Robert McDonald *Making Vancouver: 1863–1913* (University of British Columbia Press). A scholarly account of the city during the busiest period in its history.

Peter C. Newman *Caesars of the Wilderness* (Penguin, o/p). Highly acclaimed and readable account of the rise and fall of the Hudson's Bay Company, including material on the history of the company in and around Vancouver.

Doris Shadbolt *The Art of Emily Carr* (Douglas & McIntyre). A definitive account of the work of Emily Carr by the foremost scholar in her field. The same author is also responsible for the notes and annotations in *Seven Journeys: The Sketchbooks of Emily Carr* (University of Washington Press).

Fiction and poetry

Emily Carr *Klee Wyck* (Douglas & McIntyre). Painter Emily Carr took up writing in the last ten years of her life, achieving considerable success, albeit in the limited field of aboriginal culture that distinguishes most of her paintings. Klee Wyck means "Laughing One", the name given to Carr by some of her aboriginal acquaintances. This work, reissued in 2004, repays the compliment, with 21 "word portraits" of various aspects of aboriginal life and culture. See p.48 for more on Carr the artist and above for other books relating to her life and work.

Denise Chong *The Concubine's Children: Portrait of a Family Divided* (Penguin). This acclaimed book is a moving narrative of a Chinese immigrant family in Vancouver. It spans some sixty years and is told in the third person by the granddaughter of Chan Sam, who abandoned China in 1913, leaving one family in the country of his birth and beginning another in his adopted city.

Wayson Choy *The Jade Peony* (Other Press). Choy is now mostly Toronto-based, but he was born in Vancouver in 1939 and published *The Jade Peony*, his first novel, in 1995. Multi-award-winning, the book is a memoir-like family saga set in Vancouver's Chinatown in the 1930s. A sequel, *All That Matters*, continued the story into subsequent decades. Choy has also written his memoirs, *Paper Shadows*.

Douglas Coupland *Jpod* (Bloomsbury). Coupland's latest novel hardly breaks new ground, effectively dealing with the same type of aimless and amoral youngsters he spotlighted in *Generation X* in 1991. This time the feckless anti-heroes are a group of Vancouver game developers who while away their time discussing, among other things, which day of the week is the nicest, the future of breakfast cereals and the possible sexuality of Ronald McDonald.

William Gibson *Spook Country* (Berkley). Gibson settled in Vancouver in 1972, having come from the US to

avoid the Vietnam draft in 1967. Until this, his eighth novel, he had largely avoided writing about his adopted city, and had made his name primarily as a science-fiction writer. *Spook Country* (2007) is a loose follow-up to *Pattern Recognition* (2003), one of the first novels to tackle 9/11, and involves three complex narrative strands that eventually converge on contemporary Vancouver.

Jack Hodgins Hodgins is a prolific and versatile writer of adult and children's fiction (and non-fiction) whose narrative concerns often reach far beyond his native Vancouver Island. Several books, however, reference Victoria and parts of his home island, notably *Innocent Cities* (1990), many of the characters from which are based on actual Victoria residents, while *The Invention of the World* (1977) is based on cult leader Brother Twelve and his followers, who hailed from outside Nanaimo, on Vancouver Island.

Pauline Johnson *Legends of Vancouver* (Dover Publishing). Johnson was born in 1861, part English, part Mohawk, and won considerable acclaim for her ballads and other popular verse, as well as her recitations. She retired to Vancouver in 1909. *Legends of Vancouver*, published two years later, is a collection of local aboriginal myths.

W. P. Kinsella *Shoeless Joe* (Mariner Books). Kinsella was born in the Prairies but now spends most of his time in Vancouver, where he is acclaimed as a writer and raconteur. *Shoeless Joe* is perhaps less well known than the film that it inspired – the baseball fable *Field of Dreams* (1989).

Joy Kogawa *Obasan* (Anchor). Kogawa's Vancouver and western Canadian novel picks up Japanese-Canadian Naomi at the age of 35, and then has her look back at events in the 1940s and onwards, when her mother left Canada to see relatives just before the attack on Pearl Harbor. The mother never returns, and Naomi begins to explore her history, and that of Japanese-Canadians during the war, in a series of narratives, letters, dreams and other devices that reaches a dramatic conclusion.

Jen Sookfong Lee *The End of East* (Thomas Dunne Books). Lee grew up in East Vancouver, and her debut novel, published in 2008, draws on her experience of Chinatown and Canadian-Chinese culture to paint a moving portrait of three generations of a Chinese family, concentrating on the return of the disaffected Sammy Chan to Vancouver. Jobless, and abandoned by her sisters, Chan is forced to confront a future in a city she has come to resent.

Malcolm Lowry *Hear Us O Lord from Heaven Thy Dwelling Place* (Carroll & Graf). Lowry spent almost half his writing life (1939–54) in log cabins and beach houses he built for himself around Vancouver. *Hear Us O Lord* is a difficult read to say the least: a fragmentary novella that, amongst other things, describes a disturbing sojourn on Canada's wild Pacific coast.

Alice Munro Munro is one of the world's finest short-story writers, and has spent periods of her life based in different parts of the city. Several short stories are set in or inspired by areas of the North Shore and Kitsilano, though all are remarkable for their protagonists' indifference, even antipathy, to the beauty of the city and its surroundings.

New Oxford Book of Canadian Short Stories in English (ed. Margaret Atwood & Robert Weaver; Oxford University Press). A broad selection which delves beyond the better-known names of Alice Munro and Margaret Atwood, with space being given to diaspora writers. While the intention is to celebrate Canadian writing, some of the works offer a strangely negative view of the country.

New Oxford Book of Canadian Verse (ed. Margaret Atwood; Oxford University Press). Canadian poets are increasingly finding a distinctive voice, but few except this collection's editor have made much impact outside their native country. Atwood's own sharp, witty examinations of nationality and gender are among the best in this anthology.

Oxford Companion to Canadian Literature (Oxford University Press, o/p). At almost 900 pages, this is the last word on the subject, though it is more useful as a work of reference than as a primer for the country's literature.

Linda Svendsen *Marine Life* (Harper-Collins, Canada/Penguin, US, o/p). Spare and powerful linked stories, most fairly downbeat, set against a Vancouver backdrop.

Vancouver Short Stories (ed. Carole Gerson; University of British Columbia Press, Canada). Not much fiction has come out of Vancouver; this collection, published in 1985, of a few choice bits serves as a good starting point.

The Vancouver Stories: West Coast Fiction from Canada's Best Writers (Raincoast Books). Published in 2005, this volume complements and updates *Vancouver Short Stories* (see above), with contributions from writers such as Douglas Coupland too young to have featured in the earlier collection.

Ethel Wilson *Swamp Angel* (New Canadian Library). Published in 1954, this is a Canadian classic, and tells the story of a woman who leaves Vancouver and a disastrous second marriage to seek redemption and a new life in the wilds of British Columbia.

Specialist guides

John Acorn & Nancy Baron *Birds of the Pacific Northwest* (Lone Pine Publishing, Canada). A large selection of books is available for birdwatchers in BC, but this provides the best general introduction, with first-rate illustrations. See p.192 for information on birdwatching around Vancouver.

Volker Bodegom *Bicycling Vancouver* (Lone Pine Publishing, Canada). Guide to cycling for pleasure in and around the city.

Victoria Bushnell *Kids' Vancouver: Things to See and Things to Do for Kids of Every Age* (Raincoast Books). A guide that provides exactly what it says it will on the cover.

Jean Cousins *Easy Hiking Around Vancouver: An All-Season Guide* (Greystone Books). Describes 55 hikes with trailheads less than an hour's drive from Vancouver.

Greg Dombowsky *Diver's Guide: Vancouver Island South* (Heritage House, Canada). Handbook to the region's best dive sites.

Teri Lydiard *The British Columbia Bicycling Guide* (Gordon Soules, US). Small but extremely detailed pointer to some tempting routes, backed up with good maps.

Andrea Pistolesi *Vancouver: Sunrise to Sunset* (Bonechi, Canada). Vancouver's bookshops offer a plethora of glossy illustrated titles with photographs of the city; this sumptuous book is the best.

Ian Sheldon *Seashore of British Columbia* (Lone Pine Publishing, Canada). This title is too general for specialists but provides a good introduction to the mammals, foreshore plants, birds and other aspects of the region's coastal habitats.

Collin Varner and Christine Allen *Gardens of Vancouver* (Raincoast Books). A green-fingered guide to the city's gardens.

Travel store

ROUGH GUIDES World Coverage

Travel

Andorra The Pyrenees, Pyrenees & Andorra Map, Spain
Antigua The Caribbean
Argentina Argentina, Argentina Map, Buenos Aires, South America on a Budget
Aruba The Caribbean
Australia Australia, Australia Map, East Coast Australia, Melbourne, Sydney, Tasmania
Austria Austria, Europe on a Budget, Vienna
Bahamas The Bahamas, The Caribbean
Barbados Barbados DIR, The Caribbean
Belgium Belgium & Luxembourg, Bruges DIR, Brussels, Brussels Map, Europe on a Budget
Belize Belize, Central America on a Budget, Guatemala & Belize Map
Benin West Africa
Bolivia Bolivia, South America on a Budget
Brazil Brazil, Rio, South America on a Budget
British Virgin Islands The Caribbean
Brunei Malaysia, Singapore & Brunei [1 title], Southeast Asia on a Budget
Bulgaria Bulgaria, Europe on a Budget
Burkina Faso West Africa
Cambodia Cambodia, Southeast Asia on a Budget, Vietnam, Laos & Cambodia Map [1 Map]
Cameroon West Africa
Canada Canada, Pacific Northwest, Toronto, Toronto Map, Vancouver
Cape Verde West Africa
Cayman Islands The Caribbean
Chile Chile, Chile Map, South America on a Budget
China Beijing, China, Hong Kong & Macau, Hong Kong & Macau DIR, Shanghai
Colombia South America on a Budget
Costa Rica Central America on a Budget, Costa Rica, Costa Rica & Panama Map
Croatia Croatia, Croatia Map, Europe on a Budget
Cuba Cuba, Cuba Map, The Caribbean, Havana
Cyprus Cyprus, Cyprus Map
Czech Republic The Czech Republic, Czech & Slovak Republics, Europe on a Budget, Prague, Prague DIR, Prague Map
Denmark Copenhagen, Denmark, Europe on a Budget, Scandinavia
Dominica The Caribbean
Dominican Republic Dominican Republic, The Caribbean
Ecuador Ecuador, South America on a Budget
Egypt Egypt, Egypt Map
El Salvador Central America on a Budget
England Britain, Camping in Britain, Devon & Cornwall, Dorset, Hampshire and The Isle of Wight [1 title], England, Europe on a Budget, The Lake District, London, London DIR, London Map, London Mini Guide, Walks In London & Southeast England
Estonia The Baltic States, Europe on a Budget
Fiji Fiji
Finland Europe on a Budget, Finland, Scandinavia
France Brittany & Normandy, Corsica, Corsica Map, The Dordogne & the Lot, Europe on a Budget, France, France Map, Languedoc & Roussillon, The Loire, Paris, Paris DIR, Paris Map, Paris Mini Guide, Provence & the Côte d'Azur, The Pyrenees, Pyrenees & Andorra Map
French Guiana South America on a Budget
Gambia The Gambia, West Africa
Germany Berlin, Berlin Map, Europe on a Budget, Germany, Germany Map
Ghana West Africa
Gibraltar Spain
Greece Athens Map, Crete, Crete Map, Europe on a Budget, Greece, Greece Map, Greek Islands, Ionian Islands
Guadeloupe The Caribbean
Guatemala Central America on a Budget, Guatemala, Guatemala & Belize Map
Guinea West Africa
Guinea-Bissau West Africa
Guyana South America on a Budget
Holland see The Netherlands
Honduras Central America on a Budget
Hungary Budapest, Europe on a Budget, Hungary
Iceland Iceland, Iceland Map
India Goa, India, India Map, Kerala, Rajasthan, Delhi & Agra [1 title], South India, South India Map
Indonesia Bali & Lombok, Southeast Asia on a Budget
Ireland Dublin DIR, Dublin Map, Europe on a Budget, Ireland, Ireland Map
Israel Jerusalem
Italy Europe on a Budget, Florence DIR, Florence & Siena Map, Florence & the best of Tuscany, Italy, The Italian Lakes, Naples & the Amalfi Coast, Rome, Rome DIR, Rome Map, Sardinia, Sicily, Sicily Map, Tuscany & Umbria, Tuscany Map, Venice, Venice DIR, Venice Map
Jamaica Jamaica, The Caribbean
Japan Japan, Tokyo
Jordan Jordan
Kenya Kenya, Kenya Map
Korea Korea
Laos Laos, Southeast Asia on a Budget, Vietnam, Laos & Cambodia Map [1 Map]
Latvia The Baltic States, Europe on a Budget
Lithuania The Baltic States, Europe on a Budget
Luxembourg Belgium & Luxembourg, Europe on a Budget
Malaysia Malaysia Map, Malaysia, Singapore & Brunei [1 title], Southeast Asia on a Budget
Mali West Africa
Malta Malta & Gozo DIR
Martinique The Caribbean
Mauritania West Africa
Mexico Baja California, Baja California, Cancún & Cozumel DIR, Mexico, Mexico Map, Yucatán, Yucatán Peninsula Map
Monaco France, Provence & the Côte d'Azur
Montenegro Montenegro
Morocco Europe on a Budget, Marrakesh DIR, Marrakesh Map, Morocco, Morocco Map,
Nepal Nepal
Netherlands Amsterdam, Amsterdam DIR, Amsterdam Map, Europe on a Budget, The Netherlands
Netherlands Antilles The Caribbean
New Zealand New Zealand, New Zealand Map

DIR: Rough Guide **DIRECTIONS** for short breaks

Nicaragua Central America on a Budget
Niger West Africa
Nigeria West Africa
Norway Europe on a Budget, Norway, Scandinavia
Panama Central America on a Budget, Costa Rica & Panama Map, Panama
Paraguay South America on a Budget
Peru Peru, Peru Map, South America on a Budget
Philippines The Philippines, Southeast Asia on a Budget,
Poland Europe on a Budget, Poland
Portugal Algarve DIR, The Algarve Map, Europe on a Budget, Lisbon DIR, Lisbon Map, Madeira DIR, Portugal, Portugal Map, Spain & Portugal Map
Puerto Rico The Caribbean, Puerto Rico
Romania Europe on a Budget, Romania
Russia Europe on a Budget, Moscow, St Petersburg
St Kitts & Nevis The Caribbean
St Lucia The Caribbean
St Vincent & the Grenadines The Caribbean
Scotland Britain, Camping in Britain, Edinburgh DIR, Europe on a Budget, Scotland, Scottish Highlands & Islands
Senegal West Africa
Serbia Montenegro Europe on a Budget
Sierra Leone West Africa
Singapore Malaysia, Singapore & Brunei [1 title], Singapore, Singapore DIR, Southeast Asia on a Budget
Slovakia Czech & Slovak Republics, Europe on a Budget
Slovenia Europe on a Budget, Slovenia
South Africa Cape Town & the Garden Route, South Africa, South Africa Map
Spain Andalucía, Andalucía Map, Barcelona, Barcelona DIR, Barcelona Map, Europe on a Budget, Ibiza & Formentera DIR, Gran Canaria DIR, Madrid DIR, Lanzarote & Fuerteventura DIR Madrid Map, Mallorca & Menorca, Mallorca DIR, Mallorca Map, The Pyrenees, Pyrenees & Andorra Map, Spain, Spain & Portugal Map, Tenerife & La Gomera DIR
Sri Lanka Sri Lanka, Sri Lanka Map
Suriname South America on a Budget
Sweden Europe on a Budget, Scandinavia, Sweden
Switzerland Europe on a Budget, Switzerland
Taiwan Taiwan
Tanzania Tanzania, Zanzibar
Thailand Bangkok, Southeast Asia on a Budget, Thailand, Thailand Map, Thailand Beaches & Islands
Togo West Africa
Trinidad & Tobago The Caribbean, Trinidad & Tobago
Tunisia Tunisia, Tunisia Map
Turkey Europe on a Budget, Istanbul, Turkey, Turkey Map
Turks and Caicos Islands The Bahamas, The Caribbean
United Arab Emirates Dubai DIR, Dubai & UAE Map [1 title]
United Kingdom Britain, Devon & Cornwall, Edinburgh DIR England, Europe on a Budget, The Lake District, London, London DIR, London Map, London Mini Guide, Scotland, Scottish Highlands & Islands, Wales, Walks In London & Southeast England
United States Alaska, Boston, California, California Map, Chicago, Colorado, Florida, Florida Map, The Grand Canyon, Hawaii, Los Angeles, Los Angeles Map, Los Angeles and Southern California, Maui DIR, Miami & South Florida, New England, New England Map, New Orleans & Cajun Country, New Orleans DIR, New York City, NYC DIR, NYC Map, New York City Mini Guide, Oregon & Washington, Orlando & Walt Disney World® DIR, San Francisco, San Francisco DIR, San Francisco Map, Seattle, Southwest USA, USA, Washington DC, Yellowstone & the Grand Tetons National Park, Yosemite National Park
Uruguay South America on a Budget
US Virgin Islands The Bahamas, The Caribbean
Venezuela South America on a Budget
Vietnam Southeast Asia on a Budget, Vietnam, Vietnam, Laos & Cambodia Map [1 Map],
Wales Britain, Camping in Britain, Europe on a Budget, Wales
First-Time Series FT Africa, FT Around the World, FT Asia, FT Europe, FT Latin America
Inspirational guides Earthbound, Clean Breaks, Make the Most of Your Time on Earth, Ultimate Adventures, World Party
Travel Specials Camping in Britain, Travel with Babies & Young Children, Walks in London & SE England

ROUGH GUIDES Don't Just Travel

Computers Cloud Computing, FWD this link, The Internet, iPhone, iPods & iTunes, Macs & OS X, Website Directory
Film & TV American Independent Film, British Cult Comedy, Comedy Movies, Cult Movies, Film, Film Musicals, Film Noir, Gangster Movies, Horror Movies, Sci-Fi Movies, Westerns
Lifestyle Babies & Toddlers, Brain Training, Food, Girl Stuff, Green Living, Happiness, Men's Health, Pregnancy & Birth, Running, Saving & Selling Online, Sex, Weddings
Music The Beatles, The Best Music You've Never Heard, Blues, Bob Dylan, Book of Playlists, Classical Music, Heavy Metal, Jimi Hendrix, Led Zeppelin, Nirvana, Opera, Pink Floyd, The Rolling Stones, Soul and R&B, Velvet Underground, World Music
Popular Culture Anime, Classic Novels, Conspiracy Theories, Crime Fiction, The Da Vinci Code, Graphic Novels, Hidden Treasures, His Dark Materials, Hitchhiker's Guide to the Galaxy, The Lost Symbol, Manga, Next Big Thing, Shakespeare, True Crime, Tutankhamun, Unexplained Phenomena, Videogames
Science The Brain, Climate Change, The Earth, Energy Crisis, Evolution, Future, Genes & Cloning, The Universe, Weather

For more information go to www.roughguides.com

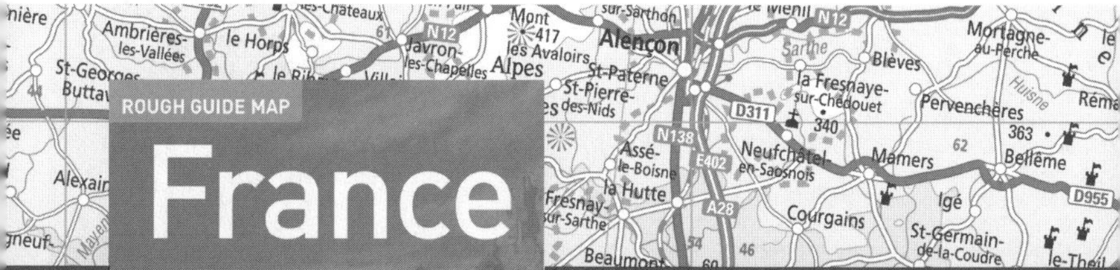

Small print and

Index

A Rough Guide to Rough Guides

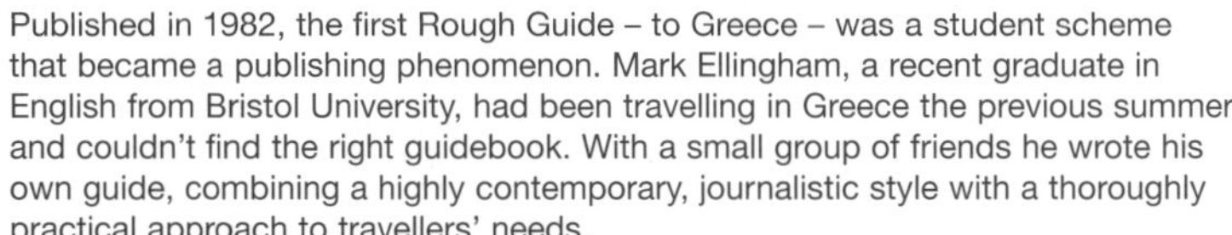

Published in 1982, the first Rough Guide – to Greece – was a student scheme that became a publishing phenomenon. Mark Ellingham, a recent graduate in English from Bristol University, had been travelling in Greece the previous summer and couldn't find the right guidebook. With a small group of friends he wrote his own guide, combining a highly contemporary, journalistic style with a thoroughly practical approach to travellers' needs.

The immediate success of the book spawned a series that rapidly covered dozens of destinations. And, in addition to impecunious backpackers, Rough Guides soon acquired a much broader and older readership that relished the guides' wit and inquisitiveness as much as their enthusiastic, critical approach and value-for-money ethos.

These days, Rough Guides include recommendations from shoestring to luxury and cover more than 200 destinations around the globe, including almost every country in the Americas and Europe, more than half of Africa and most of Asia and Australasia. Our ever-growing team of authors and photographers is spread all over the world, particularly in Europe, the US and Australia.

In the early 1990s, Rough Guides branched out of travel, with the publication of Rough Guides to World Music, Classical Music and the Internet. All three have become benchmark titles in their fields, spearheading the publication of a wide range of books under the Rough Guide name.

Including the travel series, Rough Guides now number more than 350 titles, covering: phrasebooks, waterproof maps, music guides from Opera to Heavy Metal, reference works as diverse as Conspiracy Theories and Shakespeare, and popular culture books from iPods to Poker. Rough Guides also produce a series of more than 120 World Music CDs in partnership with World Music Network.

Visit www.roughguides.com to see our latest publications.

Rough Guide travel images are available for commercial licensing at www.roughguidespictures.com

Rough Guide credits

Text editor: Christina Valhouli
Layout: Sachin Gupta
Cartography: Katie Lloyd-Jones
Picture editor: Mark Thomas
Production: Rebecca Short
Proofreader: Serena Stephenson
Cover design: Daniel May, Chloë Roberts
Photographer: Tim Draper
Editorial: Ruth Blackmore, Andy Turner, Keith Drew, Edward Aves, Alice Park, Lucy White, Jo Kirby, James Smart, Natasha Foges, Róisín Cameron, James Rice, Lara Kavanagh, Emma Traynor, Emma Gibbs, Kathryn Lane, Monica Woods, Mani Ramaswamy, Harry Wilson, Lucy Cowie, Alison Roberts, Joe Staines, Peter Buckley, Matthew Milton, Tracy Hopkins, Ruth Tidball; **Delhi** Madhavi Singh, Karen D'Souza, Lubna Shaheen
Design & Pictures: **London** Scott Stickland, Dan May, Diana Jarvis, Mark Thomas, Nicole Newman, Sarah Cummins, Emily Taylor; **Delhi** Umesh Aggarwal, Ajay Verma, Jessica Subramanian, Ankur Guha, Pradeep Thapliyal, Sachin Tanwar, Anita Singh, Nikhil Agarwal.
Production: Liz Cherry
Cartography: **London** Ed Wright; **Delhi** Rajesh Chhibber, Ashutosh Bharti, Rajesh Mishra, Animesh Pathak, Jasbir Sandhu, Karobi Gogoi, Alakananda Roy, Swati Handoo, Deshpal Dabas
Online: **London** Faye Hellon, Jeanette Angell, Fergus Day, Justine Bright, Clare Bryson, Aine Fearon, Adrian Low, Ezgi Celebi; **Delhi** Amit Verma, Rahul Kumar, Narender Kumar, Ravi Yadav, Debojit Borah, Rakesh Kumar, Ganesh Sharma, Shisir Basumatari
Marketing & Publicity: **London** Liz Statham, Louise Maher, Jess Carter, Vanessa Godden, Vivienne Watton, Anna Paynton, Rachel Sprackett, Laura Vipond; **New York** Katy Ball, Judi Powers; **Delhi** Ragini Govind
Reference Director: Andrew Lockett
Operations Assistant: Becky Doyle
Operations Manager: Helen Atkinson
Publishing Director (Travel): Clare Currie
Commercial Manager: Gino Magnotta
Managing Director: John Duhigg

Publishing information

This fourth edition published May 2010 by
Rough Guides Ltd,
80 Strand, London WC2R 0RL
14 Local Shopping Centre, Panchsheel Park, New Delhi 110017, India
Distributed by the Penguin Group
Penguin Books Ltd,
80 Strand, London WC2R 0RL
Penguin Group (USA)
375 Hudson Street, NY 10014, USA
Penguin Group (Australia)
250 Camberwell Road, Camberwell, Victoria 3124, Australia
Penguin Group (Canada)
195 Harry Walker Parkway N, Newmarket, ON, L3Y 7B3 Canada
Penguin Group (NZ)
67 Apollo Drive, Mairangi Bay, Auckland 1310, New Zealand
Cover concept by Peter Dyer.

Typeset in Bembo and Helvetica to an original design by Henry Iles.
Printed in Singapore

280pp includes index
A catalogue record for this book is available from the British Library
ISBN: 978-1-84836-504-9

1 3 5 7 9 8 6 4 2

Help us update

We've gone to a lot of effort to ensure that the fourth edition of **The Rough Guide to Vancouver** is accurate and up-to-date. However, things change – places get "discovered", opening hours are notoriously fickle, restaurants and rooms raise prices or lower standards. If you feel we've got it wrong or left something out, we'd like to know, and if you can remember the address, the price, the hours, the phone number, so much the better.

Please send your comments with the subject line "**Rough Guide Vancouver Update**" to ©mail@roughguides.com. We'll credit all contributions and send a copy of the next edition (or any other Rough Guide if you prefer) for the very best emails.

Have your questions answered and tell others about your trip at Ⓦwww.roughguides.com

SMALL PRINT

Acknowledgements

The author wishes to thank Shea Dean, Yuki Takagaki, Steven Horak and Christina Valhouli; James and Vicky Ballentyne; Air Canada; Charlotte Fraser; Fairmont Hotels; Claire Griffin; Four Seasons Hotels; Kathleen Eccles; Anna Whittaker and Virgin Holidays; Tracy Long and British Airways Holidays.

Readers' letters

Thanks to all the readers who have taken the time to write in with comments and suggestions (and apologies if we've inadvertently omitted or misspelt anyone's name):

Ken and Sue Napier, Gary Elflett, Professor Charles Brook.

Photo credits

All photos © Rough Guides except the following:

Introduction
Downtown Vancouver © Chris Cheadie/Getty
View of Coal Harbour © Stuart McCall/Getty
View of Vancouver © Paul Harrison
Grouse Mountain © Ron Watts/Getty
Harbour at dusk © Ken Stralton/Getty

Things not to miss
01 Vancouver Museum © Stock Connection/Alamy
02 Whale-watching © Picture contact/Alamy
03 Ice hockey © Jeff Vinnick/Getty
13 Whistler Mountain © Ron Niebrugge/Alamy

The Great Outdoors colour section
Snowshoeing, Seymour Mountain © All Canada Photo's/Getty
Snowboarding © Jon Faulknor/istock
Black bear © Suzann Julien/Getty
Humpback whale © Edzard de Ranitz/istock
View of the Fraser River © Andrew Stevens/Alamy
Killer whales off northern Vancouver © Rolf Hicker/Alamy

Eating out in Vancouver colour section
Scallops © Stanley Cheng/Alamy
Salmon roll © Stanley Cheng/Alamy
Wine-tasting © Lloyd Sutton/Alamy
Grapes on vine © Jurgen Vogt/Alamy

Black and whites
p.59 Dr Sun Yat-San Garden © Paul Harrison
p.66 View of the Seawall Promenade © Paul Harrison
p.81 Heritage Harbour © Paul Harrison
p.88 Museum of Anthropology © All Canada Photos/Alamy
p.201 Chinese Dragons © Gunter Marx/Alamy
p.242 Hiking Whistler Mountain © Mike Crane Photography/Alamy

Index

Map entries are in colour.

H

I

K

L

M

N

O

W

Map symbols

maps are listed in the full index using coloured text

International boundary
Chapter boundary
Trans-Canada highway
5 Interstate
99 Highway
Main road
Minor road
Pedestrianized street (town maps)
Railway
SkyTrain
Cable car & station
Footpath
Ferry route
River
Wall
Bridge
Mountain range
Mountain peak
Airport
Bus/shuttle stop
Point of interest
Tourist infocentre
Post office
Hospital
Parking
Public convenience
Helijet terminal
Golf course
Skiing area
Monument
Totem pole
Public gardens
Museum
SkyTrain/subway station
Stadium
Building
Church
Cemetery
Park/national park/reserve
Reservation

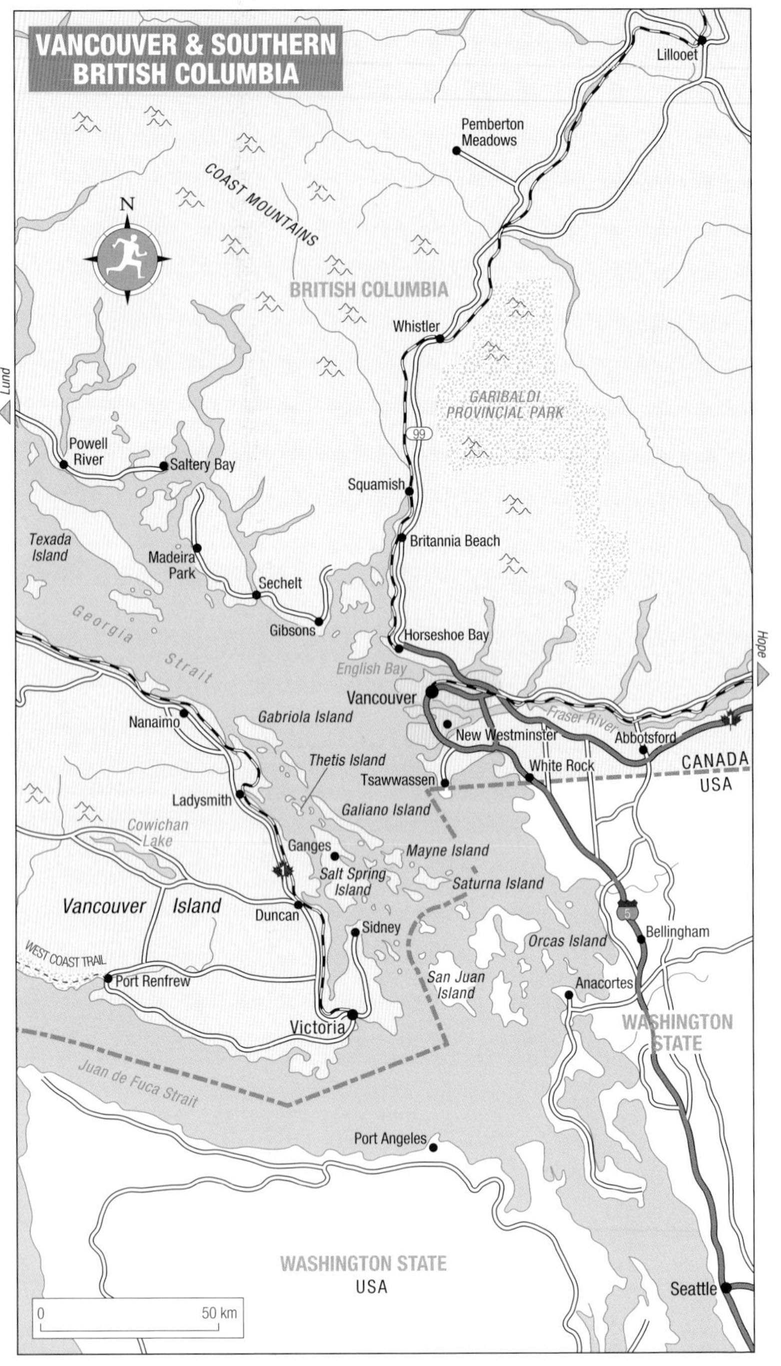

VANCOUVER & SOUTHERN BRITISH COLUMBIA
N
Lillooet
Pemberton Meadows
COAST MOUNTAINS
BRITISH COLUMBIA
Whistler
GARIBALDI PROVINCIAL PARK
99
Lund
Powell River
Saltery Bay
Squamish
Britannia Beach
Texada Island
Madeira Park
Sechelt
Gibsons
Georgia Strait
Horseshoe Bay
Hope
English Bay
Vancouver
Fraser River
Nanaimo
Gabriola Island
New Westminster
Abbotsford
1
Thetis Island
White Rock
CANADA
Tsawwassen
USA
Ladysmith
Galiano Island
Cowichan Lake
Ganges
Mayne Island
Salt Spring Island
Saturna Island
Vancouver Island
Duncan
5
Sidney
Bellingham
Orcas Island
WEST COAST TRAIL
Port Renfrew
San Juan Island
Anacortes
Victoria
WASHINGTON STATE
Juan de Fuca Strait
Port Angeles
WASHINGTON STATE
USA
Seattle
0
50 km

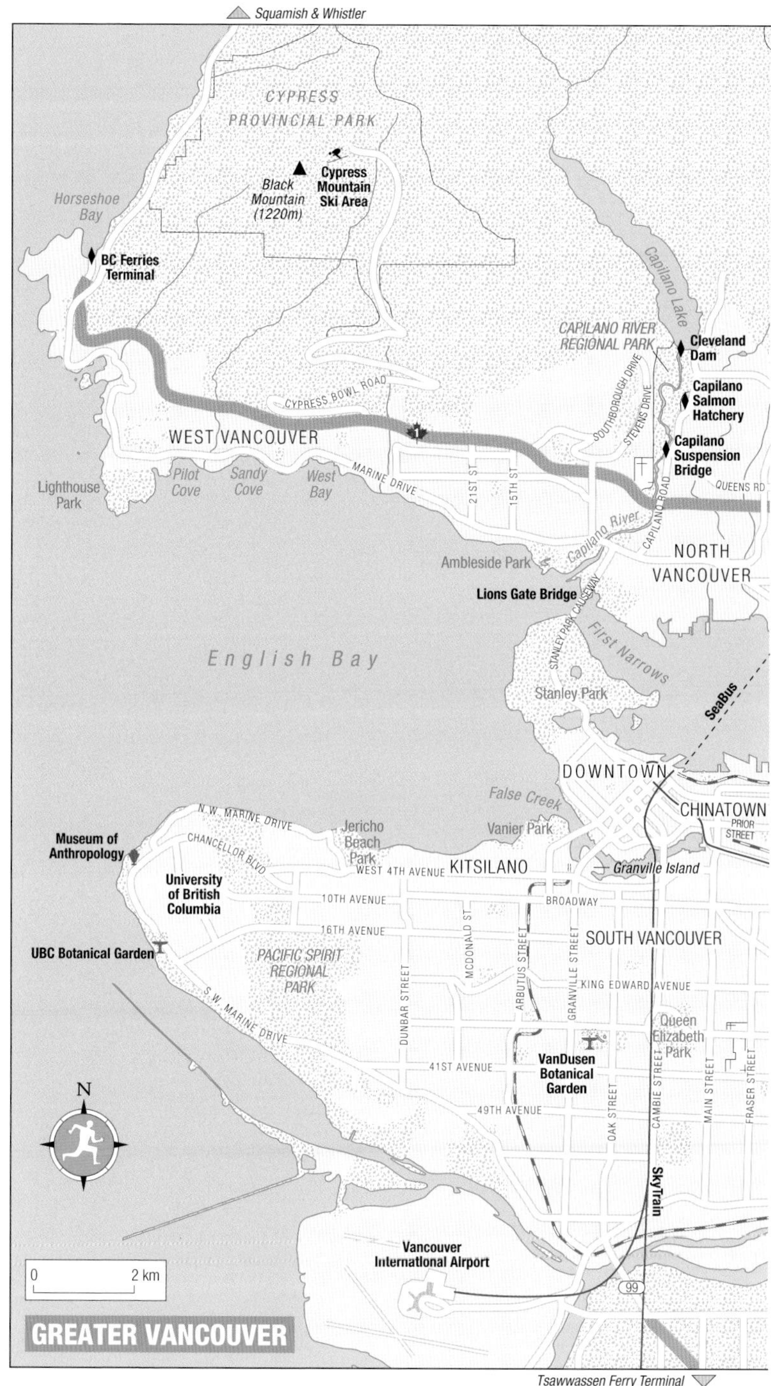

Squamish & Whistler
CYPRESS PROVINCIAL PARK
Black Mountain (1220m)
Cypress Mountain Ski Area
Horseshoe Bay
BC Ferries Terminal
Capilano Lake
CAPILANO RIVER REGIONAL PARK
Cleveland Dam
Capilano Salmon Hatchery
Capilano Suspension Bridge
SOUTHBOROUGH DRIVE
STEVENS DRIVE
CYPRESS BOWL ROAD
WEST VANCOUVER
1
Lighthouse Park
Pilot Cove
Sandy Cove
West Bay
MARINE DRIVE
21ST ST
15TH ST
QUEENS RD
CAPILANO ROAD
Capilano River
Ambleside Park
NORTH VANCOUVER
Lions Gate Bridge
STANLEY PARK CAUSEWAY
First Narrows
English Bay
Stanley Park
SeaBus
DOWNTOWN
False Creek
CHINATOWN
PRIOR STREET
N.W. MARINE DRIVE
Jericho Beach Park
Vanier Park
Museum of Anthropology
CHANCELLOR BLVD
WEST 4TH AVENUE
KITSILANO
Granville Island
University of British Columbia
10TH AVENUE
BROADWAY
16TH AVENUE
SOUTH VANCOUVER
UBC Botanical Garden
PACIFIC SPIRIT REGIONAL PARK
MCDONALD ST
ARBUTUS STREET
GRANVILLE STREET
KING EDWARD AVENUE
Queen Elizabeth Park
S.W. MARINE DRIVE
DUNBAR STREET
41ST AVENUE
VanDusen Botanical Garden
N
49TH AVENUE
OAK STREET
CAMBIE STREET
MAIN STREET
FRASER STREET
SkyTrain
Vancouver International Airport
0
2 km
99
GREATER VANCOUVER
Tsawwassen Ferry Terminal

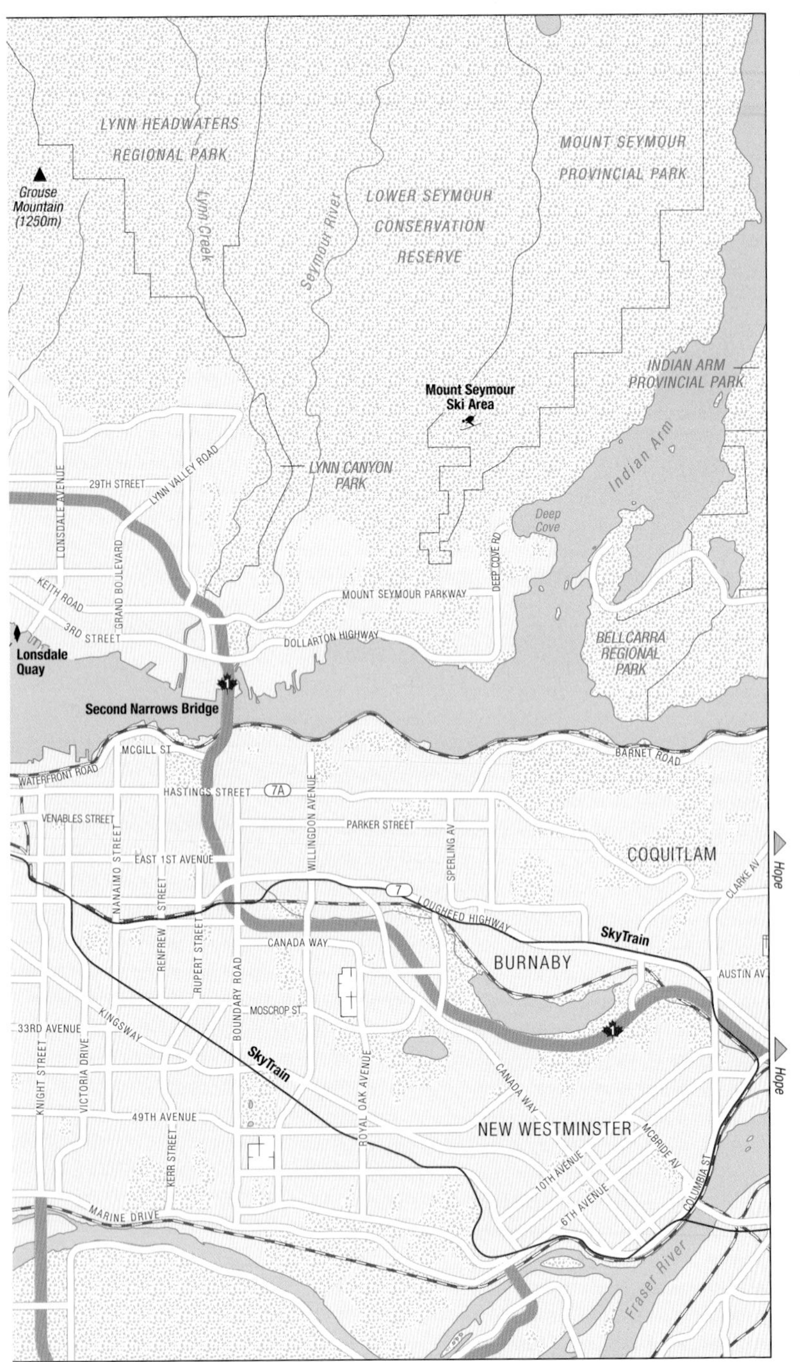

LYNN HEADWATERS
REGIONAL PARK
Grouse
Mountain
(1250m)
Lynn Creek
Seymour River
LOWER SEYMOUR
CONSERVATION
RESERVE
MOUNT SEYMOUR
PROVINCIAL PARK
INDIAN ARM
PROVINCIAL PARK
Mount Seymour
Ski Area
LYNN CANYON
PARK
Indian Arm
Deep
Cove
29TH STREET
LYNN VALLEY ROAD
LONSDALE AVENUE
GRAND BOULEVARD
KEITH ROAD
3RD STREET
DEEP COVE RD
MOUNT SEYMOUR PARKWAY
DOLLARTON HIGHWAY
BELLCARRA
REGIONAL
PARK
Lonsdale
Quay
Second Narrows Bridge
MCGILL ST
BARNET ROAD
WATERFRONT ROAD
HASTINGS STREET
7A
VENABLES STREET
WILLINGDON AVENUE
PARKER STREET
SPERLING AV
COQUITLAM
Hope
EAST 1ST AVENUE
NANAIMO STREET
RENFREW STREET
RUPERT STREET
7
LOUGHEED HIGHWAY
CLARKE AV
SkyTrain
CANADA WAY
BURNABY
AUSTIN AV
BOUNDARY ROAD
MOSCROP ST
33RD AVENUE
KINGSWAY
SkyTrain
Hope
KNIGHT STREET
VICTORIA DRIVE
ROYAL OAK AVENUE
CANADA WAY
49TH AVENUE
NEW WESTMINSTER
KERR STREET
10TH AVENUE
MCBRIDE AV
COLUMBIA ST
6TH AVENUE
MARINE DRIVE
Fraser River

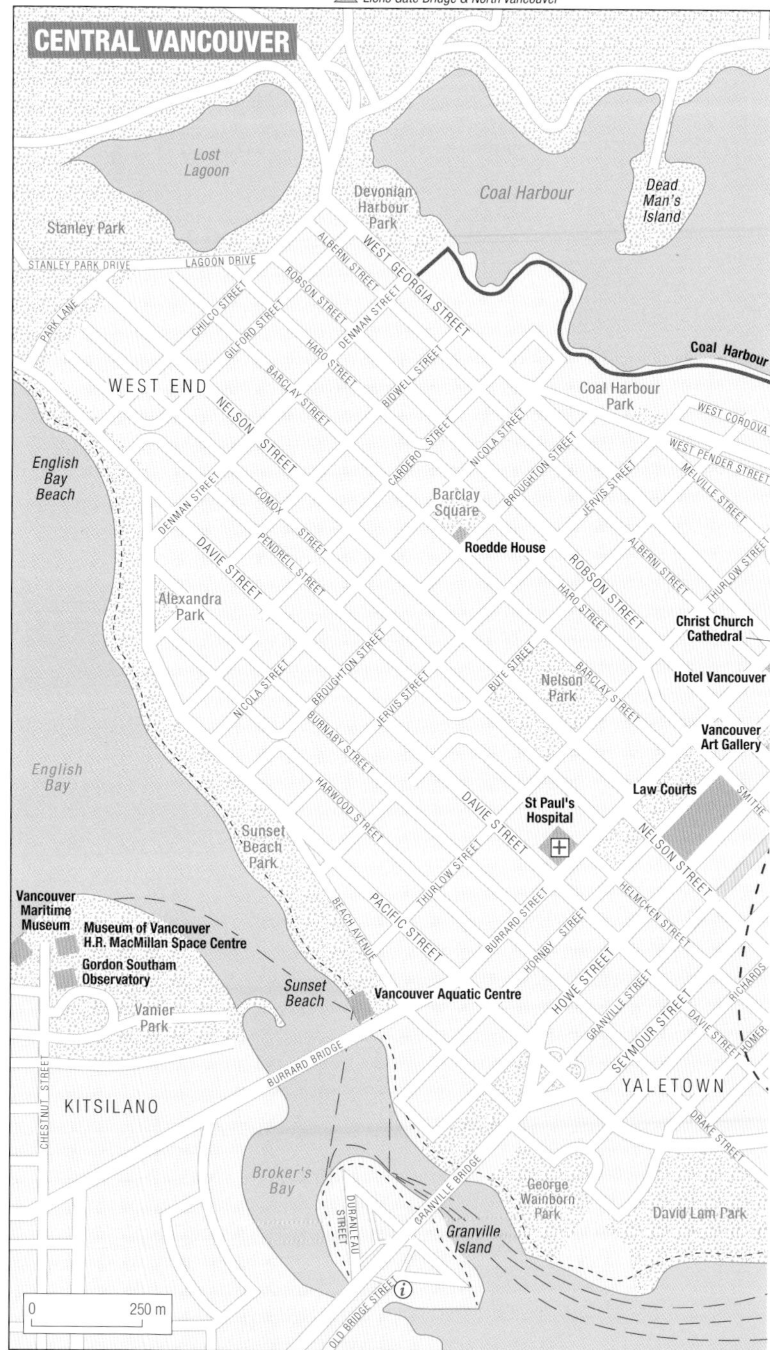

Lions Gate Bridge & North Vancouver
CENTRAL VANCOUVER
Lost Lagoon
Stanley Park
Devonian Harbour Park
Coal Harbour
Dead Man's Island
STANLEY PARK DRIVE
LAGOON DRIVE
PARK LANE
CHILCO STREET
GILFORD STREET
ROBSON STREET
ALBERNI STREET
WEST GEORGIA STREET
DENMAN STREET
HARO STREET
BARCLAY STREET
BIDWELL STREET
WEST END
NELSON STREET
Coal Harbour
Coal Harbour Park
WEST CORDOVA
WEST PENDER STREET
MELVILLE STREET
English Bay Beach
DENMAN STREET
COMOX STREET
CARDERO STREET
NICOLA STREET
BROUGHTON STREET
JERVIS STREET
Barclay Square
Roedde House
DAVIE STREET
PENDRELL STREET
ROBSON STREET
ALBERNI STREET
THURLOW STREET
HARO STREET
Alexandra Park
Christ Church Cathedral
Hotel Vancouver
NICOLA STREET
BROUGHTON STREET
JERVIS STREET
BUTE STREET
Nelson Park
BARCLAY STREET
Vancouver Art Gallery
BURNABY STREET
HARWOOD STREET
English Bay
Law Courts
SMITHE
DAVIE STREET
St Paul's Hospital
NELSON STREET
Sunset Beach Park
THURLOW STREET
HELMCKEN STREET
PACIFIC STREET
BEACH AVENUE
BURRARD STREET
HORNBY STREET
Vancouver Maritime Museum
Museum of Vancouver
H.R. MacMillan Space Centre
Gordon Southam Observatory
Sunset Beach
Vancouver Aquatic Centre
HOWE STREET
GRANVILLE STREET
SEYMOUR STREET
DAVIE STREET
RICHARDS
HOMER
Vanier Park
BURRARD BRIDGE
CHESTNUT STREET
KITSILANO
YALETOWN
DRAKE STREET
Broker's Bay
DURANLEAU STREET
GRANVILLE BRIDGE
George Wainborn Park
David Lam Park
Granville Island
OLD BRIDGE STREET
0
250 m

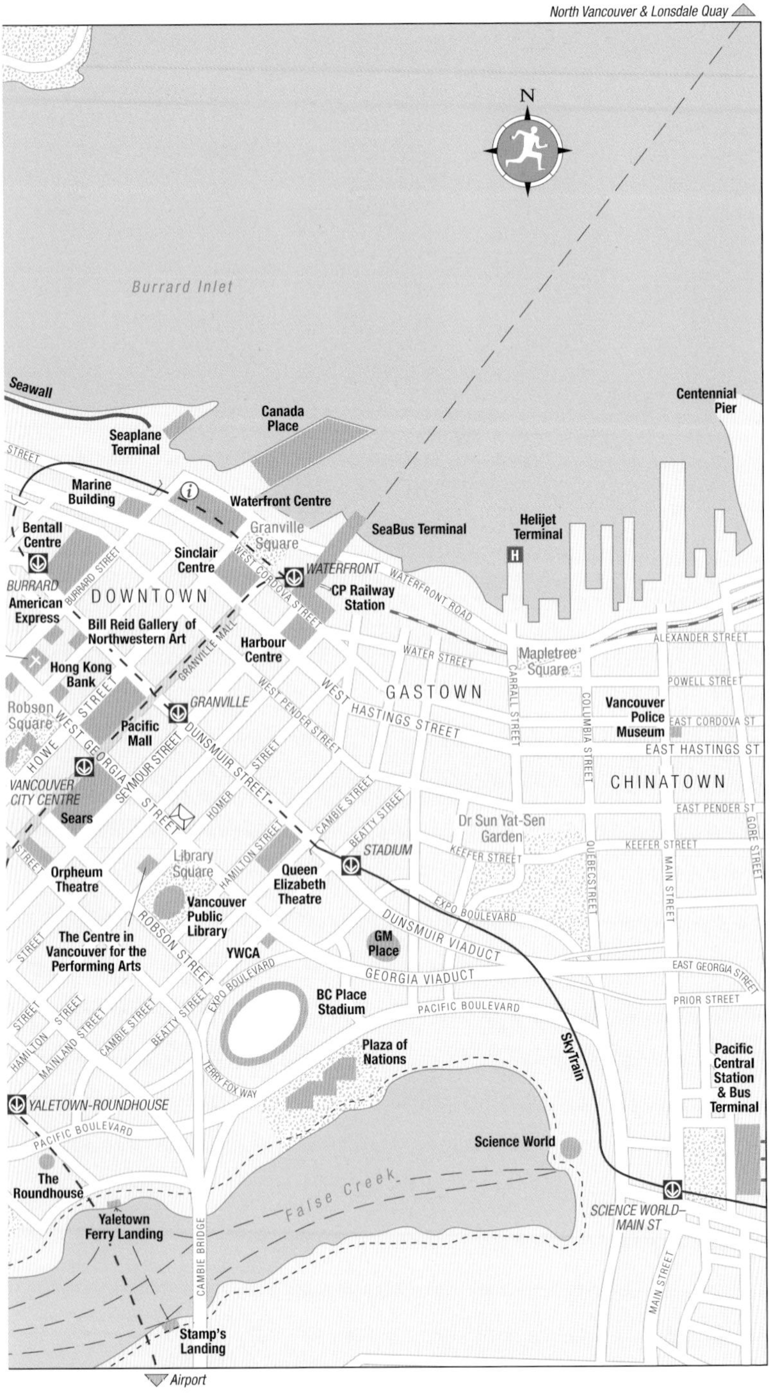

North Vancouver & Lonsdale Quay

N

Burrard Inlet

Seawall

Canada Place

Centennial Pier

Seaplane Terminal

Marine Building

Waterfront Centre

Bentall Centre

Granville Square

SeaBus Terminal

Helijet Terminal

Sinclair Centre

WATERFRONT

CP Railway Station

WATERFRONT ROAD

BURRARD

American Express

DOWNTOWN

Bill Reid Gallery of Northwestern Art

Harbour Centre

ALEXANDER STREET

Hong Kong Bank

WATER STREET

Maple Tree Square

GASTOWN

POWELL STREET

Robson Square

GRANVILLE

Pacific Mall

WEST HASTINGS STREET

Vancouver Police Museum

EAST CORDOVA ST

EAST HASTINGS ST

VANCOUVER CITY CENTRE

CHINATOWN

Sears

EAST PENDER ST

Dr Sun Yat-Sen Garden

KEEFER STREET

STADIUM

Orpheum Theatre

Library Square

Queen Elizabeth Theatre

Vancouver Public Library

EXPO BOULEVARD

The Centre in Vancouver for the Performing Arts

YWCA

GM Place

DUNSMUIR VIADUCT

GEORGIA VIADUCT

EAST GEORGIA STREET

BC Place Stadium

PRIOR STREET

PACIFIC BOULEVARD

Plaza of Nations

SkyTrain

Pacific Central Station & Bus Terminal

YALETOWN-ROUNDHOUSE

TERRY FOX WAY

PACIFIC BOULEVARD

Science World

The Roundhouse

False Creek

SCIENCE WORLD–MAIN ST

Yaletown Ferry Landing

CAMBIE BRIDGE

MAIN STREET

Stamp's Landing

Airport

BURRARD STREET, WEST CORDOVA STREET, GRANVILLE MALL, WEST PENDER STREET, WEST GEORGIA STREET, HOWE STREET, SEYMOUR STREET, DUNSMUIR STREET, HOMER STREET, RICHARDS STREET, CAMBIE STREET, BEATTY STREET, HAMILTON STREET, ROBSON STREET, MAINLAND STREET, CARRALL STREET, COLUMBIA STREET, QUEBEC STREET, MAIN STREET, GORE STREET

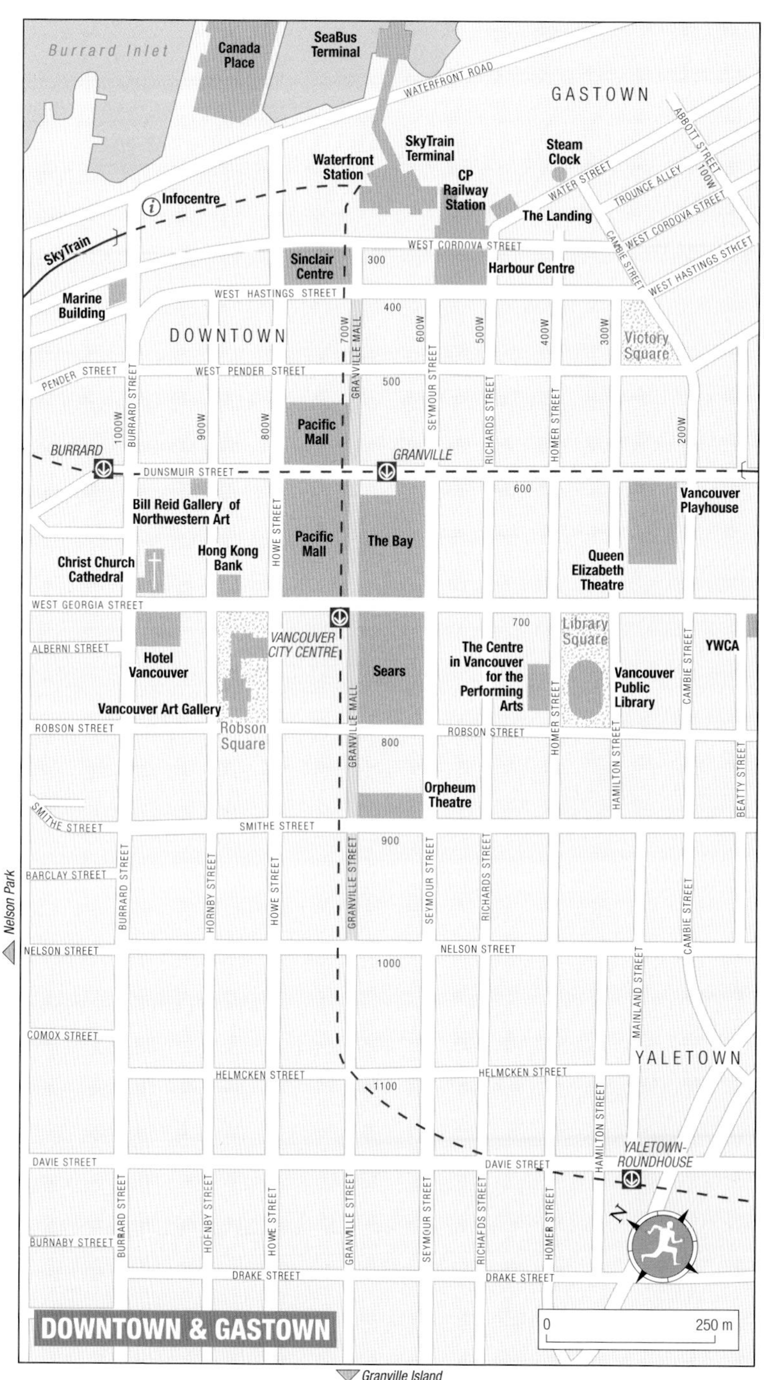

Burrard Inlet
Canada Place
SeaBus Terminal
WATERFRONT ROAD
GASTOWN
SkyTrain Terminal
Waterfront Station
Steam Clock
CP Railway Station
Infocentre
The Landing
WATER STREET
TROUNCE ALLEY
ABBOTT STREET
100W
WEST CORDOVA STREET
CAMBIE STREET
WEST HASTINGS STREET
SkyTrain
Sinclair Centre
300
Harbour Centre
Marine Building
WEST HASTINGS STREET
400
Chinatown
DOWNTOWN
700W
GRANVILLE MALL
600W
500W
400W
300W
Victory Square
PENDER STREET
WEST PENDER STREET
500
BURRARD STREET
1000W
900W
800W
Pacific Mall
SEYMOUR STREET
RICHARDS STREET
HOMER STREET
200W
BURRARD
GRANVILLE
DUNSMUIR STREET
600
Bill Reid Gallery of Northwestern Art
Vancouver Playhouse
Christ Church Cathedral
Hong Kong Bank
HOWE STREET
Pacific Mall
The Bay
Queen Elizabeth Theatre
WEST GEORGIA STREET
700
Library Square
YWCA
ALBERNI STREET
VANCOUVER CITY CENTRE
The Centre in Vancouver for the Performing Arts
CAMBIE STREET
Hotel Vancouver
Sears
Vancouver Public Library
Vancouver Art Gallery
ROBSON STREET
Robson Square
ROBSON STREET
HOMER STREET
HAMILTON STREET
800
Orpheum Theatre
BEATTY STREET
SMITHE STREET
SMITHE STREET
900
BARCLAY STREET
BURRARD STREET
HORNBY STREET
HOWE STREET
GRANVILLE STREET
SEYMOUR STREET
RICHARDS STREET
CAMBIE STREET
Nelson Park
NELSON STREET
NELSON STREET
1000
MAINLAND STREET
COMOX STREET
YALETOWN
HELMCKEN STREET
HELMCKEN STREET
1100
HAMILTON STREET
YALETOWN-ROUNDHOUSE
DAVIE STREET
DAVIE STREET
BURRARD STREET
HORNBY STREET
HOWE STREET
GRANVILLE STREET
SEYMOUR STREET
RICHARDS STREET
HOMER STREET
N
BURNABY STREET
DRAKE STREET
DRAKE STREET
DOWNTOWN & GASTOWN
0
250 m
Granville Island

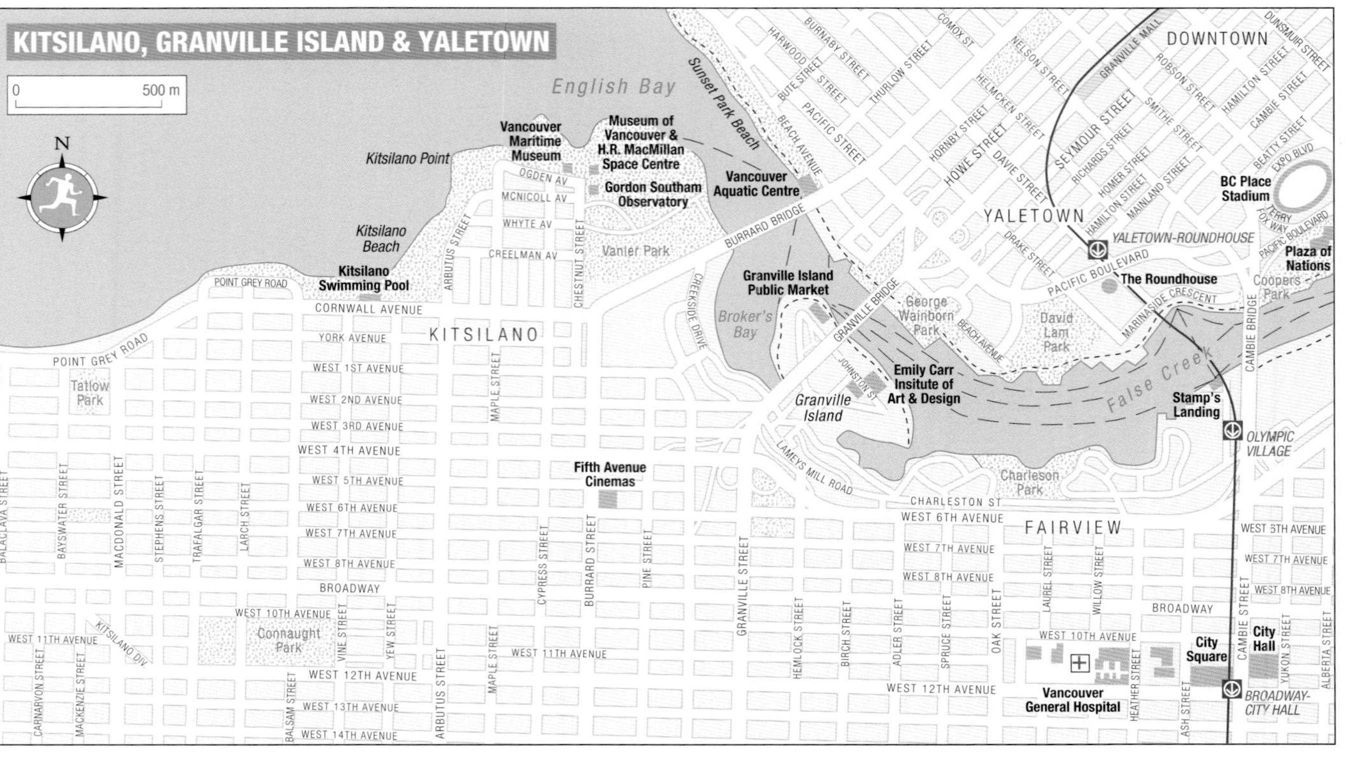

KITSILANO, GRANVILLE ISLAND & YALETOWN
0
500 m
N
English Bay
Sunset Park Beach
Kitsilano Point
Kitsilano Beach
Kitsilano Swimming Pool
Vancouver Maritime Museum
Museum of Vancouver & H.R. MacMillan Space Centre
Gordon Southam Observatory
Vancouver Aquatic Centre
Vanier Park
Granville Island Public Market
Broker's Bay
Granville Island
Emily Carr Insitute of Art & Design
George Wainborn Park
David Lam Park
False Creek
Stamp's Landing
Charleson Park
Coopers' Park
Plaza of Nations
BC Place Stadium
The Roundhouse
YALETOWN-ROUNDHOUSE
OLYMPIC VILLAGE
BROADWAY-CITY HALL
City Hall
City Square
Vancouver General Hospital
Fifth Avenue Cinemas
Tatlow Park
Connaught Park
DOWNTOWN
YALETOWN
KITSILANO
FAIRVIEW
BURRARD BRIDGE
GRANVILLE BRIDGE
CAMBIE BRIDGE
POINT GREY ROAD
CORNWALL AVENUE
YORK AVENUE
WEST 1ST AVENUE
WEST 2ND AVENUE
WEST 3RD AVENUE
WEST 4TH AVENUE
WEST 5TH AVENUE
WEST 6TH AVENUE
WEST 7TH AVENUE
WEST 8TH AVENUE
BROADWAY
WEST 10TH AVENUE
WEST 11TH AVENUE
WEST 12TH AVENUE
WEST 13TH AVENUE
WEST 14TH AVENUE
OGDEN AV
MCNICOLL AV
WHYTE AV
CREELMAN AV
ARBUTUS STREET
CHESTNUT STREET
CREEKSIDE DRIVE
JOHNSTON ST
LAMEYS MILL ROAD
CHARLESTON ST
BALACLAVA STREET
BAYSWATER STREET
MACDONALD STREET
STEPHENS STREET
TRAFALGAR STREET
LARCH STREET
CARNARVON STREET
MACKENZIE STREET
KITSILANO DIV.
BALSAM STREET
VINE STREET
YEW STREET
MAPLE STREET
CYPRESS STREET
BURRARD STREET
PINE STREET
GRANVILLE STREET
HEMLOCK STREET
BIRCH STREET
ADLER STREET
SPRUCE STREET
OAK STREET
LAUREL STREET
WILLOW STREET
HEATHER STREET
ASH STREET
CAMBIE STREET
YUKON STREET
ALBERTA STREET
HARWOOD STREET
BUTE STREET
BURNABY STREET
PACIFIC STREET
BEACH AVENUE
THURLOW STREET
COMOX ST
NELSON STREET
HELMCKEN STREET
HORNBY STREET
HOWE STREET
DAVIE STREET
DRAKE STREET
GRANVILLE MALL
SEYMOUR STREET
RICHARDS STREET
HOMER STREET
HAMILTON STREET
MAINLAND STREET
ROBSON STREET
SMITHE STREET
CAMBIE STREET
BEATTY STREET
EXPO BLVD
DUNSMUIR STREET
TERRY FOX WAY
PACIFIC BOULEVARD
MARINASIDE CRESCENT